The AmigaDOS Manual

THIRD EDITION

The AmigaDOS Manual

THIRD EDITION

Commodore-Amiga, Inc.

BANTAM BOOKS
TORONTO • NEW YORK • LONDON • SYDNEY • AUCKLAND

THE AmigaDOS MANUAL, 3RD EDITION
A Bantam Book / July 1991

All rights reserved.
Copyright © 1991 by Commodore Capital, Inc.
Cover design © 1991 by Bantam Books, Inc.
Interior design by Nancy Sugihara
Composed by Williams Printing Company

This book may not be reproduced in whole or in part, by mimeograph or any
other means, without permission. For information address: Bantam Books.

Throughout this book, tradenames and trademarks of some
companies and products have been used, and no such uses
are intended to convey endorsement of or other affiliations with the book.

ISBN 0-553-35403-5

Published simultaneously in the United States and Canada.

Bantam Books are published by Bantam Books, a division of Bantam Doubleday Dell Publishing Group, Inc. Its trademark, consisting of the words "Bantam Books" and the portrayal of a rooster, is Registered in U.S. Patent and Trademark Office and in other countries. Marca Registrada, Bantam Books, Inc., 666 Fifth Avenue, New York, New York 10103.

PRINTED IN THE UNITED STATES OF AMERICA

0 9 8 7 6 5 4 3 2 1

Preface

This book, *The AmigaDOS Manual*, has three parts:

The User's Manual
The Developer's Manual
The Technical Reference Manual

The *User's Manual* contains information of interest to every Amiga user. There are many more commands that AmigaDOS understands than are accessible from the Workbench. If a user activates AmigaDOS Command Line Interface, these new commands become accessible.

The *Developer's Manual* describes how to use AmigaDOS from within a program rather than from a command line interface. It also fully documents the Amiga Linker.

The *Technical Reference Manual* describes the data structures that AmigaDOS uses internally. It includes descriptions of how DOS disk data are stored, and the format of the "object-files" that AmigaDOS uses. A developer or expert user would find the information in this technical section very useful.

Together these three parts comprise the essential guide to AmigaDOS.

Acknowledgments

The third edition of the AmigaDOS Manual was written by Dan Baker, Randell Jesup, John Orr, John Toebes, and Isabelle Vesey and edited by Jono Hardjowirogo and Dan Baker. The original manual was written by Tim King.

A special thanks to Bruce Barrett, Patria Brown, Pamela Clare, Alan Coslett, Andy Finkel, Paul Floyd, Jessica King, Liz Laban, Rob Peck, Carolyn Scheppner, and Keith Stobie. Without their generous contributions and suggestions this manual would not have been possible.

Contents

The AmigaDOS Manual, 3rd Edition

Preface v

Acknowledgments vii

PART I THE USER'S MANUAL 1

Introduction 3

How to Open a Shell Window 3

Workbench and CLI, Their Relationship and Differences 4

Chapter 1 Introducing AmigaDOS 5

About AmigaDOS Processes 5

Console Handling 6

Using the Filing System 8

    Naming Files 8 · Using Directories 9 · Setting the Current Directory 10 · Setting the Current Device 12 · Attaching a Filenote 13 · Understanding Device Names 13 · Using Directory Conventions and Logical Devices 16

Using AmigaDOS Commands 19

    Running Commands in the Background 20 · Executing Command Files 20 · Directing Command Input and Output 21 · Interrupting AmigaDOS 21

Restart Validation Process 21

Commonly Used Commands 22

    Using the Shell 22

Some AmigaDOS Commands 23

    For a New User 23 · How to Begin 24 · Copying a Disk 24 · Formatting a Disk 25 · Making a Disk Bootable 25 · Making a CLI Disk 26 · Relabeling a Disk 26 · Looking at the Directory 27 · Using the LIST Command 27 · Using the PROTECT Command 28 · Getting Information About the File System 29 · Changing Your Current Directory 29 · Setting the Date and Time 30 · Redirecting the Output of a Command 30 · Typing a Text File to the Screen 31 · Changing the Name of a File 31 · Deleting Files 31 · Copying Files 32 · Creating a New Directory 33 · Is My File Somewhere on This Disk? 34 · Automating the Boot Sequence 35 · Assigning Disk 35

Closing Comments 37

Chapter 2 AmigaDOS Commands 39

Command Arguments and Command Options 39

Command Conventions 40

Format 41

Template 42

AmigaDOS Command Specifications 43

    ADDBUFFERS 43 · ADDMONITOR 44 · ALIAS 45 · ASK 46 · ASSIGN 47 · AUTOPOINT 51 · AVAIL 51 · BINDDRIVERS 52 · BINDMONITOR 52 · BLANKER 53 · BREAK 54 · CALCULATOR 55 · CD 56 · CHANGETASKPRI 57 · CLOCK 57 · CMD 58 · COLORS 59 · COPY 60 · CPU 62 · DATE 64 · DELETE 65 · DIR 66 · DISKCHANGE 68 · DISKCOPY 69 · DISKDOCTOR 70 · DISPLAY 71 · ECHO 73 · ED 74 · EDIT 78 · ELSE 82 · ENDCLI 82 · ENDIF 83 · ENDSHELL 83 · ENDSKIP 84 · EVAL 84 · EXCHANGE 86 · EXECUTE 87

Summary of DOT Commands 90

    FAILAT 91 · FAULT 93 · FILENOTE 93 · FIXFONTS 94 · FKEY 94 · FONT 95 · FORMAT 96 · GET 97 · GETENV 97 ·

GRAPHICDUMP 98 · ICONEDIT 99 · ICONTROL 99 · ICONX 100 ·
IF 100 · IHELP 102 · INFO 103 · INITPRINTER 104 · INPUT 104 ·
INSTALL 105 · IPREFS 106 · JOIN 106 · KEYSHOW 107 · LAB 107 ·
LIST 107 · LOADWB 110 · LOCK 111 · MAKEDIR 112 ·
MAKELINK 112 · MEMACS 113 · MORE 118 · MOUNT 119 ·
NEWCLI 119 · NEWSHELL 120 · NOCAPSLOCK 121 ·
NOFASTMEM 122 · OVERSCAN 122 · PALETTE 123 · PATH 123 ·
POINTER 125 · PRINTER 125 · PRINTERGFX 126 · PRINTFILES 126 ·
PROMPT 127 · PROTECT 128 · QUIT 129 · RELABEL 130 ·
REMRAD 131 · RENAME 131 · RESIDENT 132 · RUN 134 ·
SAY 135 · SCREENMODE 136 · SEARCH 136 · SERIAL 138 ·
SET 138 · SETCLOCK 139 · SETDATE 140 · SETENV 141 ·
SETFONT 141 · SETMAP 142 · SETPATCH 143 · SKIP 143 ·
SORT 144 · STACK 145 · STATUS 146 · TIME 146 · TYPE 147 ·
UNALIAS 147 · UNSET 148 · UNSETENV 148 · VERSION 148 ·
WAIT 149 · WBCONFIG 150 · WBPATTERN 151 · WHICH 152 ·
WHY 153

AmigaDOS Command Quick Reference   153

Chapter 3   AmigaDOS Error Messages   157

Chapter 4   Glossary   163

PART II   THE DEVELOPER'S MANUAL   167

Chapter 5   Programming on the Amiga   169

Introduction   169

Program Development for the Amiga   169

    Getting Started   169 · Calling Resident Libraries   170

    Creating an Executable Program   170

Running a Program Under the CLI   171
   Initial Environment in Assembler   171 · Initial Environment in C   172 · Failure of Routines   172 · Terminating a Program   172

Running a Program Under the Workbench   173

Basic Input and Output Programming   173
   Using File Handlers   177 · Buffered I/O   179
   Standard Command Line Parsing   181

Chapter 6   Calling AmigaDOS   187

Syntax   187
   Register Value   187 · Case   187 · Boolean Returns   188 · Values   188

AmigaDOS Functions   188
   AbortPkt   188 · AddBuffers   189 · AddDosEntry   190 · AddPart   191 · AddSegment   192 · AllocDosObject   193 · AssignAdd   193 · AssignLate   194 · AssignLock   195 · AssignPath   196 · AttemptLockDosList   196 · ChangeMode   197 · CheckSignal   198 · Cli   199 · Close   199 · CompareDates   200 · CreateDir   201 · CreateNewProc   201 · CreateProc   202 · CurrentDir   203 · DateStamp   204 · DateToStr   205 · Delay   206 · DeleteFile   207 · DeleteVar   207 · DeviceProc   208 · DoPkt   209 · DupLock   210 · DupLockFromFH   211 · EndNotify   212 · ErrorReport   212 · ExAll   213 · Examine   216 · ExamineFH   217 · Execute   218 · Exit   219 · ExNext   220 · Fault   221 · FGetC   222 · FGets   223 · FilePart   224 · FindArg   225 · FindCliProc   225 · FindDosEntry   226 · FindSegment   227 · FindVar   228 · Flush   228 · Format   229 · FPutC   230 · FPuts   231 · FRead   231 · FreeArgs   232 · FreeDeviceProc   233 · FreeDosEntry   233 · FreeDosObject   234 · FWrite   235 · GetArgStr   235 · GetConsoleTask   236 · GetCurrentDirName   236 · GetDeviceProc   237 · GetFileSysTask   238 · GetProgramDir   239 · GetProgramName   239 · GetPrompt   240 · GetVar   241 · Info   242 · Inhibit   243 · Input   243 · InternalLoadSeg   244 · InternalUnLoadSeg   245 · IoErr   246 · IsFileSystem   247 · IsInteractive   247 · LoadSeg   248 · Lock   249 · LockDosList   249 · LockRecord   250 · LockRecords   251 · MakeDosEntry   252 · MakeLink   253 · MatchEnd   254 · MatchFirst   254 · MatchNext   256 · MatchPattern   257 · MatchPatternNoCase   257 ·

MaxCli 258 · NameFromFH 259 · NamFromLock 259 ·
NewLoadSeg 260 · NextDosEntry 261 · Open 262 ·
OpenFromLock 263 · Output 263 · ParentDir 264 · ParentOfFH 265 ·
ParsePattern 265 · ParsePatternNoCase 266 · PathPart 267 ·
PrintFault 268 · PutStr 268 · Read 269 · ReadArgs 270 ·
ReadItem 272 · ReadLink 273 · Relabel 274 · RemAssignList 275 ·
RemDosEntry 275 · RemSegment 276 · Rename 277 · ReplyPkt 277 ·
RunCommand 278 · SameDevice 279 · SameLock 280 · Seek 280 ·
SelectInput 281 · SelectOutput 282 · SendPkt 282 · SetArgStr 283 ·
SetComment 284 · SetConsoleTask 284 · SetCurrentDirName 285 ·
SetFileDate 286 · SetFileSize 286 · SetFileSysTask 287 · SetIoErr 288 ·
SetMode 288 · SetProgramDir 289 · SetProgramName 290 ·
SetPrompt 290 · SetProtection 291 · SetVar 292 · SetVBuf 293 ·
SplitName 294 · StartNotify 295 · StrToDate 296 · StrToLong 297 ·
SystemTagList 298 · UnGetC 299 · UnLoadSeg 300 · UnLock 301 ·
UnLockDosList 302 · UnLockRecord 302 · UnLockRecords 303 ·
VFPrintf 304 · VFWritef 304 · VPrintf 305 · WaitForChar 306 ·
WaitPkt 307 · Write 308 · WriteChars 308

AmigaDOS Function Quick Reference 310

Chapter 7 The Linker 315

Introduction 315

Using the Linker 316

   Command Line Syntax 317 · WITH Files 318 · Errors and Other
   Exceptions 320 · MAP and XREF Output 320

Overlaying 321

   OVERLAY Directive 321 · References to Symbols 324 ·
   Cautionary Points 325

Error Codes and Messages 325

Chapter 8 AmigaDOS Device Input and Output 327

AmigaDOS Devices 328
Communicating with AmigaDOS Devices 331

PART III THE TECHNICAL REFERENCE MANUAL 333

Chapter 9 The Filing System 335

AmigaDOS File Structure 335
Root Block 336
    FFS Root Block 338
User Directory Blocks 341
    Hashing Algorithm 342 · FFS User Directory Blocks 344
File Header Block 345
    OFS and FFS File Header Block 346 · Hard and Soft Links 346
File List Block 347
    OFS and FFS File List Block 347
Data Block 348
    OFS Data Block 349 · FFS Data Block 349

Chapter 10 Amiga Binary File Structure 351

Introduction 351
    Terminology 351
Object File Structure 353
    hunk_unit (999/3E7) 354 · hunk_name (1000/3E8) 355 · hunk_code (1001/3E9) 355 · hunk_data (1002/3EA) 356 · hunk_bss (1003/3ED) 357 · hunk_reloc32 (1004/3EC) 357 · hunk_reloc32short (1020/3FC) 358 · hunk_reloc16 (1005/3ED) 359 · hunk_reloc8 (1006/3EE) 359 · hunk_dreloc32 (1015/3F7) 359 · hunk_dreloc16

(1016/3F8) 359 · hunk_dreloc8 (1017/3F9) 359 · hunk_ext
(1007/3EF) 360 · hunk_symbol (1008/3F0) 362 · hunk_debug
(1009/3F1) 363 · hunk_end (1010/3F2) 364

Load Files 364

hunk_header (1011/3F3) 365 · hunk_overlay (1013/3F5) 367 · hunk_break (1014/3F6) 367

Examples 368

Amiga Library File Structure 371

Example Library File 372 · The New Library File Structure 373 · hunk_lib (1019/3FB) 373 · hunk_index (1020/3FC) 373 · Example of hunk_lib 375 · Example of hunk_index 375

Chapter 11   AmigaDOS Data Structures   381

Introduction 381

Process Data Structures 382

Redirecting System Requesters 386

DOS Library 387

Info Substructure 389

Memory Allocation 392

Segment Lists 393

File Handles 393

Locks 394

AmigaDOS Packets 395

Packet Types 397

Basic Input/Output 399 · Directory/File Manipulation/Information 403 · Volume Manipulation/Information 416 · Handler Maintenance and Control 417 · Handler Internal 420 · Obsolete Packets 421 · Console Only Packets 421 · Summary of Defined Packet Numbers 421

Using Packets Directly 424

Chapter 12 Additional Information for the Advanced Developer 429

Hunk Overlay Table—Overview 430
    Designing an Overlay Tree 430 · Describing the Tree 431
Creating a New Device to Run Under AmigaDOS 434
Making New Disk Devices 435
Using AmigaDOS Without Workbench/Intuition 435

Index 437

Part I

THE USER'S MANUAL

Introduction

This manual describes the AmigaDOS and its commands. The Command Line Interpreter (CLI) reads AmigaDOS commands typed into a CLI window and translates them into actions performed by the computer. In this sense, the CLI is similar to more "traditional" computer interfaces: you type in commands and the interface displays text in return.

How to Open a Shell Window

To activate the CLI, also known as the Shell, boot the Amiga, and use the mouse to select the Workbench disk icon. Or, if you are using an Amiga with pre-installed hard disk software, use the mouse to select the system 2.0 icon. When the Workbench window opens, select the Shell icon (a box containing "1>"). A Shell window will open.

To use the Shell, select the Shell window and type the desired AmigaDOS commands. The Shell window may be sized and moved just like most others. To close the Shell window, type "ENDSHELL", or click on the close gadget in the upper-left-hand corner of the window.

Workbench and CLI, Their Relationship and Differences

Type "DIR" to display a list of files (and directories) in the current disk directory. This is a list of files that makes up your Workbench. You may notice that there are more files in this directory than there are icons on the Workbench. Workbench only displays file "X" if that file has an associated "X.info" file. Workbench uses the ".info" file to manipulate the icon.

For example, the diskcopy program has two files. The file "Diskcopy" contains the program and "Diskcopy.info" contains the Workbench information about it. In the case of painting data files like "mount.pic" the file "mount.pic.info" contains icon information and the name of the program (default) that should process it (GraphiCraft). In this case, when the user "opens" the data file (mount.pic) Workbench runs the program and passes the data file name (mount.pic) to it.

AmigaDOS subdirectories correspond to Workbench drawers. Random access block devices such as disks (DF0:) correspond to the disk icons you have seen.

Not all programs or commands can be run under both the Workbench and the Shell environment. Many of the AmigaDOS commands described in Chapter 2 of this manual can be run only from the Shell.

Throughout this book, the terms "CLI" and "Shell" are used to refer to the special window where you can type in AmigaDOS commands.

Chapter 1

Introducing AmigaDOS

This chapter provides a general overview of the AmigaDOS operating system, including descriptions of terminal handling, the directory structure, and command use. At the end of the chapter, you'll find a simple example session with AmigaDOS.

About AmigaDOS Processes

AmigaDOS is a **multitasking** disk operating system designed for the Amiga. You normally run AmigaDOS for a single user. The multitasking facility lets many jobs take place simultaneously. You can also use the multitasking facility to suspend one job while you run another.

Each AmigaDOS **process** represents a particular process of the operating system—for example, the filing system. Only one process is running at a time, while other processes are either waiting for something to happen or have been interrupted and are waiting to be resumed. Each process has a **priority** associated with it, and the process with the highest priority that is free to run does so. Processes of lower priority run only when those of higher priority are waiting for some reason—for example, waiting for information to arrive from the disk.

The standard AmigaDOS system uses a number of processes that you did not start, for example, the process that handles the serial line. These processes are known as system processes. Other system processes handle the console and the filing system on a disk drive. If the hardware configuration contains more than one disk drive, there is a process for each drive.

AmigaDOS provides a process that you can use, called a **Command Line Interface** or **Shell**. There may be several Shell processes running simultaneously, numbered from 1 onward. The Shell processes read **commands** and then executes them. To make additional Shell processes, you use the NEWSHELL or RUN commands. To remove a Shell process use the ENDSHELL command. (You can find a full description of these commands in Chapter 2.)

Console Handling

You can direct information that you enter at the terminal to a Command Line Interface (Shell) that tells AmigaDOS to load a program, or you can direct the information to a program running under that Shell. In either case, a **console** (or **terminal**) **handler** processes input and output. This handler also performs local line editing and certain other functions. You can type ahead as many as 512 characters—the maximum line length.

To correct mistakes, you press the BACKSPACE key. This erases the last character you typed. To rub out an entire line, hold down the CTRL key while you press X. This **control combination** is referred to from this point on in the manual as CTRL-X. You may also use the left and right cursor keys to move within the command line to insert or remove characters if you make a mistake.

You can also search for the most recent occurrence of a specific command by typing the command line, or the beginning of it, then pressing Shift-up cursor (or Ctrl-R). For instance, if you type DIR and press Shift-up cursor, you will be returned to the last command to perform a DIR of any directory. Pressing Shift-down cursor moves you to the bottom of the history buffer, leaving the cursor on a blank line.

In addition to command line editing, the Shell also provides command history, which allows you to recall previously-entered command lines, edit them, and re-enter them. This is useful when you want to repeat a command or enter several very similar commands.

The Shell uses a 2K command-line buffer to retain command lines. The exact number of lines varies depending on lengths of the lines actually stored. When the buffer fills up, the oldest lines are lost. You access lines in the buffer through the up and down cursor keys:

up cursor	Moves backward in the history buffer (earlier lines).
down cursor	Moves forward in the history buffer (later lines).

If you type anything, AmigaDOS waits until you have finished typing before displaying any other output. Because AmigaDOS waits for you to finish, you can type ahead without your input and output becoming intermixed.

AmigaDOS recognizes that you have finished a line when you press the RETURN key. You can also tell AmigaDOS that you have finished with a line by cancelling it. To cancel a line, you can either press CTRL-X or press BACKSPACE until all the characters on the line have been erased. Once AmigaDOS is satisfied that you have finished, it starts to display the output that it was holding back. If you wish to stop the output so that you can read it, simply type any character (pressing the space bar is the easiest), and the output stops. To restart output, press BACKSPACE, CTRL-X, or RETURN. Pressing RETURN causes AmigaDOS to try to execute the command line typed after the current program exits.

AmigaDOS recognizes CTRL-\ as an end-of-file indicator. In certain circumstances, you use this combination to terminate an input file. (For a circumstance when you would use CTRL-\, see "Understanding Device Names," below.)

If you find that strange characters appear on the screen when you type anything on the keyboard, you have probably pressed CTRL-O by mistake. AmigaDOS recognizes this control combination as an instruction to the console device (CON:) to display the alternative character set. To undo this condition, you press CTRL-N. Any further characters should then appear as normal. You could press ESC-C to reset the console. This clears the screen and displays normal text.

The table below summarizes the editing capabilities of the Amiga's Shell interface.

Shell Editing Commands

left cursor	Moves cursor one character to the left.
right cursor	Moves cursor one character to the right.
Shift-left cursor	Moves cursor to the beginning of the line.
Shift-right cursor	Moves cursor to the end of the line.
Backspace	Deletes the character to the left of the cursor.
Del	Deletes the character highlighted by the cursor.
Ctrl-H	Deletes the last character (same as Backspace).
Ctrl-M	Processes the command line (same as Return).
Ctrl-J	Adds a line feed.
Ctrl-W	Deletes the word to the left of the cursor.
Ctrl-X	Deletes the current line.
Ctrl-K	Deletes everything from the cursor forward to the end of the line.
Ctrl-Y	Replaces the characters deleted with Ctrl-K.
Ctrl-U	Deletes everything from the cursor backward to the start of the line.
Space bar (or any printable character)	Suspends output (stops scrolling).

Backspace	Resumes output (continues scrolling).
Ctrl-C	Sends a BREAK command to the current process (halts the process).
Ctrl-D	Sends a BREAK command to the current script (halts the script).
Ctrl-S	Suspends output.
Ctrl-Q	Resumes output if it was suspended with Ctrl-S.
Ctrl-\	Closes the Shell window.

Finally, AmigaDOS recognizes all commands and **arguments** typed in either upper or lower case. AmigaDOS displays a **filename** with the characters in the case used when it was created, but finds the file no matter what combination of cases you use to specify the filename.

Using the Filing System

This section describes the AmigaDOS filing system. In particular, it explains how to name, organize, and recall your files.

A file is the smallest named object used by AmigaDOS. The simplest identification of a file is by its filename, discussed below in "Naming Files." However, it may be necessary to identify a file more fully. Such an identification may include the device or volume name, and/or directory name(s) as well as the filename. These will be discussed in following sections.

Naming Files

AmigaDOS holds information on disks in a number of **files**, named so that you can identify and recall them. The filing system allows filenames to have up to 30 characters, where the characters may be any printing character except slash (/) and colon (:). This means that you can include space( ), equals (=), plus (+), and double quote ("), all special characters recognized by the CLI, within a filename. However, if you use these special characters, you must enclose the entire filename within double quotes. To introduce a double quote character within a filename, you must type an asterisk (*) immediately before that character. In addition, to introduce an asterisk, you must type another asterisk. This means that a file named

```
A*B = C"
```

should be typed as follows:

```
A**B = C*""
```

for the CLI to accept it.

Note: This use of the asterisk is in contrast to many other operating systems where it is used as a universal **wild card**. An asterisk by itself in AmigaDOS represents the keyboard and the current window. For example,

```
COPY filename to *
```

copies the filename to the screen. On the Amiga, the universal wild card is #?.

When spaces are used within a file, directory, or device name, quotes are required when accessing the name. For example, copy "df0:My file" to ram.

Avoid spaces before or after filenames because they may cause confusion.

Using Directories

The filing system also allows the use of **directories** as a way to group files together into logical units. For example, you may use two different directories to separate program source from program documentation, or to keep files belonging to one person distinct from those belonging to another.

Each file on a disk must belong to a directory. An empty disk contains one directory, called the **root directory**. If you create a file on an empty disk, then that file belongs to this root directory. However, directories may themselves contain further directories. Each directory may therefore contain files, or yet more directories, or a mixture of both. Any filename is unique only within the directory it belongs to, so that the file "fred" in the directory "bill" is a completely different file from the one called "fred" in the directory "mary".

This filing structure means that two people sharing a disk do not have to worry about accidentally overwriting files created by someone else, as long as they always create files in their own directories.

WARNING: When you create a file with a filename that already exists, AmigaDOS deletes the previous contents of that file. No message to that effect appears on the screen.

You can also use this directory structure to organize information on the disk, keeping different sorts of files in different directories.

An example might help to clarify this. Consider a disk that contains two directories, called "bill" and "mary." The directory "bill" contains two files, called "text" and "letter". The directory "mary" contains a file called "data" and two directories called "letter" and "invoice". These sub-directories each contain a file called "jun18". Figure l-A represents this structure as follows:

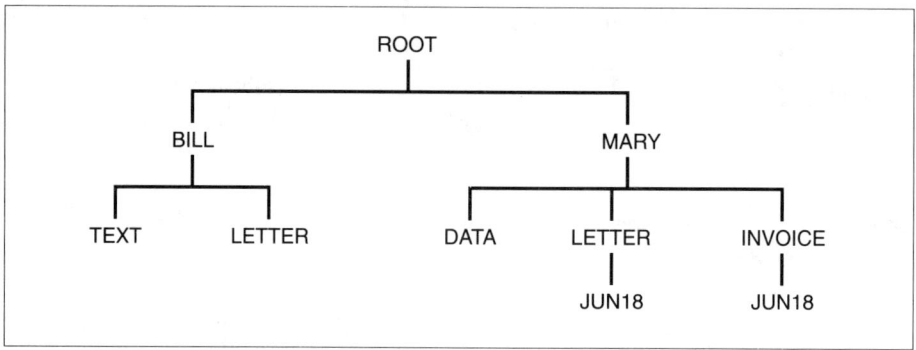

Figure l-A.
Using directory structure.

Note: The directory "bill" has a file called "letter", while the directory "mary" contains a directory called "letter". However, there is no confusion here because both files are in different directories. There is no limit to the depth that you can "nest" directories.

To specify a file fully, you must include the directory that owns it, the directory owning that directory, and so on. To specify a file, you give the names of all the directories on the path to the desired file. To separate each directory name from the next directory or filename, you type a following slash (/). Thus, the full specification of the data files on the disk shown in Figure l-A above is as follows:

```
bill/text
bill/letter
mary/data
mary/letter/jun18
mary/invoice/jun18
```

Setting the Current Directory

A full file description can get extremely cumbersome to type, so the filing system maintains the idea of a **current directory**. The filing system searches for files in this current directory. To specify the current directory, you use the CD (<u>C</u>urrent <u>D</u>irectory) command. If you have set "mary" as your current directory, then the following names would be sufficient to specify the files in that directory:

```
data
letter/jun18
invoice/jun18
```

You can set any directory as the current directory. To specify any files within that directory, simply type the name of the file. To specify files within subdirectories, you need to type the names of the directories on the path from the current directory specified.

All the files on the disk are still available even though you've set up a current directory. To instruct AmigaDOS to search through the directories from the root (top level) directory of a volume (disk or partition), you type a colon (:) at the beginning of the file description. Thus, when your file description has the current directory set to "mary", you can also obtain the file "data" by typing the description ":mary/data". Using the current directory method simply saves typing, because all you have to do is specify the filename "data".

To obtain the other files on the disk, first type ":bill/text" and ":bill/letter", respectively. Another way might be to CD or type / before a filename. Slash does not mean "root" as in some systems, but refers to the directory above the current directory. AmigaDOS allows multiple slashes. Each slash refers to the level above. So a Unix™ ../ is a / in AmigaDOS. Similarly, an MS-DOS™..\ is a / in AmigaDOS. Thus, if the current directory is ":mary/letter", you may specify the file ":mary/invoice/jun18" as "/invoice/jun18". To refer to the files in ":bill", you could type:

```
CD :bill
```

or

```
CD //bill
```

Then you could specify any file in "bill" with a single filename. Of course, you could always use the 11 feature to refer directly to a specific file. For example,

```
TYPE //bill/letter
```

displays the file without your first setting "bill" as the current directory. To go straight to the root level, always type a colon (:) followed by a directory name. If you use slashes, you must know the exact number of levels back desired.

Setting the Current Device

Finally, you may have many disk drives available. Each disk device has a name, in the form DFn (for example, DFl), where the "n" refers to the number of the device. (Currently, AmigaDOS accepts the device names DF0 to DF3.) Each individual disk is also associated with a unique name, known as a volume name (see below for more details).

In addition, the logical device SYS: is assigned to the disk you started the system up from. You can use this name in place of a disk device name (like DF0:).

The current directory is also associated with a **current drive**, the drive where you may find the directory. As you know, prefacing a file description with a colon serves to identify the root directory of the current drive. However, to give the root directory of a specific drive, you precede the colon with the drive name. Thus, you have yet another way of specifying the file "data" in directory "mary", that is "DFl:mary/data". This assumes that you have inserted the disk into drive DFl. So, to reference a file on the drive DF0 called "project-report" in directory "peter", you would type "DF0:peter/project-report", no matter which directory you had set as the current one.

Note: When you refer to a disk drive or any other device, on its own or with a directory name, you should always type the colon, for example, DFl:.

Figure l-B illustrates the structure of a file description. Figure l-C gives some examples of valid file descriptions.

Left of the:	Right of the:	Right of a/
Device name	Directory name	Subdirectory name
or	or	or
Volume name	Filename	Filename

Figure l-B.
The structure of a file description.

```
SYS:commands
DF0:bill
DF1:mary/letter
DF2:mary/letter/jun18
DOC:report/section1/figures
FONTS:silly-font
C:cls
```

Figure l-C.
Examples of file descriptions.

To gain access to a file on a particular disk, you can type its unique name, which is known as the disk's **volume name**, instead of the device name. For instance, if the file is on the disk "MCC", you can specify the same file by typing the name "MCC:peter/project-report". You can use the volume name to refer to a disk regardless of the drive it is in. You assign a volume name to a disk when you format it (for further details, see "FORMAT" in Chapter 2). You can also change the volume name using the RELABEL command.

A device name, unlike a volume name, is not really part of the name. For example, AmigaDOS can read a file you created on DF0: from another drive, such as DF1:, if you place the disk in that drive, assuming of course that the drives are interchangeable. That is, if you create a file called "bill" on a disk in drive DF0:, the file is known as "DF0:bill". If you then move the disk to drive DF1:, AmigaDOS can still read the file, which is then known as "DF1:bill".

Attaching a Filenote

Although a filename can give some information about its contents, it is often necessary to look in the file itself to find out more. AmigaDOS provides a simple solution to this problem. You can use the command called FILENOTE to attach an associated comment. You can make up a comment of up to 80 characters (you must enclose comments containing spaces in double quotes). Anything can be put in a file comment: the day of the file's creation, whether or not a bug has been fixed, the version number of a program, and anything else that may help to identify it.

You must associate a comment with a particular file—not all files have them. To attach comments, you use the FILENOTE command. If you create a new file, it will not have a comment. Even if the new file is a copy of a file that has a comment, the comment is not copied to the new file. However, any comment attached to a file which is overwritten is retained. To write a program to copy a file and its comment, you'll have to do some extra work to copy the comment. For details, see Chapter 6.

When you rename a file, the comment associated with it doesn't change. The RENAME command only changes the name of a file. The file's contents and comment remain the same regardless of the name change. For more details, see "LIST" and "FILENOTE" in Chapter 2.

Understanding Device Names

Devices have names so that you can refer to them by name. Disk names such as DF0: are examples of **device names**. Note that you may refer to device names, like filenames, using either upper or lower case. For disks, you follow the device name by a filename because AmigaDOS supports files on these devices.

Furthermore, the filename can include directories because AmigaDOS also supports directories.

You can also create files in memory with the device called RAM:. RAM: implements a filing system in memory that supports any of the normal filing system commands.

Note: If you are running AmigaDOS 1.3 or an earlier version, RAM: requires the library L:/ram-handler to be on the disk. (Under 2.0 the RAM-handler is in the ROMs.)

Once the RAM: device exists, you can, for instance, create a directory to copy all the commands into memory. To do this, type the following commands:

```
MAKEDIR ram:c
COPY sys:c TO ram:c
ASSIGN C: RAM:C
```

You could then look at the output with DIR RAM:. It would include the directory "c" (DIR lists this as c(dir).) This would make loading commands very quick but would leave little room in memory for anything else. Any files in the RAM: device are lost when you reset the machine.

AmigaDOS also provides a number of other devices that you can use instead of a reference to a disk file. The following paragraphs describe these devices including NIL:, SER:, PAR:, PRT:, CON:, and RAW:. In particular, the device NIL: is a dummy device. AmigaDOS simply throws away output written to NIL:. While reading from NIL:, AmigaDOS gives an immediate "end-of-file" indication. For example, you would type the following:

```
EDIT abc TO nil:
```

to use the editor to browse through a file, while AmigaDOS throws away the edited output.

You use the device called SER: to refer to any device connected to the serial line (often a printer). Thus, you would type the following command sequence:

```
COPY xyz TO ser:
```

to instruct AmigaDOS to send the contents of the file "xyz" down the serial line. Note that the serial device only copies in multiples of 400 bytes at a time. Copying with SER: can therefore appear granular.

The device PAR: refers to the parallel port in the same way.

AmigaDOS also provides the device PRT: (for PRinTer). PRT: is the printer you chose in the Preferences program. In this program, you can define your printer to be connected through either the serial or parallel port. Thus, the command sequence:

```
COPY xyz TO PRT:
```

prints the file "xyz," no matter how the printer is connected.

All output sent to PRT: is translated through the printer driver selected in Preferences. The printer driver will translate standard ANSI escape codes into the specific code required by the printer. PRT: translates every linefeed character in a file to carriage return plus linefeed. Some printers, however, require files without translation. To send a file with the linefeeds as just linefeeds, you use PRT:RAW instead of PRT:.

AmigaDOS supports multiple windows. To make a new window, you can specify the device CON:. The format for CON: is as follows:

```
CON:x/y/width/height/[title]
```

where "x" and "y" are coordinates, "width" and "height" are integers describing the width and height of the new window, and "title", which is optional, is a string. The title appears on the window's title bar. You must include all the slashes (/), including the last one. Your title can include up to 30 characters (including spaces). If the title has spaces, you must enclose the whole description in double quotes (") as shown in the following example:

```
"CON:20/10/300/100/my window"
```

Under 2.0 and later versions of AmigaDOS, CON: windows have additional special features. Refer to Chapter 8 for a complete description.

There is another window device called RAW:, but it is of little use to the general user. (See Chapter 8 for further details.) You can use RAW: to create a raw window device similar to CON:. However, unlike CON:, RAW: does no character translation and does not allow you to change the contents of a line. That is to say, RAW: accepts input and returns output in exactly the same form that it was originally typed. This means characters are sent to a program immediately without letting you erase anything with the BACKSPACE key. You usually use RAW: from a program where you might want to do input and output without character translation.

WARNING: RAW: is intended for the advanced user. Do not use RAW: experimentally.

There is one special name, which is * (asterisk). You use this to refer to the current window, both for input or for output. You can use the COPY command to copy from one file to another. Using *, you can copy from the current window to another window, for example,

```
COPY * TO CON:20/20/350/150/
```

from the current window to the current window, for example,
```
COPY * TO *
```

or from a file to the current window, for example,

```
COPY bill/letter TO *
```

AmigaDOS finishes copying when it comes to the end of the file. To tell AmigaDOS to stop copying from *, you must give the CTRL-\ combination. Note that * is NOT the universal wild card.

Using Directory Conventions and Logical Devices

In addition to the aforementioned physical devices, AmigaDOS supports a variety of useful **logical devices**. AmigaDOS uses these devices to find the files that your programs require from time to time. (So that your programs can refer to a standard device name regardless of where the file actually is.) All of these "logical devices" may be reassigned by you to reference any directory.

The logical devices described in this section are as follows (Figure 1-D):

Name	Description	Directory
SYS:	System disk root directory	SYS:
C:	Commands directory	SYS:C
L:	Library directory	SYS:L
S:	Script directory	SYS:S
LIBS:	Directory for Open Library calls	SYS:LIBS
DEVS:	Directory for Open Device calls	SYS:DEVS
FONTS:	Loadable fonts for Open Fonts	SYS:FONTS
	Temporary workspace	RAM:T

Figure l-D.
Logical devices.

Logical device name: SYS:
Typical directory name: Workbench:

"SYS" represents the SYStem disk root directory. When you first start up the Amiga system, AmigaDOS assigns SYS: to the root directory name of the disk in DF0:. If, for instance, the disk in drive DF0: has the volume name Workbench, then AmigaDOS assigns SYS: to Workbench:. After this assignment, any programs that refer to SYS: use that disk's root directory.

Logical device name: C:
Typical directory name: Workbench:c
'C' represents the Commands directory. When you type a command to the CLI (DIR <cr>, for example), AmigaDOS first searches for that command in your current directory. If the system cannot find the command in the current directory, it then looks for "C:DIR". So that, if you have assigned "C:" to another directory (for example, "Boot_disk:c"), AmigaDOS reads and executes from "Boot_disk:c/DIR".

Logical device name: L:
Typical directory name: Workbench:l
"L" represents the Library directory. This directory keeps the overlays for large commands and nonresident parts of the operating system. For instance, the disk based run-time libraries (Aux-Handler, Port-Handler, and so forth) are kept here. AmigaDOS requires this directory to operate.

Logical device name: S:
Typical directory name: Workbench:s
"S" represents the Script directory. This directory contains command scripts that the EXECUTE command searches for and uses. EXECUTE first looks for the script (or batch) file in your current directory. If EXECUTE cannot find it there, it looks in the directory that you have assigned S: to.

Logical device name: LIBS:
Typical directory name: Workbench:LIBS
The system looks here for the library if it is not already loaded in memory.

Logical device name: DEVS:
Typical directory name: Workbench:DEVS
Open Device calls look here for the device if it is not already loaded in memory.

Logical device name: FONTS:
Typical directory name: Workbench:FONTS
Open Fonts look here for your loadable fonts if they are not already loaded in memory.

Note: In addition to the above assignable directories, many programs open files in the "T" directory. You use this directory to store temporary files. Programs such as editors place their temporary work files, or backup copies of the last file edited, in this directory. If you run out of space on a disk, this is one of the first places you should look for files that are no longer needed.

When the system is first booted, AmigaDOS initially assigns C: to the :C directory. This means that if you boot with a disk that you had formatted by issuing the command:

```
FORMAT DRIVE DF0: NAME "My.Boot.Disk"
```

SYS: is assigned to "My.Boot.Disk". The "logical device" C: is assigned to the C directory on the same disk (that is, My.Boot.Disk:c). Likewise, the following assignments are made:

```
C:          My.Boot.Disk:c
L:          My.Boot.Disk:l
S:          My.Boot.Disk:s
LIBS:       My.Boot.Disk:libs
DEVS:       My.Boot.Disk:devs
FONTS:      My.Boot.Disk:fonts
```

If a directory is not present, the corresponding logical device is assigned to the root directory.

If you have a non-bootable hard disk (here called DH0:) and you want to use the system files on it, you must issue the following commands to the system:

```
ASSIGN SYS:      DH0:
ASSIGN C:        DH0:C
ASSIGN L:        DH0:L
ASSIGN S:        DH0:S
ASSIGN LIBS:     DH0:LIBS
ASSIGN DEVS:     DH0:DEVS
ASSIGN FONTS:    DH0:FONTS
```

If your hard disk is bootable, you don't need to make these assigns since the system handles it for you.

Please keep in mind that assignments are global to all Shell processes. Changing an assignment within one window changes it for all windows.

If you want to use your own special font library, type:

```
ASSIGN FONTS: "Special font disk:myfonts"
```

If you want your commands to load faster (and you have memory "to burn"), type:

```
makedir ram:c
copy sys:c ram:c all
assign c: ram:c
```

This copies all of the normal AmigaDOS commands to the RAM disk and reassigns the commands directory so that the system finds them there. Another way to speed up AmigaDOS commands is by making them resident. See the description of the RESIDENT command in Chapter 2.

Using AmigaDOS Commands

An AmigaDOS command consists of the command name and its arguments, if any. To execute an AmigaDOS command, you type the command name and its arguments after the Shell prompt.

When you type a command name, the command runs as part of the Command Line Interface (Shell). You can type other command names ahead, but AmigaDOS does not execute them until the current command has finished. When a command has finished, the current Shell prompt appears. In this case, the command is running interactively.

The Shell prompt is initially n> where n is the number of the Shell process. However, it can be changed to something else with the PROMPT command. (For further details on the PROMPT command, see Chapter 2.)

WARNING: If you run a command interactively and it fails, AmigaDOS continues to execute the next command you typed anyway. Therefore, it can be dangerous to type many commands ahead. For example, if you type

```
COPY a TO b
DELETE a
```

and the COPY command fails (perhaps because the disk is full), then DELETE executes and you lose your file.

Running Commands in the Background

You can instruct AmigaDOS to run a command, or commands, in the background. To do this, you use the RUN command. This creates a new Shell as a separate process of the same priority. In this case, AmigaDOS executes subsequent command lines at the same time as those that have been RUN. For example, you can examine the contents of your directory at the same time as sending a copy of your text file to the printer. To do this, type

```
RUN TYPE text_file to PRT:
LIST
```

RUN creates a new Shell and carries out your printing while you list your directory files on your original Shell window.

You can ask AmigaDOS to carry out several commands using RUN. RUN takes each command and carries it out in the given order. The line containing commands after RUN is called a command line. To terminate the command line, press RETURN. To extend your command line over several lines, type a plus sign (+) before pressing RETURN on every line except the last. For example,

```
RUN JOIN text_file1 text_file2 AS text_file +
SORT text_file TO sorted_text +
TYPE sorted_text to PRT:
```

If you want to start a command using RUN and then close the Shell window from which it was launched, you will have to redirect input and output. To do this use: RUN<NIL:>NIL: command.

Executing Command Files

You can also use the EXECUTE command to execute command lines in a file instead of typing them in directly. The Shell reads the sequence of commands from the file until it finds an error or the end of the file. If it finds an error, AmigaDOS does not execute subsequent commands on the RUN line or in the file used by EXECUTE, unless you have used the FAILAT command. See Chapter 2 for details on the FAILAT command. The Shell only gives prompts after executing commands that have run interactively.

Directing Command Input and Output

AmigaDOS provides a way for you to redirect standard input and output. You use the > and < symbols as commands. When you type a command, AmigaDOS usually displays the output from that command on the screen. To tell AmigaDOS to send the output to a file, you can use the > command. To tell AmigaDOS to accept the input to a program from a specified file rather than from the keyboard, you use the < command. The < and > commands act like traffic cops who direct the flow of information. For example, to direct the output from the DATE command and write it to the file named "text_file", you would type the following command line:

```
DATE > text__file
```

If you want to redirect output to a file that already exists use >>. For example, to direct the output of the TYPE command to a file that already exists use

```
TYPE >>more__text original__text
```

The text stored in the file original __text will be appended to any text that is already stored in the file my__text. Under 2.0 and later versions of AmigaDOS, if you redirect output to a file using >> and the file does not exist, then the file will be created for you.

Interrupting AmigaDOS

AmigaDOS allows you to indicate four levels of attention interrupt with CTRL-C, CTRL-D, CTRL-E, and CTRL-F. To stop the current command from whatever it was doing, press CTRL-C. In some cases, such as EDIT, pressing CTRL-C instructs the command to stop what it was doing and then to return to reading more EDIT commands. To tell the CLI to stop a command sequence initiated by the EXECUTE command as soon as the current command being executed finishes, press CTRL-D. CTRL-E and CTRL-F are only used by certain commands in special cases. See Chapter 2 for details.

Note: It is the programmer's responsibility to detect and respond to these interruption flags. AmigaDOS will not kill a program by itself.

Restart Validation Process

When you first insert a disk for updating, AmigaDOS creates a process at low priority. This validates the entire structure on the disk. Until the restart process has completed this job, you cannot create files on the disk. It is possible, however, to read files.

Older versions of AmigaDOS (1.3 and earlier) do some additional processing when a new disk is inserted. When the restart process completes, AmigaDOS checks to see if you have set the system date and time. To set the date and time, you use the DATE command, the SETCLOCK command, or the TIME command (see Chapter 2). If you do not specify the system date, AmigaDOS sets the system date to the date and time of the most recently created file on the inserted disk. This ensures that newer versions of files have more recent dates, even though the actual time and date will be incorrect.

Under V1.3 and earlier versions of AmigaDOS, if you ask for the date and the time before the validation is complete, AmigaDOS displays the date and time as unset. You can then either wait for the validation to complete or use DATE to enter the correct date and time.

Commonly Used Commands

This manual describes the various AmigaDOS commands. The Command Line Interpreter (Shell) reads AmigaDOS commands typed into a Shell window and translates them into actions performed by the computer. In this sense the Shell is similar to more "traditional" computer interfaces: you type in commands and the interface displays text in return.

Using the Shell

To use the Shell interface, select the Shell window and type the desired Shell commands (described within this manual). The Shell window(s) may be sized and moved just like many others. To close the Shell window, type "END-SHELL".

Not all programs or commands can be run under both the Workbench and the Shell environment. Many of the AmigaDOS commands described in Chapter 2 can be run only from the Shell.

Throughout this book, the terms "CLI" and "Shell" are used to refer to the special window where you can type in AmigaDOS commands. Although the terms are used to mean the same thing, there is a slight difference. Just keep in mind that the CLI and the Shell both refer to the place where you can type in AmigaDOS commands.

Some AmigaDOS Commands

Although all of the commands that are available through the Shell are explained in detail in Chapter 2 of this book, we have found that most users will use very few of the advanced options. Therefore we have provided a summary here showing various commands in their most common form.

The commands summarized below (along with the actual AmigaDOS command name) ask AmigaDOS to do such operations as:

- Copy a disk (DISKCOPY)
- Format a new disk (FORMAT)
- Make a formatted disk bootable (INSTALL)
- Create a CLI disk
- Relabel a disk (RELABEL)
- Look at the directory of a disk (DIR)
- Get information about files (LIST)
- Prevent a file from accidental deletion (PROTECT)
- Get Information about a file system (INFO)
- Change a current directory (CD)
- Set the date and time (DATE)
- Redirect the output of a command (>)
- Type a text file to the screen (TYPE)
- Rename a file (RENAME)
- Delete a file (DELETE)
- Create a new directory (MAKEDIR)
- Copy files on a dual-drive system (COPY)
- Copy files on a single-drive system (COPY)
- Find files on a disk (DIR OPT A)
- Do something automatically at boot time (using Startup-Sequence)
- Tell AmigaDOS where to look for certain things (ASSIGN)
- Open a new Shell window (NEWSHELL)
- Close an existing Shell window (ENDSHELL)

For a New User

For a new user, we suggest that you read and try each of these items in sequence. Each command that is shown below leaves a test disk in a known state so that the command that immediately follows will work exactly as shown. Later, when you are more familiar with the system, the subsection titles shown below will serve to refresh your memory.

How to Begin

Before you begin this section, be sure you have two blank, double-sided disks, and your Workbench disk. Before you begin, write-protect your master disk, and write-enable the blank disks. Most of the commands given below assume that you have a single-drive system; however, for convenience of those with dual-drive systems, the dual-drive version of the command is occasionally given.

Commands that instruct AmigaDOS to execute are shown in the following sections, indented from the left margin. After typing each command, press the RETURN key to return control to AmigaDOS. Although the commands are all shown in capital letters, this is simply to distinguish them from the rest of the text. AmigaDOS will accept the commands in lower case as well as upper case.

In the sections that follow, the notations "df0:" and "drive 0" refer to the disk drive that is built into the Amiga. The notation "df1:" refers to the first external 3½-inch disk drive. (Some systems use "df2:" to refer to the external drive.)

You will occasionally see a semicolon on a command line that you are told to type. What follows the semicolon is treated as a comment by AmigaDOS. Since AmigaDOS ignores the rest of the line, you don't need to type the comment along with the command. It is for your information only.

For most commands, you can get a very limited form of help by typing the command name, followed by a question mark (?) and pressing RETURN. It shows you the "template" of a command, containing the sequence of parameters it expects and the keywords it recognizes.

Copying a Disk

You can use this sequence to back up your system master disk or any other disk.

For a one-disk system:

```
DISKCOPY FROM df0: TO df0:
```

For a two-disk system:

```
DISKCOPY FROM df0: TO df1:
```

Follow the instructions as they appear. For a single-drive system, you'll be instructed to insert the master (FROM) disk. Then, as the copying progresses, AmigaDOS asks you to insert the copy (TO) disk, swapping master and copy in and out until all of the disk has been duplicated. For a two disk system, you'll be instructed to put the master disk into drive df0: (the built-in drive) and the copy disk onto which to copy into df1: (the first external drive).

Remove your master disk and put your master disk in a safe place. Leave the copy write-enabled so that you can store information on it. Insert the copy you have just made into the built-in drive and reboot your system from the copy. (See "Making a Disk Bootable," below.)

After the reboot, reenter the CLI mode again.

Formatting a Disk

To try this command, your Workbench or CLI disk copy should be in drive 0, and you should have a blank disk available.

Sometimes rather than simply copy a disk, you'll want to prepare a data disk for your system. Then later you can copy selected files to this data disk. Format your second blank disk by using the FORMAT command:

```
FORMAT DRIVE df0: NAME "AnyName"
```

Follow the instructions. You can format disks in either drive 0 (df0:, built in to your Amiga) or an extemal drive.

After the format is completed, wait for the disk activity light to go off and remove the freshly formatted disk. Reinsert your Workbench. The formatted disk can now be used to hold data files. It is not bootable, however.

Making a Disk Bootable

To try this command, your Workbench disk copy should be in drive 0, and you should have your freshly formatted disk available.

A bootable disk is one that you can use to start up your Amiga following the Kickstart process. You can change a formatted disk into a bootable disk by typing the command:

```
INSTALL ?
```

Note: To use this command on a single-drive system, you MUST use the question mark! Otherwise AmigaDOS will try to do the install on the disk currently in drive 0.

AmigaDOS responds:

```
DRIVE/A, NO BOOT/S, CHECK/S
```

Remove your Workbench disk copy and insert the formatted disk. Then type:

```
df0:
```

and press RETURN. AmigaDOS writes boot sectors to the disk in df0:. Now, if you wait until the disk activity light goes out, you can then perform a full reset (CTRL-Amiga-Amiga). When the system reboots, you will go directly into the CLI rather than into the Workbench.

Your formatted disk now contains a CLI and nothing else. This means that although you see the interpreter, it can't perform any of the commands shown in this section. A CLI needs several files before its commands can be performed. All of the command files are located in the C directory of your master disk.

Making a CLI Disk

There is another way to make a bootable disk that gives you a more useful disk in that it leaves the CLI command directories intact. Here is a step-by-step process to change a writable copy of a Workbench diskette into a CLI disk:

1. Copy your Workbench disk.

2. Open the Shell as described above.

3. Select the Shell window and type the command:

```
RENAME FROM s/startup-sequence TO s/NO-startup-sequence
```

Now if you wait for the disk activity light to go off and perform a full reset, your Workbench disk copy will have become a CLI disk. To restore the Workbench, perform the rename again, but with the name sequence reversed. You see, if AmigaDOS can't find a file with the exact name "Startup-sequence" in the "s" directory, it will enter command mode and wait for you to type a command.

Relabeling a Disk

Before you try this command, your Workbench or CLI disk copy should be in drive 0.

If, after either copying or formatting a disk, you are not satisfied with the volume name you have given it, you can change the name of the volume by using the RELABEL command:

```
relabel df0: DifferentName
```

This command changes the volume of the disk in drive df0: to "Different Name."

Looking at the Directory

Before you try this command, your Workbench or CLI disk copy should be in drive 0.

You look at the contents of a disk with the command:

```
DIR or DIR df0:
```

This lists the contents of your current directory. You can list the contents of a different directory by specifying the pathname for that directory. For example, the command:

```
DIR df0:c or DIR c
```

lists the contents of the c(directory) on drive df0. Directories are equivalent to the drawers you see when the Workbench screen is visible.

You can look at the directory of a different disk unit, if you have one, by specifying its name. For example:

```
DIR df1:
```

lists the contents of a disk inserted in drive df1:.

You can even look at the directory of a disk that isn't currently in the drive by specifying its volume name. For example, the contents of that freshly formatted disk whose name we changed can be displayed by the command:

```
DIR DifferentName:
```

AmigaDOS will ask you to insert disk DifferentName into the drive so that DIR can read it and report the contents of the directory. Don't do it yet, however, because there are no files present for DIR to read. We'll add some files later.

Using the LIST Command

To try this command, your Workbench or CLI disk copy should be in drive 0.

The DIR command tells you the names of files that are in your directory. The LIST command provides additional information about those files. Type the command:

```
LIST
```

AmigaDOS provides information about all files in the current directory, including how large each file is, the protection flags for each file, whether it is a file or a directory, and the date and time of its creation.

If you specify the name of a directory with LIST, it lists information about the files within that directory:

```
LIST c
```

In the second column after the file name you will see the protection flags for the file. The acronym "rwed" refers to protection flags, for read, write, execute, and delete. When each flag is set, using the PROTECT command, a file is supposed to be readable, writable, executable, or deleteable.

Using the Protect Command

To try this command, your Workbench or CLI disk copy should be in drive 0.

This command protects (or unprotects) a file from being deleted accidentally. Try the command:

```
DATE > myfile
PROTECT myfile
LIST myfile
```

You will see that all of the protect-flags have been set to "--------". Now if you try:

```
DELETE myfile
```

AmigaDOS responds

```
"Not Deleted - file is protected from deletion"
```

To reenable deletion of the file, type:

```
PROTECT myfile d
```

For more information about file protection flags, see the discussion of the PROTECT command in Chapter 2.

Getting Information About the File System

Your Workbench or CLI disk copy should still be in drive 0. Type the command

```
INFO
```

It tells you how much space is used and how much is free on your disks, whether they are read-only or read-write, and the name of the volume. You can make more space on the disk by deleting files. You can change the name of the volume by using the RELABEL command.

If you want to get information about a disk that isn't in your single-drive at the moment, issue the command as

```
INFO ?
```

AmigaDOS responds

```
DEVICE:
```

AmigaDOS has loaded the INFO command from your CLI disk and shows you the template for the command. The response "DEVICE:" says that you can enter any device name to get information about it. But you don't have to type anything other than a RETURN key to have it perform the command. Remove your CLI disk and insert the disk on which you want INFO to operate. Wait for the disk activity light to go on and off. Then press RETURN. AmigaDOS gives you INFO about this other disk. This works for DIR as well as INFO.

Changing Your Current Directory

Until now, we have only stayed at the "root" or topmost hierarchical level of the disk directory. You will find more information about the directory tree structure in "Using Directories" earlier. To see the level at which you are currently positioned in your directory tree, you use the command:

```
CD
```

To change to a different current directory, you tell the system which directory is to become the current one. For example, when you did a DIR command on df0: the CLI disk you saw an entry "c(dir)". If you want to make this directory the current one, you issue the command:

```
CD df0:c
```

Now when you issue the command DIR, it shows the contents of this level of the filing system. The command CD (alone) shows you the name of your current directory. You go up to the root directory (the top level) by specifying:

```
CD :
```

on the current volume (if you refer to your disks by volume name) or

```
CD df0:
```

on the built-in drive.

Setting the Date and Time

You can set the AmigaDOS clock by using the DATE command:

```
DATE 12:00:00 12-oct-85
```

Now the system clock counts up from this date and time. If your system has a battery-backed, real-time clock, you can set it using the DATE command as described followed by the command:

```
SETCLOCK SAVE
```

The SETCLOCK SAVE command copies AmigaDOS time to the real-time clock.

Redirecting the Output of a Command

Before you try this command, your Workbench or CLI disk should be in drive 0.

Normally the output of all commands goes to the monitor screen. You can change where the system puts the output by using the redirect command ">". The forward arrow symbol means send the output toward this output file name. Here's an example:

```
DATE > datefile
```

Execute the command so that you can use the datefile described below. This command creates (or overwrites) a file named "datefile" in your current directory.

Typing a Text File to the Screen

You can see the contents of a text file by using the TYPE command:

```
TYPE datefile
```

This command will display whatever you have in the specified file. If you wish to stop the output momentarily to read something on the screen, press the space bar. To restart it press the BACKSPACE key. If you wish to end the TYPE command, hold down the CTRL key, and press the C key.

Changing the Name of a File

Before you try this command, your Workbench or CLI disk copy should be in drive 0.

You can change the name of a file by using the RENAME command:

```
RENAME FROM datefile TO newname
```

or

```
RENAME datefile newname
```

Now use TYPE to verify that the new name refers to the same contents.

```
TYPE newname
```

Notice that the alternate form of the command doesn't require that you use the FROM and TO. Most of the AmigaDOS commands have an alternate form, abbreviated from that shown in this tutorial section. The longer form has been used primarily to introduce you to what the command does. Be sure to examine the summary pages to familiarize yourself with the alternate command forms that are available.

Deleting Files

To try this command, your Workbench or CLI disk should be in drive 0.

You may be working on several versions of a program or text file, and eventually wish to delete versions of that file that you don't need anymore. The DELETE command lets you erase files and releases the disk space to AmigaDOS for reuse.

Note: If you DELETE files, it is not possible to retrieve them. Be certain that you really do wish to delete them.

Here is a sample command sequence, that creates a file using the redirection command, types it to verify that it is really there, then deletes it.

```
DIR > directorystuff
TYPE directorystuff
DELETE directorystuff
TYPE directorystuff
```

To the final command in the above sequence, AmigaDOS responds:

```
Can't Open directorystuff
```

indicating that the file can't be found, because you deleted it.

Copying Files

Before you enter this command, your Workbench or CLI disk should be in drive 0.

On a dual-drive system, copying files is easy:

```
COPY FROM df0:sourcepath TO df1:destinationpath
```

or

```
COPY df0:sourcepath df1:destinationpath
```

On a single-drive system, copying files is a little more complex. You must copy certain system files from your system diskette into the system memory. This is also called the RAM: device, or ramdisk. Copy the file(s) to the ramdisk, change your directory to the ramdisk, then copy from the ramdisk onto the destination disk. Here is a sample sequence.

Be sure your Workbench or CLI disk is in the internal disk drive. Issue the commands:

```
COPY df0:c/cd RAM:
COPY df0:c/copy RAM:
CD RAM:
```

Insert the source data disk into the drive. (For this example, copy the EXECUTE command from the Workbench or CLI disk, which is already in the drive.) Type:

```
COPY df0:c/execute ram:execute
            or
COPY df0:c/execute ram:
```

Remove the source disk, and insert the destination disk into the drive. The destination disk can be any Amiga disk that has been formatted. Type:

```
COPY ram:execute df0:execute
```

The EXECUTE command has now been copied from the source disk to the destination disk.

Remove the destination disk and insert your CLI or Workbench disk again. Type:

```
CD df0:
```

and you are back where you started. The only other command you may want to perform is:

```
DELETE RAM:cd RAM:copy RAM:execute
```

which releases the ramdisk memory to the system for other uses.

Creating a New Directory

You can create a new directory (newdrawer) within the current directory by using the MAKEDIR command:

```
MAKEDIR newdrawer
```

Now if you issue the DIR command, you will see that there is an entry for:

```
newdrawer (dir)
```

You can also use the RENAME command to move a file from one directory (drawer) to another on the same disk:

```
MAKEDIR newdrawer
RENAME FROM newname TO newdrawer/newname
```

moves the file from the current directory into the newdrawer you have created. To check that it has really been moved, issue the command:

```
DIR
```

Then type:

```
DIR newdrawer
```

AmigaDOS looks in the newdrawer, and shows you that the file named "newname" is there.

Is My File Somewhere on This Disk?

Before you enter this command, your Workbench or CLI disk copy should be in drive 0.

Sometimes you wish to see everything on the disk, instead of only one directory at a time. You can use the DIR command with one of its options:

```
DIR OPT A
```

which lists all directories and subdirectories on the disk. Keep in mind the <space><BACKSPACE> combination to pause and restart the listing.

To get a closer look at the disk's contents, you might redirect the output to a file:

```
DIR > mydiskdir ALL
```

Notice that the redirect-the-output command character and filename MUST come before the list of options for the DIR command.

Now, if you wish, you can TYPE the file mydiskdir and press the space bar to pause the listing. Use the RETURN key to resume the listing. Or, you can use ED to view the file, as follows:

```
ED mydiskdir
```

Use the cursor keys to move up and down in the file.
Use the key combination ESC then T <RETURN> to move to the top of the file.
Such a combination can be referred to as "ESC-T", meaning ESC followed by T.
Use the key combination ESC-B <RETURN> to move to the bottom of the file.
Use the key combination ESC-M then a number <RETURN> to move to a specific line number within the file.
Use the key combination ESC-Q <RETURN> to QUIT without changing the file
or
Use ESC-X <RETURN> to write any changes to your file back into the original file name.

Automating the Boot Sequence

There is a file in the "s" subdirectory on your Workbench or CLI disk called startup-sequence. This is a script file. It contains a sequence of CLI commands that AmigaDOS performs whenever you reboot the system. Also in your Workbench disk startup-sequence are LOADWB (load the Workbench program) and ENDCLI which basically leaves the Workbench program in control. You can make up your own startup-sequence file using ED or MEMACS to create a custom version of an execute command sequence. The EXECUTE command summary and tutorial section in Chapter 2 has details about various commands that you can have in this file. Note that startup-sequence can also be used to auto-run a program.

> **WARNING:** Take care to modify only a copy of your disk—never modify the master disk—if you decide to change the startup-sequence. If you are using AmigaDOS 2.0 or a later version, you should add commands only to the s: user-startup file rather than the s: startup-sequence file.

Note: The 2.0 startup-sequence looks for a file called s:user-startup and executes it if one is found. Whenever possible, place all your startup additions and assignments in a file called s:user-startup rather than modify the s:startup-sequence.

Assigning Disk

Before you enter this command, your Workbench or CLI disk copy should be in drive 0.

Occasionally, you might wish to change to a different disk and then continue your work. For example, you may have booted the system using a Workbench disk, then wish to change to a CLI disk. If the CLI disk has a directory on it that contains the executable commands you want to perform, (for example, a c directory), you can change to that disk by using the ASSIGN command.

If you don't use ASSIGN, you will have to swap disks to get commands done. Here is an example. The intent is to change disks and begin using "mydisk:" as the main disk. Before you begin, you must first create a disk called "mydisk". To do this, make a copy of Workbench (refer to the instructions for copying a disk given at the beginning of this section). Then use the RELABEL command described earlier to change the name of the new copy to "mydisk".

```
CD mydisk:
```

AmigaDOS responds "insert mydisk into any drive". Insert it, then type:

```
DIR
```

AmigaDOS prompts "insert Workbench [or whatever the boot disk name was] in any drive". It knows, from boot time, that the DIR command is in the boot disk, c directory. AmigaDOS reads the DIR command, then asks "insert mydisk in any drive". Any other AmigaDOS command also results in the need for a disk swap. To avoid this, use the ASSIGN command as follows:

```
ASSIGN c: mydisk:c
```

AmigaDOS asks "insert mydisk into any drive". From now on, all commands to AmigaDOS will be sought from the command (c) directory of mydisk and AmigaDOS won't ask for the original disk back for simple commands.

Once you've done this, you'll probably want to type:

```
CD mydisk:
```

There are other things that AmigaDOS can assign. If you issue the command

```
ASSIGN LIST
```

you will see the other things as well. If you run a program that requires a serial device (modem, printer) or a parallel device (printer), AmigaDOS looks in the directory currently assigned to DEVS: to locate the device. If all of the system directories are on this new main disk, you can avoid having AmigaDOS ask you to reinsert the original disk by providing a script file on your disks that reassigns all devices to that disk. The contents of this script file for a disk named "mydisk" are as follows:

```
ASSIGN SYS: mydisk:
ASSIGN S: mydisk:s
ASSIGN DEVS: mydisk:devs
ASSIGN L: mydisk:l
ASSIGN FONTS: mydisk:fonts
ASSIGN LIBS: mydisk:libs
```

To create this script file, use the command:

```
COPY FROM * TO reassign
```

Then type the above ASSIGN lines. After you've typed the last line, enter the key combination CTRL-\ which ends the file. The "*" stands for the keyboard and current CLI window, so this method of creating a file is one possible alternative to using ED or EDIT.

Once you have created the script file, you can run it by typing:

```
EXECUTE    REASSIGN
```

Now all the ASSIGN that the system uses are set up for "mydisk" instead of the original boot disk.

Closing Comments

Chapter 2 contains a reference section that shows the templates for each of the commands in AmigaDOS. You can look at the description for each command to find more information. Once you are familiar with the commands, and the forms in which you can use them, the quick reference listing at the end of the chapter will be useful to remind you of the commands that are available.

Chapter 2

AmigaDOS Commands

This chapter gives complete specifications of all the AmigaDOS 2.0 commands. All the AmigaDOS commands have been improved, and several new commands have been added. Many commands are now internal (built into the Shell) for speed, convenience, and reduced memory usage. This chapter includes:

- Command conventions, an explanation of the symbols and abbreviations used in the command descriptions
- Specifications for each command, including the Workbench and Preferences programs
- A table of error messages

A Quick Reference list of the AmigaDOS commands is included at the end of this chapter.

Command Arguments and Command Options

When you invoke an AmigaDOS command, you usually do more than type the command name at a Shell prompt. Many commands require arguments or support options that send the Amiga additional information about what you want to do. For example, if you type:

```
1> DIR Utilities
```

you are telling the Amiga to generate a list of files and subdirectories stored in the Utilities directory. In this command line, Utilities is a command argument. However, if you typed:

```
1> DIR Utilities FILES
```

only a list of the files in the Utilities directory would be shown; subdirectories would not be listed. Here, FILES is a command option.

Command Conventions

In the "Command Specifications" section, each AmigaDOS command is explained following a standard outline:

- Examples: When examples are given, the command and any screen output are indented from the main text. A generic 1> prompt indicates what should be typed at the Shell prompt. All command names and arguments are capitalized for clarity. Case does not matter when entering commands. To execute the command line, you must press Return.
- Format: All the arguments and options accepted by a command.
- Path: The directory where the command is normally stored. For most commands this will be the C: directory. The exceptions are the Internal commands which are copied into memory and the Workbench programs.
- Purpose: A short explanation of the command's function.
- Specification: A description of the command and all of its arguments.
- Template: A built-in reminder of the command's format. The template is embedded in the program's code. If you type a command followed by a question mark (DIR ?), the template will appear on the screen.

Remember, commands and arguments should be separated by spaces. (It does not have to be just one space; multiple spaces are acceptable.) No other punctuation should be used unless it is called for in the syntax of the specific command.

Format

Each AmigaDOS command is described by a Format listing and a command Template. In Format listings, arguments are enclosed in different kinds of brackets to indicate the type of argument. The brackets are not to be typed as part of the command.

< > Angle brackets enclose arguments that must be provided. For instance, <filename> means that you must enter the appropriate filename in that position. Unless square brackets surround the argument (see below), the argument is required. The command will not work unless it is specified.

[ ] Square brackets enclose arguments and keywords that are optional. They will be accepted by the command but are not required.

{ } Braces enclose items that can be given once or repeated any number of times. For example, {<args>} means that several items may be given for this argument.

| A vertical bar is used to separate options of which you can choose only one. For example, [OPT R | S | RS] means that you can choose the R option, the S option, or both (RS) options.

The format for the COPY command is:

```
COPY [FROM] {<name|pattern>} [TO] <name|pattern> [ALL]
[QUIET] [BUF|BUFFER = <n>] [CLONE] [DATE] [NOPRO] [COM]
```

The [FROM] keyword is optional. If it is not specified, the command reads the filename or pattern to copy by its position on the command line.

The {<name|pattern>} argument must be provided. You must substitute either a filename or pattern. The braces indicate that more than one argument can be given.

The [TO] keyword is optional. If it is not specified, the command reads the filename or device to copy to by its position on the command line.

The <name|pattern> argument must be provided. You can only specify one destination.

The [ALL], [QUIET], [CLONE], [DATE], [NOPRO], and [COM] arguments are optional.

The [BUF|BUFFER = <n>] argument is optional. If given, you can use either BUF or BUFFER and a numerical argument. For instance, both BUF=5 and BUFFER=5 are acceptable.

Template

The command Template is a more condensed command description than the Format listing and is built into the system. If you type a question mark (?) after a command, the Template will appear to remind you of the proper syntax.

In Template listings, command arguments and options are separated by commas and followed by a special code which indicates the type of argument. The code is not to be typed as part of the command, it just tells you what kind of argument the command takes. Here's a list of the codes:

/A   Always required. The argument must always be given.

/K   Keyword required. The argument's keyword must be included along with the argument. (Normally the keyword is optional.)

/S   Switch keyword. The argument works as a switch. You must type the keyword in the command line to turn the switch on.

/N   Number. The argument is numeric.

/M   Multiple arguments are accepted. This is the Template equivalent of braces. There is no limit on the number of possible arguments. Any number is accepted. (The /M replaces the multiple-comma method of indicating how many elements the command could operate on used in earlier versions of AmigaDOS.)

/F   Final argument. The string must be the final argument on the command line. The remainder of the command line is taken as the desired string. Quotation marks are not needed around the string, even if it contains spaces.

=   An equals sign indicates that two different forms of the keyword are equivalent. Either will be accepted. The equals sign is not typed as part of the command.

For example, if you type in the command COPY?, the Template for the COPY command will be displayed:

```
FROM/A/M,TO/A,ALL/S,QUIET/S,BUF=BUFFER/K/N,CLONE/S,
DATES/S,NOPRO/S,COM/S
```

FROM/A/M indicates that the first argument must be given and multiple arguments are acceptable. TO/A indicates that the second argument must always be given. ALL/S, QUIET/S, CLONE/S, DATES/S, NOPRO/S, COM/S are switch arguments. If the keyword is present in the line, the switch will be turned on. BUF=BUFFER/K/N indicates that the argument is numeric (/N). The argument is optional but if given, must include both the keyword(/K) and the argument. Both BUF and BUFFER are acceptable keywords.

AmigaDOS Command Specifications

ADDBUFFERS

Format: ADDBUFFERS <drive> [<n>]
Template: DRIVE/A,BUFFERS/N
Purpose: To command the file system to add cache buffers
Path: C:ADDBUFFERS
Specification: ADDBUFFERS adds <n> buffers to the list of buffers available for <drive>. Allocating additional buffers makes disk access significantly faster. However, each additional buffer reduces free memory by approximately 500 bytes. The default buffer allocation is 5 for floppy drives and usually 30 for hard disks.

The number of buffers you should add depends on the amount of extra memory available. There is no fixed upper limit, but adding too many buffers can actually reduce overall system performance by taking radom access memory (RAM) away from other system functions.

> A buffer is a temporary storage area in memory.

If a negative number is specified, that many buffers are subtracted from the current allocation. The minimum number of buffers is one; however, using only one is not recommended.

Thirty buffers are generally recommended for a floppy drive in a 512K system. The optimal number for a hard disk depends on the type and size of your drive. If you have the Commodore 2091 you should use the default value recommended by the HDToolbox. (This value can be displayed by selecting the Advanced Options gadget on the Partitioning screen.) As a general rule, you can use 30 to 50 buffers for every megabyte of RAM in your system.

If only the <drive> argument is specified, ADDBUFFERS displays the number of buffers currently allocated for that drive.
Examples: Add 25 buffers to drive DF1:.

```
1> ADDBUFFERS DF1: 25
DF1: has 30 buffers
```

Display the number of buffers currently allocated to drive DF0:.

```
1> ADDBUFFERS DF0:
DF0: has 20 buffers
```

ADDMONITOR

Format:	ADDMONITOR NUM=%d NAME=%s
Template:	NUM/N/A,NAME/A,HBSTRT/K,HBSTOP/K, HSSTRT/K,HSSTOP/K,VBSTRT/K,VBSTOP/K, VSSTRT/K,VSSTOP/K,MINROW/K,MINCOL/K, TOTROWS/K,TOTCOLS/K,BEAMCONO/K
Purpose:	To inform the Amiga that a non-RGB-style monitor has been added to your system
Path:	SYS:System/AddMonitor

Specification: ADDMONITOR must be run if you have attached an A2024 or Multiscan monitor or a monitor that is different from your country's video standard (PAL for NTSC countries, and vice versa).

AddMonitor takes two arguments: NUM and NAME. The acceptable values are listed below:

	NUM=	NAME=
For an NTSC monitor	1	NTSC
For a PAL monitor	2	PAL
For a Multiscan	3	Multiscan
For an A2024	4	A2024

The additional options control special hardware features of the Amiga. Certain graphics hardware may require these options in order to function correctly. If so, options should be explained in the documentation accompanying the hardware.

After using AddMonitor, you must use the ScreenMode editor to select the new display mode. To have the system recognize your monitor on booting, drag the appropriate icon from the MonitorStore drawer to the Monitors drawer.

Examples: If you've attached a Multiscan monitor, type:

```
1> ADDMONITOR NUM=3 NAME=Multiscan
```

If you've attached an A2024 monitor, type:

```
1> ADDMONITOR NUM=4 NAME=A2024
```

You must then use the ScreenMode Preferences editor to select the appropriate display mode for your monitor.

ALIAS

Format: ALIAS [<name>] [<string>]
Template: NAME,STRING/F
Purpose: To set or display command aliases
Path: Internal
Specification: ALIAS permits you to create aliases, or alternative names, for AmigaDOS commands. Using an alias is like replacing a sentence with a single word. With ALIAS, you can abbreviate frequently used commands or replace a standard command name with a different name.

When AmigaDOS encounters <name>, it replaces it with the defined <string>, integrates the result with the rest of the command line, and attempts to interpret and execute the resulting line as an AmigaDOS command. So <name> is the alias and <string> is the command to be substituted for the alias.

ALIAS <name> displays the <string> that will be substituted for the alias. ALIAS alone lists all current aliases.

Aliases are local to the Shell in which they are defined. If you create another Shell with the NEWSHELL command, it shares the same aliases as its parent Shell. However, if you create another Shell with the Execute Command menu item, it will not recognize aliases created in your original Shell. To create a global alias that will be recognized by all shells, insert the alias in the S:Shell-startup file.

An alias must be at the beginning of the command line, and you can specify arguments on the command line after the alias. However, you cannot use an alias for a series of command arguments. For instance, you cannot create a script using the LFORMAT option of the LIST command by creating an alias to represent the LFORMAT argument.

You can substitute a filename or other instruction within an alias by placing square brackets ([ ]) in the <string>. Any argument typed after the alias will be inserted at the brackets. To remove an ALIAS, use the UNALIAS command.

Examples:

```
1> ALIAS d1 DIR DF1:
```

Typing d1 results in a directory of the contents of the disk in DF1:, just as if you had typed DIR DF1:.

```
1> ALIAS hex TYPE [] HEX NUMBER
```

creates an alias called hex that displays the contents of a specified file in hexadecimal format. The brackets indicate where the filename will be inserted. If you then typed:

```
1> hex Myfile
```

the contents of MyFile would be displayed in hexadecimal format with line numbers.

ASK

Format: ASK <prompt>
Template: PROMPT/A
Purpose: To obtain user input when executing a script file
Path: Internal
Specification: ASK is used in scripts to write the <prompt> to the current window, then wait for keyboard input. Valid responses are Y (yes), N (no), and Return (no). If Y is pressed, ASK sets the condition flag to 5 (WARN). If N is pressed, the condition flag is set to 0. To check the response, an IF statement can be used.

If the <prompt> contains spaces, it must be enclosed in quotation marks.
Example: Assume a script contained the following commands:

```
ASK Continue?
IF WARN
  ECHO Yes
ELSE
  ECHO No
ENDIF
```

When the ASK command is reached, Continue? will appear on the screen. If Y is pressed, Yes will be displayed on the screen. If N is pressed, No will be displayed.
See also: IF, ELSE, ENDIF, WARN

ASSIGN

Format: ASSIGN [<name>:{dir}] [LIST] [EXISTS] [DISMOUNT] [DEFER] [PATH] [ADD] [REMOVE] [VOLS] [DIRS] [DEVICES]

Template: NAME,TARGET/M,LIST/S,EXISTS/S,DISMOUNT/S, DEFER/S, PATH/S,ADD/S,REMOVE/S,VOLS/S,DIRS/S, DEVICES/S

Purpose: To control assignment of logical device names to file system directories

Path: C:ASSIGN

Specification: ASSIGN allows directories to be referenced via short, convenient logical device names rather than their usual names or complete paths. ASSIGN gives an alternative directory name, much as ALIAS permits alternative command names. The ASSIGN command can create, remove assignments, or list some or all current assignments.

If the <name> and {dir} arguments are given, ASSIGN will assign the given name to the specified directory. Each time the assigned logical device name is referred to, AmigaDOS will access the specified directory. If the <name> given is already assigned to a directory, the new directory will replace the previous directory. (Always be sure to include a colon after the <name> argument.)

If only the <name> argument is given, any existing ASSIGN of a directory to that logical device is cancelled.

You can assign several logical device names to the same directory by using multiple ASSIGN commands. You can assign one logical device name to several directories by specifying each directory after the <name> argument or by using the ADD option. When the ADD option is specified, any existing directory assigned to <name> is not cancelled. Instead, the newly specified directory is added to the assign list, and the system searches for both directories when <name> is encountered. If the original directory is not available, ASSIGN will be satisfied with the newly added directory.

To delete a name from the assign list, use the REMOVE option.

If no arguments are given with ASSIGN, or if the LIST keyword is used, a list of all current assignments will be displayed. If the VOLS, DIRS, or DEVICES switch is specified, ASSIGN limits the display to volumes, directories, or devices, respectively.

When the EXIST keyword is given along with a logical device name, AmigaDOS will search the ASSIGN list for that name and display the volume and directory assigned to that device. If the device name is not found, the condition flag is set to 5 (WARN). This option is commonly used in scripts.

Normally, when the {dir} argument is given, AmigaDOS immediately looks for that directory. If the ASSIGN commands are part of S:startup-sequence, the directories need to be present on a mounted disk during the boot procedure. If an assigned directory cannot be found, a requester appears asking for the volume containing that directory. However, two new options, DEFER and PATH, wait until the directory is actually needed before searching for it.

The DEFER option creates a "late-binding" ASSIGN. This assign only takes effect when the assigned object is first referenced, rather than when the assignment is made. This eliminates the need to insert disks during the boot procedure that contain the directories that are assigned during the startup-sequence. When the DEFER option is used, the disk containing the assigned directory is not needed until the object is actually called on.

For example, if you assign FONTS: to DF0:Fonts with the DEFER option, the system will associate FONTS: with whatever disk is in DF0: at the time FONTS: is called. If you have a Workbench disk in DF0: at the time the FONTS: directory is needed, the system will associate FONTS: with that particular Workbench disk. If you later remove that Workbench disk and insert another disk containing a Fonts directory, the system will specifically request the original Workbench disk the next time FONTS: is needed.

The PATH option creates a "nonbinding" ASSIGN. A nonbinding ASSIGN acts like a DEFERred ASSIGN except that it is reevaluated each time the assigned name is referenced. This arrangement prevents the system from expecting a particular volume in order to use a particular directory (such as the situation described in the example above). For instance, if you assign FONTS: to DF0:Fonts with the PATH option, any disk in DF0: will be searched when FONTS: is referenced. As long as the disk contains a Fonts directory, it will satisfy the ASSIGN. You cannot assign multiple directories with the PATH option.

The PATH option is especially useful to users with floppy disk systems as it eliminates the need to reinsert the original Workbench disk used to boot the system. As long as the drive you have assigned with the PATH option contains a disk with the assigned directory name, the system will use that disk.

WARNING: The DISMOUNT option (called REMOVE in V1.3) disconnects a volume or device from the list of mounted devices. It does not free up resources; it merely removes the name from the list. There is no way to cancel a DISMOUNT without rebooting. DISMOUNT is primarily for use during software development. Careless use of this option may cause a software failure.

Examples:

```
1> ASSIGN FONTS: MyFonts:Fontdir
```

assigns the system FONTS: directory to Fontdir on MyFonts:.

```
1> ASSIGN LIST
```

Volumes:

```
Ram Disk [Mounted]
Workbench2.0 [Mounted]
MyFonts [Mounted]
```

Directories:

```
CLIPS      Ram Disk:Clipboards
ENV        Ram Disk:Env
T          Ram Disk:T
ENVARC     Workbench2.0:Prefs/Env-Archive
SYS        Workbench2.0:
C          Workbench2.0:C
S          Workbench2.0:S
L          Workbench2.0:L
FONTS      MyFonts:Fontdir
DEVS       Workbench2.0:Devs
LIBS       Workbench2.0:Libs
```

Devices:

```
PIPE AUX SPEAK RAM CON
RAW PAR SER PRT DF0 DF1
```

shows a list of all current assignments.

```
1> ASSIGN FONTS: EXISTS
FONTS MyFonts:FontDir
```

is an inquiry into the assignment of FONTS:. AmigaDOS responds by showing that FONTS: is assigned to the FontDir directory of the MyFonts volume.

```
1> ASSIGN LIBS: SYS:Libs BigAssem:Libs PDAssem:Libs
```

is a multiple-directory assignment that creates a search path containing three Libs directories. These directories are searched in sequence each time LIBS: is invoked.

```
1> ASSIGN DEVS: DISMOUNT
```

removes the DEVS: assignment from the system.

```
1> ASSIGN WorkDisk: DF0: DEFER
1> ASSIGN WorkDisk: EXISTS
WorkDisk <DF0:>
```

set up a late-binding assignment of the logical device WorkDisk:. The disk does not have to be inserted in DF0: until the first time you refer to the name WorkDisk:. Notice that ASSIGN shows DF0: enclosed in angle brackets to indicate that it is DEFERred. After the first reference to WorkDisk:, the volume name of the disk that was in DF0: at the time will replace <DF0:>.

```
1> ASSIGN C: DF0:C PATH
1> ASSIGN C: EXISTS
C          [DF0:C]
```

references the C directory of whatever disk is in DF0: at the time a command is searched for. Notice that ASSIGN shows DF0:C in square brackets to indicate that it is a nonbinding ASSIGN.

```
1> ASSIGN LIBS: ZCad:Libs ADD
```

adds ZCad:Libs to the list of directories assigned as LIBS:.

```
1> ASSIGN LIBS: ZCad:Libs REMOVE
```

removes ZCad:Libs from the list of directories assigned as LIBS:.

AUTOPOINT

Format:	AUTOPOINT [CX_PRIORITY=<n>]
Template:	CX_PRIORITY/K/N
Purpose:	To automatically select any window the pointer is over
Path:	Extras2.0:Tools/Commodities/AutoPoint

Specification: When AUTOPOINT is run, any window that the pointer is over is automatically selected. You do not need to click the selection button to activate it.

The CX_PRIORITY=<n> argument sets the priority of AutoPoint in relation to all the other Commodity Exchange programs. (This is the same as entering a CX_PRIORITY=<n> Tool Type in the icon's Information window.) All the Commodity Exchange programs are set to a default priority of 0. If you specify an <n> value higher than 0, AutoPoint takes priority over any other Commodity Exchange program.

To exit AutoPoint when it has been started from a Shell, type Ctrl-E or use the BREAK command.

Example:

```
1> AUTOPOINT
```

starts the AutoPoint program.

AVAIL

Format:	AVAIL [CHIP I FAST I TOTAL] [FLUSH]
Template:	CHIP/S,FAST/S,TOTAL/S,FLUSH/S
Purpose:	To report the amount of Chip and Fast memory available
Path:	C:AVAIL

Specification: AVAIL gives a summary of the system RAM, both Chip and Fast. For each memory type, AVAIL reports the total amount, how much is available, how much is currently in use, and the largest contiguous memory block not yet allocated.

By using the CHIP, FAST and/or TOTAL options, you can have AVAIL display only the number of free bytes of Chip, Fast, or total RAM available, instead of the complete summary. This value can be used for comparisons in scripts. The FLUSH option causes all unused libraries and device modules to be expunged from memory.

Examples:
```
1> AVAIL
   Type Available    In-Use      Maximum      Largest
   chip 233592       282272      515864       76792
   fast 341384       182896      524280       197360
   tot  574976       465168      1040144      274152

1> AVAIL CHIP
   233592
```
MyDisplay would appear in the Choose Display Mode gadget of the ScreenMode editor instead of Hires.

> The Amiga uses two different types of RAM. Chip RAM is used for graphics and sound data. Fast RAM is general-purpose RAM used by all types of programs.

BINDDRIVERS

Format: BINDDRIVERS
Template: (none)
Purpose: To bind device drivers to hardware
Path: C:BINDDRIVERS
Specification: BINDDRIVERS is used to load and run device drivers for add-on hardware that is configured by the expansion library. These device drivers must be in the SYS:Expansion directory for BINDDRIVERS to find them.

BINDDRIVERS is normally placed in the Startup-sequence file. If drivers for expansion hardware are in the Expansion directory, you must have a BINDDRIVERS command in your Startup-sequence or the hardware will not be configured when the system is booted.

BINDMONITOR

Format: BINDMONITOR
Template: MONITORID/A, MONITORNAME/A
Purpose: To assign names to the different display modes

Path: SYS:System/BindMonitor

Specification: BINDMONITOR assigns names to the different display modes supported by the graphics library. The acceptable arguments match the Tool Types of the Mode_Names icon.

```
           Acceptable BINDMONITOR Arguments
0x00000 Lores               0x00004 Lores-Interlaced
0x08000 Hires               0x08004 Hires-Interlaced
0x08020 SuperHires          0x08024 SuperHires-Interlaced
0x11000 NTSC:Lores          0x11004 NTSC:Lores-Interlaced
0x19000 NTSC:Hires          0x19004 NTSC:Hires-Interlaced
0x19020 NTSC:SuperHires     0x19024 NTSC:SuperHires-Interlaced
0x21000 PAL:Lores           0x21004 PAL:Lores-Interlaced
0x29000 PAL:Hires           0x29004 PAL:Hires-Interlaced
0x29020 PAL:SuperHires      0x29024 PAL:SuperHires-Interlaced
0x31004 VGA-ExtraLores      0x31005 VGA-ExtraLores-Interlaced
0x39004 VGA-Lores           0x39005 VGA-Lores-Interlaced
0x39024 Productivity        0x39025 Productivity Interlaced
0x41000 A2024_10Hz          0x49000 A2024_15Hz
```

For instance, ROM recognizes 0x08000 as a 640 x 200 line display. However, BindMonitor links 0x08000 with the name Hires. The names associated with the display modes appear in the Choose Display Mode gadget of the ScreenMode editor.

Example:

```
1> BINDMONITOR 0x08000MyDisplay
```

MyDisplay would appear in the Choose Display Mode gadget of the ScreenMode editor instead of Hires.

BLANKER

Format: BLANKER [SECONDS=<n>] [CX_POPKEY=<key (s)>] [CX_POPUP=<yes|no>] [CX_PRIORITY=<n>]

Template: SECONDS/K/N,CX_POPKEY/K,CX_POPUP/K,CX_PRIORITY/K/N

Purpose: To cause the monitor screen to go blank if no input has been received within a specified period of time

Path: Extras2.0:Tools/Commodities/Blanker

Specification: BLANKER is a Commodity Exchange program that causes the screen to go blank if no mouse or keyboard input has been received in the specified number of seconds. The SECONDS=<n> argument allows you to specify the number of seconds that must pass. The acceptable range is from 1 to 9999. Default is 60 seconds.

- CX_POPKEY=<key(s)>allows you to specify the hot key for the program. If more than one key is specified, be sure to enclose the entire argument in double-quotes (i.e., "CX_POPKEY=Shift F1").
- CX_POPUP=no will prevent the Blanker window from opening. (By default the program window opens when the command is invoked.)
- CX_PRIORITY=<n> sets the priority of Blanker in relation to all other Commodity Exchange programs. All the Commodity Exchange programs are set to a default priority of 0.

To kill Blanker when it is run through the Shell, press Ctrl-E.

Examples:

```
1> BLANKER SECONDS=45
```

The Blanker window will open, and 45 will be displayed inside its text gadget. If no mouse or keyboard input is received during a 45-second interval, the screen will go blank.

```
1> BLANKER CX_POPUP=no
```

The Blanker program will start. If no input is received within 60 seconds (the default), the screen will go blank. The Blanker window will not open.

BREAK

Format: BREAK <process> [ALL | C | D | E | F]
Template: PROCESS/A/N,ALL/S,C/S,D/S,E/S,F/S
Purpose: To set attention flags in the specified process
Path: C.BREAK
Specification: BREAK sets the specified attention flags in the <process> indicated. C sets the Ctrl-C flag, D sets the Ctrl-D flag, and so on. ALL sets all

the flags from Ctrl-C to Ctrl-F. By default, AmigaDOS only sets the Ctrl-C flag.

The action of BREAK is identical to selecting the relevant process by clicking in its window and pressing the appropriate Ctrl-key combination(s).

Ctrl-C is used as the default for sending a BREAK signal to halt a process. A process that has been aborted this way will display ***BREAK in the shell window. Ctrl-D is used to halt execution of a script file. Ctrl-E is used to exit Commodity Exchange programs. Ctrl-F is not currently used.

> Use the STATUS command to display the current process numbers.

Examples:

```
1> BREAK 7
```

sets the Ctrl-C attention flag of process 7. This is identical to selecting process 7 and pressing Ctrl-C.

```
1> BREAK 5 D
```

sets the Ctrl-D attention flag of process 5.

See also: STATUS

CALCULATOR

Format: CALCULATOR
Template: (none)
Purpose: To provide an on-screen calculator
Path: SYS:Utilities/Calculator
Specification: CALCULATOR starts the Calculator program. You can cut-and-paste the output of the Calculator into any console window, like the Shell or ED.

To exit the program, select the window's close gadget.

Example:

```
1> CALCULATOR
```

CD

Format:	CD [<dir | pattern>]
Template:	DIR
Purpose:	To set, change, or display the current directory
Path:	Internal

Specification: CD with no arguments displays the name of the current directory. When a valid directory name is given, CD makes the named directory the current directory.

CD does not search through the disk for the specified directory. It expects it to be in the current directory. If it is not, you must give a complete path to the directory. If CD cannot find the specified directory in the current directory or in the given path, a Can't find <directory> error message is displayed.

If you want to move up a level in the filing hierarchy to the parent directory of the current directory, type CD followed by a space and a single slash (/). Moving to another directory in the parent can be done at the same time by including its name after the slash. If the current directory is a root directory, CD / will have no effect. Multiple slashes are allowed; each slash refers to an additional higher level. When using multiple slashes, leave no spaces between them.

To move directly to the root directory of the current device, use CD followed by a space and a colon.

CD also supports pattern matching. If more than one directory matches the given pattern, an error message is displayed.

Examples:

    1> CD DF1:Work

sets the current directory to the Work directory on the disk in drive DF1:.

    1> CD SYS:Com/Basic

makes the subdirectory Basic in the Com directory the current directory.

    1> CD //

moves up two levels in the directory structure and makes SYS: the current directory.

    1> CD SYS:Li#?

uses the #? pattern to match with the Libs directory.

CHANGETASKPRI

Format:	CHANGETASKPRI <priority> [<process>]
Template:	PRI=PRIORITY/A/N,PROCESS/K/N
Purpose:	To change the priority of a currently running process
Path:	C:CHANGETASKPRI

Specification: Since the Amiga is multitasking, it uses priority numbers to determine the order in which current tasks should be serviced. Normally, most tasks have a priority of 0, and the time and instruction cycles of the central processing unit (CPU) are divided equally among them. CHANGETASKPRI changes the priority of the specified shell process. (If no process is specified, the current shell process is assumed.) Any tasks started from <process> inherit its priority.

The range of acceptable values for <priority> is the integers from −128 to 127, with higher values yielding a higher priority (a greater proportion of CPU time is allocated). However, do not enter values above +10, or you may disrupt important system tasks. Too low a priority (less than 0) can result in a process taking unreasonably long to execute.

Example:

```
1> CHANGETASKPRI 4 Process 2
```

The priority of Process 2 is changed to 4. Any tasks started from this shell will also have a priority of 4. They will have priority over any other user tasks created without using CHANGETASKPRI (those tasks will have a priority of 0).
See also: STATUS

CLOCK

Format:	CLOCK [DIGITAL] [[LEFT] <n>] [[TOP <n>] [[WIDTH] <n>] [[HEIGHT <n>] [24HOUR] [SECONDS] [DATE]
Template:	DIGITAL/S,LEFT/N,TOP/N,WIDTH/N,HEIGHT/N, 24HOUR/S, SECONDS/S,DATE/S
Purpose:	To provide an on-screen clock
Path:	SYS:Utilities/Clock

Specification: The DIGITAL option opens a digital clock. The LEFT, TOP, WIDTH, and HEIGHT options allow you to specify the size and position of the clock. The keywords are optional; however, the clock understands numeric arguments by their position, as outlined below:

First number: The clock will open <n> pixels from the left edge of the screen.
Second number: The clock will open <n> pixels from the top of the screen.
Third number: The clock will be <n> pixels wide.
Fourth number: The clock will be <n> pixels high.

For instance, if you only wanted to specify the width and height of the Clock, you would have to use the WIDTH and HEIGHT keywords. If you only typed two numbers, the clock would interpret them as the LEFT and TOP positions.

Note: WIDTH and HEIGHT are not available if you use the DIGITAL option. You cannot change the size of the digital clock, although you can specify its position.

The 24HOUR option opens the clock in 24-hour mode. If not specified, the clock opens in 12-hour mode. If the SECONDS option is specified, the seconds are displayed. If the DATE option is specified, the date is displayed.

Examples: To open a clock that is 75 pixels from the left edge of the screen, 75 pixels from the top edge of the screen, 300 pixels wide and 100 pixels high, type:

```
1> CLOCK 75 75 300 100
```

To use the SECONDS, DATE, and 24HOUR options, type:

```
1> CLOCK SECONDS DATE 24HOUR
```

To open a digital clock that is 320 pixels from the left edge of the screen and in the screen's title bar (0 pixels from the top), type:

```
1> CLOCK DIGITAL 3200
```

CMD

Format:	CMD <devicename> <filename> [OPT s | m | n]
Template:	DEVICENAME/A,FILENAME/A,OPT/K
Purpose:	To redirect printer output to a file
Path:	Extras2.0:Tools/CMD

Specification: The <devicename> can be serial, parallel, or printer, and should be the same device as specified in the Printer editor. <Filename> is the name of the file to which the redirected output should be sent.

The CMD options are as follows:

s   Skip any short initial write (usually a reset if redirecting a screen dump).
m   Intercept multiple files until a BREAK command or Ctrl-C is typed.
n   Notify user of progress (messages are displayed on the screen).

Example:

```
1> CMD parallel ram:cmd_file
```

Any output sent to the parallel port will be rerouted to a file in RAM: called cmd_file.

COLORS

Format: COLORS [<bitplanes> <screentype>]
Template: BITPLANES,SCREENTYPE
Purpose: To change the colors of the frontmost screen
Path: Extras2.0:Tools/Colors
Specification: COLORS lets you change the colors of the frontmost screen. By specifying values for the <bitplanes> and <screentype> options you can open a custom test screen. The acceptable values for <bitplanes> and <screentype> are listed below:

<bitplanes>   Specifies the depth of the test screen:
              1   2 colors.
              2   4 colors.
              3   8 colors.
              4   16 colors.
              5   32 colors.
<screentype> Specifies the resolution of the test screen:
              0   320 x 200 pixels.
              1   320 x 400 pixels.
              2   640 x 200 pixels.
              3   640 x 400 pixels.

The value for <bitplanes> is restricted to 4 or less if the value for <screentype> is equal to either 2 or 3.

Example:

```
1> COLORS 3 2
```

A new custom screen is opened, and it displays a window for the color program. The screen has eight colors and a 640 x 200 pixel (Hires) resolution.

COPY

Format: COPY [FROM] {<name I pattern>} [TO] <name I pattern> [ALL] [QUIET] [BUF I BUFFER=<n>] [CLONE] [DATES] [NOPRO] [COM][NOREQ]

Template: FROM/M,TO/A,ALL/S,QUIET/S,BUF=BUFFER/K/N, CLONE/S, DATES/S, NOPRO/S,COM/S,NOREQ/S

Purpose: To copy files or directories

Path: C:COPY

Specification: COPY copies the file or directory specified with the FROM argument to the file or directory specified by the TO argument. You can copy several items at once by giving more than one FROM argument; each argument should be separated by spaces. You can use pattern matching to copy or exclude items whose names share a common set of characters or symbols.

If a TO filename already exists, COPY overwrites the TO file with the FROM file. If you name a destination directory that does not exist, COPY creates a directory with that name. You can also use a pair of double quotes ("") to refer to the current directory when specifying a destination. (Do NOT put any spaces between the double quotes.)

If the FROM argument is a directory, only the directory's files will be copied; its subdirectories will not be copied. Use the ALL option to copy the complete directory, including its files, subdirectories, and the subdirectories' files. If you want to copy a directory and you want the copy to have the same name as the original, you must include the directory name in the TO argument.

COPY prints to the screen the name of each file as it is copied. This can be overridden by the QUIET option.

The BUF= option is used to set the number of 512-byte buffers used during the copy. (Default is 200 buffers, approximately 100K of RAM.) It is often useful to limit the number of buffers when copying to RAM:. BUF=0 uses a buffer the same size as the file to be copied.

Normally, copy gives the TO file the date and time the copy was made. Any comments attached to the original FROM file are ignored. The protection bits of the FROM file are copied to the TO file. Several options allow you to override these defaults:

> DATES: The creation date of the FROM file is copied to the TO file.
>
> COM: Any comment attached to the FROM file is copied to the TO file.
>
> CLONE: The date, comments, and protection bits of the FROM file are copied to the TO file.
>
> NOPRO: The protection bits of the FROM file are not copied to the TO file. The TO file will be given standard protection bits of r, w, e, and d.

Normally, COPY displays a requester if the COPY cannot continue for some reason. When the NOREQ option is given, all requesters are suppressed. This is useful in scripts and can prevent a COPY failure from stopping the script while it waits for a response. For instance, if a script calls for a certain file to be copied and the system cannot find that file, normally the script would display a requester and would wait until a response was given. With the NOREQ option, the COPY command would be aborted and the script would continue.

Examples:

```
1> COPY File1 TO :Work/File2
```

copies File1 in the current directory to File2 in the Work directory.

```
1> COPY ~(#?.info) TO DF1:Backup
```

copies all the files not ending in .info in the current directory to the Backup directory on the disk in DF1:. This is a convenient use of pattern matching to save storage space when icons are not necessary.

```
1> COPY Work:Test TO ""
```

copies the files in the Test directory on Work to the current directory; subdirectories in Test will not be copied.

```
1> COPY Work:Test TO DF0:Test ALL
```

copies all the files and any subdirectories of the Test directory on Work to the Test directory on DF0:. If a Test directory does not already exist on DF0:, AmigaDOS will create one.

```
1> COPY DF0: TO DF1: ALL QUIET
```

copies all files and directories on the disk in DF0: to DF1:, without displaying on the screen any file/directory names as they are copied. (This procedure is quite slow in comparison to DiskCopy.)

CPU

Format: CPU [CACHE] [BURST] [NOBURST] [DATACACHE] [DATABURST] [NODATACACHE] [NODATABURST] [INSTCACHE] [INSTBURST] [NOINSTCACHE] [NOINSTBURST] [FASTROM] [NOFASTROM] [NOMMUTEST] [CHECK 68010 | 68020 | 68030 | 68881 | 68882 | 68851 | MMU | FPU]

Template: CACHE/S,BURST/S,NOCACHE/S,NOBURST/S,DATACACHE/S,DATABURST/S,NODATACACHE/S, NODATABURST/S,INSTCACHE/S,INSTBURST/S,NOINSTCACHE/S,NOINSTBURST/S,FASTROM/S,NOFASTROM/S,NOMMUTEST/S,CHECK/K

Purpose: To set or clear the CPU caches, check for a particular processor, load the read only memory (ROM) image into fast, 32-bit memory, or set an illegal memory access handler which will output information over the serial port at 9600 baud if a task accesses page zero (lower 256 bytes) or memory above 16M

Path: C:CPU

Specification: The CPU allows you to adjust various options of the microprocessor installed in your Amiga. The CPU also shows the processor and options that are currently enabled.

   Note: Many options only work with certain members of the 680X0 processor family. The 68020 has a special type of memory known as instruction cache. When instruction cache is used, instructions are executed more quickly. The 68030 has two types of cache memory: instruction and data. If you have Static Column Dynamic RAM (SCRAM) installed, you can also use a special access mode for both instruction and data cache, known as burst mode. This procedure may further improve access speed in some cases. The CPU options, outlined below, specify the types of memory to be used. If mutually exclusive options are specified, the safest option is used.

- CACHE: Turns on both data and instruction cache (only for 68030).
- NOCACHE: Turns off data and instruction cache.
- BURST: Turns on burst mode for both data and instructions (only for 68030 with SCRAM).
- NOBURST: Turns off burst mode for data and instructions.
- DATACACHE: Turns on data cache (only for 68030).
- NODATACACHE: Turns off data cache.
- DATABURST: Turns on burst mode for data (only for 68030 with SCRAM).
- NODATABURST: Turns off burst mode for data.
- INSTCACHE: Turns on instruction cache.
- INSTBURST: Turns on burst mode for instructions (if SCRAM installed).
- NOINSTCACHE: Turns off instruction cache.
- NOINSTBURST: Turns off burst mode for instructions.
- FASTROM: Copies data from ROM into 32-bit RAM, making access to this data significantly faster. The CPU then write-protects the RAM area so that the data cannot be changed.
- NOFASTROM: Turns off FASTROM.
- NOMMUTEST: Allows the MMU to be changed without checking to see if it is currently in use.

The CHECK option, when given with a keyword (68010, 68020, 68030, 68881, 68882, or 68851) checks for the presence of the keyword.

Examples:

```
1> CPU
System: 68030 68881 (INST: NoCache Burst) (DATA: Cache
NoBurst)

1> CPU Burst Cache Check MMU
System: 68030 68881 (INST: Cache Burst) (DATA: Cache
Burst)

1> CPU NoBurst DataCache NoInstCache
```

```
System: 68030 68881 (INST: NoCache NoBurst) (DATA: Cache
NoBurst)
1> CPU Burst Cache FastROM
System: 68030 68881 FastROM (INST: Cache Burst) (DATA:
Cache Burst)

1> CPU NoFastRom NoDataCache
System: 68030 68881 (INST: Cache Burst) (DATA: NoCache
Burst)
```

DATE

Format: DATE [<day>] [<date>] [<time>] [TO | VER <filename>]
Template: DAY,DATE,TIME,TO=VER/K
Purpose: To display or set the system date and/or time
Path: C:DATE
Specification: DATE with no argument displays the currently set system time and date, including the day of the week. Time is displayed using a 24-hour clock.

DATE <date> sets just the date. The format for <date> is DD-MMM-YY (day-month-year). The hyphens between the arguments are required. A leading zero in the date is not necessary. The first three letters of the month (in English) must be used, as well as the last two digits of the year.

If the date is already set, you can reset it by specifying a day name (this sets the date forward to that day of the week). You can also use tomorrow or yesterday as the <day> argument.

DATE <time> sets the time. The format for <time> is HH:MM:SS (hours:minutes:seconds). Seconds are optional.

If your Amiga does not have a battery backed-up hardware clock and you do not set the date, the system, on booting, sets the date to the date of the most recently created file on the boot disk.

If you specify the TO or VER option, followed by a filename, the output of the DATE command is sent to that file, overwriting any existing contents.

Note: Adjustments made with DATE only change the software clock. They will not survive past power-down. To set the battery backed-up hardware clock from the Shell, you must set the date and then use SETCLOCK SAVE.
Examples:

```
1> DATE
```

displays the current date and time.

```
1> DATE 6-sep-82
```

sets the date to September 6, 1982. The time is not reset. (The earliest date you can set is January 1, 1978.)

```
1> DATE tomorrow
```

resets the date to 1 day ahead.

```
1> DATE TO Fred
```

sends the current date to the file Fred.

```
1> DATE 23:00
```

sets the current time to 11:00 p.m.

DELETE

Format: DELETE {<name | pattern>} [ALL] [Q | QUIET] [FORCE]
Template: FILE/M/A,ALL/S,QUIET/S,FORCE/S
Purpose: To delete files or directories
Path: C:DELETE
Specification: DELETE attempts to delete (erase) the specified file(s). If more than one file was specified, AmigaDOS continues to the next file in the list.

You can use pattern matching to delete files. The pattern may specify directory levels as well as filenames. All files that match the pattern are deleted. To abort a multiple-file DELETE, press Ctrl-C.

AmigaDOS does not request confirmation of deletions. An error in a pattern-matching DELETE can have severe consequences, as deleted files are unrecoverable. Be sure you understand pattern matching before you use this feature, and keep backups of important files.

> **Warning:** If you try to delete a directory that contains files, you will receive a message stating that the directory could not be deleted as it is not empty. To override this, use the ALL option. DELETE ALL deletes the named directory, its subdirectories, and all files.

Filenames are displayed on the screen as they are deleted. To suppress the screen output, use the QUIET option.

If the d (deletable) protection bit of a file has been cleared, that file cannot be deleted unless the FORCE option is used.

Examples:

```
1> DELETE Old-file
```

deletes the Old-file file in the current directory.

```
1> DELETE Work/Prog1 Work/Prog2 Work
```

deletes the files Prog1 and Prog2 in the Work directory, and then deletes the Work directory (if there are no other files left in it).

```
1> DELETE T#?/#?(1|2)
```

deletes all files that end in 1 or 2 in directories that start with T.

```
1> DELETE DF1:#? ALL FORCE
```

deletes all the files on DF1:, even those set as not deletable.

DIR

Format: DIR [<dir|pattern>] [OPT A|I|AI|D|F] [ALL] [DIRS] [FILES] [INTER]
Template: DIR,OPT/K,ALL/S,DIRS/S,FILES/S,INTER/S
Purpose: To display a sorted list of the files in a directory
Path: C:DIR
Specification: DIR displays the file and directory names contained in the specified directory, or the current directory if no name is given. Directories are listed first, followed by an alphabetical list of the files in two columns. Pressing Ctrl-C aborts a directory listing.

The options are:

ALL   Displays all subdirectories and their files.
DIRS   Displays only directories.
FILES   Displays only files.
INTER   Enters an interactive listing mode.

Note: The ALL, DIRS, FILES, and INTER keywords supersede the OPT A, D, F, and I options, respectively. The older keywords are retained for compatibility with earlier versions of AmigaDOS. Do not use OPT with the full keywords—ALL, DIRS, FILES, or INTER.

The interactive listing mode stops after each name and displays a question mark at which you can enter commands. The acceptable responses are shown below:

Return: Displays the next name on the list.

E: Enters a directory; the files in that directory will be displayed.

B: Goes back one directory level.

DEL or DELETE: Deletes a file or empty directory. DEL does not refer to the Del key; type the letters D, E, then L.

T: Types the contents of a file.

C or COMMAND: Allows you to enter additional AmigaDOS commands.

Q: Quits interactive editing.

?: Displays a list of the available interactive-mode commands.

The COMMAND option allows almost any AmigaDOS command to be executed during the interactive directory list. When you want to issue a command, type C (or COM) at the question mark prompt. DIR will ask you for the command. Type the desired command, then press Return. The command will be executed and DIR will continue. You can also combine the C and the command on one line, by putting the command in quotes following the C.

For instance, C "type prefs.info hex" is equivalent to pressing Q to exit interactive listing mode and return to a regular shell prompt, and then typing:

```
1> TYPE Prefs.info HEX
```

The Prefs.info file would be typed to the screen in hexadecimal format.

> **Warning:** It is dangerous to format a disk from the DIR interactive mode, as the format takes place immediately, without any confirmation requesters appearing. Also, starting another interactive DIR from interactive mode results in garbled output.

Examples:

    1> DIR Workbench2.0:

displays a list of the directories and files on the Workbench2.0 disk.

    1> DIR MyDisk:#?.memo

displays all the directories and files on MyDisk that end in .memo.

    1> DIR Extras2.0: ALL

displays the complete contents of the Extras2.0 disk — all directories, subdirectories, and files.

    1> DIR Workbench2.0: DIRS

displays only the directories on Workbench2.0.

    1> DIR Workbench2.0: INTER

provides an interactive list of the contents of Workbench2.0.

DISKCHANGE

Format:	DISKCHANGE <device>
Template:	DEVICE/A
Purpose:	To inform the Amiga that you have changed a disk in a disk drive
Path:	C:DISKCHANGE

Specification: The DISKCHANGE command is only necessary when you are using 5 1/4-inch floppy disk drives or removable media drives without automatic diskchange hardware. Whenever you change the disk or cartridge of such a drive, you must use DISKCHANGE to inform the system of the switch.

DISKCHANGE can also be used if you edit a disk icon image and wish to see the new icon on the Workbench screen immediately. This is the only way to display an altered hard disk icon without rebooting.

Example: If a requester appears and asks you to insert a new disk into your 5 1/4-inch drive, known as DF2:, you must insert the disk, then type:

```
1> DISKCHANGE DF2:
```

AmigaDOS then recognizes the new disk, and you can proceed.

DISKCOPY

Format:	DISKCOPY [FROM] <disk> TO <disk> [NOVERIFY] [MULTI] [NAME<name>]
Template:	DISK/A,TO/A,DISK/A,NOVERIFY/S,MULTI/S,NAME/S
Purpose:	To copy the contents of one disk to another
Path:	SYS:System/DiskCopy

Specification: The DISKCOPY command copies the entire contents of one volume to another. The FROM keyword does not have to be specified. However, the TO keyword must be given for DISKCOPY to work.

The <disk> argument can be either the volume name or drive name, such as Workbench2.0 or DF0:. An altered floppy disk icon can be displayed by removing the disk from the drive and reinserting it.

Normally during a diskcopy, the Amiga copies and verifies each cylinder of data. The NOVERIFY option allows you to skip the verification process, making the copy faster.

The MULTI option loads the data on the source disk into memory, allowing you to make multiple copies without having to read the data from the source disk each time.

By default, the destination disk will have the same name as the source disk. If you specify the NAME option, you can give the destination disk a different name from the source disk.

Examples:

    1> DISKCOPY DF0: to DF2:

copies the contents of the disk in drive DF0: to the disk in drive DF2: overwriting the contents of the disk in drive DF2:

    1> DISKCOPY DF0: to DF2: NOVERIFY NAME NewDisk

copies the contents of the disk in drive DF0: to the disk in drive DF2: and gives the disk in drive DF2: the name NewDisk. The disk is not verified as it is copied.

DISKDOCTOR

Format: DISKDOCTOR <drive>
Template: DRIVE/A
Purpose: To attempt to repair a corrupted disk
Path: C:DISKDOCTOR
Specification: DISKDOCTOR attempts to repair a corrupted disk enough to allow you to retrieve files from it and copy them onto a good disk. If AmigaDOS has detected a corrupted disk, it displays a requester stating that the disk could not be validated or that it has a read/write error. By using DISKDOCTOR, you can try to restore the file structure of the disk.

You can use DISKDOCTOR on both the standard file system and the FastFileSystem. However, to use DISKDOCTOR with the FastFileSystem, you must make sure that the DosType keyword in the MountList is set to 0x444F5301. Do not use DISKDOCTOR on a FastFileSystem partition if the DosType keyword is not set correctly. Not all FastFileSystem partitions will have an entry in the Mount List; for these auto-mounting partitions it is not necessary to adjust the Mount List before using DISKDOCTOR.

DISKDOCTOR versions 1.3.5 or earlier do not work with FFS floppies.

Warning: Before running DISKDOCTOR, it is a good idea to copy all files from the disk, as DISKDOCTOR will write to the corrupted disk. This can prevent the use of other disk repair utilities. After running DISKDOCTOR, you should copy the restored files to a new disk, then reformat the corrupted disk.

DISKDOCTOR checks for enough memory before starting operations and changes the boot block to type DOS.

It may be necessary to run DISKDOCTOR several times before a disk is usable once again. If DISKDOCTOR was not able to read the root block of the disk, the disk will be renamed Lazarus.

Example: If you receive a message stating that Volume Workbench is not validated or Error validating disk/Disk is unreadable, you can use DISKDOCTOR to retrieve the disk's files. For instance, if the corrupted disk is in DF1:, type:

```
1> DISKDOCTOR DF1:
```

AmigaDOS will ask you to insert the disk to be corrected and press Return. DISKDOCTOR then reads each cylinder of the disk. If it finds an error, it displays Hard error Track <xx>, Surface <xx>. As each file and directory is replaced, the filename is displayed on the screen. When DISKDOCTOR is finished, it displays:

```
Now copy files required to a new disk and reformat this
disk.
```

If a hard error is found, there may be actual physical damage to the disk. If, after reformatting, the disk still shows problems, it should be discarded.

DISPLAY

Format: DISPLAY {<filename> | FROM <filelist>}[OPT mlbpenv] [t=<n>]
Template: FILENAME/A/M,FROM/K,OPT/K,T/N
Purpose: To display graphics saved in IFF ILBM format
Path: SYS:Utilities/Display
Specification: DISPLAY displays graphics saved using the IFF ILBM format. You can type a series of files on the command line, and they will be shown in the order given. You can also create a script containing a list of all the IFF files you'd like to display and use the FROM <filelist> argument.

The options are listed below. Remember, the OPT keyword must be used.

m   Clicking the selection button displays the next file in the filelist; clicking the menu button displays the previous file.

l Instead of exiting after the last picture, Display returns to the first file and starts again.

b Pictures stay on their own unactivated screen behind the Workbench screen. This is useful when printing pictures while doing something else.

p Prints each file that is displayed. You can also press Ctrl-P while the file is on the screen.

e This option tells Display to treat a 6-bitplane image as Extra Halfbrite. This is for users who may be using an early HAM paint package that does not save a CAMG chunk. Normally if there is no CAMG, Display treats the image as a HAM picture.

n Borders will not be transparent when genlocked.

v Pictures will be displayed with full-video display clip. This means that the picture fills the maximum possible position on the right edge of the screen, going a little beyond the Overscan settings in Preferences. However, when using this option, the screen cannot be dragged sideways, and Display cannot center the picture.

> A CAMG chunk is part of an IFF file that describes in which viewmode the picture should be displayed.

The t=<n> argument specifies the number of seconds the IFF file will be displayed. This allows for automatic advancing through files.

Examples:

```
1> DISPLAY file1 file2 file3
```

displays the files in the order given. To advance from one file to the next, press Ctrl-C.

```
1> DISPLAY from Scriptlist
```

displays the files listed in the Scriptlist file. Pressing Ctrl-C advances to the next file.

```
1> DISPLAY from Scriptlist OPT mp
```

displays the files listed in the Scriptlist file. Clicking the selection button advances to the next file in the list. Clicking the menu button displays the previous file. Each file is printed as it is displayed.

```
1> DISPLAY from Scriptlist OPT t=5
```

displays each file in the Scriptlist file for 5 seconds.

ECHO

Format: ECHO [<string>] [NOLINE] [FIRST <n>] [LEN <n>] [TO<device/file>]
Template: /M,.NOLINE/S,FIRST/K/N,LEN/K/N,TO/K
Purpose: To display a string
Path: Internal
Specification: ECHO writes the specified string to the current output window or device, usually the screen. By default this is the screen, but it could be any device or file. When the string contains spaces, the whole string must be enclosed in double quotes. (ECHO is commonly used in scripts.)

When the NOLINE option is specified, ECHO does not automatically move the cursor to the next line after printing the string.

The FIRST and LEN options allow the echoing of a substring. FIRST <n> indicates the character position to begin the echo; LEN <n> indicates the number of characters of the substring to echo, beginning with the first character. If the FIRST option is omitted and only the LEN keyword is given, the substring printed consists of the rightmost <n> characters of the main string. For instance, if your string is 20 characters long and you specify LEN 4, the 17th, 18th, 19th, and 20th characters of the string will be echoed.

Examples:

```
1> ECHO "hello out there!"
hello out there!

1> ECHO "hello out there!" NOLINE FIRST 0 LEN 5
hello1>
```

ED

Format:	ED [FROM] <filename> [SIZE <n>] [WITH<file>] [WINDOW <window specification>] [TABS<n>] [WIDTH<n>] [HEIGHT<n>] [COLS<n>] [ROWS<n>]
Template:	FROM/A,SIZE/N,WITH/K,WINDOW/K,TABS/N,WIDTH= COLS/N, HEIGHT=ROWS/N
Purpose:	To edit text files (a screen editor)
Path:	C:ED

Specification: ED is a full-screen text editor suitable for preparing source code or other text files. You can use ED to create a new file or alter an existing one. Text is displayed on screen and can be scrolled vertically or horizontally using the cursor keys. To add new text, you simply type it in. To delete existing text, you use the delete keys. You can also position the cursor and select text with the mouse.

The FROM argument specifies the file you want to edit. If the file exists, it is loaded into ED and the first few lines are displayed on-screen ready for editing. If the file does not exist, ED creates the file and presents a blank screen ready for text to be entered.

You can adjust the size of the text buffer that ED uses with the SIZE argument. The initial size of the text buffer is based on the size of the file you edit with a minimum of 40,000 bytes.

The optional WITH argument is the name of an ED command file created to set up particular function key assignments, or even to perform automated editing operations on an existing file when you call it. The command file can contain any sequence of ED extended mode commands. Each command must be on a separate line. A complete list of ED extended mode commands is given below.

The WINDOW, WIDTH, and HEIGHT arguments are for defining your terminal type if you are using a non-Amiga console, or if you simply want to adjust the ED window size. WINDOW describes the console type, such as RAW:0/0/640/256/<title>, AUX:, or even *. WIDTH and HEIGHT give the number of characters to display horizontally and vertically.

The TABS arguments specifies the tab stop interval. This interval is the number of spaces to the right of the current position that the cursor moves when the tab key is pressed. The default value is 3.

Examples:

```
1> ED mytext
```

starts up ED and loads the text file mytext for editing.

```
1> ED mytext SIZE 50000 TABS 8
```

starts up ED and loads the file mytext for editing. The text buffer used by ED is set to 50,000 bytes and the tabs are set to eight characters.

Moving the Cursor

The cursor can be positioned anywhere in your text by moving the pointer to the desired spot and clicking the selection button. If you prefer to use the keyboard, you can use the cursor keys, Tab, and several Ctrl-key combinations.

To move the cursor one position in any direction, press the appropriate cursor key. If the cursor is on the right edge of the screen, ED scrolls the text to the left so you can see the rest of the line. ED scrolls text vertically one line at a time and horizontally ten characters at a time. You cannot move the cursor off the top or bottom of the file or off the left or right edge of a line. If you try, ED displays a Top of File or Bottom of File message.

Some additional ways to move the cursor are listed below:

Shift-up cursor	Top of the file
Shift-down cursor	Bottom of the file
Shift-left cursor	Left edge of the ED window (regardless of the margin setting)
Shift-right cursor	End of the current line

ED Immediate Mode Command Quick Reference

The list below gives all the ED immediate mode commands. You give these commands by holding down the control (Ctrl) key and pressing one of the letter keys.

CTRL-A	Insert line.
CTRL-B	Delete line.
CTRL-D	Scroll text down 12 lines.
CTRL-E	Move to top or bottom of screen.
CTRL-F	Flip case.
CTRL-G	Repeat the last extended mode command (see list below).
CTRL-H	Delete character left of cursor.
CTRL-I	Move cursor right to next tab position.
CTRL-M	Return.

CTRL-O	Delete word or spaces.
CTRL-R	Cursor to end of previous word.
CTRL-T	Cursor to start of next word.
CTRL-U	Scroll text up 12 lines.
CTRL-V	Verify screen.
CTRL-Y	Delete from cursor to end of line.
CTRL-[	Escape (enter extended command mode).
CTRL-]	Cursor to end or start of line.

ED Extended Mode Command Quick Reference

This is a full list of the ED extended mode commands. To give an extended mode command, you first press the escape (ESC) key. A special command line appears at the bottom of the screen indicating that ED is ready to accept your command. Next type in a command from the list below and press return. ED will perform the command.

For instance, to save a file you have created, press the escape key, then type SA and return. ED will save the file using the filename you specified when you started ED. To exit ED without saving anything, press the escape key, then type Q and return.

In the list below /s/ indicates a string, /s/t/ indicates two exchange strings, and n indicates a number.

A /s/	Insert a line with the text s after the current line.
B	Move to the bottom of the text.
BE	Mark a block end at cursor.
BF /s/	Backward find, searches for the string s in the reverse direction.
BS	Mark a block start at cursor.
CE	Move cursor to the end of the line.
CL	Move cursor one position left.
CR	Move cursor one position right.
CS	Move the cursor to the start of the line.
D	Delete the current line.
DB	Delete block. You must first use BS and BE to mark the block.
DC	Delete character at cursor.
DF R	Display function key R.
DL	Deletes the character to the left of the cursor.
DW	Deletes to the end of the current word.
E /s/t/	Exchange all occurrences of the string s with the string t.
EL	Deletes to the end of the current line.
EM	Enable New Menus.
EP	Move to end of page.

EQ /s/t/	Exchange the string s with the string t but query first.
EX	Extend right margin.
F /s/	Find string s.
FC	Switches case of letters.
I /s/	Insert a line with the string s before the current line.
IB	Insert a copy of marked block. You must first use BS and BE to mark the block.
IF /s/	Insert the file s at the current position.
J	Join current line with the next line.
LC	Distinguish between upper case and lower case in searches.
M n	Move to line number n.
N	Move to the start of the next line.
NW	Creates a new file replacing the existing one.
OP	Opens a file.
P	Move to the start of the previous line.
PD	Next page.
PU	Previous page.
Q	Qui ED without saving.
RF	Loads and executes a command file of extended mode commands.
RK	Reset function keys and control keys to defaults.
RP	Repeat command until error.
S	Split line at cursor.
SA /s/	Save text to the file s.
SB	Show current marked block on screen.
SF n/s/	Set function key r to string s.
SH	Show information.
SI nm/s/t/	Set menu item n to type m with text s and t.
SL n	Set left margin to nth column.
SM	Prints the given string on the status line.
SR n	Set right margin to nth column.
ST n	Set tab distance to n.
T	Move to the top of text.
TB	Move to next tab position.
U	Undo changes on the current line.
UC	Do not distinguish between upper case and lower case in searches.
WB /s/	Write marked block to file /s/. You must first use BS and BE to mark the block.
WN	Move to start of next word.
WP	Move to space after previous word.
X	Exit ED saving text to the file specified when ED was started.
XQ	Exits ED unless changes have been made to the file.

EDIT

Format:	EDIT [FROM] <filename> [[TO] <filename>] [WITH <filename>] [VER <filename>] [[OPT P <lines> I W <chars>] I [PREVIOUS <lines> I WIDTH <chars>]]
Template:	FROM/A,TO,WITH/K,VER/K,OPT/K,WIDTH/N,PREVIOUS/N
Purpose:	To edit text files by processing the source file sequentially (a line editor)
Path:	C:EDIT

Specification: EDIT is a line-oriented text editor that can be used to process files sequentially under the control of editing commands. Edit moves through the input, or source file, line by line making any changes and passing the result to the output, or destination file.

The argument FROM represents the source file that you want to edit. This must be a file that already exists.

The TO argument is the name of the destination file. This is the file to which EDIT sends the output including any editing changes. If you omit the TO argument, EDIT uses a temporary file and, when editing is complete, copies the temporary file to the original file, overwriting it.

The WITH argument allows you to specify a command file from which to get EDIT commands. Ordinarily, EDIT functions interactively, reading commands that you type from the keyboard. You may put EDIT commands in a file instead and have them executed automatically using the WITH argument to specify the command file.

The VER argument gives the name of the file to which EDIT will send error messages and line verifications. If you omit the VER argument EDIT will print its messages on the screen.

EDIT has the capability to move backward in the source file a limited number of lines. This is possible because EDIT doesn't write the lines to the destination file immediately, but instead holds them in an output buffer. The PREVIOUS argument specifies the number of lines that EDIT can move backward in the source file.

The WIDTH argument sets the maximum line length that EDIT can handle. Together the PREVIOUS and WIDTH arguments determine the size of the buffer that EDIT will use (buffer size = PREVIOUS * WIDTH). Unless you specify otherwise, PREVIOUS is set to 40 and WIDTH to 120.

Examples:

```
1> EDIT FROM program1 TO program1new WITH myeditcommands
```

starts EDIT with program1 as the source file and program1new as the destination file. The EDIT commands in the file myeditcommands would be executed automatically as if they had been typed at the keyboard.

```
1> EDIT FROM program1 PREVIOUS 50 WIDTH 240 VER verfile
```

starts EDIT with program1 as the source file. Any changes made with EDIT will be written back to this same file since the TO argument is omitted. The EDIT buffer is set up so that you can move back 50 previous lines. The line width is limited to 240 characters. All verification and error messages from EDIT will be sent to the file verfile.

EDIT Command Quick Reference

Here's a complete list of EDIT commands. The list uses the following abbreviations:

t	A string with delimiters (such as /any string/).
n	Line number in source file; a period (.) refers to the current line in the source file, an asterisk (*) refers to the last line.
sw	Switch (+ is on and is off).
qs	A string or a qualified string with delimiters. There are five qualifiers: B (beginning), E (ending), L (last), P (precisely), and U (upper case). For instance the qualified string "B/any string/" matches "any string" if it occurs at the beginning of a line. The qualified string U/x/ will match either upper or lowercase "x".

POSITIONING COMMANDS

M n	Move to line n.
M +	Move to highest line in buffer.
M	Move to lowest line in buffer.
N	Next line.
P	Previous line.

SEARCH COMMANDS

F qs	Find string qs.
BF qs	Find string qs moving backward through source file.

DF qs   Find string qs and delete any intervening lines.

CHARACTER POSITIONING COMMANDS

<   Move character pointer left.
>   Move character pointer right.
Delete character at pointer.
$ Lower case character at pointer.
%   Upper case character at pointer.
j   Turn character at pointer to space.
PA qs   Position character pointer after qs.
PB qs   Position character pointer before qs.
PR   Reset character pointer to start of line.

CURRENT LINE COMMANDS

A qs t   Put string t after qs.
AP qs t   Put string t after qs, position character pointer after t.
B qs t   Put string t before qs.
BP qs t   Put string t before qs, position character pointer after qs.
CL t   Concatenate current line, string t, and next line.
D n   Delete line number n; if a second number is given, delete from n1 to n2 inclusive; if no number is given, delete the current line.
DF qs   Delete from current line to line containing qs.
DFA qs   Delete from after qs to end of line.
DFB qs   Delete from before qs to end of line.
DTA qs   Delete from start of line to after qs.
DTB qs   Delete from start of line to before qs.
E qs t   Exchange string qs with string t.
EP qs   Exchange string qs with string t and position character pointer after t.
I n   Insert material typed at keyboard before line n (type Z to terminate keyboard input).
I t   Insert material from file t before the current line.
R n   Replace line n with material typed at keyboard (type Z to terminate keyboard input); if a second line number is given, replace lines from n1 to n2 with new material.
R n t   Replace line n with material from file t; if a second line number is given, replace lines from n1 to n2 with file.
SA qs   Split line after qs.
SB qs   Split line before qs.

GLOBAL COMMANDS

GA qs t	For each qs found as file is processed, place t after qs.
GB qs t	For each qs found as file is processed, place t before qs.
GE qs t	For each qs found as file is processed, replace qs with t.
CG n	Cancel global n (cancel all if n omitted).
DG n	Disable global n (disable all if n omitted).
EG n	Enable global n (enable all if n omitted).
SHG	Display info on globals used.

TEXT VERIFICATION COMMANDS

?	Verify current line.
!	Verify with character indicators.
T	Type to end of file.
T n	Type n lines.
TL n	Type n lines with line numbers.
TN	Type until buffer changes.
TP	Move to top of buffer then type lines to end of buffer.
V sw	Set verification on or off.

FILE COMMANDS

FROM t	Take source from file t.
FROM	Revert to original source file.
TO t	Place output lines in file t.
TO	Revert to original destination file.
CF t	Close file t.

OTHER COMMANDS

'	Repeat previous A, B, or E command.
= n	Set line number to n.
C t	Take commands from file t.
H n	Set halt at line n. If n is * then halt and unset H.
REWIND	Rewind source file.
Q	Exit from command level; windup if at level 1.
SHD	Show data.
STOP	Quit without saving changes.
TR sw	Set or unset trailing space removal.
W	Windup (exit saving changes).
Z t	Set input terminator to string t.

ELSE

Format: ELSE
Template: (none)
Purpose: To specify an alternative for an IF statement in a script file
Path: Internal
Specification: ELSE is used in an IF block of a script to specify an alternative action in case the IF condition is not true. If the IF condition is not true, execution of the script will jump from the IF line to the line after ELSE; all intervening commands will be skipped. If the IF condition is true, the commands immediately following the IF statement are executed up to the ELSE. Then, execution skips to the ENDIF statement that concludes the IF block.
Example: Assume a script, called Display, contained the following block:

```
IF exists <name>
  TYPE <name> OPT n
ELSE
  ECHO "<name> is not in this directory"
ENDIF
```

To execute this script, you could type:

```
1> EXECUTE Display work/prg2
```

If the work/prg2 file can be found in the current directory, the TYPE <name> OPT n command will be executed. The work/prg2 file will be displayed on the screen with line numbers.

If the work/prg2 file cannot be found in the current directory, the script will skip ahead to the ECHO "<name> is not in this directory" command. The message work/prg2 is not in this directory will be displayed in the Shell window.
See also: IF, ENDIF, EXECUTE

ENDCLI

Format: ENDCLI
Template: (none)
Purpose: To end a Shell process
Path: Internal

Specification: ENDCLI ends a Shell process.
See also: ENDSHELL

ENDIF

Format:	ENDIF
Template:	(none)
Purpose:	To terminate an IF block in a script file
Path:	Internal

Specification: ENDIF is used in scripts at the end of an IF block. If the IF condition is not true, or if the true condition commands were executed and an ELSE has been encountered, the execution of the script will skip to the next ENDIF command. Every IF statement must be terminated by an ENDIF.

The ENDIF applies to the most recent IF or ELSE command.
See also: ELSE, IF

ENDSHELL

Format:	ENDSHELL
Template:	(none)
Purpose:	To end a Shell process
Path:	Internal
Specification:	ENDSHELL ends a Shell process

ENDCLI also closes a Shell window.

ENDSHELL should only be used when the Workbench is loaded or another Shell is running. If you have quit the Workbench and you close your only Shell, you will be unable to communicate with the Amiga. Your only recourse is to reboot.

The Shell window may not close if any processes that were launched from the Shell are still running. Even though the window stays open, the Shell will not accept new input. You must terminate those processes before the window will close. For instance, if you opened an editor from the Shell, the Shell window will not close until you exit the editor.

In some cases you can launch a process from the Shell and then close the Shell if the process is started with RUN>:<command>.

ENDSKIP

Format:	ENDSKIP
Template:	(none)
Purpose:	To terminate a SKIP block in a script file
Path:	Internal

Specification: ENDSKIP is used in scripts to terminate the execution of a SKIP block. (A SKIP block allows you to jump over intervening commands if a certain condition is met.) When an ENDSKIP is encountered, execution of the script resumes at the line following the ENDSKIP. The condition flag is set to 5 (WARN).

See also: SKIP

EVAL

Format:	EVAL <value1> [<operation>] [<value2>] [TO <file>] [LFORMAT=<string>]
Template:	VALUE1/A,OP,VALUE2/M,TO/K,LFORMAT/K
Purpose:	To evaluate simple expressions
Path:	C:EVAL

Specification: EVAL is used to evaluate and print the answer of an integer expression. The fractional portion of input values and final results, if any, is truncated (cut off).

<Value1> and <value2> may be in decimal, hexadecimal, or octal numbers. Decimal numbers are the default. Hexadecimal numbers are indicated by either a leading 0x or #X. Octal numbers are indicated by either a leading 0 or a leading #. Alphabetical characters are indicated by a leading single quote (').

The output format defaults to decimal; however, you can use the LFORMAT keyword to select another format. The LFORMAT keyword specifies the formatting string used to print the answer. You may use %X (hexadecimal), %O (octal), %N (decimal), or %C (character). The %X and %O options require a number of digits specification (that is, %X8 gives eight digits of hex output). When using the LFORMAT keyword, you can specify that a new line should be printed by including a *N in your string.

The supported operations and their corresponding symbols are shown in the table below:

Operation	Symbol
Addition	+
Subtraction	-
Multiplication	*
Division	/
Modulo	mod
AND	&
OR	|
NOT	~
Left shift	<<
right shift	>>
negation	-
exclusive OR	xor
bitwise equivalence	eqv

EVAL can be used in scripts to act as a counter for loops. In that case, the TO option, which sends the output of EVAL to a file, is very useful.

Parentheses may be used in the expressions.

Examples:

```
1> EVAL 4 * -5
-20
1> EVAL 0x4f / 010 LFORMAT="The answer is %X4*N"
The answer is 0009
1>
```

This expression divides hexadecimal 4f (79) by octal 10 (8), yielding 0009, the integer portion of the decimal answer 9.875. (The 1> prompt would have appeared immediately after the 0009 if *N had not been specified in the LFORMAT string.)

Assume you were using the following script, called Loop:

```
.Key loop/a
; demo a loop using eval and skip
Bra {
.Ket }
ECHO >ENV:Loop {loop}
LAB start
ECHO "Loop #" noline
TYPE ENV:Loop
EVAL <ENV:Loop >NIL: to=T:Qwe{$$} value2=1 op=- ?
TYPE >ENV:Loop T:Qwe{$$}
```

```
IF val $loop GT 0
SKIP start back
ENDIF
ECHO "done"
```

If you were to type:

```
1> EXECUTE Loop 5
Loop #5
Loop #4
Loop #3
Loop #2
Loop #1
done
```

The first ECHO command sends the number given as the loop argument, entered as an argument of the EXECUTE command, to the ENV:Loop file.

The second ECHO command coupled with the TYPE command, displays Loop # followed by the number given as the loop argument. In this case, it displays Loop #5.

The EVAL command takes the number in the ENV:Loop file as <value1>. <Value2> is 1, and the operation is subtraction. The output of the EVAL command is sent to the T:Qwe($$) file. In this case, the value would be 4.

The next TYPE command sends the value in the T:Qwe($$) file to the ENV:Loop file. In this case, it changes the value in ENV:Loop from 5 to 4.

The IF statement states that as long as the value for Loop is greater than 0, the script should start over. This results in the next line being Loop #4.

The script will continue until Loop is equal to 0.

EXCHANGE

Format: EXCHANGE [CX_POPKEY=<key>] [CX_POPUP=no] [CX_PRIORITY=<n>]
Template: CX_POPKEY/K,CX_POPUP/K,CX_PRIORITY/K/N
Purpose: To monitor and control the Commodity Exchange programs
Path: SYS:Utilities/Exchange
Specification: EXCHANGE is a Commodity Exchange program that monitors and controls all the other Commodity Exchange programs. CX_POPKEY=<key(s)> allows you to specify the hot key for the program. If more

than one key is specified, be sure to enclose the entire argument in double quotes (i.e., "CX_POPKEY=Shift F1"). CX_POPUP=no keeps the Exchange window from opening.

CX_PRIORITY=<n> sets the priority of Exchange in relation to all the other Commodity Exchange programs. All the Commodity Exchange programs are set to a default priority of 0.

To kill Exchange, press Ctrl-E.

Example:

```
1> EXCHANGE "CX_POPKEY=Shift F1"
```

The Exchange program will be started and its window will appear on the screen. If you Hide the window, then want to bring it back again, the hot key combination is Shift-F1.

EXECUTE

Format: EXECUTE <script> [{<arguments>}]
Template: FILE/A
Purpose: To execute a script with optional argument substitution
Path: C:EXECUTE
Specification: EXECUTE is used to run scripts of AmigaDOS commands. The lines in the script are executed just as if they had been typed at a Shell prompt. If the s protection bit of a file is set and the file is in the search path, you only need type the filename — the EXECUTE command is not needed.

You can use parameter substitution in scripts by including special keywords in the script. When these keywords are used, you can pass variables to the script by including the variable in the EXECUTE command line. Before the script is executed, AmigaDOS checks the parameter names in the script against any arguments given on the command line. If any match, AmigaDOS substitutes the values you specified on the command line for the parameter name in the script. You can also specify default values for AmigaDOS to use if no variables are given. If you have not specified a variable, and there is no default specified in the script, then the value of the parameter is empty (no substitution is made).

The permissible keywords for parameter substitution are explained below. Each keyword must be prefaced with a dot character (.).

The .KEY (or .K) keyword specifies both keyword names and positions in a script. It tells EXECUTE how many parameters to expect and how to interpret them. In other words, .KEY serves as a template for the parameter values you specify. Only one .KEY statement is allowed per script. If present, it should be the first line in the file.

The arguments on the .KEY line can be given with the /A and /K directives, which work the same as in an AmigaDOS template. Arguments followed by /A are required; arguments followed by /K require the name of that argument as a keyword. For example, if a script starts with .KEY filename/A it indicates that a filename must be given on the EXECUTE command line after the name of the script. This filename will be substituted in subsequent lines of the script. For instance, if the first line of a script is:

```
.KEY filename/A, TOname/K
```

You must specify a filename variable. The TOname variable is optional, but if specified the TOname keyword must be used. For instance if the first line of a script is:

```
1> EXECUTE Script Textfile TOname NewFile
```

Before execution, AmigaDOS scans the script for any items enclosed by BRA and KET characters (< and >). Such items may consist of a keyword or a keyword and a default value. Wherever EXECUTE finds a keyword enclosed in angle brackets, it tries to substitute a parameter. However, if you want to use a string in your script file that contains angle brackets, you will have to define substitute "bracket" characters with the .BRA and .KET commands. .BRA <ch> changes the opening bracket character to <ch>, while .KET changes the closing bracket character to <ch>.
For example:

```
.KEY filename
ECHO "This line does NOT print <angle> brackets."
.BRA {
.KET }
ECHO "This line DOES print <angle> brackets."
ECHO "The specified filename is {filename}."
```

would result in the following output:

```
1> EXECUTE script TestFile
This line does NOT print brackets.
This line DOES print <angle> brackets.
```

```
The specified filename is TestFile.
```

The first ECHO statement causes AmigaDOS to look for a variable to substitute for the <angle> parameter. If no argument was given on the EXECUTE command line, the null string is substituted. The .BRA and .KET commands then tell the script to use braces to enclose parameters. So, when the second ECHO statement is executed, the angle brackets will be printed. The third ECHO statement illustrates that the braces now function as the bracket characters.

When enclosing a keyword in bracket characters, you can also specify a default string to be used if a variable is not supplied on the command line. There are two ways to specify a default. The first way requires that you specify the default every time you reference a parameter. You must separate the two strings with a dollar sign ($).

For example, in the following statement:

```
ECHO "<word1$defword1> is the default for Word1."
```

defwordl is the default value specified for wordl. It will be printed if no other variable is given for wordl. However, if you want to specify this default several times in your script, you would have to use <wordl$defwordl> each time.

The .DOLLAR <ch> command allows you to change the default character from $ to <ch>. (You can also use .DOL <ch>.) For instance:

```
.DOL #
ECHO "<word1#defword1> is the default for Word1."
```

The second way to define a default uses the .DEF command. This allows you to specify a default for each specific keyword. For example:

```
.DEF word1 "defword1"
```

assigns defwordl as the default for the wordl parameter throughout the script. The following statement:

```
ECHO "<word1> is the default for Word1."
```

results in the same output as the previous ECHO statement:

```
defword1 is the default for Word1.
```

You can embed comments in a script by including them after a semicolon (;) or by typing a dot (.), followed by a space, then the comment.

Summary of Dot Commands

.KEY	Argument template used to specify the format of arguments; may be abbreviated to .K
.DOT <ch>	Change dot character from . to <ch>
.BRA <ch>	Change opening "bracket" character from < to <ch>
.KET <ch>	Change closing "bracket" character from > to <ch>
.DOLLAR <ch>	Change default character from $ to <ch>; may be abbreviated to .DOL
.DEF <keyword value>	Give default to parameter
.<space>	Comment line
.\	Blank comment line

When you EXECUTE a command line, AmigaDOS looks at the first line of the script. If it starts with a dot command, AmigaDOS scans the script looking for parameter substitution and builds a temporary file in the T: directory. If the file does not start with a dot command, AmigaDOS assumes that no parameter substitution is necessary and starts executing the file immediately without copying it to T:. If you do not need parameter substitution, do not use dot commands as they require extras disk accesses and increase execution time.

AmigaDOS provides a number of commands that are useful in scripts, such as IF, ELSE, SKIP, LAB, and QUIT. These commands, as well as the EXECUTE command, can be nested in a script. That is, a script can contain EXECUTE commands.

To stop the execution of a script, press Ctrl-D. If you have nested script files, you can stop the set of EXECUTE commands by pressing Ctrl-C. Ctrl-D only stops the current script from executing.

The current Shell number can be referenced by the characters <$$>. This procedure is useful in creating unique temporary files, logical assignments, and PIPE names.

Examples: Assume the script List contains the following:

```
.K filename
RUN COPY <filename> TO PRT: +
ECHO "Printing of <filename> done"
```

The following command:

```
1> EXECUTE List Test/Prg
```

acts as though you had typed the following commands at the keyboard:

```
1> RUN COPY Test/Prg TO PRT: +
1> ECHO "Printing of Test/Prg done"
```

Another example, Display, uses more of the features described above:

```
.Key name/A
IF EXISTS <name>
TYPE <name> NUMBER  ;if the file is in the given
directory,
;type it with line numbers
ELSE
ECHO "<name> is not in this directory"
ENDIF
```

The command:

```
1> RUN EXECUTE Display Work/Prg2
```

should display the Work/Prg2 file, with line numbers on the screen, if it exists on the current directory. If the file is not there, the screen displays an error message. Because of the /A, if a filename is not given on the command line after display, an error will occur.

See also: ECHO, FAILAT, IF, LAB, QUIT, RUN, SKIPT

FAILAT

Format: FAILAT [<n>]
Template: RCLIM/N
Purpose: To instruct a command sequence to fail if a program gives a return code greater than or equal to the given value
Path: Internal
Specification: Commands indicate that they have failed in some way by setting a return code. A nonzero return code indicates that the command has

encountered an error of some sort. The return code, normally 5, 10, or 20, indicates how serious the error was. A return code greater than or equal to a certain limit (the fail limit) terminates a sequence of noninteractive commands (commands you specify after RUN or in a script).

You may use the FAILAT command to alter the fail limit RCLIM (Return Code Limit) from its initial value of 10. If you increase the limit, you indicate that certain classes of error should not be regarded as fatal and that execution of subsequent commands may proceed after an error. The argument must be a positive number. The fail limit is reset to the initial value of 10 on exit from the command sequence.

If the argument is omitted, the current fail limit is displayed.

Example: Assume a script contains the following lines:

```
COPY DF0:MyFile to RAM:
ECHO "MyFile being copied."
```

If MyFile cannot be found, the script is aborted and the following message appears in the Shell window:

```
COPY: object not found
COPY failed returncode 20:
```

However, if you changed the return code limit to higher than 20, the script would continue even if the COPY command fails. For instance, if you changed the script to read:

```
FAILAT 21
COPY DF0:MyFile to RAM:
ECHO "MyFile being copied."
```

even if MyFile cannot be found, the script will continue. The following message appears in the Shell window:

```
COPY: object not found
MyFile being copied.
```

See also: ECHO, EXECUTE

FAULT

Format:	FAULT <error number(s)>
Template:	/N/M
Purpose:	To print the messages(s) for the specified error code(s)
Path:	Internal

Specification: FAULT prints the message(s) corresponding to the error number(s) supplied. Up to ten error numbers can be specified at once. If several error numbers are given with FAULT, they may be separated by commas or spaces.

Example: If you received the error message Error when opening DF1:TestFile 205 and needed more information, you would type:

```
1> FAULT 205
FAULT 205: object not found
```

This tells you that the error occurred because TestFile could not be found on DF1:.

FILENOTE

Format:	FILENOTE [FILE] <file l pattern> [[COMMENT] <comment>] [ALL] [QUIET]
Template:	FILE/A,COMMENT,ALL/S,QUIET/S
Purpose:	To attach a comment to a file
Path:	C:FILENOTE

Specification: FILENOTE attaches an optional comment of up to 79 characters to the specified file or to all files matching the given pattern.

If the <comment> includes spaces, it must be enclosed in double quotes. To include double quotes in a filenote, each literal quote mark must be immediately preceded by an asterisk (*), and the entire comment must be enclosed in quotes, regardless of whether the comment contains any spaces.

If the <comment> argument is omitted, any existing filenote will be deleted from the named file.

Creating a comment with FILENOTE is the same as entering a comment into the Comment gadget of an icon's Information window. Changes made with FILENOTE will be reflected in the Information window, and vice versa.

When an existing file is copied to (specified as the TO argument of a COPY command), it will be overwritten, but its comment will be retained. Any comment attached to a FROM file will not be copied unless the CLONE or COM option of COPY is specified. If the ALL option is given, FILENOTE adds the <comment> to all the files in the specified directory. If the QUIET option is given, screen output is suppressed.

Examples:

```
1> FILENOTE Sonata "allegro non troppo"
```

attaches the filenote allegro non troppo to the Sonata file.

```
1> FILENOTE Toccata "*"presto*""
```

Here the filenote is "presto"

FIXFONTS

Format:	FIXFONTS
Template:	(none)
Purpose:	To update the .font files of the FONTS: directory
Path:	SYS:System/FixFonts

Specification: FIXFONTS runs the FixFonts program. (FIXFONTS does not support any arguments.) Your disk light will come on while the FONTS: directory is updated. When the update is finished, the light goes out and a Shell prompt appears.

Example:

```
1> FIXFONTS
```

FKEY

Format:	FKEY [F1-F10=<string>] [SF1-SF10=<string>] [CX_PRIORITY=n] [CX_POPUP=yes|no][CX_POPKEY=<key>]
Template:	KEY,CX_PRIORITY/K/N,CX_POPUP/K, CX_POPKEY/K
Purpose:	To assign text to function and shifted functions keys
Path:	Extras2.0:Tools/Commodities/FKey

Specification: FKEY is a Commodities Exchange program that allows you to assign a text string to the function keys and shifted function keys. The output of the function keys is viewable through the Execute Command menu item or in a Shell window.

Example:

```
1> RUN FKEY F4=INFO\n CX_POPUP=no
```

assigns the INFO command to the F4 key. The FKey program is started but the CX_POPUP=no option keeps the window from opening. Pressing F4 while working in a Shell window is the same as typing the INFO command and pressing Return.

FONT

Format:	FONT [FROM <filename>] [EDIT] [USE] [SAVE] [WORKBENCH] [SCREEN] [SYSTEM]
Template:	FROM,EDIT/S,USE/S,SAVE/S,WORKBENCH/S,SCREEN/S, SYSTEM/S
Purpose:	To specify the font(s) used by the system
Path:	SYS:Prefs/Font

Specification: FONT with no arguments or with the EDIT argument opens the Font editor.

The FROM argument must be used in combination with at least one WORKBENCH, SCREEN, or SYSTEM switch. (You can use more than one switch.) This allows you to specify a particular font to be used in the designated area(s) of the screen. The FROM file must be one that was previously saved with the Save As menu item of the Font editor's Project menu. Even if the font in the FROM file was originally saved as one type of text, it can be used in a different area of the screen by specifying the appropriate switch. For instance, if the FROM file was created when you saved a font as Screen text, that font can be used as the Workbench icon text by specifying the WORKBENCH switch after the filename.

If you specify the USE option, the font will be loaded into the appropriate area and used, just as if you had opened the Font editor, selected the appropriate radio button, chosen the font, and selected the Use gadget. If you specify the SAVE option, that font will be saved.

If you do not specify USE or SAVE, EDIT is assumed, and the Font editor is opened. If a FROM file and a WORKBENCH, SCREEN, or SYSTEM switch is

specified, the Font editor will open with the font saved in the FROM file displayed next to the selected radio button(s). If no switch is specified with the FROM file, the editor will display the last used configuration.
Examples:

    1> FONT Prefs/Presets/Font.screen WORKBENCH

opens the Font editor. The font previously saved in the Font.screen file will be displayed in the Workbench icon text gadget. You must select the Save, Use, or Cancel gadget to close the editor.

    1> FONT Prefs/Presets/Font.screen WORKBENCH USE

uses the font in Font.screen as the Workbench icon text. The Font editor is not opened. The font choice will be lost if the system is rebooted.

    1> FONT Prefs/Presets/Font.screen SCREEN WORKBENCH USE

uses the font saved in the Font.screen file as both the Screen text and the Workbench icon text.

FORMAT

Format: FORMAT DRIVE <drive> NAME <name> [NOICONS] [QUICK] [FFS] [NOFFS]
Template: DRIVE/A/K,NAME/A/K,NOICON/S,QUICK/S,FFS/S, NOFFS/S
Purpose: To format a disk for use with the Amiga
Path: SYS:System/Format
Specification: To format a disk, you must specify both the DRIVE and the NAME keywords. The name can be from 1 to 31 characters in length. If you include spaces in the name, it must be enclosed in double quotes.

The NOICONS option prevents a Trashcan icon from being added to the newly formatted disk.

The QUICK option specifies that FORMAT will only format and create the root block (and track), the boot block (and track), and create the bitmap blocks. This is useful when reformatting a previously formatted floppy disk.

Normally, floppy disks are formatted with the old file system. For hard disks, FORMAT uses information specified by the HDToolbox program or in the

MountList to determine the DOS type and file system. The FFS option marks the disk as being used with the FastFileSystem and overrides the MountList keywords or any other default file systems.

Examples:

```
1> FORMAT DRIVE DF0: NAME EmptyDisk
```

formats the disk in drive DF0:, erases any data, and names the disk EmptyDisk. To reformat, or erase, a disk that already contains data, use the QUICK option.

```
1> FORMAT DRIVE DF2: NAME NewDisk QUICK
```

GET

Format: GET <name>
Template: NAME/A
Purpose: To get the value of a local variable
Path: Internal
Specification: GET is used to retrieve and display the value of a local environment variable. The value is displayed in the current window. Local environment variables are only recognized by the Shell in which they are created, or by any Shells created from a NEWSHELL command executed in the original Shell. If you open an additional Shell by opening the Shell icon or by using the Execute Command menu item, previously created local environment variables will not be available.

Example:

```
1> GET editor
Extras2.0:Tools/MEmacs
```

See also: SET

GETENV

Format: GETENV <name>
Template: NAME/A
Purpose: To get the value of a global variable

Path: Internal

Specification: GETENV is used to retrieve and display the value of a global environment variable. The value is displayed in the current window. Global variables are stored in ENV: and are recognized by all Shells.

Example:

```
1> GETENV editor
Extras2.0:Tools/MEmacs
```

See also: SETENV

GRAPHICDUMP

Format: GRAPHICDUMP [TINY I SMALL I MEDIUM I LARGE I <xdots>:<ydots>]

Template: TINY/S,SMALL/S,MEDIUM/S,LARGE/S, <xdots>:<ydots>/S

Purpose: To print the frontmost screen

Path: Extras2.0:Tools/GraphicDump

Specification: GRAPHICDUMP sends a dump of the frontmost screen to the printer about 10 seconds after issuing the command. The size options, which correspond to the program's acceptable Tool Types, determine the width of the printout:

TINY	1/4 the total width allowed by the printer.
SMALL	1/2 the total width allowed by the printer.
MEDIUM	3/4 the total width allowed by the printer.
LARGE	the full width allowed by the printer.

The height of the printout is such that the perspective of the screen is maintained.

To specify specific dimensions, substitute the absolute width in dots for <xdots> and the absolute height for <ydots>.

Examples:

```
1> GRAPHICDUMP SMALL
```

produces a printout of the frontmost screen that is about one-half the total width allowed by the printer.

```
1> GRAPHICDUMP 600:300
```

produces a printout that is 600 dots wide by 300 dots high.

ICONEDIT

Format: ICONEDIT
Template: (none)
Purpose: To edit the appearance and type of icons
Path: Extras2.0:Tools/IconEdit
Specification: ICONEDIT opens the IconEdit program. The command does not support any arguments.
Example:

```
1> ICONEDIT
```

ICONTROL

Format: ICONTROL [FROM <filename>] [EDIT] [USE] [SAVE]
Template: FROM,EDIT/S,USE/S,SAVE/S
Purpose: To specify parameters used by the Workbench
Path: SYS:Prefs/IControl
Specification: ICONTROL without any arguments or with the EDIT argument opens the IControl editor. The FROM argument lets you specify a file to open. This must be a file that was previously saved with the Save As menu item of the IControl editor. For instance, if you have saved a special configuration of the IControl editor to a file in the Presets drawer, you can use the FROM argument to open that file. If the USE switch is also given, the editor will not open, but the settings in the FROM file will be used. If the SAVE switch is given, the editor will not open, but the settings in the FROM file will be saved.
Example:

```
1> ICONTROL Prefs/Presets/IControl.pre USE
```

uses the settings that were saved in the IControl.pre file. The editor is not opened.

ICONX

Format: ICONX
Template: (none)
Purpose: To allow execution of a script file from an icon
Path: C:ICONX
Specification: ICONX allows you to execute a script file of AmigaDOS commands via an icon.

To use ICONX, create or copy a project icon for the script. Open the icon's Information window and change the Default Tool of the icon to C:ICONX. Add the WINDOW= and DELAY= Tool Types if you chose, and select Save to store the changed .info file. The script can then be executed by double-clicking on the icon.

When the icon is opened, ICONX changes the current directory to the directory containing the project icon before executing the script. An input/output window for the script file will be opened on the Workbench screen. The icon's WINDOW= Tool Type can be used to specify the size of the window. You can add a delay (specified in seconds) after the execution of the file is complete with the DELAY= Tool Type. This keeps the window open to allow time for reading the output. If a 0 is specified for DELAY=, ICONX waits for a Ctrl-C before exiting. Extended selection can be used to pass files that have icons to the script. Their filenames appear to the script as keywords. To use this facility, the .KEY keyword must appear at the start of the script. In this case, the AmigaDOS EXECUTE command is used to execute the script file.

See also: EXECUTE

IF

Format: IF [NOT] [WARN] [ERROR] [FAIL] [<string> EQ | GT | GE <string>] [VAL] [EXISTS <filename>]
Template: NOT/S,WARN/S,ERROR/S,FAIL/S,,EQ/K,GT/K,GE/K, VAL/S,EXISTS/K
Purpose: To evaluate conditional operations in script files

Path: Internal

Specification: In a script file, IF, when its conditional is true, carries out all the subsequent commands until an ENDIF or ELSE command is found. When the conditional is not true, execution skips directly to the ENDIF or to the ELSE. The conditions and commands in IF and ELSE blocks can span more than one line before their corresponding ENDIFs.

Following are some of the ways you can use the IF, ELSE, and ENDIF commands:

```
IF <condition>      IF <condition>      IF <condition>
<command(s)>        <command(s)>        <command(s)>
ENDIF               ELSE                IF <condition>
                    <command(s)>        <command(s)>
                    ENDIF               ENDIF
                                        ENDIF
```

ELSE is optional, and nested IFs jump to the nearest ENDIF.

The additional keywords are as follows:

NOT: Reverses the interpretation of the result.
WARN: True if previous return code is greater than or equal to 5.
ERROR: True if previous return code is greater than or equal to 10; only available if you set FAILAT to greater than 10.
FAIL: True if previous return code is greater than or equal to 20; only available if you set FAILAT to greater than 20.
<a> EQ <b>: True if the text of a and b is identical (disregarding case).
EXISTS <file>: True if the file exists.

If more than one of the three condition-flag keywords (WARN, ERROR, FAIL) are given, the one with the lowest value is used.

IF supports the GT (greater than) and GE (greater than or equal to) comparisons. Normally, the comparisons are performed as string comparisons. However, if the VAL option is specified, the comparison is a numeric comparison.

Note: You can use NOT GE for LT and NOT GT for LE.

You can use local or global variables with IF by prefacing the variable name with a $ character.

Examples:

```
IF EXISTS Work/Prog
  TYPE Work/Prog
ELSE ECHO "It's not here"
ENDIF
```

If the file Work/Prog exists in the current directory, then AmigaDOS displays it. Otherwise, AmigaDOS displays the message It's not here and continues after the ENDIF.

```
IF ERROR
  SKIP errlab
ENDIF
ECHO "No error"
LAB errlab
```

If the previous command produced a return code greater than or equal to 10 then AmigaDOS skips over the ECHO command to the errlab label.
See also: EXECUTE, FAILAT, LAB, QUIT, SKIP

IHELP

Format: IHELP[CYCLE=<key>] [MAKEBIG=<key>] [MAKESMALL= <key>][CYCLESCREEN=<ke-y>] [ZIPWINDOW=<key>] [CX_PRIORITY=<n>]
Template: CYCLE/K,MAKEBIG/K,MAKESMALL/K,CYCLESCREEN/K, ZIPWINDOW/K,CX_PRIORITY/K/N
Purpose: To enable the keyboard to take over certain mouse operations
Path: Extras2.0:Tools/Commodities/IHelp
Specification: IHELP is a Commodities Exchange program that lets you assign functions normally performed by the window gadgets to keys. The arguments supported by IHelp are the same as the Tool Types that can be entered into the icon's Information window. If a <key> argument specifies multiple keys, be sure to enclose the entire argument in double quotes. A list of the arguments follows:

CYCLE: Cycles any open tool or project screens from the back of the screen to the front.

MAKEBIG: Makes the active window as large as possible without moving it.

MAKESMALL: Makes the active window as small as possible.

CYCLESCREEN: Cycles through all open screens.

ZIPWINDOW: Zooms the active window. (This is the same as selecting the window's zoom gadget.)

The CX_PRIORITY=<n> argument sets the priority of IHelp in relation to all the other Commodity Exchange programs. All the Commodity Exchange programs are set to a default priority of 0. For instance, if IHelp has a priority of 3, it will intercept any keys specified for the arguments before any other Exchange programs.

Example:

```
1>IHELP "CYCLE=Alt F7" "MAKESMALL=Control S" "MAKEBIG=
Control B"
```

If you were to press Alt-F7, any project or tool windows would cycle from front to back. The Ctrl-S combination makes the selected window small, while the Ctrl-B combination makes the selected window bigger.

INFO

Format: INFO [<device>]
Template: DEVICE
Purpose: To give information about the file system(s)
Path: C:INFO
Specification: INFO displays a line of information about each disk or partition. This includes the maximum size of the disk, the used and free space, the number of soft disk errors that have occurred, and the status of the disk.

With the DEVICE argument, INFO provides information on just one device or volume.

Example:

```
1> INFO

Unit  Size  Used  Free  Full  Errs  Status       Name

DF0:  879K  1738   20   98%    0    Read Only    Workbench2.0
DF1:  879K   418  1140  24%    0    Read/Write   Text-6
```

```
Volumes available:
Workbench2.0 [Mounted]
Text-6 [Mounted]
```

INITPRINTER

Format: INITPRINTER
Template: (none)
Purpose: To initialize a printer for print options specified in the Preferences editors
Path: Extras2.0:Tools/InitPrinter
Specification: INITPRINTER runs the InitPrinter program. (It does not support any arguments.) You will hear the printer reset, then the Shell prompt will return.
Example:

```
1> INITPRINTER
```

INPUT

Format: INPUT [FROM <filename>] [EDIT] [USE] [SAVE]
Template: FROM,EDIT/S,USE/S,SAVE/S
Purpose: To specify different speeds for the mouse and keyboard
Path: SYS:Prefs/Input
Specification: INPUT without any arguments or with the EDIT argument opens the Input editor. The FROM argument lets you specify a file to open. This must be a file that was previously saved with the Save As menu item of the Input editor. For instance, if you have saved a special configuration of the Input editor to a file in the Presets drawer, you can use the FROM argument to open that file. If the USE switch is also given, the editor will not be opened, but the settings in the FROM file will be used. If the SAVE switch is given, the editor will not open, but the settings in the FROM file will be saved.
Example:

```
1> INPUT Prefs/Presets/Input.fast SAVE
```

loads and saves the settings from the Input.fast file. Even if the system is rebooted, those settings will still be in effect. The editor does not open.

INSTALL

Format: INSTALL [DRIVE] <DF0: | DF1: | DF2: | DF3:> [NOBOOT] [CHECK] [FFS]
Template: DRIVE/A,NOBOOT/S,CHECK/S,FFS/S
Purpose: To write the boot block to a formatted floppy disk, specifying whether it should be bootable
Path: C:INSTALL
Specification: INSTALL clears a floppy disk's boot block area and writes a valid boot block onto the disk. By default, the disk will be given the boot block of the filing system specified when the disk was initially formatted, either the old filing system (OFS) or the FastFileSystem (FFS). To force FastFileSystem, use the FFS switch.

The NOBOOT option removes the boot block from an AmigaDOS disk, making it not bootable.

> **Warning:** The NOBOOT option will write a boot block on a non-AmigaDOS disk. INSTALL uses the default DOS type, OFS, when writing to a non-AmigaDOS disk.

The CHECK option checks for valid boot code. It reports whether a disk is bootable or not and whether standard Commodore-Amiga boot code is present on the disk. The condition flag is set to 0 if the boot code is standard (or the disk isn't bootable), 5 (WARN) otherwise.
Examples:

```
1> INSTALL DF0: CHECK
No bootblock installed
```

indicates that there is a non-bootable floppy in DF0:.

```
1> INSTALL DF0:
```

makes the disk in drive DF0: a bootable disk.

```
1> INSTALL DF0: CHECK
```

```
Appears to be FFS bootblock
```

indicates that there is an FFS floppy in DF0:.

IPREFS

Format: IPREFS
Template: (none)
Purpose: To communicate Preferences information stored in the individual editor files to the Workbench
Path: C:IPREFS
Specifications: IPREFS reads the individual system Preferences files and passes the information to the Workbench so that it can reply accordingly. IPREFS is generally run in the Startup-sequence after the Preferences files are copied to ENV:. Each time a user selects Save or Use from within an editor, IPREFS is notified and passes the information along to Workbench. If necessary, IPREFS resets Workbench to implement those changes. If any project or tool windows are open, IPREFS displays a requester asking you to close any nondrawer windows.

JOIN

Format: JOIN {<file | pattern>} AS | TO <filename>
Template: FILE/M/A,AS=TO/K/A
Purpose: To concatenate two or more files into a new file
Path: C:JOIN
Specification: JOIN copies all the listed files, in the order given, to one new file. This destination file cannot have the same name as any of the source files. You must supply a destination filename. The original files remain unchanged. Any number of files may be JOINed in one operation.

TO can be used as a synonym for AS.

Example:

```
1> JOIN Part1 Part2 Part3 AS Textfile
```

KEYSHOW

Format: KEYSHOW
Template: (none)
Purpose: To display the current Keymap
Path: Extras2.0:Tools/KeyShow
Specification: KEYSHOW opens the KeyShow window. (The command does not support any arguments.) To exit the program, select the window's close gadget.
Example:

```
1> KEYSHOW
```

LAB

Format: LAB [<string>]
Template: (none)
Purpose: To specify a label in a script file
Path: Internal
Specification: LAB is used in scripts to define a label that is looked for by the SKIP command. The label <string> may be of any length but must consist of alphanumeric characters. No symbols are allowed. If the <string> contains spaces, it must be enclosed in quotes.
See also: EXECUTE, IF, SKIP

LIST

Format: LIST [{<dir | pattern>}] [P | PAT <pattern>] [KEYS] [DATES] [NODATES] [TO <name>] [SUB <string>] [SINCE <date>] [UPTO <date>] [QUICK] [BLOCK] [NOHEAD] [FILES] [DIRS] [LFORMAT <string>] [ALL]
Template: DIR/M,P=PAT/K,KEYS/S,DATES/S,NODATES/S,TO/K, SUB/K, SINCE/K, UPTO/K,QUICK/S, BLOCK/S, NOHEAD/S, FILES/S, DIRS/S, LFORMAT/K,ALL/S
Purpose: To list specified information about directories and files
Path: C:LIST

Specification: LIST displays information about the contents of the current directory. If you specify a <dir>, <pattern>, or <filename> argument, LIST will display information about the specified directory, all directories or files that match the pattern, or the specified file, respectively.

Unless other options are specified, LIST displays the following:

Name: The name of the file or directory.

Size: The size of the file in bytes. If there is nothing in this file, the field will read empty. For directories, this entry reads Dir.

Protection: The protection bits that are set for this file are shown as letters. The clear (unset) bits are shown as hyphens. Most files show the default protection bits, ----rwed for readable/writable/executable/ deletable. See the PROTECT command for more on protection bits.

Date and time: The date and time the file was created or last altered.

Comment: The comment, if any, placed on the file using the FILENOTE command. It is preceded by a colon (:).

LIST has options that will change the way the output is displayed. These options are explained below:

KEYS: Displays the block number of each file header or directory.

DATES: Displays dates in the form DD-MMM-YY (the default unless you use QUICK).

NODATES: Will not display date and time information.

TO <name>: Specifies an output file or device for LIST; by default, LIST outputs to the current window.

SUB <string>: Lists only files containing the substring <string>.

SINCE <date>: Lists only files created on or after a certain date.

UPTO <date>: Lists only files created on or before a certain date.

QUICK: Lists only the names of files and directories.

BLOCK: Displays file sizes in blocks, rather than bytes.

NOHEAD: Suppresses the printing of the header information.

FILES: Lists files only (no directories).

DIRS: Lists directories only (no files).

LFORMATP: Defines a string to specially format LIST output.

ALL: Lists all files in directories and subdirectories.

The LFORMAT option modifies the output of LIST and can be used as a quick method of generating script files. When LFORMAT is specified, the QUICK and NOHEAD options are automatically selected. When using LFOR-

MAT you must specify an output format specification string; this string is incorporated into the script file. If you want the output to be saved, you must redirect it to a file by using the > operator or specifying a TO file.

The format for the output format specification string is LFORMAT= <string>. To include the output of LIST in this string, use the substitution operator %S. The path and filename can be made part of the string this way. Whether the path or the filename is substituted for an occurrence of %S depends on how many occurrences are in the LFORMAT line, and their order, as follows:

Substituted with each occurrence

Occurrences

of %S	1st	2nd	3rd	4th
1	filename			
2	path	filename		
3	path	filename	filename	
4	path	filename	path	filename

Some new options allow you to specify fields to be printed in the LFORMAT output. These options are:

%A	Prints file attributes (protection bits).
%B	Prints size of file in blocks.
%C	Prints any comments attached to the file.
%D	Prints the date associated with the file.
%K	Prints the file key block.
%L	Prints the length of file in bytes.
%N	Prints the name of the file.
%P	Prints the file parent path.
%T	Prints the time associated with the file.

You can put a length specifier and/or a justification specifier between the percent size (%) and the field specifier.

Examples:

```
1> LIST Dirs
Monitors    Dir —    rwed    27-June-90    11:43:59
T           Dir —    rwed    Wednesday     11:37:43
Trashcan    Dir —    rwed    21-Jun-90     17:54:20
```

Only the directories in the current directory, in this case SYS:, are listed. (A shortened version of the typical output is shown above.)

```
1> LIST Li#? TO RAM:Libs.file
```

LIST will search for any directories or files that start with LI. The output of LIST will be sent to the Libs.file in RAM:.

```
1> LIST DF0:Documents UPTO 09-Oct-90
```

Only the files or directories on the Documents directory of DF0: that have not been changed since October 9, 1990, will be listed.

```
1> LIST >RAM:Scriptnotes #? LFORMAT="filenote %S%S Testnote"
```

A new script file, Scriptnotes, is created in RAM:. The contents will include a list of all the files in the current directory. When Scriptnotes is executed, it will add the filenote Testnote to each file. For instance, if the current directory is S:, the contents of Scriptnotes as produced by this command might look like this:

```
filenote s:HDBackup.config Testnote
filenote s:DPat Testnote
filenote s:Ed-startup Testnote
filenote s:PCD Testnote
filenote s:Shell-startup Testnote
filenote s:SPat Testnote
filenote s:Startup-sequence Testnote
```

LOADWB

Format: LOADWB [-DEBUG] [DELAY] [CLEANUP] [NEWPATH]
Template: -DEBUG/S,DELAY/S,CLEANUP/S,NEWPATH/S
Purpose: To start Workbench
Path: C:LOADWB
Specification: LOADWB starts the Workbench. Normally, this is done when booting, by placing the LOADWB command in the Startup-sequence file. If you shut down the Workbench, LOADWB can be used from a Shell to restart it.

Workbench snapshots the current paths in effect when the LOADWB command is executed. It uses these paths for each Shell started from Workbench.

Example: If you have quit the Workbench and are working through a Shell, typing:

```
1> LOADWB
```

will bring the Workbench back. Typing LOADWB when the Workbench is already loaded has no effect. LOADWB NEWPATH will cause Workbench to take a new snapshot of the current paths. LOADWB -DEBUG will start Workbench with a special menu that can be used by programmers to flush memory. This is handy for debugging code.

LOCK

Format: LOCK <drive> [ON | OFF] [<passkey>]
Template: DRIVE/A,ON/S,OFF/S,PASSKEY
Purpose: To set the write-protect status of a disk
Path: C:LOCK

Specification: LOCK sets or unsets the write-protect status of a disk or partition. The LOCK remains on until the system is rebooted or until the LOCK is turned off with the LOCK OFF command.

An optional passkey may be specified. If the passkey is used to lock a hard disk partition, the same passkey must be specified to unlock the partition. The passkey may be any number of characters in length.

Example:

```
1> LOCK Work: ON SecretCode
```

The Work: partition is locked. You can read the contents of Work: with commands like DIR, LIST or MORE, but you cannot alter the contents of the partition. If you try to edit the contents of a file on Work:, a requester will appear stating that Work: is write-protected. For instance, if you try to create a new directory, the following message will appear:

```
1> MAKEDIR WORK:Test
Can't create directory Work:Test
Disk is write-protected
```

To unlock the partition, type:

```
1> LOCK Work: OFF SecretCode
```

MAKEDIR

Format: MAKEDIR {<name>}
Template: NAME/M
Purpose: To create a new directory
Path: C:MAKEDIR
Specification: MAKEDIR creates a new, empty directory(s) with the name(s) you specify. The command works within only one directory level at a time, so any directories on the given path(s) must already exist. The command fails if a directory or a file of the same name already exists in the directory above it in the hierarchy. MAKEDIR does not create a drawer icon for the new directory.

Examples:

```
1> MAKEDIR Tests
```

creates a directory Tests in the current directory.

```
1> MAKEDIR DF1:Xyz
```

creates a directory Xyz in the root directory of the disk in DF1:.

```
1> CD DF0:
1> MAKEDIR Documents Payables Orders
```

creates three directories, Documents, Payables, and Orders, on the disk in DF0:.

MAKELINK

Format: MAKELINK [FROM] <file> [TO] <file> [HARD]
Template: FROM/A,TO/A,HARD/S
Purpose: To create a link between files
Path: C:MAKELINK
Specification: MAKELINK creates a file on a disk that is a pointer to another file, this is known as a link. When an application or command calls the FROM file, the TO file is actually used. By default, MAKELINK supports hard links—the FROM file and TO file must be on the same volume.

Note: Soft links, which can be links across volumes, are not currently implemented.

MEMACS

Format: MEMACS [<filename>] [goto <n>] [OPT W]
Template: None.
Purpose: To create and edit text files
Path: SYS:Utilities/Tools/MEMACS
Specification: MEMACS is a screen-oriented editor that allows you to create and edit multiple text files simultaneously. You can use MEMACS to create a new file or alter an existing one. Text is displayed on screen and can be scrolled vertically or horizontally using the cursor keys. To add new text, you simply type it in. To delete existing text, you use the delete keys.

The filename argument specifies the file you want to edit. If the file exists, the MEMACS screen appears and the named file is loaded into memory for editing. If the file does not exist, MEMACS creates the file and presents a blank screen ready for text to be entered.

The optional goto argument specifies a line number to position the cursor on when MEMACS is started. The OPT W argument tells MEMACS to open on the Workbench screen. If this argument is omitted, MEMACS opens its own screen which takes a little more memory.

Examples:

```
1> MEMACS myfile OPT W
```

starts up MEMACS on the Workbench screen with myfile loaded and ready to be edited. If myfile does not already exist, it is created.

```
1> MEMACS myfile goto 17
```

starts up MEMACS on its own screen with myfile loaded and ready to be edited. The cursor will be positioned on line 17 instead of at the beginning of the file. If myfile does not already exist, it is created.

MEMACS Command Quick Reference

Here is a list of commands you can give the MEMACS text editor once it is started. In this list, a carat symbol (^) means press the control key (Ctrl) at the same time as the letter. For instance, ^X means hold down the control key and press X. Esc means press the Escape key at the same time as the letter. For instance, EscW means hold down the Escape key and press W.

FILING COMMANDS (PROJECT MENU)

^X F   Rename. Changes the name of the current file being edited; MEMACS will prompt you for the new name to use.

^X^R   Read-file. This commands replaces the current file with a new one. MEMACS will prompt you for the new file to use.

^X^V   Visit-file. This command lets you work with multiple files at the same time. MEMACS will prompt you for the name of the visit file. Enter a filename and press return and a new MEMACS window opens showing the visit file you requested ready for editing.

^X^I   Insert-file. MEMACS will prompt you for the name of the file to insert. Enter a filename and press return and the new file is inserted at the cursor position.

^X^S   Save-file. MEMACS saves the file, overwriting the old one.

^X^W   Save-file-as. MEMACS saves the file but first prompts you for a filename to use for the save.

^X^M   Save-mod. Saves the current file and any visit files only if they have been changed. The original files are overwritten.

^X^F   Save-exit. Saves any changes and exits. The original file is overwritten.

^ -   New-CLI. A new Shell will open so you can enter AmigaDOS commands. Enter ENDSHELL or ENDCLI to close the Shell and return to MEMACS.

^X !   CLI-command. MEMACS prompts you for an AmigaDOS command to pass to the Shell. Any messages from AmigaDOS are displayed on the lower half of the screen. Use ENDSHELL or ENDCLI to return to MEMACS. (Use ^X 1 to close the Shell output window.)

^C   Quit. Quit MEMACS. The file is not saved.

EDITING COMMANDS

^W   Kill-region (Cut). This command cuts a marked block (or region) from the text and copies it into the kill buffer.

^Y   Yank (Paste). This command copies a previously cut block from the kill buffer into the text at the cursor position.

^@	Set-mark. This command sets the beginning position of a marked block for cut and paste operations. The ending position of the block does not have to be set; it follows the cursor.
EscW	Copy-region. This command copies the marked block to the kill buffer.
^X^L	Lower-region. This command makes the marked block all upper case.
^X^U	Upper-region. This command makes the marked block all lower case.
^X^B	List-buffers. MEMACS will display the list of all files currently being edited and the size of the buffers used to hold them.
^XB	Select-buffer. MEMACS prompts you for the name of the buffer you wish to edit. Enter a name and press return.
Esc^Y	Insert-buffer. MEMACS prompts you for the name of a file to insert at the cursor position. Enter a name and press return.
^XK	Kill-buffer. MEMACS prompts you for the name of a buffer to delete. Enter a name and press return.
^XJ	Justify-buffer. Removes all blank spaces and tabs from the left-hand side of the current text file.
^L	Redisplay. This command redraws the display screen.
^Q	Quote-char. Use this key combination first if you want to type the control character, escape, or return in your text or for searches.
^J	Indent. Moves the cursor to the next line and automatically indents the same amount of space as the previous line.
^T	Transpose. Swaps the position of two adjacent characters.
^G	Cancel. Ends a long command such as query search and replace.

WINDOW COMMANDS

^X1	One-window. Makes the current buffer a single full-size screen.
^X2	Split-window. Splits the current buffer in half so that you can look at two separate parts of the text at the same time.
^XN	Next-window. Moves the cursor to the next window.
^XP	Prev-window. Moves the cursor to the previous window.
^XZ	Expand-window. In a split-window screen this command adds a line to the current window and subtracts a line from the adjacent window.
^X^Z	Shrink-window. In a split-window screen this command subtracts a line from the current window and adds a line to the adjacent window.
Esc^V	Next-w-page. In a split-window screen this command makes text in the adjacent window scroll up a page.

^XV   Prev-w-page. In a split-window screen this command makes text in the adjacent window scroll down a page.

MOVE COMMANDS

Esc<   Top-of-buffer. Moves the cursor to the top of the text buffer.
Esc>   End-of-buffer. Moves the cursor to the last line in the text buffer.
Esc,   Top-of-window. Moves the cursor to the top of the window.
Esc.   End-of-window. Moves the cursor to the last line in the window.
^X^G   Go-to-line. MEMACS Prompts you to enter a line number and moves the cursor to that line.
^X^X   Swap-dot&mark. Swaps the cursor position with a mark set earlier. This lets you quickly toggle between two positions in the text.
^V   Next-page. Scrolls the text up a page.
EscV   Prev-page. Scrolls the text down a page.
EscF   Next-word. Moves the cursor to the end of the next word.
EscB   Previous-word. Moves the cursor to the first letter of the previous word.
^Z   Scroll-up. Scrolls the text down one line.
EscZ   Scroll-down. Scrolls the text up one line.

LINE COMMANDS

^O   Open-line. Splits the line at the cursor making one line into two. The cursor stays in position at the end of the upper line.
^X^D   Kill-line. Deletes the line the cursor is on and copies the text to the kill buffer for later paste (yank) operations.
^K   Kill-to-eol. Deletes text between the cursor and the end of the line and copies it to the kill buffer for paste (yank) operations.
^A   Start-of-line. Positions the cursor at the beginning of the line.
^E   End-of-line. Positions the cursor at the end of the line.
^N   Next-line. Moves the cursor down a line.
^P   Previous-line. Moves the cursor up a line.
Esc!   Line-to-top. Moves the line the cursor is on to the top of the window.
^X^O   Delete-blanks. Deletes all blank lines between the cursor and the next line containing any text.
^X=   Show-line#. Displays the cursor position line and column number, and the relative amount of text above the cursor as a percent.

WORD COMMANDS

EscD   Delete-forw. Deletes text between the cursor and the end of word.

EscH	Delete-back. Deletes text between the cursor and the start of word.
EscU	Upper-word. Changes text between the cursor and the end of word to upper case.
EscL	Lower-word. Changes text between the cursor and the end of word to lower case.
EscC	Cap-word. Change the letter under the cursor to a capital and all remaining letters in the word to lower case.
Esc^	Switch-case. Change the case of all letters between the cursor and end of word.

SEARCH COMMANDS

^S	Search-forward. MEMACS prompts you for a text string to search for. Type in a word and press return. If the word you entered is found MEMACS positions the cursor on it.
^R	Search-backward. MEMACS prompts you for a text string to search for. Type in a word and press return. If the word is found anywhere in the preceding text MEMACS positions the cursor on it.
EscR	Search-replace. MEMACS first prompts you for a text string to search for and then for a text string to replace it with. Type in the words you want to change and press return.
EscQ	Query-sr. Same as searchreplace except that, for each occurrence of the string found, MEMACS positions the cursor on it and gives you the choice of making the replacement or not.
EscF	Fence-Match. Moves the cursor to the next occurrence of the character currently under the cursor.

EXTRA COMMANDS

^U	Set-arg. Lets you type in a number for the next command you use. This is especially important for the Set command.
EscS	Set. Allows you to set various MEMACS parameters. MEMACS prompts you for the name of the parameter to set as follows:

Screen	Toggles between a Workbench screen and a custom screen.
Interlace	Toggles interlace mode on and off.
Mode	+cmode or -cmode toggles C editing mode features. +wrap or -wrap toggles word wrap mode on or off.
Left	Sets left margin.
Right	Sets right margin.
Tab	Sets the increment for tab spacing.

Indent	Sets the indent level for cmode usage.
Case	Toggles case-sensitive search mode on or off.
Backup	ON for automatic backups in <filename>.bak. SAFE for backups with protection from overwriting. OFF to turn off automatic backups.
^X(	Start-macro. Tells MEMACS to start recording any subsequent keystrokes.
^X)	Stop-macro. Tells MEMACS to stop recording keystrokes.
^XE	Execute-macro. Automatically repeats all keystrokes and menu operations performed between Start-macro and Stop-macro.
^X^K	Set-key. Allows you to define keyboard shortcuts. MEMACS prompts you for the key to define. Press a function key, help key, or numeric keypad key and MEMACS displays its current definition. You can type in a new definition or just press return.
EscK	Reset-keys. Restores function keys, help key, and numeric keypad keys to their default definitions.
EscE	Execute-file. Lets you execute a file of MEMACS commands as a script. MEMACS prompts you for the name of the file to execute. Type in a name and press return. The script file you execute must contain only MEMACS commands with command names typed in exactly as they appear in the menus.
^[^[	Execute-line. Lets you execute a single line of MEMACS commands. MEMACS prompts you for the command line. Type in only MEMACS commands with command names entered exactly as they appear in the menus.

MORE

Format: MORE <filename>
Template: FILENAME/K
Purpose: To display the contents of an ASCII file
Path: SYS:Utilities/More
Specification: MORE displays the contents of the file <filename>. If the file is not in the current directory, you must specify the complete path. If you don't specify a file, MORE will display a file requester.

MORE also accepts input from a PIPE. Since standard input from the Pipe-Handler is of unknown length, the Backspace, >, and %n commands are disabled when the MORE input is from a PIPE.

If the EDITOR environment variable is defined and you are using MORE from the Shell, you can bring up an editor to use on the file you are viewing (type Shift-E). The EDITOR variable should have the complete path to the editor specified, that is, C:ED.

Example:

```
1> MORE DF0:TestFile
```

displays the contents of the ASCII file called TestFile on the disk in drive DF0:.

MOUNT

Format: MOUNT <device> [FROM <filename>]
Template: DEVICE/A,FROM/K
Purpose: To make a device connected to the system available
Path: C:MOUNT
Specification: MOUNT causes AmigaDOS to recognize devices connected to the system. When the MOUNT command is issued, MOUNT looks in the DEVS:MountList file (or the optional FROM file) for the parameters of the device that is being mounted. MOUNT commands are usually placed in the Startup-sequence file.

Example: Sample uses of MOUNT in the Startup-sequence include

```
MOUNT Speak:
MOUNT Aux:
MOUNT Pipe:
```

These commands MOUNT the Speak.handler, Aux.handler, and Pipe.handler found in the L: directory.

NEWCLI

Format: NEWCLI
Template: (none)
Purpose: To start a new Shell process
Path: Internal

Specification: NEWCLI starts a new Shell process. It is the same as using the NEWSHELL command. See the specifications for NEWSHELL for more information.

NEWSHELL

Format: NEWSHELL [<window specification>] [FROM <filename>]
Template: WINDOW,FROM
Purpose: To open a new interactive Shell window
Path: C:NEWSHELL
Specification: NEWSHELL invokes a new, interactive Shell. The new window becomes the currently selected window and process. The new window has the same current directory, prompt string, and stack size as the one from which it was invoked. However, each Shell window is independent, allowing separate input, output, and program execution.

The window can be sized, dragged, zoomed, and depth-adjusted just like most other Amiga windows. To create a custom window, you can include the WINDOW argument. You may specify the initial dimensions, location, and title of the window with this <window specification> syntax:

```
CON:x/y/width/height/title/options
```
where:

- x   is the number of pixels from the left edge of the screen to the left border of the Shell window.
- y   is the number of pixels from the top of the screen to the top of the Shell window.
- width   is the width of the Shell window, in pixels.
- height   is the height of the Shell window, in pixels.
- title   is the text that appears in the Shell window title bar.

NEWSHELL uses the default startup file S:Shell-startup, unless a FROM filename is specified. You might have several different Shell-startup files, each having different command aliases, for example. You can call such customized Shell environments with FROM.

The NEWCLI command has the same effect as NEWSHELL; it invokes a new Shell process.

Examples:

```
1> NEWSHELL
```

A new Shell window will open.

```
1> NEWSHELL CON:0/0/640/200/Myshell/CLOSE
```

A window starting in the upper left corner of the screen and measuring 640 pixels wide and 200 pixels high will open. The window is titled Myshell, and it has a close gadget. If you add the command to your User-startup file, a Shell window opens automatically when your Amiga is booted.

```
1> NEWSHELL FROM S:Programming.startup
```

opens a new Shell, but instead of executing the Shell-startup file, the Programming.startup file is executed. You could have aliases and prompt commands in the Programming-startup file that you only use when you are programming.

NOCAPSLOCK

Format: NOCAPSLOCK [CX_PRIORITY=<n>]
Template: CX_PRIORITY/K/N
Purpose: To disable the Caps Lock key
Path: Extras2.0:Tools/Commodities/NoCapsLock
Specification: NOCAPSLOCK is a Commodity Exchange program that temporarily disables the Caps Lock key.

CX_PRIORITY=<n> sets the priority of NoCapsLock in relation to all the other Commodity Exchange programs. All the Commodity Exchange programs are set to a default priority of 0.

To kill NoCapsLock, press Ctrl-E.

Example:

```
1> NOCAPSLOCK
```

NOFASTMEM

Format: NOFASTMEM
Template: (none)
Purpose: To force the Amiga to use only resident Chip RAM
Path: SYS:System/NoFastMem
Specification: NOFASTMEM disables any Fast (or expansion) RAM used by the system. The expansion memory can be turned on again by sending the NoFastMem program a break, either via the BREAK command or by typing Ctrl-C. Ctrl-C will only work if you don't start the program with the RUN command.

Example:

```
1> NOFASTMEM
```

OVERSCAN

Format: OVERSCAN [FROM <filename>] [EDIT] [USE] [SAVE]
Template: FROM,EDIT/S,USE/S,SAVE/S
Purpose: To change the sizes of the display areas for text and graphics
Path: SYS:Prefs/Overscan
Specification: OVERSCAN without any arguments or with the EDIT argument opens the Overscan editor. The FROM argument lets you specify a file to open. This must be a file that was previously saved with the Save As menu item of the Overscan editor. For instance, if you have saved a special configuration of the Overscan editor to a file in the Presets drawer, you can use the FROM argument to open that file. If the USE switch is also given, the editor will not open, but the settings in the FROM file will be used. If the SAVE switch is given, the editor will not open, but the settings in the FROM file will be saved.

Example:

```
1> OVERSCAN Prefs/Presets/Overscan.graphics SAVE
```

loads and saves the Overscan sizes saved in the Overscan.graphics file.

PALETTE

Format: PALETTE [FROM <filename>] [EDIT] [USE] [SAVE]
Template: FROM,EDIT/S,USE/S,SAVE/S
Purpose: To change the colors of the Workbench screen
Path: SYS:Prefs/Palette
Specification: PALETTE without any arguments or with the EDIT argument opens the Palette editor. The FROM argument lets you specify a file to open. This must be a file that was previously saved with the Save As menu item of the Palette editor. For instance, if you have saved a special configuration of the Palette editor to a file in the Presets drawer, you can use the FROM argument to open that file. If the USE switch is also given, the editor will not be opened, but the settings in the FROM file will be used. If the SAVE switch is given, the editor will not open, but the settings in the FROM file will be saved.
Example:

```
1> PALETTE Prefs/Presets/Palette.grey USE
```

loads and uses the colors saved in the Palette.grey file. If the system is rebooted, the previously saved colors are used.

PATH

Format: PATH [{<dir>}] [ADD] [SHOW] [RESET] [QUIET] [REMOVE]
Template: PATH/M,ADD/S,SHOW/S,RESET/S,QUIET/S, REMOVE/S
Purpose: To control the directory list that the Shell searches to find commands
Path: Internal
Specification: PATH lets you see, add to, or change the search path that AmigaDOS follows when looking for a command or program to execute. When a directory is in the search path, you no longer need to specify the complete path to any files or subdirectories within that directory. You can just enter the filename, and AmigaDOS will look through the directories in the search path until it finds the file.

Enter the PATH command alone, or with the SHOW option, and the directory names in the current search path will be displayed. Normally, when PATH is displaying the directory names, a requester appears if a volume that is part of the search path cannot be found. For instance, if you added a floppy disk to the search path, then removed that disk from the disk drive, a requester would ask you to insert the disk.

If you specify the QUIET option, PATH will not display requesters for volumes that are not currently mounted. If PATH encounters an unmounted volume, it simply displays the volume name. The names of any directories on that volume included in the PATH are not displayed.

The ADD option specifies directory names to be added to the current PATH. You can add up to ten directories with one PATH ADD command (the ADD keyword is optional); names of the directories must be separated by at least one space. When you issue the PATH command, AmigaDOS searches for each of the ADDed directories.

To replace the existing search path with a completely new one, use PATH RESET followed by the names of the directories. The existing search path, except for the current directory and SYS:C, is erased and the new one is substituted.

The REMOVE option eliminates the named directory from the search path.

Examples:

```
1> PATH EXTRAS2.0:Tools ADD
```

adds the Tools directory on the Extras2.0 disk to the search path of the Shell. If the Extras2.0 disk is not in a disk drive, a requester will ask you to insert it in any drive.

If you remove Extras2.0 from the drive, and type:

```
1> PATH
```

a list of directories in the search path will be displayed. A requester will ask you to insert Extras2.0. However, if you had typed:

```
1> PATH QUIET
```

The list of directories in the search path will be displayed; however, when the path comes to Extras2.0:Tools, only the volume name, Extras2.0:, will appear in the list.

See also: ASSIGN

POINTER

Format: POINTER [FROM <filename>] [EDIT] [USE] [SAVE]
Template: FROM,EDIT/S,USE/S,SAVE/S
Purpose: To change the appearance of the screen pointer
Path: SYS:Prefs/Pointer
Specification: POINTER without any arguments or with the EDIT argument opens the Pointer editor. The FROM argument lets you specify a file to open. This must be a file that was previously saved with the Save As menu item of the Pointer editor. For instance, if you have saved a special version of the pointer to a file in the Presets drawer, you can use the FROM argument to open that file. If the USE switch is also given, the editor will not be opened, but the settings in the FROM file will be used. If the SAVE switch is given, the editor will not open, but the settings in the FROM file will be saved.
Example:

```
1> POINTER Prefs/Presets/Pointer.star USE
```

loads and uses the pointer saved in the Pointer.star file. If the system is rebooted, the previously saved pointer appears.

PRINTER

Format: PRINTER [FROM <filename>] [EDIT] [USE] [SAVE]
Template: FROM,EDIT/S,USE/S,SAVE/S
Purpose: To specify a printer and print options
Path: SYS:Prefs/Printer
Specification: PRINTER without any arguments or with the EDIT argument opens the Printer editor. The FROM argument lets you specify a file to open. This must be a file that was previously saved with the Save As menu item of the Printer editor. For instance, if you have previously saved a printer configuration in a file in the Presets drawer, you can use the FROM argument to open that file. If the USE switch is also given, the editor will not be opened, but the settings in the FROM file will be used. If the SAVE switch is given, the editor will not open, but the settings in the FROM file will be saved.
Example:

```
1> PRINTER Prefs/Presets/Printer.epson SAVE
```

loads and saves the specifications saved in the Printer.epson file.

PRINTERGFX

Format: PRINTERGFX [FROM <filename>] [EDIT] [USE] [SAVE]
Template: FROM,EDIT/S,USE/S,SAVE/S
Purpose: To specify graphic printing options
Path: SYS:Prefs/PrinterGfx
Specification: PRINTERGFX without any arguments or with the EDIT argument opens the PrinterGfx editor. The FROM argument lets you specify a file to open. This must be a file that was previously saved with the Save As menu item of the PrinterGfx editor. For instance, if you have saved a special set of PrinterGfx options to a file in the Presets drawer, you can use the FROM argument to open that file. If the USE switch is also given, the editor will not be opened, but the settings in the FROM file will be used. If the SAVE switch is given, the editor will not open, but the settings in the FROM file will be saved.
Example:

```
1> PRINTERGFX Prefs/Presets/PrinterGfx.halftone USE
```

loads and uses the specifications saved in the PrinterGfx.halftone file. If the system is rebooted, the last saved specifications will be loaded.

PRINTFILES

Format: PRINTFILES {[-f] <filename>}
Template: -f/S,FILENAME/A/M
Purpose: To send file(s) to the printer
Path: Extras2.0:Tools/PrintFiles
Specification: PRINTFILES prints the specified file. The -f flag turns on the form feed mode. When printing multiple files, be sure to specify the flag before each filename.
Example:

```
1> PRINTFILES -f DF0:testfile -f DF0:docfile
```

prints the testfile and docfile files, stored on the disk inserted in drive DF0:. The -f argument adds a form feed between the two files so that they each start on a new page.

PROMPT

Format: PROMPT [<prompt>]
Template: PROMPT
Purpose: To change the prompt string of the current Shell
Path: Internal
Specification: PROMPT allows you to customize the prompt string, the text printed by the Shell at the beginning of a command line. The prompt string may contain any characters, including escape sequences. (In the examples in this manual, the prompt string is shown as 1>.)

The default prompt string is:

```
"%N.%S> "
```

which displays the Shell number, a period, the current directory, a right angle-bracket, and a space.

The substitutions available for the <prompt> string are:

%N   Displays the Shell number.
%S   Displays the current directory.
%R   Displays the return code for the last operation.

A space is not automatically added to the end of the string. If you want a space between the prompt and typed-in text, place it in the string, and enclose the string in double quotes.

You can embed commands in the prompt string by enclosing the command in backward quotes (`).

PROMPT alone, without a string argument, resets the prompt to the default.
Examples:

```
1> PROMPT %N
1
```

Only the Shell number is shown. The > is removed from the prompt.

```
1> PROMPT "%N.%S.%R> "
1.SYS:.0>
```

The Shell number, current directory, and return code of the previous command are shown. A space is included after the >.

```
1> PROMPT " `date`>"
Tuesday 11-Sep-90 14:36:39>
```

The DATE command is executed and used as the prompt. The prompt is not updated as the time changes. You would have to execute the PROMPT command again to update the Shell prompt.

PROTECT

Format: PROTECT [FILE] <file | pattern> [FLAGS] [+ | -] [<flags>] [ADD | SUB] [ALL] [QUIET]
Template: FILE/A,FLAGS,ADD/S,SUB/S,ALL/S,QUIET/S
Purpose: To change the protection bits of a file
Path: C:PROTECT
Specification: All files have a series of protection bits stored with them which control their attributes. These bits can be altered to indicate the type of file and the file operations permitted. PROTECT is used to set or clear the protection bits of a file.

The protection bits are represented by letters:

- r   The file can be read.
- w   The file can be written to (altered).
- e   The file is executable (a program).
- d   The file can be deleted.
- s   The file is a script.
- p   The file is a pure command and can be made resident.
- a   The file has been archived.

To see the protection bits associated with a file, use the LIST command. The protection field is displayed with set (on) bits shown by their letters and clear (off) bits shown by hyphens. For instance, a file that is readable, writable, and deletable will have - - - -rw-d in the protection field.

To specify the entire protection field at once, simply give the letters of the bits you want set as the FLAGS argument, without any other keywords. The named bits will be set, and all the others will be cleared.

The symbols + and - (or the equivalent keywords ADD and SUB) are used to control specific bits without affecting the state of unspecified bits. Follow + or - with the letter(s) of the bit(s) to set or clear, respectively, and only those bits will be changed. Don't put a space after the symbol or between the letters. The order of the letters does not matter. ADD and SUB work similarly, but there must be a space between the keyword and the letter(s). You cannot both set and clear bits in the same command.

The ALL option adds or removes the specified protection bits from all the files in the specified directory. The QUIET option suppresses the screen output.
Examples:

```
1> PROTECT DF0:Memo +rw
```

sets only the protection bits r (readable) and w (writable) to the file Memo on DF0:. No other protection bits are changed.

```
1> PROTECT L:#? e SUB
```

clears the e (executable) protection bit from all the files in the L: directory.

```
1> PROTECT Work:Paint rwed
```

The protection status of Paint becomes "- - - -rwed".
See Also: LIST

QUIT

Format: QUIT [<return code>]
Template: RC/N
Purpose: To exit from a script file with a specified return code
Path: Internal
Specification: QUIT is used to stop the execution of the script upon the specified return code. The default return code is zero. It is recommended that you use the standard return code values of 5, 10, and 20.

Example:

```
ASK "Do you want to stop now?"
IF WARN
QUIT 5
ENDIF
ECHO "OK, the script is continuing."
```

If you press Y at the prompt, the script will be aborted, as WARN is equal to a return code of 5. If you press N or press Return:

```
OK, the script is continuing.
```

will be displayed in the Shell window.

RELABEL

Format: RELABEL [DRIVE] <drive> [NAME] <name>
Template: DRIVE/A,NAME/A
Purpose: To change the volume name of a disk
Path: C:RELABEL
Specification: RELABEL changes the volume name of the disk in the given drive to the <name> specified. Volume names are set initially when you format a disk.

If you have a floppy disk system with only one disk drive, be sure to specify the disks by volume name, instead of drive name.

Examples:

```
1> RELABEL Workbench2.0: My2.0Disk
```

changes the name of the Workbench2.0 disk to My2.0Disk. Notice that you don't need the colon after the second name.

```
1> RELABEL DF2: DataDisk
```

changes the name of the disk in DF2: to DataDisk.

REMRAD

Format: REMRAD [<drive>] [FORCE]
Template: DEVICE,FORCE/S
Purpose: To remove the recoverable ramdrive.device
Path: C:REMRAD
Specification: If you want to remove the recoverable ramdrive.device (usually mounted as RAD:) from memory, and you do not want to turn the system off, you can use the REMRAD command. If you have mounted more than one recoverable ramdrive.device, use the DRIVE specification.

REMRAD commands the ramdrive.device to delete all of its files and become inactive. The next time the Amiga is rebooted, the ramdrive.device is removed from memory completely. If the device is in use at the time the REMRAD command is given, the operation aborts with a drive in use message. To remove it even if it is in use, you must use the FORCE option.

RENAME

Format: RENAME [{FROM}] <name> [TO | AS] <name> [QUIET]
Template: FROM/A/M,TO=AS/A, QUIET/S
Purpose: To change the name of a file or directory
Path: C:RENAME
Specification: RENAME renames the FROM file or directory with the specified TO name. FROM and TO must be on the same disk. If the name refers to a directory, RENAME leaves the contents of the directory unchanged. (The directories and files within that directory keep the same names and contents.)

If you rename a directory, or if you use RENAME to give a file another directory name (for example, you rename :Bill/Letter to :Mary/Letter), AmigaDOS changes the position of that directory or file in the filing system hierarchy.

> The colon before the directory indicates that the directory is in the root directory.

Examples:

```
1> RENAME Work/Prog1 AS :Arthur/Example
```

renames the file Prog1 as Example, and moves it from the Work directory to the Arthur directory. The Arthur directory must exist in the root directory for this command to work.

```
1> RENAME 7.2Fax 8.16Fax 9.22Fax TO Faxes
```

moves the 7.2Fax, 8.16Fax, and 9.22Fax files to the Faxes directory. The Faxes directory must already exist.

RESIDENT

Format: RESIDENT [<resident name>] [<filename>] [REMOVE] [ADD] [REPLACE] [PURE | FORCE][SYSTEM]
Template: NAME,FILE,REMOVE/S,ADD/S,REPLACE/S,PURE=FORCE/S, SYSTEM/S
Purpose: To display and modify the list of resident commands
Path: Internal
Specification: RESIDENT is used to load commands and add them to the resident list maintained by the Shell. This allows the command to be executed without it having to be reloaded from disk each time. This eliminates the time it takes to load the command and reduces memory use when multitasking.

To be made resident, a command should be both reentrant and reexecutable. A reentrant command can properly support independent use by two or more programs at the same time. A reexecutable command does not have to be reloaded to be executed again. Commands that have these characteristics are called pure and have the p (pure) protection bit set.

> LIST the C: directory to check for the presence of the p protection bit to determine which commands are pure.

Many of the commands in the C: directory, as well as the More command in Utilities, are pure commands and can be made resident. If a command does not have its pure bit set, it probably cannot be made resident safely. (Just setting the pure bit does not make a command or program pure.)

The REPLACE option is the default option and does not need to be explicitly stated. If RESIDENT is invoked with no options, it lists the programs on the resident list. If no <resident name> is specified (that is, just a filename is specified), RESIDENT will use the filename portion as the name on the resident list.

Note: The full path to the file must be used.

If a <resident name> is specified and RESIDENT finds a program with that name already on the list, it will attempt to replace the command. That <resident name> must then be used to reference the resident version of the command. The replacement will succeed only if the already-resident command is not in use.

To override REPLACEment and make several versions of a command resident simultaneously, use the ADD option, giving a different <resident name> for each version loaded.

If the SYSTEM option is specified, the command is added to the system portion of the resident list. Any commands added to the resident list with the SYSTEM option cannot be removed. To list SYSTEM files on the RESIDENT list, you must specify the SYSTEM option.

The PURE option forces RESIDENT to load commands that are not marked as pure (that is, they do not have their pure bit set), and can be used experimentally to test the pureness of other commands and programs.

WARNING: Use the PURE option with caution. Remember that for a command to be made RESIDENT, it must be both reentrant and reexecutable. Although it is unlikely, some of your programs may be pure enough to be fully reentrant and usable by more than one process at the same time. Other programs may not be fully reentrant but may be pure enough to be reexecutable. Such commands can be made RESIDENT, but you must be extremely careful to use the command in only one process at a time.

The availability of Internal commands can also be controlled with RESIDENT. To deactivate an Internal command (for instance, if an application has its own command of the same name), use RESIDENT <Command> REMOVE. AmigaDOS will no longer recognize the Internal command. The AmigaDOS command can be reactivated with the REPLACE option.

Examples:

```
1> RESIDENT C:COPY
```

makes the COPY command resident (replaces any previous version).

```
1> RESIDENT Copy2 DF1:C/COPY ADD
```

adds another version of COPY to the resident list, under the name Copy2.

```
1> RESIDENT Xdir DF1:C/Xdir PURE
```

makes an experimental, nonpure version of the DIR command resident.

```
1> RESIDENT CD REMOVE
```

makes the Internal CD command unavailable.

```
1> RESIDENT CD REPLACE
```

restores the CD command to the system.

See also: PROTECT

RUN

Format:	RUN <command> [+ {<command>}]
Template:	COMMAND/F
Purpose:	To execute commands as background processes
Path:	C:RUN

Specification: RUN is used to launch background processes. A background process does not open its own window for input or output and does not take over the parent Shell.

RUN attempts to execute the <command> and any arguments entered on the command line. You can RUN multiple commands by separating them with plus signs (+). If you press Return after a plus sign, RUN will interpret the next line as a continuation of the same command line.

To allow the closing of the Shell window in which the process was started, redirect the output of RUN with RUN >NIL: <command>. A new background Shell has the same search path and command stack size as the Shell from which RUN was given.

You can RUN commands stored on the resident list. For speed, resident commands are checked before commands in the command path. A Shell started with RUN NEWSHELL still uses the default startup file, S:Shell-startup.

Examples:

```
1> RUN COPY Text PRT:+
DELETE Text +
ECHO "Printing finished"
```

prints the Text file by copying it to the printer device, deletes it, then displays the given message. Plus signs are used to concatenate the command lines.

```
1> RUN EXECUTE Comseq
```

executes, in the background, all the commands in the file Comseq.

SAY

Format: SAY [-m] [-f] [-r] [-n] [-s <n>] [-p <n>] [-x <filename>]
Template: -m/S,-f/S,-r/S,-n/S,-s/K/N,-p/K/N,-x/K
Purpose: To speak phrases or files through the Amiga
Path: SYS:Utilities/Say
Specification: SAY utilizes the Amiga's speech capabilities. It supports the same options as when run through the Workbench, except that when run through the Shell, you can specify a file and its contents will be spoken. The options are:

-m	Specifies a male voice.
-f	Specifies a female voice.
-r	Specifies a robot voice.
-n	Specifies a natural voice.
-s <n>	Type the -s option, followed by a number from 40 to 400 to control the speed of the voice. Do not put a space between the -s and the number.
-p <n>	Type the -p option, followed by a number from 65 to 320 to control the pitch of the voice.
-x <filename>	Type the -x option followed by a filename, and the Amiga will "read" the contents of that file.

Do not forget the hyphen before each alphabetical option.

Example:

```
1> SAY -m -s125 -p65 -x s:startup-sequence
```

The Amiga will read the contents of the Startup-sequence file in a male voice at a moderately paced speed.

SCREENMODE

Format: SCREENMODE [FROM <filename>] [EDIT] [USE] [SAVE]
Template: FROM,EDIT/S,USE/S,SAVE/S
Purpose: To select a display mode
Path: SYS:Prefs/ScreenMode
Specification: SCREENMODE without any arguments, or with the EDIT argument, opens the ScreenMode editor. The FROM argument lets you specify a file to open. This must be a file that was previously saved with the Save As menu item of the ScreenMode editor. For instance, if you have previously saved your ScreenMode settings to a file in the Presets drawer, you can use the FROM argument to open that file. If the USE switch is also given, the editor is not opened, but the settings in the FROM file are used. If the SAVE switch is given, the editor will not open, but the settings in the FROM file will be saved.

Example:

```
1> SCREENMODE Prefs/Presets/ScreenMode.Hires USE
```

You will be prompted to close all nondrawer windows, and the system will reset and use the settings saved in the ScreenMode.Hires file. The editor window will not open. When the system is rebooted, the display mode returns to the last selection saved.

SEARCH

Format: SEARCH [FROM] <name|pattern> [SEARCH|NAME] <string|pattern> [ALL] [NONUM] [QUIET] [QUICK] [FILE] [PATTERN]
Template: FROM/M,SEARCH/A,ALL/S,NONUM/S,QUIET/S, QUICK/S,FILE/S,PATTERN/S
Purpose: To look for the specified text string in the file of the specified directory or directories
Path: C:SEARCH

Specification: SEARCH looks through all the files in the FROM directory for the given SEARCH string. (The FROM and SEARCH keywords are optional.) If the ALL switch is given, SEARCH also looks through all the subdirectories of the FROM directory. SEARCH displays the name of the file being searched and any line that contains the text sought. You must place quotation marks around any search text containing a space. The search is case-indifferent (capitalization is ignored).

The options are as follows:

NONUM   Line numbers are not printed with the strings.
QUIET   Searches quietly; filenames being searched are not displayed.
QUICK   Uses a more compact output format.
FILE   Looks for a file by the specified name, rather than for a string in the file.
PATTERN Uses pattern matching in the search.

SEARCH leaves a 0 in the condition flag if the object is found, and a 5 (WARN) otherwise. This makes it useful in scripts. To abandon the search of the current file and continue to the next file, if any, type Ctrl-D. SEARCH is aborted when a Ctrl-C is typed.

Examples:

```
1> Search DEVS: alternative
(dir)
  Keymaps (dir)
  Printers (dir)
clipboard.device..
MountList..

14 /* This is an example of an alternative type of non-
filing device mount.
narrator.device..
parallel.device..
printer.device..
serial.device..
system-configuration..
```

searches through the DEVS: directory for the word alternative. It is found on line 14 of the MountList file.

```
1> SEARCH Universe: "Intelligent life" ALL
```

searches for Intelligent life (or intelligent life) in every file on the volume Universe:.

```
1> SEARCH Work:#?.source SEARCH Progtest.c?? FILE PATTERN
```

locates all Progtest.c files with a two-character suffix in directories ending in .source in the Work volume.

SERIAL

Format: SERIAL [FROM <filename>] [EDIT] [USE] [SAVE]
Template: FROM,EDIT/S,USE/S,SAVE/S
Purpose: To set the specifications for communication through the serial port
Path: SYS:Prefs/Serial
Specification: SERIAL without any arguments or with the EDIT argument opens the Serial editor. The FROM argument lets you specify a file to open. This must be a file that was previously saved with the Save As menu item of the Serial editor. For instance, if you have saved a special configuration of the Serial editor to a file in the Presets drawer, you can use the FROM argument to open that file. If the USE switch is also given, the editor will not open, but the settings in the FROM file will be used. If the SAVE switch is given, the editor will not open, but the settings in the FROM file will be saved.
Example:

```
1> SERIAL Prefs/Presets/Serial.9600 USE
```

loads and uses the specifications saved in the Serial.9600 file. If the system is rebooted, the last saved settings will take effect.

SET

Format: SET [<name>] [<string>]
Template: NAME,STRING/F
Purpose: To set a local variable
Path: Internal

Specification: SET with <name> and <string> arguments creates a new environment variable. The first word after SET is taken as the <name>. Everything else on the command line is taken as the <string> argument. Quotation marks are not required.

SET with no arguments list the current local variables.

An environment variable created with SET is local to the Shell in which it was created. If you create a new Shell with the NEWSHELL command, that Shell will also recognize any variables created in its parent Shell. However, if you create a new Shell with the Execute Command menu item or by opening the Shell icon, variables created with SET are not recognized.

You can call environment variables in a script or on a command line by placing a dollar sign ($) in front of the variable name. To remove a local variable definition, use the UNSET command.

Examples:

```
1> SET origin This process launched from icon
```

creates the local variable origin which stores a reminder that a Shell was invoked from an icon rather than a NEWSHELL.

```
1> ECHO $origin
This process launched from icon.
```

See also: GET, UNSET

SETCLOCK

Format:	SETCLOCK LOAD | SAVE | RESET
Template:	LOAD/S,SAVE/S,RESET/S
Purpose:	To set or read the battery backed-up hardware clock
Path:	C:SETCLOCK

Specification: SETCLOCK SAVE sets the date and time of the battery backed-up hardware clock from the current system time (saved with the Time editor or with the DATE command). SETCLOCK SAVE is typically used after a DATE command.

SETCLOCK LOAD sets the current system time from the battery backed-up clock. It is typically included in the Startup-sequence to automatically load the correct time when the Amiga is booted. The RESET option resets the clock com-

pletely. This may be necessary if a poorly written program that does not follow the rules turns the clock off or sets the test bit of the clock.
Example:

```
1> DATE 17-Aug-92 05:45:54
1> SETCLOCK SAVE
```

saves the date, August 17, 1992, and the time, 5:45 a.m., to the battery backed-up hardware clock. That clock keeps time even when the Amiga is powered off. When the system is booted, the SETCLOCK LOAD command in the Startup-sequence sets the system clock with the time saved in the hardware clock.
See also: DATE

> The battery backed-up clock keeps the time even when the Amiga is turned off. Amiga 500s do not have battery backed-up clocks, unless an A501 RAM expansion cartridge has been installed.

SETDATE

Format: SETDATE <file | pattern> [<weekday-name>] [<date>] [<time>] [ALL]
Template: FILE/A,WEEKDAY,DATE,TIME,ALL/S
Purpose: To change a file or directory's timestamp
Path: C:SETDATE
Specification: SETDATE changes the timestamp (date and time of creation or last change) of a file or directory. SETDATE <file> changes the date/time of the file to the current system date/time. SETDATE does not affect the software or hardware clocks. The output of the DATE command may be used as input to SETDATE.
Examples:

```
1> SETDATE TestFile
```

changes the date and time associated with TestFile to the current date and time.

```
1> SETDATE TestFile 16-09-89 15:25:52
```

change the date and time associated with TestFile to September 16, 1989, 3:25 p.m.
See also: DATE

SETENV

Format:	SETENV [<name>] [<string>]
Template:	NAME,STRING/F
Purpose:	To set a global variable
Path:	Internal

Specification: SETENV with <name> and <string> arguments creates a new global environment variable. The first word after SETENV is taken as the <name>. Everything else on the command line is taken as the <string> argument. Quotation marks are not required.

SETENV with no arguments list the current global variables. Global variables are stored in ENV: and are used by all processes. However, if a local variable (defined by SET) and a global variable share the same name, the local variable will be used.

Environment variables are called by scripts or other commands by including a dollar sign ($) in front of the variable name.

To remove a global variable definition, use the UNSETENV command.

Examples:

```
1> SETENV Editor Extras2.0:Tools/MEmacs
```
creates the environment variable Editor which can be used with the More utility. This specifies the editor as being MEmacs, located in the Tools drawer of the Extras2.0 disk. The variable Editor is available in any Shell.

```
1> SETENV Editor C:ED
```

Same as above, only the editor specified is the editor ED.
See also: GETENV, UNSETENV

SETFONT

Format:	SETFONT <font> <size> [SCALE] [PROP] [ITALIC] [BOLD] [UNDERLINE]
Template:	NAME/A,SIZE/N/A,SCALE/S,PROP/S,ITALIC/S,BOLD/S, UNDERLINE/S
Purpose:	To change the Shell font
Path:	C:SETFONT

Specification: SETFONT lets you change the font used in a particular Shell window, overriding the System Default Text setting specified in the Font editor. SETFONT is only effective in the window in which it is invoked.

You must specify both a font name and a size when using the SETFONT command. The other options are:

SCALE	Enables bitmap font scaling.
PROP	Allows proportional fonts.
ITALIC	The font will be italic.
BOLD	The font will be boldface.
UNDERLINE	The font will be underlined.

Invoking SETFONT clears the Shell window of its current contents and displays a new prompt, in the new font, at the top of the window.

Example:

```
1> SETFONT Topaz 13 BOLD UNDERLINE
```

The Shell window will clear, and the new prompt will be in 13 point Topaz, underlined and boldface.

SETMAP

Format:	SETMAP <keymap>
Template:	KEYMAP/A
Purpose:	To change the keymap used by the Amiga
Path:	SYS:System/SetMap

Specification: SETMAP specifies the keymap used by the Amiga. The available files are listed below:

Keymap	Keyboard
cdn	French Canadian
ch1	Swiss French
ch2	Swiss German
d	German
dk	Danish
e	Spanish
f	French
gb	Great Britain

i	Italian
is	Icelandic
n	Norwegian
s	Swedish
usa0	(For programs developed before V1.0)
usa	American
usa2	Dvorak

To have the system always use a specific keymap, add the SETMAP command to your Startup-sequence file.

Example:
To change to a French Canadian keymap, type:

```
1> SETMAP cdn
```

The keymap file must be in DEVS:Keymaps for SetMap to find it.

SETPATCH

Format: SETPATCH [QUIET]
Template: QUIET/S
Purpose: To make ROM patches in system software
Path: C:SETPATCH
Specification: SETPATCH installs temporary modifications to the operating system. If needed, it must be run at the beginning of the Startup-sequence file. Updated versions of SETPATCH will be made available when necessary as AmigaDOS development continues.

SKIP

Format: SKIP [<label>] [BACK]
Template: LABEL,BACK/S
Purpose: To skip to a label when executing script files
Path: Internal
Specification: SKIP is used in scripts to allow you to skip ahead in the script to a <label> defined by a LAB statement. If no <label> is specified, SKIP jumps to the next LAB statement.

SKIP always searches forward from the current line of the file. However, when the BACK option is used, SKIP starts searching for the label from the beginning of the file. This allows SKIPs to points prior to the SKIP command.

You can only SKIP back as far as the last EXECUTE statement. If there are no EXECUTE statements in a script, you will SKIP back to the beginning of the file.

If SKIP does not find the label you specified, the command sequence terminates and the message Label <label> not found by Skip is displayed.

Example: Assume you have the following script, called CheckFile:

```
.KEY name
IF exists <name>
  SKIP message
ELSE
ECHO "<name> is not in this directory."
ENDIF
LAB message
  ECHO "The <name> file does exist."
```

You can run the script by typing:

```
1> EXECUTE CheckFile Document
```

If the Document file exists in the current directory, the execution of the script will skip ahead to the LAB command. The message The Document file does exist will be displayed in the Shell window.

If the Document file is not in the current directory, the execution of the script will jump to the line after the ELSE statement, and the message Document that is not in this directory will be displayed.

See also: EXECUTE, LAB

SORT

Format:	SORT [FROM] <file|pattern> [TO] <filename> [COLSTART <n>] [CASE] [NUMERIC]
Template:	FROM/A,TO/A,COLSTART/K,CASE/S,NUMERIC/S
Purpose:	To alphabetically sort the lines of a file
Path:	C:SORT
Specification:	SORT will sort the FROM file alphabetically, line-by-line, sending the sorted results to the TO file. SORT assumes the file is a normal text file in which lines are separated by Returns or line feeds. SORT normally

disregards capitalization. If the CASE switch is given, capitalized items will be output first.

The COLSTART keyword allows you to specify the character column at which the comparison will begin. SORT compares the lines from that point on, and comparison will wrap around to the beginning of the line if the lines being compared match to the end.

When the NUMERIC option is specified, the lines are interpreted as numbers from the first column rightward, stopping at the first non-numeric character. Lines not beginning with numbers are treated as 0. The lines are output in numerical order. If the CASE switch is given with NUMERIC, CASE is ignored.

Example:

```
1> SORT DF0:Glossary DF0:Glossary.alpha
```

sorts the lines in the Glossary file, arranges them alphabetically, and outputs them to a new file called Glossary.alpha. The case of the words is disregarded.

STACK

Format:	STACK [<n>]
Template:	SIZE/N
Purpose:	To display or set the stack size within the current Shell
Path:	Internal

Specification: When you run a program, it uses a certain amount of stack, a special area in memory allocated for the program. The stack required for a program should be given in the program's documentation. However, if a program causes system failure, you may wish to experiment with various stack sizes.

Commands that perform operations that consist of multiple levels may require additional stack space.

Stack sizes generally range from 4000 to 25,000 bytes. If the stack size is too small, a system failure may occur. A stack size that is too large may take too much memory away from other system functions.

WARNING: If you run out of stack space, you may receive a Software Failure message. If you have altered the stack for the program that caused the Software Failure message, try increasing the stack size.

STATUS

Format: STATUS [<process>] [FULL] [TCB] [CLI | ALL] [COMMAND <command>]

Template: PROCESS/N,FULL/S,TCB/S,CLI=ALL/S,COM=COMMAND/K

Purpose: To list information about Shell/CLI processes

Path: C:STATUS

Specification: STATUS without any arguments lists the numbers of the current Shell/CLI processes and the program or command, if any, running in each. The <process> argument specifies a process number, and STATUS will only give information about that process.

For information on the stacksize, global vector size, priority, and current command for each process, use the FULL keyword. The TCB keyword is similar, but omits the command information.

With the COMMAND option, you can tell STATUS to search for a command. STATUS then scans the Shell list, looking for the specified <command>. If the command is found, the Shell number is output, and the condition flag is set to 0. Otherwise the flag is set to 5 (WARN). This is useful in script files.

Examples:

```
1> STATUS 1
Process 1: Loaded as command: status

1> STATUS 1 FULL
Process 1: stk 4000, gv 150, pri 0 Loaded as command: status
1> STATUS >RAM:Xyz COMMAND=COPY

1> BREAK <RAM:Xyz >NIL: ?
```

sends a break to the process executing COPY.

See also: BREAK

TIME

Format: TIME [EDIT]

Template: EDIT/S

Purpose: To set the system clock
Path: SYS:PREFS/TIME
Specification: TIME without any arguments or with the EDIT argument opens the Time editor.
Example:

```
1> TIME
```

TYPE

Format: TYPE {<file | pattern>} [TO <name>] [OPT H | N] [HEX] [NUMBER]
Template: FROM/A/M,TO/K,OPT/K,HEX/S,NUMBER/S
Purpose: To display a text file
Path: C:TYPE
Specification: TYPE will output the contents of the named file to the current window, if no destination is given, or to a specified output file. If more than one filename is specified, and the TO keyword is not used, the filenames will be typed in sequence.

The OPT H and OPT N options are also available by the HEX and NUMBER keywords, respectively. The HEX option causes the file to be typed as columns of hexadecimal numbers, with an ASCII character interpretation column. This option is useful for analyzing object files. The NUMBER option numbers the lines as they are output.

To pause output, press the Space bar. To resume output, press Backspace, Return, or Ctrl-X. To stop output, press Ctrl-C (***BREAK is displayed).
Example:

```
1> TYPE DEVS:MountList
```

The contents of the MountList file in the DEVS: directory are displayed on the screen.

UNALIAS

Format: UNALIAS [<name>]
Template: NAME

Purpose: To remove an alias
Path: Internal
Specification: UNALIAS removes the named alias from the alias list. With no arguments, UNALIAS lists the current aliases.
See also: ALIAS

UNSET

Format: UNSET [<name>]
Template: NAME
Purpose: To remove a local variable
Path: Internal
Specification: UNSET removes the named local variable from the variable list for the current process.
   With no arguments, UNSET lists the current variables.
See also: SET

UNSETENV

Format: UNSETENV [<name>]
Template: NAME
Purpose: To remove a global variable
Path: Internal
Specification: UNSETENV removes the named global variable from the current variable list.
   With no arguments, UNSETENV lists the current variables.
See also: SETENV

VERSION

Format: VERSION [<library | device | file>] [<version #>] [<revision #>] [<unit #>]
Template: NAME,VERSION,REVISION,UNIT,FILE/S,INTERNALS,RES/S,FULL/S
Purpose: To find software version and revision numbers

Path: C:VERSION

Specification: VERSION finds the version and revision number of a library, device, command, or Workbench disk. VERSION can also test for a specific version/revision and set the condition flags if the version/revision is greater. This is useful in scripts.

VERSION with no <library I device I file> argument prints the Kickstart version number and the Workbench version number and sets the environment variables. If a name is specified, version attempts to open the library, device, drive, or file and read the version information.

When a <version #> (and possibly a <revision #>) is specified, VERSION sets the condition flag to 0 if the version (and revision) number of the Kickstart, library, or device driver is greater than or equal to the specified values. Otherwise, the flag is set to 5 (WARN). (If a revision number is not specified, no comparison on the revision number is performed.)

The <unit #> option allows you to specify a unit number other than 0. This may be necessary for accessing multiunit devices.

Examples:

```
1> VERSION
Kickstart version 36.202 Workbench version 36.77


1> VERSION Prefs/Font
Prefs/Font version 36.191
```

WAIT

Format:	WAIT [<n>] [SEC I SECS] [MIN I MINS] [UNTIL <time>]
Template:	/N,SEC=SECS/S,MIN=MINS/S,UNTIL/K
Purpose:	To wait for the specified time
Path:	C:WAIT

Specification: WAIT is used in command sequences or after RUN to wait for a certain period, or to wait until a certain time. Unless you specify otherwise, the waiting period is 1 second.

The <n> argument specifies the number of seconds (or minutes, if MINS is given) to wait.

Use the keyword UNTIL to wait until a particular time of the day, given in the format HH:MM.

Examples:

```
1> WAIT 10 MINS
```

waits 10 minutes.

```
1> WAIT UNTIL 21:15
```

waits until 9:15 p.m.

WBCONFIG

Format:	WBCONFIG [FROM <filename>] [EDIT] [USE] [SAVE]
Template:	FROM,EDIT/S,USE/S,SAVE/S
Purpose:	To control the appearance of the backdrop window and the option of bringing windows to the front by double-clicking in them
Path:	SYS:Prefs/WBConfig

Specification: WBCONFIG without any arguments or with the EDIT argument opens the WBConfig editor. The FROM argument lets you specify a file to open. This must be a file that was previously saved with the Save As menu item of the WBConfig editor. For instance, if you have saved a special configuration of the WBConfig editor to a file in the Presets drawer, you can use the FROM argument to open that file. If the USE switch is also given, the editor will not open, but the settings in the FROM file will be used. If the SAVE switch is given, the editor will not open, but the settings in the FROM file will be saved.

Example:

```
1> WBCONFIG Prefs/Presets/Backdrop.on USE
```

loads the settings saved in the Backdrop.on file. If the system is rebooted, the last saved specifications will be loaded.

WBPATTERN

Format:	WBPATTERN [FROM <filename>] [EDIT] [USE] [SAVE] [WORKBENCH] [WINDOW]
Template:	FROM,EDIT/S,USE/S,SAVE/S,WORKBENCH/S, WINDOW/S
Purpose:	To create background patterns for the Workbench and windows
Path:	SYS:Prefs/WBPattern

Specification: WBPATTERN with no arguments or with the EDIT argument opens the WBPattern editor.

The FROM argument must be used in combination with a WORKBENCH or WINDOW switch. (You can use more than one switch.) This allows you to specify a particular pattern to be used in the designated area(s) of the screen. The FROM file must be one that was previously saved with the Save As menu item of the WBPattern editor's Project menu. Even if the pattern in the FROM file was originally saved for one area of the screen, it can be used in a different area of the screen by specifying the appropriate switch. For instance, if the FROM file was created when you saved a pattern for the Workbench, that pattern can be used in the windows by specifying the WINDOW switch after the filename.

If you specify the USE option, the pattern will be loaded into the appropriate area and used, just as if you had opened the WBPattern editor, selected the appropriate radio button, created the pattern, and selected the Use gadget. If you specify the SAVE option, that pattern will be saved.

If you do not specify USE or SAVE, EDIT is assumed, and the WBPattern editor is opened. If a FROM file and a WORKBENCH or WINDOW switch is specified, the Font editor will open, the pattern saved in the FROM file is displayed, and the appropriate radio button is selected. If no switch is specified with the FROM file, the editor displays the last used pattern.

Examples:

```
1> WBPATTERN FROM SYS:Prefs/Presets/Diamonds WORKBENCH
SAVE
```

loads and saves the pattern saved in the Diamond file as the background pattern for the Workbench.

```
1> WBPATTERN FROM SYS:Prefs/Presets/Dots WINDOWS
```

opens the WBPattern editor. The pattern saved in the Dots file appears in the magnified view, and the Windows radio button is selected. You must select the Save, Use, or Cancel gadget to proceed.

WHICH

Format:	WHICH <command> [NORES] [RES] [ALL]
Template:	FILE/A,NORES/S,RES/S,ALL/S
Purpose:	To search the command path for a particular item
Path:	C:WHICH

Specification: WHICH lets you find a particular command, program, or directory by entering its name. If the named item is in the search path, WHICH displays the complete path to that item. WHICH lists resident commands as RESIDENT and internal commands as INTERNAL.

Normally, WHICH searches the resident list, the current directory, the command path(s), and the C: directory. The condition flag is set to 5 (WARN) if the file is not found.

If the NORES option is specified, the resident list is not searched. If the RES option is specified, only the resident list is searched.

The ALL switch causes the search to continue through the full search path, even after one or more instances of the named item have been found and listed. This procedure ensures that all versions of a command or program are found. It can, however, lead to multiple listings of the same command, if that command is reached by more than one route (for example, C: and the current directory).

Examples:

```
1> WHICH avail
C:avail

1> WHICH C:
Workbench2.0:C

1> WHICH alias
INTERNAL alias
```

WHY

Format: WHY
Template: (none)
Purpose: To print an error message that explains why the previous command failed
Path: Internal
Specification: Usually when a command fails the screen displays a brief message. This message typically includes the name of the file (if that was the problem) but does not go into detail.

For example, the message Can't open <filename> may appear. This could happen for a number of reasons—AmigaDOS may not be able to locate the file, the file may be of the wrong type, or there is insufficient disk space or RAM for the operation requested.

If the reason is not immediately obvious, enter WHY to get a more complete explanation.

Examples:

```
1> COPY DF0:
Bad arguments

1> WHY
Last command failed because required argument missing
```

The WHY message points to the error: A destination for the COPY was not given.

AmigaDOS Command Quick Reference

ADDBUFFERS	Commands the file system to add cache buffers.
ADDMONITOR	Informs the Amiga that a non-RGB style monitor has been added to your system.
ALIAS	Sets or displays command aliases.
ASK	Obtains user input when executing a script file.
ASSIGN	Controls assignment of logical device names to file system directories.
AUTOPOINT	Automatically selects any window the pointer is over.
AVAIL	Reports the amount of Chip and Fast memory available.

BINDDRIVERS	Binds device drivers to hardware.
BINDMONITOR	Assigns names to the different display modes.
BLANKER	Causes the monitor screen to go blank if no input has been received within a specified period of time.
BREAK	Sets attention flags in the specified process.
CALCULATOR	Provides an on-screen calculator.
CD	Sets, changes, or displays the current directory.
CHANGETASKPRI	Changes the priority of a currently running process.
CLOCK	Provides an on-screen clock.
CMD	Redirects printer output to a file.
COLORS	Changes the colors of the frontmost screen.
COPY	Copies files or directories.
CPU	Sets or clears the CPU caches, checks for a particular processor, loads the ROM image into fast, 32-bit memory, or sets an illegal memory access handler which will output information over the serial port at 9600 baud if a task accesses page zero (lower 256 bytes) or memory above 16M.
DATE	Displays or sets the system date and/or time.
DELETE	Deletes files or directories.
DIR	Displays a sorted list of the files in a directory.
DISKCHANGE	Informs the Amiga that you have changed a disk in a disk drive.
DISKCOPY	Copies the contents of one disk to another.
DISKDOCTOR	Attempts to repair a corrupted disk.
DISPLAY	Displays graphics saved in IFF ILBM format.
ECHO	Displays a string.
ED	Edits text files (a screen editor).
EDIT	Edits text files by processing the source file sequentially (a line editor).
ELSE	Specifies an alternative for an IF statement in a script file.
ENDCLI	Ends a Shell process.
ENDIF	Terminates an IF block in a script file.
ENDSHELL	Ends a Shell process.
ENDSKIP	Terminates a SKIP block in a script file.
EVAL	Evaluates simple expressions.
EXCHANGE	Monitors and controls the Commodity Exchange programs.
EXECUTE	Executes a script with optional argument substitution.
FAILAT	Instructs a command sequence to fail if a program gives a return code greater than or equal to the given value.
FAULT	Prints the messages(s) for the specified error code(s).

FILENOTE	Attaches a comment to a file.
FIXFONTS	Updates the .font files of the FONTS: directory.
FKEY	Assigns text to function and shifted functions keys.
FONT	Specifies the font(s) used by the system.
FORMAT	Formats a disk for use with the Amiga.
GET	Gets the value of a local variable.
GETENV	Gets the value of a global variable.
GRAPHICDUMP	Prints the frontmost screen.
ICONEDIT	Edits the appearance and type of icons.
ICONTROL	Specifies parameters used by the Workbench.
ICONX	Allows execution of a script file from an icon.
IF	Evaluates conditional operations in script files.
IHELP	Enables the keyboard to take over certain mouse operations.
INFO	Gives information about the file system(s).
INITPRINTER	Initializes a printer for print options specified in the Preferences editors.
INPUT	Specifies different speeds for the mouse and keyboard.
INSTALL	Writes the boot block to a formatted floppy disk, specifying whether it should be bootable.
IPREFS	Communicates Preferences information stored in the individual editor files to the Workbench.
JOIN	Concatenates two or more files into a new file.
KEYSHOW	Displays the current Keymap.
LAB	Specifies a label in a script file.
LIST	Lists specified information about directories and files.
LOADWB	Starts Workbench.
LOCK	Sets the write-protect status of a disk
MAKEDIR	Creates a new directory.
MAKELINK	Creates a link between files.
MORE	Displays the contents of an ASCII file.
MOUNT	Makes a device connected to the system available.
NEWCLI	Starts a new Shell process.
NEWSHELL	Opens a new interactive Shell window.
NOCAPSLOCK	Disables the Caps Lock key.
NOFASTMEM	Forces the Amiga to use only resident Chip RAM.
OVERSCAN	Changes the sizes of display areas for text and graphics.
PALETTE	Changes the colors of the Workbench screen.
PATH	Controls the directory list that the Shell searches to find commands.
POINTER	Changes the appearance of the screen pointer.
PRINTER	Specifies a printer and print options.

PRINTERGFX	Specifies graphic printing options.
PRINTFILES	Sends file(s) to the printer.
PROMPT	Changes the prompt string of the current Shell.
PROTECT	Changes the protection bits of a file.
QUIT	Exits from a script file with a specified return code.
RELABEL	Changes the volume name of a disk.
REMRAD	Removes the recoverable ramdrive.device.
RENAME	Changes the name of a file or directory.
RESIDENT	Displays and modifies the list of resident commands.
RUN	Executes commands as background processes.
SAY	Speaks phrases or files through the Amiga.
SCREENMODE	Selects a display mode.
SEARCH	Looks for the specified text string in the files of the specified directory or directories.
SERIAL	Sets the specifications for communication through the serial port.
SET	Sets a local variable.
SETCLOCK	Sets or reads the battery backed-up hardware clock.
SETDATE	Changes a file or directory's timestamp.
SETENV	Sets a global variable.
SETFONT	Changes the Shell font.
SETMAP	Changes the keymap used by the Amiga.
SETPATCH	Makes ROM patches in system software.
SKIP	Skips to a label when executing script files.
SORT	Alphabetically sorts the lines of a file.
STACK	Displays or sets the stack size within the current Shell.
STATUS	Lists information about Shell/CLI processes.
TIME	Sets the system clock.
TYPE	Displays a text file.
UNALIAS	Removes an alias.
UNSET	Removes a local variable.
UNSETENV	Removes a global variable.
VERSION	Finds software version and revision numbers.
WAIT	Waits for the specified time.
WBCONFIG	Controls the appearance of the backdrop window and the option of bringing windows to the front by double-clicking in them.
WBPATTERN	Creates background patterns for the Workbench and windows.
WHICH	Searches the command path for a particular item.
WHY	Prints an error message that explains why the previous command failed.

Chapter 3

AmigaDOS Error Messages

This chapter lists the possible AmigaDOS errors, along with probable causes and suggestions for recovery.

103 Not enough memory
    Probable Cause: Not enough memory in your Amiga to carry out the operation.
    Recovery Suggestion: Close any unneeded windows and applications, then reissue the command. If it still doesn't work, try rebooting. It may be that you have enough memory but it has become fragmented. It is possible that you may need to add more RAM to your system.

104 Process table full
    Probable Cause: There is a limit to the number of possible processes.
    Recovery Suggestion: Stop one or more tasks.

114 Bad template
    Probable Cause: Incorrect command line.
    Recovery Suggestion: Consult the documentation for the correct command format.

115 Bad number
    Probable Cause: The program was expecting a numeric argument.
    Recovery Suggestion: Consult the documentation for the correct command format.

116 Required argument missing
    Probable Cause: Incorrect command line.

Recovery Suggestion: Consult the documentation for the correct command format.

117 Argument after "=" missing

Probable Cause: Incorrect command line.

Recovery Suggestion: Consult the documentation for the correct command format.

118 Too many arguments

Probable Cause: Incorrect command line.

Recovery Suggestion: Consult the documentation for the correct command format.

119 Unmatched quotes

Probable Cause: Incorrect command line.

Recovery Suggestion: Consult the documentation for the correct command format.

120 Argument line invalid or too long

Probable Cause: Your command line is incorrect or contains too many arguments.

Recovery Suggestion: Consult the documentation for the correct command format.

121 File is not executable

Probable Cause: You misspelled the command name, or the file may not be a loadable (program or script) file.

Recovery Suggestion: Retype the filename and make sure that the file is a program file. Remember, to execute a script, either the s bit must be set or the EXECUTE command must be used.

122 Invalid resident library

Probable Cause: You are trying to use commands with a previous version of AmigaDOS, for example, Version 2.0 commands with Version 1.3.

Recovery Suggestion: Reboot with the current version of AmigaDOS.

202 Object is in use

Probable Cause: The specified file or directory is already being used by another application. If an application is reading a file, no other program can write to it, and vice versa.

Recovery Suggestion: Stop the other application that is using the file or directory, and reissue the command.

203 Object already exists

Probable Cause: The name that you specified already belongs to another file or directory.

Recovery Suggestion: Use another name, or delete the existing file or directory, and replace it.

204 Directory not found
   Probable Cause: AmigaDOS cannot find the directory you specified. You may have made a typing or spelling error.
   Recovery Suggestion: Check the directory name (use DIR if necessary). Reissue the command.
205 Object not found
   Probable Cause: AmigaDOS cannot find the file or device you specified. You may have made a typing or spelling error.
   Recovery Suggestion: Check the filename (use DIR) or the device name (use INFO). Reissue the command.
206 Invalid window description
   Probable Cause: This error occurs when specifying a window size for a Shell, ED, or ICONX window. You may have made the window too big or too small, or you may have omitted an argument. This error also occurs with the NEWSHELL command, if you supply a device name that is not a window.
   Recovery Suggestion: Reissue the window specification.
209 Packet request type unknown
   Probable Cause: You have asked a device handler to attempt an operation it cannot do. For example, the console handler cannot rename anything.
   Recovery Suggestion: Check the request code passed to device handlers for the appropriate request.
210 Object name invalid
   Probable Cause: There is an invalid character in the filename or the filename is too long. Remember, filenames cannot be longer than 30 characters and cannot contain control characters.
   Recovery Suggestion: Retype the name, being sure not to use any invalid characters or exceed the maximum length.
211 Invalid object lock
   Probable Cause: You have used something that is not a valid lock.
   Recovery Suggestion: Check that your code only passes valid locks to AmigaDOS calls that expect locks.
212 Object not of required type
   Probable Cause: You may have specified a filename for an operation that requires a directory name, or vice versa.
   Recovery Suggestion: Consult the documentation for the correct command format.
213 Disk not validated
   Probable Cause: If you have just inserted a disk, the disk validation process may be in progress. It is also possible that the disk is corrupt.
   Recovery Suggestion: If you've just inserted the disk, wait for the validation process to finish. This may take less than a minute for a floppy disk or up

to several minutes for a hard disk. If the disk is corrupt, it cannot be validated. In this case, try to retrieve the disk's files and copy them to another disk. You may have to use DISKDOCTOR.

214 Disk is write-protected

Probable Cause: The plastic tab is in the write-protect position.

Recovery Suggestion: If you're certain you want to write to that particular disk, remove the disk, move the tab, and reinsert the disk. Otherwise, use a different disk.

215 Rename across devices attempted

Probable Cause: RENAME only changes a filename on the same volume. You can use RENAME to move a file from one directory to another, but you cannot move files from one volume to another.

Recovery Suggestion: Use COPY to copy the file to the destination volume. Delete it from the source volume, if desired. Then use RENAME.

216 Directory not empty

Probable Cause: This error occurs if you attempt to delete a directory that contains files or subdirectories.

Recovery Suggestion: If you are sure you want to delete the complete directory, use the ALL option of DELETE.

217 Too many levels

Probable Cause: You've exceeded the limit of 15 soft links.

Recovery Suggestion: Reduce the number of soft links.

218 Device (or volume) not mounted

Probable Cause: If the device is a floppy disk, it has not been inserted in a drive. If it is another type of device, it has not been mounted with MOUNT. It is also possible that you have made a typing error when specifying the device name.

Recovery Suggestion: Insert the correct floppy disk, check the spelling of the device name, mount the device, or revise your MountList file.

219 Seek error

Probable Cause: You have attempted to call SEEK with invalid arguments.

Recovery Suggestion: Make sure that you only SEEK within the file. You cannot SEEK outside the bounds of the file.

220 Comment is too long

Probable Cause: Your filenote has exceeded the maximum number of characters (79).

Recovery Suggestion: Use a shorter filenote.

221 Disk is full

Probable Cause: There is not enough room on the disk to perform the requested operation.

Recovery Suggestion: Delete some unnecessary files or directories, or use a different disk.

222 Object is protected from deletion
   Probable Cause: The d (deletable) protection bit of the file or directory is clear.
   Recovery Suggestion: If you are certain that you want to delete the file or directory, use PROTECT to set the d bit or use the FORCE option of DELETE.
223 File is write protected
   Probable Cause: The w (writeable) protection bit of the file is clear.
   Recovery Suggestion: If you are certain that you want to overwrite the file, use PROTECT to set the w bit.
224 File is read protected
   Probable Cause: The r (readable) protection bit of the file is clear.
   Recovery Suggestion: Use PROTECT to set the r bit of the file.
225 Not a valid DOS disk
   Probable Cause: The disk in the drive is not an AmigaDOS disk, it has not been formatted, or it is corrupt.
   Recovery Suggestion: Check to make sure you are using the correct disk. If you know the disk worked before, use DISKDOCTOR or another disk recovery program to salvage its files. If the disk has not been formatted, use FORMAT to do so.
226 No disk in drive
   Probable Cause: The disk is not properly inserted in the specified drive.
   Recovery Suggestion: Insert the appropriate disk in the specified drive.
232 No more entries in directory
   Probable Cause: This indicates that the AmigaDOS call EXNEXT has no more entries in the directory you are examining.
   Recovery Suggestion: Stop calling EXNEXT.
233 Object is soft link
   Probable Cause: You tried to perform an operation on a soft link that should only be performed on a file or directory.
   Recovery Suggestion: AmigaDOS uses the Action_Read_Link packet to resolve the soft link and retries the operation.

Chapter 4

Glossary

Arguments
   Additional information supplied to commands.

Boot
   The startup process for a computer. It comes from the expression "pulling yourself up by the bootstraps."

Character pointer
   Pointer to the left edge of a line window in EDIT. You use it to define the part of a line that EDIT may alter.

Character string
   Sequence of printable characters.

Command
   An instruction you give directly to the computer.

Command Line Interface (CLI)
   A **process** that decodes user input.

Console handler
   See **terminal handler**.

Command template
   The method of defining the syntax for each **command**.

Control combination
   A combination of the CTRL key and a letter or symbol. The CTRL key is pressed down while the letter or symbol is typed. It appears in the documentation, for example, in the form CTRL-A.

Current directory
   This is either the **root directory** or the last **directory** you set yourself in with the command CD.

Current drive
   The disk drive that is inserted and declared to be current. The default is SYS:.
Default
   Initial setting, or in other words, what happens if you do nothing. In this manual default means " in the absence of something else."
Delimiter characters
   Characters used at the beginning and end of a **character string**.
Destination file
   File being written to.
Device name
   Unique name given to a device, for example, DF0: = floppy drive 0:.
Directory
   A collection of **files**.
File
   A collection of related data.
File Handle
   An internal AmigaDOS value that represents an open file or device.
Filename
   A name given to a file for identification purposes.
Immediate mode
   Commands that are executed immediately.
Keyword
   Arguments to commands that must be stated explicitly.
Logical Device
   A name you can give to a directory with the ASSIGN command that you can then use as a device name.
Memory
   This is sometimes known as RAM and is where a computer stores its data and instructions.
Multiprocessing
   The execution of two or more **processes** in parallel, that is, at the same time.
Object Code
   Binary output from an assembler or compiler and binary imput to a linker.
Output queue
   Buffer in memory holding data before being written out to **file**.
Priority
   The relative importance of a **process**.
Process
   A job requested by the operating system or the user.
Qualified string
   A string preceded by one or more qualifiers.

Queue
See **Output queue**.
Reboot
Restart.
Root directory
The top level in the filing system. **Files** and **directories** within the root directory have their names preceded by a colon (:).
Sequential files
A **file** that can be accessed at any point by starting at the beginning and scanning sequentially until the point is reached.
Source file
File being read from.
Stream
An open file or device that is associated with a file handle. For example, the input stream could be from a file and the output stream could be to the console device.
System disk
A disk containing the Workbench and AmigaDOS commands.
Syntax
The format or "grammar" you use for giving a command.
Terminal handler
A **process** handling input and output from the terminal or console.
Volume name
The unique name associated with a disk.
Wild card
Symbols used to match any pattern.

Part II

THE DEVELOPER'S MANUAL

Chapter 5

Programming on the Amiga

This chapter introduces the reader to programming in C or Assembler under AmigaDOS.

Introduction

This manual assumes that you have some familiarity with either C or Assembler. It does not attempt to teach either of these languages. An introduction to C can be found in the book *The C Programming Language* by Brian W. Kernighan and Dennis M. Ritchie, published by Prentice-Hall. There are a number of books on writing 68000 assembler, including *Programming the MC68000* by Tim King and Brian Knight, published by Addison-Wesley.

Program Development for the Amiga

This section describes how to develop programs for the Amiga. It describes what you need before you start, how you can call the system routines, and how to create a file that you can execute on the Amiga.

Getting Started

Before you start writing programs for the Amiga, you need the following items:

1. Documentation on AmigaDOS and other system routines that you can call.
2. Documentation on the language you intend to use. If you intend to use Assembler or C, then this manual tells you how to use these tools although it does not contain any specific information normally found in a language reference manual.
3. Header files containing the necessary Amiga structure definitions and the values for calling the system routines that you need. Commodore-Amiga provides these header files as included files for either C (usually ending in .h) or Assembler (ending in .i). To use a particular resident library, you must include one or more header files containing the relevant definitions. For example, to use AmigaDOS from C, you must include the file "dos.h".
4. An assembler or compiler.
5. The Amiga linker as well as the standard Amiga library (amiga.lib) containing functions, interface routines, and various absolute values.

Calling Resident Libraries

You should note that there are two ways of calling system routines from a user assembly program. C programmers simply call the function as specified. You usually call a system routine in Assembler by placing the library base pointer for that resident library in register A6 and then jumping to a suitable negative offset from that pointer. The offsets are available to you as absolute externals in the Amiga library, with names of the form _ LVOname. So, for instance, a call could be JSR _ LVOname(A6), where you have loaded A6 with a suitable library base pointer. These base pointers are available to you from the OpenLibrary () call to Exec; you can find the base pointer for Exec at location 4 (the only absolute location used in the Amiga). This location is also known as AbsExecBase which is defined in amiga.lib.

You can call certain RAM-based resident libraries and the AmigaDOS library in this way, if required. Note that the AmigaDOS library is called "dos.library". However, you do not need to use A6 to hold a pointer to the library base; you may use any other register if you need to. In addition, you may call AmigaDOS using the resident library call feature of the linker. In this case, simply code a JSR to the entry point and the linker notes the fact that you have used a reference to a resident library. When your code is loaded into memory, the loader automatically opens the library and closes it for you when you have unloaded The loader automatically patches references to AmigaDOS entry points to refer to the correct offset from the library base pointer.

Creating an Executable Program

To produce a file that you can execute on the Amiga, you should follow the four steps below. You can do each step either on the Amiga itself or on a suitable cross-development computer.

1. Get your program source into the Amiga. To do this, you can type it directly in using an editor, or you can transfer it from another computer.
2. Assemble or compile your program.
3. Link your program together, including any startup code you may require at the beginning, and scan the Amiga library and any others you may need to satisfy any external references.
4. Load your program into the Amiga and watch it run!

Running a Program Under the CLI

There are two ways you can run a program. First, you can run your program under a CLI (also known as the Shell). Second, you can run your program under the Workbench. This section describes the first of the two ways.

Running a program under the CLI (Shell) is a little like using an old-fashioned line-oriented teletype (TTY) system although you might find a Shell useful, for example, to port your program over to your Amiga as a first step in development. To load and enter your program, you simply type the name of the file that contains the binary and possibly follow this with a number of arguments.

Initial Environment in Assembler

When you load a program under a Shell, you type the name of the program and a set of arguments. You may also specify input or output redirection by means of the ">" and "<" symbols. The Shell automatically provides all this information for the program when it starts up.

When the Shell starts up a program, it allocates a stack for that program. This stack is initially 4000 bytes, but you may change the stack size with the STACK command. AmigaDOS obtains this stack from the general free memory heap just before you run the program; it is not, however, the same as the stack that the Shell uses. AmigaDOS pushes a suitable return address onto the stack that tells the Shell to regain control and unload your program. Below this on the stack at 4(SP) is the size of the stack in bytes, which may be useful if you wish to perform stack checking.

Your program starts with register A0 pointing to the arguments you, or anyone else running your program typed. AmigaDOS stores the argument line in memory within the CLI stack and this pointer remains valid throughout your program. Register D0 indicates the number of characters in the argument line. You can use these initial values to decode the argument line to find out what the user requires. Note that all registers may be corrupted by a user program.

To make the initial input and output file handles available, you call the AmigaDOS routines Input() and Output(). Remember that you may have to open the AmigaDOS library before you do this. The calls return file handles that refer to the standard input and output the user requires. This standard input and output (I/O) is usually the terminal unless you redirected the I/O by including ">" or "<" on the argument line. You should not close these file handles with your program; the CLI opened them for you and it will close them, if required.

Initial Environment in C

When programming in C, you should always include the startup code as the first element in the linker input. This means that the linker enters your program at the startup code entry point. This section of code scans the argument list and makes the arguments available in "argv", with the number of arguments in "argc" as usual. It also opens the AmigaDOS library and calls Input() and Output() for you, placing the resulting file handles into "stdin" and "stdout". It then calls the C function "main".

Failure of Routines

Most AmigaDOS routines return a zero if they fail; the exceptions are the Read and Write calls that return minus 1 on finding an error. If you receive an error return, you can call IoErr() to obtain more information on the failure. IoErr() returns an integer that corresponds to a full error code, and you may wish to take different actions depending on exactly why the call failed. A complete list of error codes and messages can be found at the end of Chapter 2.

Terminating a Program

To exit from a program, it is sufficient to give a simple RTS using the initial stack pointer (SP). In this case, you should provide a return code in register D0. This is zero if your program succeeded; otherwise, it is a positive number. If you return a nonzero number, then the CLI notices an error. Depending on the current fail value (set by the command FAILAT), a noninteractive CLI, such as one running a command script set up by the EXECUTE command, terminates. A program written in C can simply return from "main" which returns to the startup code; this clears D0 and performs an RTS.

Alternatively, an assembler program may call the AmigaDOS function Exit (), which takes the return code as an argument. This instructs your program to exit no matter what value the stack pointer has. A C program should call the exit routine provided by the compiler manufacturer. Typically, this function is called exit (); note the lower case e.

It is important at this stage to stress that AmigaDOS does not control any resources; this is left entirely up to the programmer. Any files that a user program opens must be closed before the program terminates. Likewise, any locks it obtains must be freed, any code it loads must be unloaded, and any memory it allocates returned. Of course, there may be cases where you do not wish to return all resources, for example, when you have written a program that loads a code segment into memory for later use. This is perfectly acceptable, but you must have a mechanism for eventually returning any memory, file locks, and so on.

Running a Program Under the Workbench

To run a program under the Workbench, you need to appreciate the different ways in which a program may be run on the Amiga. Under the CLI your program is running as part of the CLI process. It can inherit I/O streams and other information from the CLI, such as the arguments you provided.

If a program is running under the Workbench, then AmigaDOS starts it as a new process running at the same time as Workbench. Workbench loads the program and then sends a message to get it started. You must therefore wait for this initial message before you start to do anything. You must retain the message and return it to Workbench when your program has finished, so that Workbench can unload the code of your program.

For C programmers, this is all done by simply using a different part of the startup routine. For assembly language programmers, this work must be done yourself.

You should also note that a program running as a new process initiated by Workbench has no default input and output streams. You must ensure that your program opens all the I/O channels that it needs, and that it closes them all when it has finished.

Basic Input and Output Programming

This section covers the basics of dos.library I/O functions. Many C compilers supply their own standard I/O functions which differ from the dos.library routines described here. See your compiler manual for information on its standard I/O functions.

The original dos.library was written in BCPL, a precursor to the C programming language. Although dos.library was rewritten in C and assembler for 2.0, remnants of BCPL remain to keep dos.library backwards compatible. One of these is the BCPL pointer, or BPTR.

BCPL only thinks in 32-bit, longwords. When BCPL thinks about an individual memory address, it thinks of a four byte wide quantity rather than a single byte quantity (like the CPU), so when BCPL thinks of memory address 2, it thinks of the second (after the zeroth and the first) set of four bytes (what the CPU thinks of as addresses 8 through 11).

Because AmigaDOS uses BPTRs, programming certain areas of AmigaDOS will require converting normal adresses to and from BPTRs. To convert a normal address (which must be longword aligned) to a BPTR, divide it by four (>> 2). The dos.h include file contains macros to convert between the two address formats. Note that, because a BPTR refers to a long word (a 32-bit address), anything it addresses must be long word aligned.

Another BCPL remnant is the BCPL string, or BSTR. A BSTR is a BPTR to a BCPL style string. The first byte of a BCPL string contains the length of the string. The remaining bytes make up the actual characters of the string.

One of the basic features of AmigaDOS is file input and output. To perform file I/O, DOS requires something called a file handle. A file handle is what DOS uses to identify and keep track of an open file.

Another thing that DOS uses when reading and writing files is a Lock. AmigaDOS uses a Lock to "lock" a file, or to prevent two (or more) processes from manipulating a file at the same time. While a file is locked, other processes cannot make changes to it.

There are two types of locks, shared locks and exclusive locks. A shared lock normally is used for read-only access to a file. There can be many shared locks on a file at any given time. The purpose of a shared lock is to prevent another process from writing to a file while your process is reading it. An exclusive lock is used for write access to a file. While any locks exist on a file (shared or exclusive), no one can create a new exclusive lock on the file.

To open a file (and obtain a file handle to it), use the dos.library's Open () function:

```
BPTR myfilehandle = Open (    UBYTE *filename, LONG
accessMode );
```

where myfilehandle is a BPTR to a FileHandle structure, filename is a C string naming the file to open (relative to the current directory), and accessMode is either, MODE_OLDFILE, MODE_NEWFILE, or MODE_READWRITE.

MODE_OLDFILE opens an existing file for reading or writing. In this mode, DOS creates a read lock on the file (which changes to a write lock while you are trying to write to the file). Attempting to open a nonexistant file in this mode causes the Open() to fail (returning a NULL). MODE_NEWFILE opens a file for reading and writing, and will delete the file if it already exists. In this mode, DOS creates an exclusive lock on the file. MODE_READWRITE, a new mode added in release 2.0, opens a file (with a shared lock) for reading and writing but will not delete the file if it already exists.

The Read () and Write () functions are used to read and write blocks of data to and from a buffer:

```
LONG actualcount = Read (  BPTR filehandle, APTR buffer,
LONG length  );
LONG actualcount = Write (  BPTR filehandle, APTR buffer,
LONG length  );
```

Normally, these functions are used for reading and writing large blocks of data as they are not very efficient for small reads and writes. Release 2.0 introduced buffered reading and writing routines that are much more efficient for very small blocks of data. They are discussed later.

The Read() and Write() calls take the same arguments: a file handle for the file in question, a buffer that holds the data, and a count of how many bytes to read or write. Both functions return the actual number of bytes read or written. If Read() returns a zero, then no characters were read and the current file position is at the end of the file. If either function returns -1, an error occurred (use the dos.library function IoErr() to get the code of the most recent DOS error).

DOS maintains a current position for open files. DOS increments a file's current position for every byte it reads or writes. Read()s and Write()s are relative to the current position, so if you open an already existing file and you want to write additional data to it, you must make sure that the current file position is at the end of the file. When Open() first opens a file, the file's current position is at the beginning of the file.

Using the Seek () function, a program can move the current file position:

```
LONG oldposition = Seek (  BPTR filehandle, LONG
fileposition, LONG offset_from_where);
```

Seek ()'s fileposition field is the new file position, which is relative to the offset. The offset (offset_from_where) is one of the following:

OFFSET_END	the fileposition (which should be zero here) is relative to the end of the file.
OFFSET_CURRENT	the fileposition is relative to the current file position.
OFFSET_BEGINNING	the fileposition is relative to the beginning of the file.

Seek() returns the file position before the Seek() occurred, or a -1 to indicate an error.

To close an open file handle, use dos.library's Close() function:

```
LONG returnvalue = Close( BPTR file );
```

Under release 2.0, Close() returns either DOSTRUE (-1) for success or DOSFALSE (O) for failure. Prior to release 2.0, the return value was undefined.

The following is a very simple example of basic file I/O.

```
;/* - Execute me to compile me with Lattice 5.1Oa
LC -bl -cfistq -v -y -j73 RW.c
Blink FROM LIB:C.o,RW.o TO RW LIBRARY LIB:LC.lib,LIB:Amiga.lib
quit
*/

/*   This program opens the file "s:startup-sequence" and
**   copies it to "ram:qwe".

#include <dos/dos.h>
#include <dos/dosextens.h>
#include <clib/dos_protos.h>
#include <clib/alib_stdio_protos.h>

/*   to compile this with the 1.3 #includes, change the
above four #includes to:

#include <libraries/dos.h>
#include <libraries/dosextens.h>
*/

#ifdef LATTICE
int CXBRK(void) { return(O); }   /* Disable Lattice CTRL/C handling */
int chkabort(void) { return(O); }
```

```
#endif

/*  For most applications, the buffer size below is way too small.
**  For most programming purposes, the buffer should be MUCH larger
**  to make reading and writing more efficient.
*/
#define BUFSIZE 256

UBYTE *vers = "\0$VER: RW 1.0";

UBYTE buffer[BUFSIZE];

void main(void)
{
    BPTR myfile, startup;
    LONG count, actual;

    if (myfile = Open("ram:qwe", MODE_NEWFILE))
{

    if (startup = Open("a:startup-sequence", MODE_OLDFILE))
    {
       count = 1;
       /*  keep writing until we hit the end of the file
       **  or an error occurs. */
       while ((actual = Read(startup, buffer, BUFSIZE)) && (count > O))
           count = Write(myfile, buffer, actual);

       if (actual < O) printf("Error while reading\n");
       if (count < O) printf("Error while writing\n");
       Close(startup);
    }
    Close(myfile);
   }
}
```

Using File Handlers

Each AmigaDOS device has a process associated with it called a handler. The handler process is used by AmigaDOS to talk to Exec devices. A handler is responsible for processing a standard set of commands that AmigaDOS sends when it needs to use a device. AmigaDOS can use handlers for things such as reading and writing files, writing to the console, or sending output to a printer. DH0:, RAM:, CON:, and SER: each are controlled with their respective handler process.

One particular type of handler is the file handler. A file handler is used to maintain a filing system (i.e., files and directories) on a particular device. The handler process responsible for DF0: is one example of a file handler. This handler allows AmigaDOS to use the Exec device trackdisk.device. If you try to read a file from DF0:, DOS sends a read request to DF0:'a handler process. DF0:'a handler interprets the read command and extracts the file data from some place on the disk. DOS does not know anything about how the underlying device works, it just asks the file handler for data and the handler supplies it. This scheme makes adding new AmigaDOS devices to the system relatively easy.

Although writing handlers is beyond the scope of this section, using them is not. The handler makes it possible to think about various forms of I/O as file I/O. For example, using the Open() routine, it is possible to open a console window and write to it as if it was a file:

```
consoleFH = Open("CON:20/20/500/100/Console",
MODE_NEWFILE);
```

This opens a console window on the Workbench screen. You can write directly to the console window and read directly from it using the file handle returned by the Open() call (note that when reading from a CON: window file handle, the user must hit return before the data can be read).

Every process has a standard input and standard output file handle associated with it. For Shell-based programs, the standard I/O handles are normally the Shell's console window. It is possible to redirect the standard I/O for a program started from the Shell using the < (input) and > (output) redirection operators. With these the user can, for example, redirect output from a Shell-based program to a file, or to PRT:. The dos.library routines Input() and Output() return the current standard input and output file handles, respectively:

```
BPTR inputFH  = Input( void );
BPTR outputFH = Output( void );
```

Release 2.0 introduced two new functions, SelectInput() and SelectOutput() which allow a program to change the current standard I/O handles:

```
oldinputFH  = SelectInput ( BPTR newinputFH );
oldoutputFH = SelectOutput( BPTR newoutputFH );
```

where newinputFH/newoutputFH is an open, valid file handle, and oldinputFH/oldoutputFH is the previous standard input/output handle. Do not carelessly discard the old file handle as it is still valid and will have to be closed or reinstated eventually.

Buffered I/O

Release 2.0 introduced a series of buffered I/O routines. The buffered I/O routines improve the performance of small reads and writes by reducing the overhead involved in reading and writing small blocks of data.

The buffered I/O equivalents to Read() and Write() are:

```
LONG actualblocks = FRead( BPTR fh, APTR buffer, ULONG
blocklength, ULONG numblocks );
LONG actualblocks = FWrite( BPTR fh, APTR buffer, ULONG
blocklength, ULONG numblock );
```

These two functions are similar to their unbuffered counterparts, but their arguments differ slightly. Instead of requiring a number of bytes to read or write, FRead() and FWrite() will read/write a number (numblocks) of blocks. Each block is blocklength bytes long. These functions return the number of blocks actually written or read (or zero if EOF is read). If there is an error, both functions return the number of blocks written or read, but the number will differ from the number of blocks requested.

When switching back and forth from buffered to unbuffered I/O, you must flush the file buffer using the Flush() routine:

```
void Flush( BPTR fh );
```

Currently, DOS flushes the buffer when it is full, or when someone writes a \n, \0, \r, or \12. When using buffered I/O on your original standard input file handle, you must Flush() before reading any data.

There are some routines for buffered reading and writing single characters and strings:

```
LONG FGetC( BPTR fh );
UBYTE *FGets( BPTR fh, UBYTE *buf, ULONG buflen );
LONG FPuts( BPTR fh, UBYTE *str );
void FPutC( BPTR fh, ULONG ch );
LONG WriteChars( UBYTE *buf, unsigned long buflen );
LONG PutStr( UBYTE *str );
LONG UnGetC( BPTR fh, long character );
```

See the Autodocs (in chapter 6) for more information on these and other related functions.

There are also some buffered I/O functions for writing formatted data to a file handle:

```
LONG VFPrintf( BPTR fh, UBYTE *formatstring,
LONG *argarray );
LONG VPrintf( UBYTE *formatstring, LONG *argarray );
```

where formatstring is a C style string that contains a printf()-like formatting template with the following supported % options:

%flags][width.limit][length]type

flags	—only one allowed. '-' specifies left justification.
width	—field width. If the first character is a '0', the field will be padded with leading 0's.
	—must follow the field width, if specified
limit	—maximum number of characters to output from a string (only valid for %s).
length	—size of input data defaults to WORD for types d, x, and c, 'l' changes this to long (32-bit).
type	—supported types are:

    b —BSTR, data is 32-bit BPTR to byte count followed by a byte string, or NULL terminated byte string. A NULL BPTR is treated as an empty string (Added in V36 Exec).
    d —decimal.
    x —hexadecimal.
    s —string, a 32-bit pointer to a NULL terminated byte string. In V36, a NULL pointer is treated as an empty string.
    c —character

The argarray is a pointer to an array of arguments corresponding to the entries in the formatting template.

The only difference between these two functions is that VPrintf() writes to the current standard output file handle and VFPrintf() writes to the file handle you supply. The advantage to using these two functions over a function such as printf() is that printf() has to be linked into a program (from amiga.lib), making the program larger. VPrintf() and VFPrintf() are already in the ROMs, so using these functions does not require linking in extra code.

Standard Command Line Parsing

Release 2.0 introduced standard command line parsing. The ReadArgs() routine is the heart of this feature:

```
struct RDArgs *rda = ReadArgs( UBYTE *argtemplate,
LONG  *argarray, struct RDArgs *myrda );
```

The first argument, argtemplate, is a C style string that describes program options settable from the command line. Each option should be a full, descriptive name (for example "Quick" not "Q"). Each option can be prepended by an abbreviation of the form "abbrev=option" ("Q=Quick"). The argtemplate options are delimited by commas. Each option can also be followed by modifiers that specify characteristics of individual options. The valid modifiers are:

/S—Switch. This is considered a boolean variable, and will be set if the option name appears in the command-line. The entry is the boolean (0 for not set, non-zero for set).

/K—Keyword. This means that the option will not be filled unless the keyword appears. For example if the template is "Name/K", then unless "Name=<string>" or "Name <string>" appears in the command line, Name will not be filled.

/N—Number. This parameter is considered a decimal number, and will be converted by ReadArgs(). If a number specified is invalid, ReadArgs() will fail. The entry will be a pointer to the longword number or NULL (this is how you know if a number was specified).

/T—Toggle. This is similar to a switch (/S), but causes the boolean value to toggle.

/A—Required. This keyword tells ReadArgs() to fail if this option is not specified in the command line.

/F—Rest of line. If this is specified, the entire rest of the line is taken as the parameter for the option, even if other option keywords appear in it.

/M—Multiple. This means the option will take any number of arguments, returning them as an array of pointers. Any arguments not considered to be part of another option will be added to this option. Only one /M should appear in a template. Example: for a template "Dir/M,All/S" the commandline "foo bar all qwe" will set the boolean "all", and return an array consisting of "foo", "bar", and "qwe". The entry in the array will be a pointer to an array of string pointers, the last of which will be NULL.

There is an interaction between /M parameters and /A parameters. If there are unfilled /A parameters after parsing, ReadArgs() will grab strings from the end of a previous /M parameter list to fill the /A's. This is used for things like Copy ("From/A/M,To/A").

ReadArgs() second argument, argarray, is an array of LONGs used by ReadArgs() to store the values of the command line arguments. Before passing this array to ReadArgs(), a program must either set the array entries to reasonable default values or clear them.

If it is successful, ReadArgs() returns a pointer to a RDArgs structure (from <dos/rdargs.h>). ReadArgs() uses this structure internally to control its operation. It is possible to pass ReadArgs() a custom RDArgs structure (myrda in the ReadArgs() prototype above). For most applications, myrda will be NULL, because most applications do not need to control ReadArgs().

```
struct RDArgs {
    struct  CSource RDA_Source;   /* Select input source */
    LONG    RDA_DAList;           /* PRIVATE. */
    UBYTE   *RDA_Buffer;          /* Optional string parsing space. */
    LONG    RDA_BufSiz;           /* Size of RDA Buffer (0..n) */
    UBYTE   *RDA_ExtHelp;         /* Optional extended help */
    LONG    RDA_Flags;            /* Flags for any required control */
};
```

Any successful call to ReadArgs() (even those that use a custom RDArgs structure) must be complemented with a call to FreeArgs():

```
void FreeArgs(struct RDArgs *rda);
```

where rda is the RDArgs structure used by ReadArgs().

An application can use a custom RDArgs structure to provide an alternate command line source, an alternate temporary storage buffer, or an extended help string. The custom RDArgs structure must be allocated with AllocDosObject() and deallocated with FreeDosObject(). See the Autodocs (chapter 6) for more details on these functions.

The RDArgs.RDA_Source field is used to supply ReadArgs() with an alternate command line to parse. ReadArgs() will use it only if the RDA_Source fields are filled in. The CSource structure (from <dos/rdargs.h>) is as follows:

```
struct CSource {
    UBYTE    *CS_Buffer;
    LONG     CS_Length;
    LONG     CS_CurChr;
};
```

Where CS_Buffer is the command line to parse, CS_Length is the length of CS_Buffer, and CS_CurChr is the position in CS_Buffer from which ReadArgs() should begin its parsing. Normally CS_CurChr is initialized to zero. Note that currently the buffer must end with a newline (\n).

RDA_DAList is private and must be set to NULL before ReadArgs() uses this structure.

The RDA_Buffer and RDA_BufSiz fields allow an application to supply a fixed-size buffer in which to store parsed data. This allows the application to pre-allocate a buffer rather than requiring ReadArgs() to allocate buffer space. If either RDA_Buffer or RDA_BufSiz is NULL, ReadArgs() assumes the application has not supplied a buffer.

RDA_ExtHelp is a text string which ReadArgs() displays if the user asks for additional help. The user asks for additional help by typing a question mark when ReadArgs() prompts the user for input (which normally happens only when he or she types a question mark as the only argument on the command line).

RDA_Flags is a bit field used to toggle certain options of ReadArgs(). Currently, only one option is implemented, RDAF_NOPROMPT. When set, RDAF_NOPROMPT prevents ReadArgs() from prompting the user.

The following code, ReadArgs.c, uses a custom RDArgs structure to pass a command line to ReadArgs.

```
;/* ReadArgs.c - Execute me to compile me with Lattice 5.10a
LC -b1 -cfistq -v -y -j73 ReadArgs.c
Blink   FROM   LIB:c.o,ReadArgs.o   TO   ReadArgs   LIBRARY
LIB:LC.lib,LIB:Amiga.lib
quit
*/

#include <dos/dos.h>
#include <dos/rdargs.h>
#include <clib/dos_protos.h>
#include <clib/alib_stdio_protos.h>
#ifdef LATTICE
int CXBRK(void) { return(0); } /* Disable Lattice CTRL/C
handling */
```

```c
int chkabort(void) { return(0); }
#endif

UBYTE *vers = "\0SVER: ReadArgs 1.0";

#define TEMPLATE "S=SourceFiles/A/M,D=DebugLevel/K/N,L=link/S"
#define OPT_SOURCE    0
#define OPT_DEBUG     1
#define OPT_LINK      2
#define OPT_COUNT     3

/*  The array of LONGS where ReadArgs() will store the data from
**  the command line arguments. C guarantees that all the array
**  entries will be set to zero.
*/
LONG result[OPT_COUNT];

/* My custom RDArgs */
struct RDArgs *myrda;

ULONG StrLen(UBYTE *);

void main(void)
{
    UWORD x;
    UBYTE **sourcefiles;
/* Need to ask DOS for a RDArgs structure */
if (myrda = (struct RDArgs *)AllocDosObject(DOS_RDARGS, NULL))
{

    /* set up my parameters for ReadArgs() */

    /* use the following command line */
    myrda->RDA_Source.CS_Buffer = "file1 file2 file3
    D=1 Link file4 file5\n";
    myrda->RDA_Source.CS_Length =
            (LONG)StrLen(myrda->RDA_Source.CS_Buffer);
```

```c
        /* parse my command line */
    if (ReadArgs(TEMPLATE, result, myrda))
    {
        /*start printing out the results */

        /*  We don't need to check if there is a value in
        **  result[OPT_SOURCE] because the ReadArgs()
            template
        **  requires (using the /A modifier) that there
            be
        **  file names, so ReadArgs() will either fill in
        **  a value or ReadArgs() will fail
        */

        sourcefiles = (UBYTE **)result[OPT_SOURCE];
        /*  VPrintf() is a lot like Printf() except it's
            in
        **  ROM, and the arguments are referenced from an
        **  array rather than being extracted from the
            stack.
        */
        VPrintf("Files specified:\n", NULL);
        for (x=0; sourcefiles[x]; x++)
            VPrintf("\t%s\n", (LONG *)&sourcefiles[x]);

        /*  Is there something in the "DebugLevel"
            option?
        **  If there is, print it.
        */

        if (result[OPT_DEBUG])
            VPrintf("Debugging Level = %ld\n", (LONG
            *)result[OPT_DEBUG]);

        /*  If the link toggle was present, say something
            about it. */
        if (result[OPT_LINK])
            VPrintf("linking...\n", NULL);
        FreeArgs(myrda);
    }
    FreeDosObject(DOS_RDARGS, myrda);
}
```

```
}

ULONG StrLen(UBYTE *string)
{
    ULONG x = 0L;

    while (string[x++]);
    return(x);
}
```

Chapter 6

Calling AmigaDOS

This chapter describes the functions provided by the AmigaDOS resident library. To help you, it provides an explanation of the syntax, a full description of each function, and a quick reference card of the available functions.

Syntax

The syntax used in this chapter shows the C function call for each AmigaDOS function and the corresponding register you use when you program in assembler.

Register Values

The letter/number combination (D0...Dn) represents registers. The text to the left of an equals sign represents the result of a function. A register (that is, D0) appearing under such text indicates the register value of the result. Text to the right of an equals sign represents a function and its arguments, where the text enclosed in parentheses is a list of the arguments. A register (for example, D2) appearing under an argument indicates the register value of that argument.

Note that not all functions return a result.

Case

The letter case (that is, lower or upper case) IS significant. For example, you must enter the word "FileInfoBlock" with the first letter of each component word in upper case.

Boolean Returns

-1 (TRUE or SUCCESS), 0 (FALSE or FAILURE)

Values

All values are longwords (that is, 4-byte values or 32 bits). Values referred to as "string" are 32-bit pointers to NULL-terminated series of characters.

AmigaDOS Functions

This reference section describes the functions provided by the AmigaDOS resident library. Each function is arranged alphabetically. Under each function name there is a brief description of the function's purpose, a specification of the register values, and an explanation of the syntax of the arguments and result. To use any of these functions, you must link with amiga.lib.

A quick reference list of all AmigaDOS functions is included at the end of this chapter.

AbortPkt

Name

AbortPkt: Aborts an asynchronous packet, if possible. (V36)

Synopsis

```
AbortPkt(port, pkt)
         D1    D2

void AbortPkt (struct MsgPort *, struct DosPacket *)
```

Function

This attempts to abort a packet sent earlier with SendPkt to a handler. There is no guarantee that any given handler will allow a packet to be aborted, or if it is aborted whether function requested completed first or completely. After calling AbortPkt(), you must wait for the packet to return before reusing it or deallocating it.

Inputs

port: port the packet was sent to
pkt: the packet you wish aborted

Bugs

As of V37, this function does nothing.
See also: SendPkt(), DoPkt(), WaitPkt()

AddBuffers

Name

AddBuffers: changes the number of buffers for a filesystem

Synopsis

```
success = AddBuffers(filesystem, number)
D0                   D1          D2
BOOL AddBuffers(char *, LONG)
```

Function

Adds buffers to a filesystem. If it succeeds, the number of current buffers is returned in IoErr(). Note that "number" may be negative. The amount of memory used per buffer, and any limits on the number of buffers, are dependent on the filesystem in question. If the call succeeds, the number of buffers in use on the filesystem is returned by IoErr().

Inputs

filesystem: name of device to add buffers to (with ":").
number: number of buffers to add. May be negative.

Result

success: success or failure of command

Bugs

The V36 ROM filesystem (FFS/OFS) doesn't return the right number of buffers unless preceded by an AddBuffers(fs, -1) (in-use buffers aren't counted). This is fixed in V37.

AddDosEntry

Name

AddDosEntry: adds a DOS List entry to the lists

Synopsis

```
success = AddDosEntry(dlist)
D0                    D1
BOOL AddDosEntry(struct DosList *)
```

Function

Adds a device, volume, or assign to the DOS device list. This routine can fail if it conflicts with an existing entry (such as another assign to the same name or another device of the same name). Volume nodes with different dates and the same name CAN be added, or with names that conflict with devices or assigns.

Note: The DOS list does NOT have to be locked to call this. Do not access dlist after adding unless you have locked the DOS device list.

Inputs

dlist: device list entry to be added

Result

success: success/failure indicator

See also: RemDosEntry(), FindDosEntry(), NextDosEntry(), LockDosList(), MakeDosEntry(), FreeDosEntry()

AddPart

Name

AddPart: appends a file/dir to the end of a path

Synopsis

```
success = AddPart( dirname, filename, size )
D0                 D1       D2        D3
BOOL AddPart( UBYTE *, UBYTE *, ULONG )
```

Function

This routine adds a file, directory, or subpath name to a directory path name taking into account any required separator characters. If filename is a fully qualified path it will totally replace the current value of dirname.

Inputs

dirname: the path to add a file/directory name to.

filename: the filename or directory name to add. May be a relative pathname from the current directory (example: foo/bar). Can deal with leading "/"(s), indicating one directory up per "/", or with a ":", indicating it's relative to the root of the appropriate volume.

size: size in bytes of the space allocated for dirname. Must not be 0.

Result

success: nonzero for OK, FALSE if the buffer would have overflowed. If an overflow would have occurred, dirname will not be changed.

Bugs

Doesn't check if a subpath is legal (that is, doesn't check for ':'s) and doesn't handle leading "/"s in versions 2.0 through 2.02 (V36). Version 2.04 (V37) should fix this, allowing filename to be any path, including absolute.

See also: Filepart(), PathPart()

AddSegment

Name

AddSegment: adds a resident segment to the resident list

Synopsis

```
success = AddSegment(name, seglist, type)
D0                   D1     D2       D3
BOOL AddSegment(char *, BPTR, LONG)
```

Function

Adds a segment to the DOS resident list, with the specified Seglist and type (stored in seg_UC — normally 0). Note that currently unused types may cause it to interpret other registers (D4 and above) as additional parameters in a future release.

Do not build Segment structures yourself!

Inputs

name: name for the segment.

seglist: DOS seglist of code for segment.

type: initial usecount, normally 0.

Result

success: success or failure

Bugs

In 1.4 Beta 1, the return code was undefined, and an allocation failure would bring up a deadend Alert. In 2.0, this routine works correctly.

See also: FindSegment(), RemSegment(), LoadSeg()

AllocDosObject

Name

AllocDosObject: creates a DOS object

Synopsis

```
ptr = AllocDosObject(type, tags)
D0                    D1   D2
void *AllocDosObjectTagList(ULONG, struct TagItem *)
ptr = AllocDosObjectTags (type, Tag1, ...)
void *AllocDosObjectTags (ULONG, ULONG, ...)
```

Function

Creates one of several DOS objects, initializes it, and returns it to you. Note the DOS_STDPKT returns a pointer to the sp_Pkt of the structure.

Inputs

type: type of object requested.

tags: pointer to taglist with additional information.

Result

packet: pointer to the object or NULL
See also: FreeDosObject, <dos/dostags.h>, <dos/dos.h>

AssignAdd

Name

AssignAdd: adds a lock to an assign for multidirectory assigns

Synopsis

```
success = AssignAdd(name,lock)
D0                   D1   D2
BOOL AssignAdd(char *,BPTR)
```

Function

Adds a lock to an assign, making or adding to a multidirectory assign. Note that this only will succeed on an assign created with AssignLock(), or an assign created with AssignLate() that has been resolved (converted into a AssignLock-assign).

Note: You should not use the lock in any way after making this call successfully. It becomes the part of the assign, and will be unlocked by the system when the assign is removed. If you need to keep the lock, pass a lock from DupLock() to AssignLock().

Inputs

name: name of device to assign lock to (without trailing ":").

lock: lock associated with the assigned name.

Result

success: success/failure indicator. On failure, the lock is not unlocked.
See also: Lock(), AssignLock(), AssignPath(), AssignLate(), DupLock(), RemAssignList()

AssignLate

Name

AssignLate: creates an assignment to a specified path later

Synopsis

```
success = AssignLate(name,path)
D0                   D1    D2
BOOL AssignLate(char *,char *)
```

Function

Sets up a assignment that is expanded on the FIRST reference to the name. The path (a string) is attached to the node. When the name is referenced (Open("FOO:xyzzy")...), the string is used to determine where to set the assign to, and if the directory can be locked, the assign acts from that point on as if it had been created by AssignLock().

A major advantage is assigning data to unmounted volumes, which will be requested on access (useful in startup sequences).

Inputs

name: name of device to be assigned (without trailing ":").

path: name of late assignment to be resolved on the first reference.

Result

success: success/failure indicator of the operation

AssignLock

Name

AssignLock— creates an assignment to a locked object

Synopsis

```
success = AssignLock(name,lock)
D0                   D1   D2
BOOL AssignLock(char *,BPTR)
```

Function

Sets up an assign of a name to a given lock. Passing NULL for a lock cancels any outstanding assign to that name. If an assign entry of that name is already on the list, this routine replaces that entry. If an entry is on the list that conflicts with the new assign, then a failure code is returned.

Note: You should not use the lock in any way after making this call successfully. It becomes the assign, and will be unlocked by the system when the assign is removed. If you need to keep the lock, pass a lock from DupLock() to AssignLock().

Inputs

name: name of device to assign lock to (without trailing ":").

lock: lock associated with the assigned name.

Result

success: success/failure indicator. On failure, the lock is not unlocked.

AssignPath

Name

AssignPath: creates an assignment to a specified path

Synopsis

```
success = AssignPath(name,path)
D0                   D1    D2
BOOL AssignPath(char *,char *)
```

Function

Sets up a assignment that is expanded on EACH reference to the name. This is implemented through a new device list type (DLT_ASSIGNPATH, or the like). The path (a string) would be attached to the node. When the name is referenced (Open("FOO: xyzzy"), the string will be used to determine where to do the open. No permanent lock is part of it. For example, you could AssignPath c2: to df2:c, and references to c2: would go to df2:c, even if you change disks.

The other major advantage is assigning things to unmounted volumes, which will be requested on access (useful in startup sequences).

Inputs

name: name of device to be assigned (without trailing ":").

path: name of late assignment to be resolved at each reference.

Result

success: success/failure indicator of the operation

AttemptLockDosList

Name

AttemptLockDosList: attempts to lock the DOS lists for use

Synopsis

```
dlist = AttemptLockDosList(flags)
D0                          D1
struct DosList *AttemptLockDosList(ULONG)
```

Function

Locks the dos device list in preparation to walk the list. If the list is "busy" then this routine returns NULL. See LockDosList() for more information.

Inputs

flags: flags stating which types of nodes you want to lock.

Result

dlist: pointer to the beginning of the list or NULL. This is NOT a valid node!

ChangeMode

Name

ChangeMode: changes the current mode of a lock or filehandle

Synopsis

```
success = ChangeMode(type, object, newmode)
D0                    D1     D2      D3
BOOL ChangeMode(ULONG, BPTR, ULONG)
```

Function

This routine allows you to attempt to change the mode in use by a lock or filehandle. For example, you could attempt to turn a shared lock into an exclusive lock. The handler may well reject this request.

WARNING: If you use the wrong type for the object, the system may crash.

Inputs

   type: either CHANGE_FH or CHANGE_LOCK.

   object: a lock or filehandle.

   newmode: the new mode you want.

Result

   success: Boolean

Bugs

   This routine did not work in versions 2.0, 2.01, or 2.02 (V36). It should work in 2.04 (V37). In the earlier versions, it can crash the machine.

CheckSignal

Name

   CheckSignal: checks for break signals

Synopsis

```
signals = CheckSignal(mask)
D0                    D1
ULONG CheckSignals(ULONG)
```

Function

   Checks to see if any signals specified in the mask have been set and if so, returns them. Otherwise it returns FALSE. All signals specified in mask will be cleared.

Inputs

   mask: signals to check for

Result

   signals: signals specified in mask that were set

Cli

Name

Cli: returns a pointer to the CLI structure of the process

Synopsis

```
cli_ptr = Cli()
D0
struct CommandLineInterface *Cli(void)
```

Function

Returns a pointer to the CLI structure of the current process, or NULL if the process has no CLI structure

Result

cli_ptr: pointer to the CLI structure, or NULL

Close

Name

Close: closes an open file

Synopsis

```
success = Close( file )
D0                 D1
BOOL Close(BPTR)
```

Function

The file specified by the filehandle is closed. You must close all files you explicitly opened, but you must not close inherited filehandles that are passed to you (each filehandle must be closed once and ONLY once). If Close() fails, the filehandle is still deallocated and should not be used.

Inputs

   file: BCPL pointer to a filehandle

Results

   success: returns if Close() succeeded. Note that it might fail depending on buffering and whatever I/O must be done to close a file being written to.

   Note: this return value did not exist before V36!

   See also: Open(), OpenFromLock()

CompareDates

Name

   CompareDates: compares two datestamps

Synopsis

```
result = CompareDates(date1,date2)
D0                    D1    D2
LONG CompareDates(struct DateStamp *,struct DateStamp *)
```

Function

   Compares two times for relative magnitude. <0 is returned if date1 is later than date2, 0 if they are equal, or >0 if date2 is later than date1.
   Note: This ordering is NOT the same as in strcmp!

Inputs

   date1, date2: DateStamps to compare

Result

   result: <0, 0, or >0 based on comparison of two date stamps
   See also: DateStamp(), DateToStr(), StrToDate()

CreateDir

Name

CreateDir: creates a new directory

Synopsis

```
lock = CreateDir( name )
D0              D1
BPTR CreateDir(char *)
```

Function

CreateDir() creates a new directory with the specified name. An error is returned if it fails. Directories can only be created on devices that support them, for example, disks. CreateDir() returns an exclusive lock on the new directory, if it succeeds.

Inputs

name:- pointer to a null-terminated string

Results

lock: BCPL pointer to a lock or NULL for failure

CreateNewProc

Name

CreateNewProc: creates a new process

Synopsis

```
process = CreateNewProc(tags)
D0                      D1
struct Process *CreateNewProc(struct TagItem *)
process = CreateNewProcTagList (tags)
D0                               D1
struct Process *CreateNewProcTagList (struct TagItem *)
process = CreateNewProcTags (Tag1, ...)
```

```
struct Process *CreateNewProcTags (ULONG, ...)
```

Function

This function creates a new process according to the tags passed in. See dos/dostags.h for the tags. You must specify one of NP_Seglist or NP_Entry. NP_Seglist takes a seglist (as returned by LoadSeg). NP_Entry takes a code ptr for the routine to call. There are many options, as you can see by examining dos/dostags.h.

The defaults are for a non-CLI process, with copies of your CurrentDir, HomeDir (used for PROGDIR:), priority, consoletask, windowptr, and variables. The input and output filehandles default to opens of NIL:, stack to 4000, and others as shown in dostags.h. This is a fairly reasonable default setting for creating threads, though you may wish to modify it (for example, to give a descriptive name to the process.)

CreateNewProc() is callable from a task, though any actions that require doing DOS I/O (DupLock of currentdir) will not occur.

Inputs

tags: a pointer to a TagItem array

Result

process: the created process, or NULL

CreateProc

Name

CreateProc: creates a new process

Synopsis

```
process = CreateProc( name, pri, seglist, stackSize )
D0                   D1    D2   D3       D4
struct MsgPort *CreateProc(char *, LONG, BPTR, LONG)
```

Function

CreateProc() creates a new AmigaDOS process of name "name". AmigaDOS processes are a superset of Exec tasks.

A seglist, as returned by LoadSeg(), is passed as 'seglist'. This represents a section of code that is to be run as a new process. The code is entered at the first hunk in the segment list, which should contain suitable initialization code or a jump to such. A process control structure is allocated from memory and initialized. If you wish to fake a seglist (that will never have DOS UnLoadSeg() called on it), use this code:

```
DS.1    0    ;Align to longword
DC.L    16   ;Segment "length" (faked)
DC.L    0    ;Pointer to next segment
...start of code...
```

The size of the root stack on activation is passed as "stackSize". "pri" specifies the required priority of the new process. The result is the process msg-port address of the new process, or zero if the routine failed. The argument 'name' specifies the new process name. A zero return code indicates error. The seglist passed to CreateProc() is not freed when it exits; it is up to the parent process to free it, or for the code to unload itself.

Under V36 and later, you probably should use CreateNewProc() instead.

Inputs

name: pointer to a NULL-terminated string.

pri: signed long (range -128 to +127).

seglist: BCPL pointer to a seglist.

stackSize: integer (must be a multiple of 4 bytes).

Result

process: process identifier

CurrentDir

Name

CurrentDir: makes a directory lock the current directory

Synopsis

```
oldLock = CurrentDir( lock )
D0                    D1
```

```
BPTR CurrentDir(BPTR)
```

Function

CurrentDir() causes a directory associated with a lock to be made the current directory. The old current directory lock is returned. A value of zero is a valid result here, this 0 lock represents the root of file system that you booted from. Any call that has to Open(), Lock(), and go on a file requires the current directory to be a valid lock or 0.

Inputs

lock: BCPL pointer to a lock

Result

oldLock: BCPL pointer to a lock

See also: Lock(), Unlock(), Open(), DupLock()

DateStamp

Name

DateStamp: obtains the date and time in internal format

Synopsis

```
ds = DateStamp( ds );
D0                 D1
struct DateStamp *DateStamp (struct DateStamp *)
```

Function

DateStamp() takes a structure of three longwords that is set to the current time. The first element in the structure is a count of the number of days. The second element is the number of minutes elapsed in the day. The third is the number of ticks elapsed in the current minute. A tick happens 50 times a second. DateStamp ensures that the day and minute are consistent. All three elements are zero if the date is unset. DateStamp() currently only returns even multiples of 50 ticks. Therefore, the time you get is always an even number of ticks. Time is measured from January 1, 1978.

Inputs

ds: pointer to asterisk DateStamp.

Results

The array is filled as described.

DateToStr

Name

DateToStr: converts a DateStamp to a string

Synopsis

```
success = DateToStr( datetime )
D0                    D1
BOOL DateToStr(struct DateTime *)
```

Function

DateToStr() converts an AmigaDOS DateStamp to a human-readable ASCII string as requested by your settings in the DateTime structure.

Inputs

DateTime: a pointer to an initialized DateTime structure. The DateTime structure should be initialized as follows:

dat_Stamp: a copy of the datestamp you wish to convert to ASCII.

dat_Format: a format byte that specifies the format of the dat_StrDate. This can be any of the following. (Note: If value used is something other than those below, the default of FORMAT_DOS is used).

FORMAT_DOS: AmigaDOS format (dd-mmm-yy).
FORMAT_INT: International format (yy-mmm-dd).
FORMAT_USA: American format (mm-dd-yy).
FORMAT_CDN: Canadian format (dd-mm-yy).
FORMAT_DEF: Default format for locale.

dat_Flags: a flags byte. The only flag that affects this function is:

DTF_SUBST: if set, a string such as Today, Monday, etc., will be used instead of the dat_Format specification if possible.

DTF_FUTURE: ignored by this function.

dat_StrDay: pointer to a buffer to receive the day of the week string (Monday, Tuesday, etc.). If null, this string will not be generated.

dat_StrDate: pointer to a buffer to receive the date string, in the format requested by dat_Format, subject to possible modifications by DTF_SUBST. If null, this string will not be generated.

dat_StrTime: pointer to a buffer to receive the time of day string. If NULL, this will not be generated.

Result

success: a zero return indicates that the DateStamp was invalid, and could not be converted. Nonzero indicates that the call succeeded.

See also: StrtoDate(), libraries/datetime.h, DateStamp()

Delay

Name

Delay: delays a process for a specified time

Synopsis

```
Delay( ticks )
       D1
Void Delay(ULONG)
```

Function

The argument 'ticks' specifies how many ticks (50 per second) to wait before returning control.

Inputs

    ticks: Integer

Bugs

    Due to a bug in the timer.device in V1.2/V1.3, specifying a timeout of zero for Delay() can cause unreliable timer and floppy disk operation. This defect has been fixed in V36 and later versions.

DeleteFile

Name

    DeleteFile: deletes a file or directory

Synopsis

```
success = DeleteFile( name )
D0                    D1
BOOL DeleteFile(char *)
```

Function

    This routine attempts to delete the file or directory specified by "name". An error is returned if the deletion fails. Note that all the files within a directory must be deleted before the directory itself can be deleted.

Inputs

    name: pointer to a null-terminated string

Result

    success: Boolean

DeleteVar

Name

    DeleteVar: deletes a local or environment variable

Synopsis

```
success = DeleteVar( name, flags )
D0                     D1     D2
BOOL DeleteVar(UBYTE *, ULONG )
```

Function

Deletes a local or environment variable

Inputs

name: pointer to a variable name. Note that variable names follow filesystem syntax and semantics.

flags: combination of type of var to delete (low 8 bits), and flags to control the behavior of this routine. Currently defined flags include:

GVF_LOCAL_ONLY: delete a local (to your process) variable.
GVF_GLOBAL_ONLY: delete a global environment variable.

The default is to delete a local variable if found, otherwise a global environment variable if found (only for LV_VAR).

Result

success: if nonzero, the variable was successfully deleted; FALSE indicates failure

Bugs

LV_VAR is the only type that can be global

See also: GetVar(), SetVar(), FindVar(), DeleteFile(), dos/var.h

DeviceProc

Name

DeviceProc: returns the process MsgPort of specific I/O handler

Synopsis

```
process = DeviceProc( name )
D0                    D1
struct MsgPort *DeviceProc (char *)
```

Function

DeviceProc() returns the process identifier of the process that handles the device associated with the specified name. If no process handler can be found then the result is zero. If the name refers to an assign then a directory lock is returned in IoErr(). This lock should not be Unlock()ed or Examine()ed (if you wish to do so, DupLock() it first).

Bugs

In V36, if you try to DeviceProc() something relative to an assign made with AssignPath(), it will fail. This is because there's no way to know when to unlock the lock. If you're writing code for V36 or later, it is highly advised you use GetDeviceProc() instead, or make your code conditional on V36 to use GetDeviceProc()/ FreeDeviceProc().

DoPkt

Name

DoPkt: sends a DOS packet and wait for reply (V36)

Synopsis

```
result1 = DoPkt(port,action,arg1,arg2,arg3,arg4,arg5)
D0              D1     D2     D3   D4   D5   D6   D7
LONG = DoPkt(struct MsgPort *,LONG,LONG,LONG,LONG,
                    LONG)
```

Function

This function sends a packet to a handler and waits for it to return. Any secondary return will be available in D1 AND from IoErr(). DoPkt() will work even if the caller is an Exec task and not a process; however, it will be slower, and may fail for some additional reasons, such as being unable to allocate a signal. DoPkt() uses your pr_MsgPort for the reply, and will call pr_PktWait. (See BUGS regarding tasks, though.)

Inputs

port: pr_MsgPort of the handler process to send to.

action: the action requested of the filesystem/handler.

arg1, arg2, arg3, arg4, arg5: arguments, depending on the action, may not be required.

Result

result1: the value returned in dp_Res1, or FALSE if there was some problem in sending the packet or receiving it

Bugs

Using DoPkt() from tasks doesn't work in DOS 2.0. Use AllocDosObject(), PutMsg(), and WaitPort()/GetMsg() for a workaround, or you can call CreateNewProc() to start a process to do DOS I/O for you. Only allows five arguments to be specified. For more arguments (packets support a maximum of seven) create a packet and use SendPkt()/WaitPkt().

DupLock

Name

DupLock: duplicates a lock

Synopsis

```
lock = DupLock (lock)
D0                D1
BPTR DupLock(BPTR)
```

Function

DupLock() is passed a shared filing system lock. This is the ONLY way to obtain a duplicate of a lock—simply copying is not allowed.

Another lock to the same object is then returned. It is not possible to create a copy of an exclusive lock.

A zero return indicates failure.

Inputs

lock: BCPL pointer to a lock

Result

newLock: BCPL pointer to a lock

See also: Lock(), UnLock(), DupLockFromFH(), ParentOfFH()

DupLockFromFH

Name

DupLockFromFH: gets a lock on an open file

Synopsis

```
lock = DupLockFromFH(fh)
D0                   D1
BPTR DupLockFromFH(BPTR)
```

Function

This routine obtains a lock on the object associated with fh. This routine only works if the file was opened using a nonexclusive mode. Other restrictions may be placed on success by the filesystem.

Inputs

fh: opened file for which to obtain the lock

Result

lock: obtained lock or NULL for failure

EndNotify

Name

EndNotify: ends a notification request (V36)

Synopsis

```
EndNotify(notifystructure)
          D1
VOID EndNotify(struct NotifyRequest *)
```

Function

This routine removes a notification request. It is safe to call even if StartNotify failed. For NRF_SEND_MESSAGE, it searches your port for any messages about the object in question and removes and replies to them before returning.

Inputs

notifystructure: a structure passed to StartNotify().

ErrorReport

Name

ErrorReport: displays a Retry/Cancel requester for an error

Synopsis

```
status = ErrorReport(code, type, arg1, device)
D0                   D1    D2    D3    A0
BOOL ErrorReport(LONG, LONG, ULONG, struct MsgPort *)
```

Function

Based on the request type, this routine formats the appropriate requester to be displayed. If the code is not understood, it returns DOS_TRUE immediately. Returns DOS_TRUE if the user selects CANCEL or if the attempt to put up the requester fails, or if the process pr_WindowPtr is -1. Returns FALSE if the user selects Retry. The routine will retry on DISKINSERTED for appropriate error codes. These return values are the opposite of what AutoRequest returns.

Note: This routine sets IoErr() to code before returning.

Inputs

code: error code to put a requester up for. Current valid error codes are:

ERROR_DISK_NOT_VALIDATED
ERROR_DISK_WRITE_PROTECTED
ERROR_DISK_FULL
ERROR_DEVICE_NOT_MOUNTED
ERROR_NOT_A_DOS_DISK
ERROR_NO_DISK
ABORT_DISK_ERROR/* read/write error */
ABORT_BUSY/* you MUST replace... */

type: Current request types are:

REPORT_LOCK	arg1 is a lock (BPTR).
REPORT_FH	arg1 is a filehandle (BPTR).
REPORT_VOLUME	arg1 is a volumenode (C pointer).
REPORT_INSERT	arg1 is the string for the volumename (will be split on a ":"). With ERROR_DEVICE_NOT_MOUNTED puts up the "Please insert..." requester.

arg1: variable parameter (see type).

device (optional): address of handler task for which report is to be made. Only required for REPORT_LOCK, and only if arg1==NULL.

Result

status: Cancel/Retry indicator (0 means retry)

ExAll

Name

ExAll: examines an entire directory

Synopsis

```
continue = ExAll(lock, buffer, size, type, control)
D0               D1      D2      D3    D4    D5
BOOL ExAll(BPTR,UBYTE *,LONG,LONG,struct ExAllControl *)
```

Function

This routine examines an entire directory. Lock must be on a directory. Size is the size of the buffer supplied.

The buffer is filled with (partial) ExAllData structures, as specified by the type field.

Type is a value from those shown below that determines which information is to be stored in the buffer. Each higher value adds new data to the list as described below:

ED_NAME	fileName
ED_TYPE	type
ED_SIZE	size in bytes
ED_PROTECTION	protection bits
ED_DATE	three longwords of date
ED_COMMENT	comment (is NULL if no comment)

Thus, ED_NAME gives only filenames, and ED_COMMENT gives everything.

The ead_Next entry gives a pointer to the next entry in the buffer. The last entry will have NULL in ead_Next.

The control structure is required so that FFS can keep track if more than one call to ExAll() is required. This happens when there are more names in a directory than will fit into the buffer. The format of the control structure is as follows:

Note: the control structure MUST be allocated by AllocDosObject()

1. Entries: This field tells the calling application how many entries are in the buffer after calling ExAll(). Note: Make sure your code handles the 0 entries case, including 0 entries with continue nonzero.

2. LastKey: This field ABSOLUTELY MUST be initialized to 0 before calling ExAll() for the first time. Any other value will cause nasty things to happen. If ExAll() returns nonzero, then this field should not be touched before making the second and subsequent calls to ExAll(). Whenever ExAll() returns nonzero, there are more calls required before all names have been received.

As soon as a FALSE return is received then ExAll() has completed (if IoErr() returns ERROR_NO_MORE_ENTRIES—otherwise it returns the error that occurred, similar to ExNext.)

3. MatchString: If this field is NULL then all filenames will be returned. If this field is non-null then it is interpreted as a pointer to a string that is used to pattern match all file names before accepting them and putting them into the buffer. The default AmigaDOS caseless pattern match routine is used. This string MUST have been parsed by ParsePatternNoCase()!

4. MatchFunc: Contains a pointer to a hook for a routine to decide if the entry will be included in the returned list of entries. The entry is filled out first, and then passed to the hook. If no MatchFunc is to be called then this entry should be NULL. The hook is called with the following parameters (as is standard for hooks):

```
BOOL = MatchFunc( hookptr, data, typeptr )
                    a0      a1    a2
(a0 = ptr to hook, a1 = ptr to filled in ExAllData, a2 =
ptr to longword of type).
```

MatchFunc() should return FALSE if the entry is not to be accepted, otherwise return TRUE.

DOS will emulate ExAll() using Examine() and ExNext() if the handler does not support the ExAll packet.

Inputs

lock: lock on directory to be examined.

buffer: buffer for data returned (MUST be at least word-aligned, preferably longword-aligned).

size: size in bytes of "buffer".

type: type of data to be returned.

control: control data structure (see Function and Note, above). MUST have been allocated by AllocDosObject()!

Result

continue: whether or not ExAll() is done. If FALSE is returned, either ExAll() has completed (IoErr() == ERROR_NO_MORE_ENTRIES), or an error occurred (check IoErr()). If nonzero is returned, you MUST call ExAll() again until it returns FALSE.

Example

```
eac = AllocDosObject(DOS_EXALLCONTROL,NULL);
if (!eac) ...
...
eac->eac_LastKey = 0;
do {
  more = ExAll(lock, EAData, sizeof(EAData), ED_FOO, eac);
  if ((!more) && (IoErr() != ERROR_NO_MORE_ENTRIES)) {
     /* ExAll failed abnormally */
     break;
  }
  if (eac->eac_Entries == 0) {
     /* ExAll failed normally with no entries */
     continue;
         /* ("more" is *usually* zero) */
  }
  ead = (struct ExAllData *) EAData;
  do {
     /* use ead here */
     ...
     /* get next ead */
     ead = ead->ed_Next;
 } while (ead);

    } while (more);
    ...
    FreeDosObject(DOS_EXALLCONTROL,eac);
```

Bugs

Use only the V37 and later versions of this function.

Examine

Name

Examine: examines a directory or file associated with a lock

Synopsis

```
success = Examine( lock, FileInfoBlock )
D0                D1    D2
BOOL Examine(BPTR,struct FileInfoBlock *)
```

Function

Examine() fills in information in the FileInfoBlock concerning the file or directory associated with the lock. This information includes the name, size, creation date, and whether it is a file or directory. FileInfoBlock must be longword-aligned. Examine() gives a return code of zero if it fails.

You may make a local copy of the FileInfoBlock, as long as it is never passed back to ExNext(). The FileInfoBlock must be longword-aligned. AllocDosObject() will allocate it for you correctly.

Inputs

lock: BCPL pointer to a lock.

infoBlock: pointer to a FileInfoBlock (must be longword-aligned).

Result

success: Boolean

ExamineFH

Name

ExamineFH: gets information on an open file

Synopsis

```
success = ExamineFH(fh, fib)
D0                  D1  D2
BOOL ExamineFH(BPTR, struct FileInfoBlock *)
```

Function

Examines a filehandle and returns information about the file in the FileInfoBlock. There are no guarantees as to whether the fib_Size field will reflect any changes made to the file size it was opened, though filesystems should attempt to provide up-to-date information for it.

Inputs

fh: filehandle you wish to examine.

fib: FileInfoBlock, must be longword-aligned

Result

success: success/failure indication

Execute

Name

Execute: executes a CLI command

Synopsis

```
success = Execute( commandString, input, output )
D0                 D1             D2     D3
BOOL Execute(char *, BPTR, BPTR)
```

Function

This function attempts to execute the string commandString as a Shell command and arguments. The string can contain any valid input that you could type directly in a Shell, including input and output redirection using < and >. Execute() does not return until the commands in commandString have returned.

The input filehandle is normally zero, and in this case Execute() will perform whatever was requested in the commandString and then return. If the input file handle is non-zero then after the (possibly non-zero empty) commandString is performed subsequent input is read from the specified input filehandle until end of that file is reached.

In most cases the output filehandle must be provided, and is used by the Shell commands as their output stream unless output redirection was specified. If the output filehandle is set to zero then the current window, normally specified as *, is used. Note that programs running under the Workbench do not normally have a current window.

Execute() may also be used to create a new interactive Shell process just like those created with the NEWSHELL function. To do this you would call Execute() with an empty commandString, and pass a filehandle relating to a new window as the input filehandle. The output filehandle would be set to zero. The Shell reads commands from the new window, and uses the same window for output. This new Shell window can only be terminated by using the ENDSHELL command.

Under V37, if an input filehandle is passed, and it's either interactive or a NIL: filehandle, the pr_ConsoleTask of the new process will be set to that filehandle's process (the same applies to SystemTagList()).

For this command to work the program RUN must be present in C: in versions before V36.

Inputs

commandString: pointer to a NULL-terminated string.

input: BCPL pointer to a filehandle.

output: BCPL pointer to a filehandle.

Result

success: Boolean, indicating whether Execute() was successful in finding and starting the specified program. This is NOT the same as the return code of the commands executed.

Exit

Name

Exit: exits from a program

Synopsis

```
Exit( returnCode )
      D1
void Exit(LONG)
```

Function

Exit() is currently for use with programs written as if they were BCPL programs. This function is not normally useful for other purposes.

In general, therefore, please DO NOT CALL THIS FUNCTION!

To exit, C programs should use the C language exit() function (note the lower case letter e). Assembly programs should place a return code in D0, and execute an RTS instruction with their original stack pointer.

Implementation

The action of Exit() depends on whether the program that called it is running as a command under a CLI or not. If the program is running under the CLI the command finishes and control reverts to the CLI. In this case, returnCode is interpreted as the return code from the program.

If the program is running as a distinct process, Exit() deletes the process and releases the space associated with the stack, segment list, and process structure.

Inputs

returnCode: Integer

ExNext

Name

ExNext: examines the next entry in a directory

Synopsis

```
success = ExNext( lock, FileInfoBlock )
D0                 D1    D2
BOOL ExNext(BPTR, struct FileInfoBlock *)
```

Function

This routine is passed a directory lock and a FileInfoBlock that have been initialized by a previous call to Examine(), or updated by a previous call to ExNext(). ExNext() gives a return code of zero on failure. The most common cause of failure is reaching the end of the list of files in the owning directory. In this case, IoErr() returns ERROR_NO_MORE_ENTRIES and a good exit is appropriate.

So, follow these steps to examine a directory:

1. Pass a Lock and a FileInfoBlock to Examine(). The Lock must be on the directory you wish to examine.
2. Pass ExNext() the same Lock and FileInfoBlock.
3. Do something with the information returned in the FileInfoBlock. Note that the lib_DirEntryType field is positive for directories, negative for files.
4. Keep calling ExNext() until it returns FALSE. Check IoErr() to ensure that the reason for failure was ERROR_NO_MORE_ENTRIES.

Note: if you wish to recursively scan the file tree and you find another directory while ExNext'ing you must Lock that directory and Examine() it using a new FileInfoBlock. Use of the same FileInfoBlock to enter a directory would lose important state information such that it will be impossible to continue scanning the parent directory. While it is permissible to UnLock() and Lock() the parent directory between ExNext() calls, this is NOT recommended.

Important state information is associated with the parent lock, so if it is freed between ExNext() calls this information has to be rebuilt on each new ExNext call, and will significantly slow down directory scanning.

It is NOT legal to Examine() a file, and then to ExNext from that FileInfoBlock.You may make a local copy of the FileInfoBlock, as long as it is never passed back to the operating system.

Inputs

lock: BCPL pointer to a lock originally used for the Examine() call.

infoBlock: pointer to a FileInfoBlock used on the previous Examine() or ExNext() call.

Result

success: Boolean

Special note: The FileInfoBlock must be longword-aligned. AllocDosObject() will allocate them correctly for you.

Fault

Name

Fault: returns the text associated with a DOS error code

Synopsis

```
success = Fault(code, header, buffer, len)
D0                D1      D2      D3      D4
BOOL Fault(LONG, UBYTE *, UBYTE *, LONG)
```

Function

This routine obtains the error message text for the given error code. The header is prepended to the text of the error message, followed by a colon. Puts a null-terminated string for the error message into the buffer. By convention, error messages should be no longer than 80 characters (+1 for termination), and preferably no more than 60 characters.

The value returned by IoErr() is set to the code passed in. If there is no message for the error code, the message is "Error code <number>\n".

Inputs

code: error code.

header: header to output before error text.

buffer: buffer to receive error message.

len: length of the buffer.

Result

success: success/failure code

FGetC

Name

FGetC: reads a character from the specified input (buffered)

Synopsis

```
char = FGetC(fh)
D0             D1
LONG FGetC(BPTR)
```

Function

Reads the next character from the input stream. A -1 is returned when EOF or an error is encountered. This call is buffered. Use Flush() between buffered and unbuffered I/O on a filehandle.

Inputs

fh: filehandle to use for buffered I/O

Result

char: character read (0–255) or -1

Bugs

In V36, after an EOF was read, EOF would always be returned from FGetC() from then on. Starting in V37, it tries to read from the handler again each time (unless UnGetC (fh, -1) was called).
See also: FPutC(), UnGetC(), Flush()

FGets

Name

FGets: reads a line from the specified input (buffered)

Synopsis

```
buffer = FGets(fh, buf, len)
D0                D1   D2   D3
UBYTE *FGets(BPTR, UBYTE *, ULONG)
```

Function

This routine reads in a single line from the specified input stopping at a NEWLINE character or EOF. In either event, UP TO the number of len specified bytes minus 1 will be copied into the buffer. Hence if a length of 50 is passed and the input line is longer than 49 bytes, it returns 49 characters. It returns the buffer pointer normally, or NULL if EOF is the first thing read.

If terminated by a newline, the newline WILL be the last character in the buffer. This is a buffered read routine. The string read in IS null-terminated.

Inputs

>fh: filehandle to use for buffered IO.
>
>buf: area to read bytes into.
>
>len: number of bytes to read, must be > 0.

Result

>buffer: Pointer to buffer passed in, or NULL for immediate EOF or for an error. If NULL is returned for an EOF, IoErr() returns 0.

FilePart

Name

>FilePart: returns the last component of a path

Synopsis

```
fileptr = FilePart( path )
D0                  D1
UBYTE *FilePart( UBYTE * )
```

Function

>This function returns a pointer to the last component of a string path specification, which will normally be the file name. If there is only one component, it returns a pointer to the beginning of the string.

Inputs

>path: pointer to an path string. This pointer may be relative to the current directory or the current disk.

Result

>fileptr: pointer to the last component of the path.

Example

>FilePart("xxx:yyy/zzz/qqq") would return a pointer to the first q.
>FilePart("xxx:yyy") would return a pointer to the first y.

See also: PathPart(), AddPath()

FindArg

Name

FindArg: finds a keyword in a template

Synopsis

```
index = FindArg(template, keyword)
D0                D1        D2
LONG FindArg(UBYTE *, UBYTE *)
```

Function

This routine returns the argument number of the keyword, or -1 if it is not a keyword for the template. Abbreviations are handled.

Inputs

keyword: keyword to search for in template.

template: template string to search.

Result

index: number of entry in template, or -1 if not found

FindCliProc

Name

FindCliProc: returns a pointer to the requested CLI process

Synopsis

```
proc = FindCliProc(num)
D0              D1
struct Process *FindCliProc(LONG)
```

Function

This routine returns a pointer to the CLI process associated with the given CLI number. If the process isn't an active CLI process, NULL is returned.

Note: This should normally be called inside a Forbid(), if you must use this function at all.

Inputs

num: task number of CLI process

Result

proc: pointer to given CLI process

FindDosEntry

Name

FindDosEntry: finds a specific DOS List entry

Synopsis

```
newdlist = FindDosEntry(dlist,name,flags)
D0                       D1   D2   D3
struct DosList *FindDosEntry(struct DosList *,UBYTE
*,ULONG)
```

Function

Locates an entry on the device list. Starts with the entry dlist.

Note: must be called with the device list locked, no references may be made to dlist after unlocking.

Inputs

dlist: the device entry to start with.

name: name of device entry (without ":") to locate.

flags: search control flags. Use the flags you passed to LockDosLis()t, or a subset of them. LDF_READ/LDF_WRITE are not required for this call.

Result

newdlist: the device entry or NULL

FindSegment

Name

FindSegment: finds a segment on the resident list (V36)

Synopsis

```
segment = FindSegment(name, start, system)
D0                    D1     D2     D3
struct Segment *FindSegment(char *, struct Segment *, LONG)
```

Function

Finds a segment on the DOS resident list by name and type, starting at the segment AFTER "start", or at the beginning if start is NULL. If system is zero, it only returns nodes with a seg_UC of 0 or more. It does NOT increment the seg_UC, and it does NOT do any locking of the list. You must Forbid() lock the list to use this call.

To use an entry you have found, you must: if the seg_UC is 0 or more, increment it, and decrement it (under Forbid()!) when you're done with the seglist.

The other values for seg_UC are:
- -1: system module, such as a filesystem or shell
- -2: resident shell command
- -999: disabled internal command, ignore

Negative values should never be modified. All other negative values between 0 and -32767 are reserved to AmigaDos and should not be used.

Inputs

name: name of segment to find.

start: segment to start the search after.

system - true for system segment, false for normal segments.

Result

segment: the segment found or NULL.

FindVar

Name

FindVar: finds a local variable (V36)

Synopsis

```
var = FindVar( name, type )
D0              D1    D2
struct LocalVar * FindVar(UBYTE *, ULONG )
```

Function

Finds a local variable structure

Inputs

name: pointer to an variable name. Note variable names follow filesystem syntax and semantics.

type: type of variable to be found. (see dos/var.h.)

Result

var: pointer to a LocalVar structure or NULL

See also: DeleteVar(), GetVar(), SetVar(), dos/var.h

Flush

Name

Flush: flushes buffers for a buffered filehandle

Synopsis

```
success = Flush(fh)
D0        D1
BOOL Flush(BPTR)
```

Function

This routine flushes any pending buffered writes to the filehandle. All buffered writes will also be flushed on Close(). If the filehandle was being used for input, it drops the buffer, and tries to Seek() back to the last read position (so subsequent reads or writes will occur at the expected position in the file).

Inputs

fh: filehandle to flush

Result

success: success or failure

Format

Name

Format: causes a filesystem to initialize itself (V37)

Synopsis

```
success = Format(filesystem, volumename, dostype)
D0                D1          D2          D3
BOOL Format(UBYTE *, UBYTE *, ULONG)
```

Function

Interface for initializing new media on a device. This function causes the filesystem to write out an empty disk structure to the media, which should then be ready for use. This function assumes the media has been lowlevel formatted and verified already.

Inputs

filesystem: name of device to be formatted. ":" must be supplied.

volumename: name for volume (if supported). No ":".

dostype: type of format, if filesystem supports multiple types.

Result

success: success/failure indicator

FPutC

Name

FPutC: writes a character to the specified output (buffered) (V36)

Synopsis

```
char = FPutC(fh, char)
D0            D1   D2
LONG FPutC(BPTR, UBYTE)
```

Function

Writes a single character to the output stream. This call is buffered. Use Flush() between buffered and unbuffered I/O on a filehandle. Interactive filehandles are flushed automatically on a newline, return, "\0", or linefeed.

Inputs

fh: filehandle to use for buffered I/O.

char: character to write.

Result

char: either the character written, or EOF for an error

FPuts

Name

FPuts: writes a string to the specified output (buffered)

Synopsis

```
error = FPuts(fh, str)
D0            D1  D2
LONG FPuts(BPTR, UBYTE *)
```

Function

This routine writes an unformatted string to the filehandle. No newline is appended to the string and the length actually written is returned. This routine is buffered.

Inputs

fh: filehandle to use for buffered I/O.

str: null-terminated string to be written to default output.

Result

error: 0 normally, otherwise -1. Note that this is opposite of most other DOS functions, which return success.

FRead

Name

FRead: reads a number of blocks from an input (buffered)

Synopsis

```
count = FRead(fh, buf, blocklen, blocks)
D0            D1   D2   D3        D4
LONG FRead(BPTR, UBYTE *, ULONG, ULONG)
```

Function

Attempts to read a number of blocks, each blocklen long, into the specified buffer from the input stream. This routine may return less than the number of blocks requested, either due to EOF or read errors. This call is buffered.

Inputs

fh: filehandle to use for buffered I/O.

buf: area to read bytes into.

blocklen: number of bytes per block. Must be > 0.

blocks: number of blocks to read. Must be > 0.

Result

count - Number of _blocks_ read, or 0 for EOF. On an error, the number of blocks actually read is returned.

Bugs

Doesn't clear IoErr() before starting. If you want to find out about errors, use SetIoErr(0L) before calling.

FreeArgs

Name

FreeArgs: Free allocated memory after ReadArga() (V36)

Synopsis

```
FreeArgs(rdargs)
         D1

void FreeArgs(struct RDArgs *)
```

Function

Frees memory allocated to return arguments in from ReadArgs(). If ReadArgs allocated the RDArgs structure it will be freed.

Inputs

rdargs: structure returned from ReadArgs()
See also: ReadArgs(), ReadItem(), FindArg()

FreeDeviceProc

Name

FreeDeviceProc: releases port returned by GetDeviceProc (V36)

Synopsis

```
FreeDeviceProc(devproc)
               D1
void FreeDeviceProc(struct DevProc *)
```

Function

Frees up the structure created by GetDeviceProc(), and any associated temporary locks.

Decrements the counter incremented by GetDeviceProc(). The counter is in an extension to the 1.3 process structure. After calling FreeDeviceProc(), do not use the port or lock again! It is safe to call FreeDeviceProc(NULL).

Inputs

devproc: a value returned by GetDeviceProc()

Bugs

Counter not currently active in 2.0

FreeDosEntry

Name

FreeDosEntry: frees an entry created by MakeDosEntry().

Synopsis

```
FreeDosEntry(dlist)
             D1
void FreeDosEntry(struct DosList *)
```

Function

Frees an entry created by MakeDosEntry(). This routine should be eliminated and replaced by a value passed to FreeDosObject().

Inputs

dlist: DosList to free

FreeDosObject

Name

FreeDosObject: frees an object allocated by AllocDosObject

Synopsis

```
FreeDosObject(type, ptr)
              D1   D2
void FreeDosObject(ULONG, void *)
```

Function

Frees an object allocated by AllocDosObject(). Do NOT call for objects allocated in any other way.

Inputs

type: type passed to AllocDosObject().

ptr: ptr returned by AllocDosObject().

See also: AllocDosObject, dos/dos.h

FWrite

Name

FWrite: writes a number of blocks to an output (buffered)

Synopsis

```
count = FWrite(fh, buf, blocklen, blocks)
D0             D1   D2   D3        D4
LONG FWrite(BPTR, UBYTE *, ULONG, ULONG)
```

Function

Attempts to write a number of blocks, each blocklen long, from the specified buffer to the output stream. This routine may return less than the number of blocks requested, if there is some error such as a full disk or read/write error. This call is buffered.

Inputs

fh: filehandle to use for buffered I/O.

buf: area to write bytes from.

blocklen: number of bytes per block. Must be > 0.

blocks: number of blocks to read. Must be > 0.

Result

count: Number of _blocks_ written. On an error, the number of blocks actually written is returned.

Bugs

FWrite doesn't clear IoErr() before starting. If you want to find out about errors, use SetIoErr(0L) before calling.

GetArgStr

Name

GetArgStr: returns the arguments for the process (V36)

Synopsis

```
ptr = GetArgStr()
D0
UBYTE *GetArgStr(void)
```

Function

GetArgStr() returns a pointer to the (NULL-terminated) arguments for the program (process). This is the same string passed in a 0 on startup from CLI.

Result

ptr: pointer to arguments

GetConsoleTask

Name

GetConsoleTask: returns the default console for the process

Synopsis

```
port = GetConsoleTask()
D0
struct MsgPort *GetConsoleTask(void)
```

Function

Returns the default console task's port (pr_ConsoleTask) for the current process

Result

port: the pr_MsgPort of the console handler, or NULL

GetCurrentDirName

Name

GetCurrentDirName: returns the current directory name

Synopsis

```
success = GetCurrentDirName(buf, len)
D0                          D1    D2
BOOL GetCurrentDirName(char *, LONG)
```

Function

Extracts the current directory name from the CLI structure and puts it into the buffer. If the buffer is too small, the name is truncated appropriately and a failure code returned. If no CLI structure is present, a null name is returned in the buffer. The call fails with IoErr() = = ERROR_OBJECT_WRONG_TYPE.

Inputs

buf: buffer to hold extracted name

len: number of bytes of space in buffer

Result

success: success/failure indicator

GetDeviceProc

Name

GetDeviceProc: finds a handler to send a message to

Synopsis

```
devproc = GetDeviceProc(name, devproc)
  D0                     D1    D2
struct DevProc *GetDeviceProc(UBYTE *, struct DevProc *)
```

Function

This routine finds the handler/filesystem to send packets regarding 'name' to. This may involve getting temporary locks. It returns a structure that includes a lock and msgport to send to to attempt your operation. It also includes information on how to handle multiple-directory assigns (by passing the DevProc back to GetDeviceProc() until it returns NULL).

The initial call to GetDeviceProc() should pass NULL for devproc. If after using the returned DevProc, you get an ERROR_OBJECT_NOT_ FOUND, and (devproc->dvp_Flags and DVPF_ASSIGN) is true, you should call GetDeviceProc again, passing it the devproc structure. It will either return a modified DevProc structure, or NULL (with ERROR_NO_MORE_ENTRIES in IoErr()). Continue until it returns NULL.

This call also increments the counter that locks a handler/fs into memory. After calling FreeDeviceProc(), do not use the port or lock again!

Inputs

name: name of the object you wish to access. This can be a relative path ("foo/bar"), relative to the current volume (":foo/bar"), or relative to a device/volume/assign ("foo:bar").

devproc: a value returned by GetDeviceProc() before, or NULL.

Result

devproc: a pointer to a DevProc structure or NULL.

Bugs

Counter not currently active in 2.0. In 2.0 and 2.01, you HAD to check DVPF_ASSIGN before calling it again. This defect was fixed for the 2.02 release.

GetFileSysTask

Name

GetFileSysTask: returns the default filesystem for the process

Synopsis

```
port = GetFileSysTask()
D0
struct MsgPort *GetFileSysTask(void);
```

Function

Returns the default filesystem task's port (pr_FileSystemTask) for the current process

Result

port: the pr_MsgPort of the filesystem, or NULL

GetProgramDir

Name

GetProgramDir: returns a lock on the directory the program was loaded from

Synopsis

```
lock = GetProgramDir()
D0
BPTR GetProgramDir(void)
```

Function

GetProgramDir() returns a shared lock on the directory the program was loaded from. This can be used for a program to find data files, etc. that are stored with the program, or to find the program file itself. NULL returns are valid, and may occur, for example, when running a program from the resident list. You should NOT unlock the lock.

Result

lock: a lock on the directory the current program was loaded from, or NULL if loaded from resident list, etc.

Bugs

Should return a lock for things loaded via resident. Perhaps this routine should return currentdir if NULL.

GetProgramName

Name

GetProgramName: returns the current program name

Synopsis

```
success = GetProgramName(buf, len)
D0                       D1   D2
BOOL GetProgramName(char *, LONG)
```

Function

Extracts the program name from the CLI structure and puts it into the buffer. If the buffer is too small, the name is truncated appropriately and a failure code returned. If no CLI structure is present, a null name is returned in the buffer and failure is indicated by IoErr() = = ERROR_OBJECT_WRONG_TYPE.

Inputs

buf: buffer to hold extracted name.

len: number of bytes of space in buffer.

Result

success: success/failure indicator

GetPrompt

Name

GetPrompt: returns the prompt for the current process (V36)

Synopsis

```
success = GetPrompt(buf, len)
D0                  D1   D2
BOOL GetPrompt(char *, LONG)
```

Function

This routine extracts the prompt string from the CLI structure and puts it into the buffer. If the buffer is too small, the string is truncated appropriately and a failure code returned. If no CLI structure is present, a null string is returned in the buffer and failure is indicated by IoErr() = = ERROR_OBJECT_WRONG_TYPE.

Inputs

> buf: buffer to hold extracted prompt.
>
> len: number of bytes of space in buffer.

Result

> success: success/failure indicator

GetVar

Name

> GetVar: returns the value of a local or global variable

Synopsis

```
len = GetVar( name, buffer, size, flags )
D0              D1    D2      D3    D4
LONG GetVar( UBYTE *, UBYTE *, LONG, ULONG )
```

Function

> This routine gets the value of a local or environment variable. It is advised to only use ASCII strings inside variables, but this is not required. This avoids putting characters into the destination when a \n is hit, unless GVF_BINARY_VAR is specified. (The \n is not stored in the buffer.)

Inputs

> name: pointer to a variable name.
>
> buffer: a user-allocated area that will be used to store the value associated with the variable.
>
> size: length of the buffer region in bytes.
>
> flags: combination of type of var to get value of (low 8 bits), and flags to control the behavior of this routine. Currently defined flags include:
>
>> GVF_GLOBAL_ONLY: tries to get a global env variable.
>>
>> GVF_LOCAL_ONLY: tries to get a local variable.
>>
>> GVF_BINARY_VAR: doesn't stop at \n.

The default is to try to get a local variable first, then to try to get a global environment variable.

Result

len: size of environment variable. -1 indicates that the variable was NOT DEFINED. If the value would overflow the user buffer, the buffer is truncated. The buffer returned is null-terminated (even if GVF_BINARY_VAR is used.) The number of characters put in the buffer (not including '\0') is returned and IoErr() will return the size of the variable.

Bugs

LV_VAR is the only type that can be global. Under V36, we documented (and it returned) the size of the variable, not the number of characters transferred. For V37 this was changed to the number of characters put in the buffer, and the total size of the variable is put in IoErr().

See also: DeleteVar(), FindVar(), SetVar(), dos/var.h

Info

Name

Info: returns information about the disk

Synopsis

```
success = Info( lock, parameterBlock )
D0                D1    D2
BOOL Info(BPTR, struct InfoData *)
```

Function

Info() can be used to find information about any disk in use. 'lock' refers to the disk, or any file on the disk. The parameter block is returned with information about the size of the disk, number of free blocks and any soft errors.

Inputs

lock: BCPL pointer to a lock

parameterBlock: pointer to an InfoData structure (longword–aligned)

Result

success: Boolean

Special note: Note that InfoData structure must be longword-aligned.

Inhibit

Name

Inhibit: inhibits access to a filesystem (V36)

Synopsis

```
success = Inhibit(filesystem, flag)
D0                 D1          D2
BOOL Inhibit(char *,LONG)
```

Function

This routine sends an ACTION_INHIBIT packet to the indicated handler. This action stops all activity by the handler until uninhibited. When the handler is uninhibited, anything may have happened to the disk in the drive, or there may no longer be one.

Inputs

filesystem: name of device to inhibit (with ":").

flag: new status. DOSTRUE = inhibited, FALSE = uninhibited.

Result

success: success/failure indicator

Input

Name

Input: identifies the program's initial input file handle

Synopsis

```
file = Input()
D0
BPTR Input(void)
```

Function

Input() is used to identify the initial input stream allocated when the program was initiated. Never close the filehandle returned by Input()!

Result

file: BCPL pointer to a file handle

See also: Output(), SelectInput()

InternalLoadSeg

Name

InternalLoadSeg: low-level load routine

Synopsis

```
seglist = InternalLoadSeg(fh,table,functionarray,stack)
D0                        D0 A0        A1           A2
BPTR InternalLoadSeg(BPTR,BPTR,LONG *,LONG *)
```

Function

InternalLoadSeg() loads from fh. Table is used when loading an overlay, otherwise should be NULL. Functionarray is a pointer to an array of functions. Note that the current Seek position after loading may be at any point after the last hunk loaded. The filehandle will not be closed. If a stacksize is encoded in the file, the size is stuffed in the LONG pointed to by stack. This LONG should be initialized to your default value: InternalLoadSeg() will not change it if no stacksize is found. Clears unused portions of Code and Data hunks (as well as BSS hunks). (This also applies to LoadSeg() and NewLoadSeg()).

If the file being loaded is an overlaid file, this returns -(seglist). All other results are positive.

Note: Overlay users, InternalLoadSeg() does NOT return seglist in both D0 and D1, as LoadSeg does. The current ovs.asm uses LoadSeg(), and assumes returns are in D1. We support this for LoadSeg() ONLY.

Inputs

fh: filehandle to load from.

table: when loading an overlay, otherwise ignored.

functionarray: array of function to be used for read, alloc, and free.

```
FuncTable[0] -> Actual = ReadFunc(readhandle,buffer, length),DOSBase
                  D0                D1          A0        D0      A6
FuncTable[1] -> Memory = AllocFunc(size,flags), Execbase
                  D0               D0    D1      a6
FuncTable[2] -> FreeFunc(memory,size), Execbase
                         A1     D0      a6
```

stack: pointer to storage (ULONG) for stacksize.

Result

seglist: seglist loaded or NULL. NOT returned in D1!

Bugs

Tags really should be used.

InternalUnLoadSeg

Name

InternalUnLoadSeg: unloads a seglist loaded with InternalLoadSeg()

Synopsis

```
success = InternalUnLoadSeg(seglist,FreeFunc)
  D0                          D1       A1
BOOL InternalUnLoadSeg(BPTR,void (*)(char *,ULONG))
```

Function

Unloads a seglist using freefunc to free segments. Freefunc() is called as for InternalLoadSeg(). **Note:** This function calls Close() for overlaid seglists.

Inputs

seglist: seglist to be unloaded.

FreeFunc: function called to free memory.

Result

success: returns whether everything went OK (since this may close files). Also returns FALSE if seglist was NULL.

Bugs

Tags should really be used.

IoErr

Name

IoErr: returns extra information from the system

Synopsis

```
error = IoErr()
   D0
LONG IoErr(void)
```

Function

Most I/O routines return zero to indicate an error. When this happens, this routine may be called to determine more information. It is also used in some routines to pass back a secondary result. Note that there is no guarantee as to what IoErr() will return after a successful operation unless it is specified in the function.

Result

error - Integer.

See also: Fault(), PrintFault(), SetIoErr()

IsFileSystem

Name

IsFileSystem: returns whether a DOS handler is a filesystem

Synopsis

```
result = IsFileSystem(name)
D0                    D1
BOOL IsFileSystem(char *)
```

Function

This routine returns whether the device is a filesystem or not. A filesystem supports separate files storing information. It may also support subdirectories, but is not required to. If the filesystem doesn't support this new packet, IsFileSystem() uses Lock(":",...) as an indicator.

Inputs

name: name of device in question, with trailing ':'

Result

result: flag to indicate if device is a file system

IsInteractive

Name

IsInteractive: discovers whether a file is a virtual terminal

Synopsis

```
status = IsInteractive( file )
D0                      D1
BOOL IsInteractive(BPTR)
```

Function

The return value "status" indicates whether the file associated with the file handle "file" is connected to a virtual terminal.

Inputs

file: BCPL pointer to a file handle

Result

status: Boolean

LoadSeg

Name

LoadSeg: Scatter-load a loadable file into memory.

Synopsis

```
seglist = LoadSeg( name )
D0                 D1
BPTR LoadSeg(char *)
```

Function

The file 'name' should be a load module produced by the linker. LoadSeg scatter-loads the CODE, DATA, and BSS segments into memory, chaining together the segments with BPTR's on their first words. The end of the chain is indicated by a zero. There can be any number of segments in a file. All necessary relocation is handled by LoadSeg(). In the event of an event, any blocks loaded will be unloaded and a NULL result returned.

If the module is correctly loaded then the output will be a pointer at the beginning of the list of blocks. Loaded code is unloaded via a call to UnLoadSeg().

Inputs

name: pointer to a null-terminated string

Result

seglist: BCPL pointer to a seglist

Lock

Name

Lock: locks a directory or file

Synopsis

```
lock = Lock( name,  accessMode )
D0             D1       D2
BPTR Lock(char *, LONG)
```

Function

A filing system lock on the file or directory "name" is returned if possible.

If the accessMode is ACCESS_READ, the lock is a shared read lock; if the accessMode is ACCESS_WRITE then it is an exclusive write lock. Do not use random values for mode.

If Lock() fails (that is, if it cannot obtain a filing system lock on the file or directory) it returns a zero.

Tricky assumptions about the internal format of a lock are unwise, as are any attempts to use the fl_link or fl_Access fields.

Inputs

name: pointer to a NULL-terminated string.

accessMode: integer.

Result

lock: BCPL pointer to a lock

LockDosList

Name

LockDosList: locks the specified DOS lists for use

Synopsis

```
dlist = LockDosList(flags)
D0                 D1
struct DosList *LockDosList(ULONG)
```

Function

This routine locks the DOS device list in preparation to walk the list.

If the list is "busy" then this routine will not return until it is available. This routine "nests": you can call it multiple times, and then must unlock it the same number of times. The dlist returned is NOT a valid entry: it is a special value. Note that for 1.3 compatibility, it also does a Forbid() — this will probably be removed at some future time. The 1.3 Forbid() locking of this list had some race conditions. The pointer returned by this is NOT an actual DosList pointer — you should use one of the other DosEntry calls to get actual pointers to DosList structures (such as NextDosEntry), passing the value returned by LockDosList() as the dlist value.

Inputs

flags: flags stating which types of nodes you want to lock

Result

dlist: pointer to the head of the list. This is NOT a valid node!

LockRecord

Name

LockRecord: locks a portion of a file

Synopsis

```
success = LockRecord(fh,offset,length,mode,timeout)
D0                   D1  D2    D3    D4   D5
ULONG LockRecord(BPTR,ULONG,ULONG,ULONG,ULONG)
```

Function

This routine locks a portion of a file for exclusive access. Timeout is how long to wait in ticks (1/50 second) for the record to be available.

Valid modes are:

REC_EXCLUSIVE
REC_EXCLUSIVE_IMMED
REC_SHARED
REC_SHARED_IMMED

For the IMMED modes, the timeout is ignored. Record locks are tied to the filehandle used to create them. The same filehandle can get any number of exclusive locks on the same record, for example. These are cooperative locks, they only affect other people calling LockRecord().

Inputs

fh: file handle for which to lock the record.

offset: record start position.

length: length of record in bytes.

mode: type of lock requester.

timeout: timeout interval in ticks. 0 is legal.

Result

success: success or failure

Bugs

In 2.0 through 2.02 (V36), LockRecord() only worked in the ramdisk. Attempting to lock records on the disk filesystem causes a crash. This was fixed for V37.

LockRecords

Name

LockRecords: locks a series of records

Synopsis

```
success = LockRecords(record_array,timeout)
D0                    D1               D2
BOOL LockRecords(struct RecordLock *,ULONG)
```

Function

This locks several records within a file for exclusive access. Timeout is how long to wait in ticks for the records to be available. The wait is applied to each attempt to lock each record in the list. It is recommended that you always lock a set of records in the same order to reduce possibilities of deadlock. The array of RecordLock structures is terminated by an entry with rec_FH of NULL.

Inputs

record_array: list of records to be locked.

timeout: timeout interval. 0 is legal.

Result

success: success or failure.

Bugs

Also see: LockRecord()

MakeDosEntry

Name

MakeDosEntry: creates a DosList structure (V36)

Synopsis

```
newdlist = MakeDosEntry(name, type)
D0                      D1    D2
struct DosList *MakeDosEntry(UBYTE *, LONG)
```

Function

Create a DosList structure, including allocating a name and correctly null-terminating the BSTR. It also sets the dol_Type field, and sets all other fields to 0. This routine should be eliminated and replaced by a value passed to AllocDosObject().

Inputs

name: name for the device/volume/assign node.

type: type of node.

Result

newdlist: the new device entry or NULL

MakeLink

Name

MakeLink: Creates a filesystem link (v36)

Synopsis

```
success = MakeLink( name, dest, soft )
D0                  D1    D2    D3

BOOL MakeLink( UBYTE *, LONG, LONG )
```

Function

Create a filesystem link from 'name' to dest. For "soft-links", dest is a pointer to a null-terminated path string. For "hard-links", dest is a lock (BPTR). 'soft' is FALSE for hard-links, non-zero otherwise.

Soft-links are resolved at access time by a combination of the filesystem (by returning ERROR_IS_SOFT_LINK to dos), and by Dos (using ReadLink() to resolve any links that are hit).

Hard-links are resolved by the filesystem in question. A series of hard-links to a file are all equivalent to the file itself. If one of the links (or the original entry for the file) is deleted, the data remains until there are no links left.

Inputs

    name: Name of the link to create
    dest: CPTR to path string, or BPTR lock
    soft: FALSE for hard-links, non-zero for soft-links

Result

    Success - boolean

Bugs

    In V36, soft-links didn't work in the ROM filesystem. This was fixed for V37.
    See also: ReadLink(), Open(), Lock()

MatchEnd

Name

    MatchEnd: free storage allocated for MatchFirst()/MatchNext()

Synopsis

```
MatchEnd(AnchorPath)
            D1
VOID MatchEnd(struct AnchorPath *)
```

Function

    This routine returns all storage associated with a given search.

Inputs

    AnchorPath: anchor used for MatchFirst()/MatchNext() MUST be longword aligned!

MatchFirst

Name

    MatchFirst: finds file that matches pattern

Synopsis

```
error = MatchFirst(pat, AnchorPath)
D0                  D1          D2
BOOL MatchFirst(UBYTE *, struct AnchorPath *)
```

Function

This routine locates the first file or directory that matches a given pattern. MatchFirst() is passed your pattern (you do not pass it through ParsePattern(); MatchFirst() does that for you), and the control structure. MatchFirst() normally initializes your AnchorPath structure for you, and returns the first file that matched your pattern, or an error. Note that MatchFirst()/MatchNext() are unusual for DOS in that they return 0 for success, or the error code (see dos/dos.h), instead of having the application get the error code from IoErr().

When looking at the result of MatchFirst()/MatchNext(), the ap_Info field of your AnchorPath has the results of an Examine() of the object. You normally get the name of the object from fib_FileName, and the directory it's in from ap_Current->an_Lock. To access this object, normally you would temporarily CurrentDir() to the lock, do an action to the file/dir, and then CurrentDir() back to your original directory. This makes certain you affect the right object even when two volumes of the same name are in the system. You can use ap_Buf (with ap_Strlen) to get a name to report to the user.

The patterns are fairly extensive, and approximate some of the ability of Unix/grep regular expression patterns. Here are the available tokens:

?	Matches a single character.
#	Matches the following expression 0 or more times.
(ab | cd)	Matches any one of the items separated by '|'.
~	Negates the following expression. It matches all strings that do not match the expression (aka ~(foo) matches all strings that are not exactly "foo").
[abc]	Character class: matches any of the characters in the class.
a–z	Character range (only within character classes).
%	Matches 0 characters always (useful in "(foo | bar | %)").
*	Synonym for "#?", not available by default in 2.0. Available as an option that can be turned on.

"Expression" in the above list means either a single character (ex: "#?"), or an alternation (ex: "#(ab \| cd \| ef)"), or a character class (ex: "#[a-zA-Z]").

Inputs

pat: pattern to search for.

AnchorPath: place holder for search. MUST be longword aligned!

Result

error: 0 for success or error code. (Opposite of most DOS calls.)

MatchNext

Name

MatchNext: finds the next file or directory that matches pattern

Synopsis

```
error = MatchNext(AnchorPath)
D0                D1
BOOL MatchNext(struct AnchorPath *)
```

Function

Locates the next file or directory that matches a given pattern. See dos/dosasl.h for more information. Various bits in the flags allow the application to control the operation of MatchNext().

Inputs

AnchorPath: place holder for search. MUST be longword aligned!

Result

error: 0 for success or error code. (Opposite of most DOS calls.)

MatchPattern

Name

MatchPattern — Checks for a pattern match with a string

Synopsis

```
match = MatchPattern(pat, str)
D0                   D1   D2
BOOL MatchPattern(UBYTE *, UBYTE *)
```

Function

Checks for a pattern match with a string. The pattern must be a tokenized string output by ParsePattern(). All matching is currently case-sensitive. You must have at least 1500 free bytes of stack to call this function since it uses deep recursion.

Inputs

pat: special pattern string to match as returned by ParsePattern().

str: string to match against given pattern.

Result

match: success or failure of pattern match. On failure, IoErr() will return 0 or ERROR_TOO_MANY_LEVELS (V37).

MatchPatternNoCase

Name

MatchPatternNoCase: Checks for a pattern match with a string (V36)

Synopsis

```
match = MatchPatternNoCase(pat, str)
D0                         D1   D2

BOOL MatchPatternNoCase(UBYTE *, UBYTE *)
```

Function

Checks for a pattern match with a string. The pattern must be a tokenized string output by ParsePatternNoCase(). This routine is case-insensitive.

NOTE: This routine is highly recursive. You must have at least 1500 free bytes of stack to call this (it will cut off its recursion before going any deeper than that and return failure). That's_currently_enough for about 100 levels deep of #, (, ~, and so on.

Inputs

pat: special pattern string to match as returned by ParsePatternNoCase()
str: String to match against given pattern

Result

match: success or failure of pattern match. On failure, IoErr() will return 0 or ERROR_TOO_MANY_LEVELS (starting with V37—before that there was no stack checking).

See also: ParsePatternNoCase(), MatchPattern(), MatchFirst(), MatchNext()

MaxCli

Name

MaxCli: returns the highest CLI process number possibly in use

Synopsis

```
number = MaxCli()
D0
LONG MaxCli(void)
```

Function

Returns the highest CLI number that may be in use. CLI numbers are reused, and are usually as small as possible. To find all CLIs, scan using FindCliProc() from 1 to MaxCli(). The number returned by MaxCli() may change as processes are created and destroyed.

Result

number: the highest CLI number that _may_ be in use.

NameFromFH

Name

NameFromFH: get the name of an open filehandle (V36)

Synopsis

```
success = NameFromFH(fh, buffer, len)
D0                   D1   D2      D3
BOOL NameFromFH(BPTR, char *, LONG)
```

Function

Returns a fully qualified path for the filehandle. This routine is guaranteed not to write more than len characters into the buffer. The name will be NULL-terminated. See NameFromLock() for more information.

Inputs

fh: lock of object to be examined.

buffer: buffer to store name.

len: length of buffer.

Result

success: success/failure indicator

NameFromLock

Name

NameFromLock: returns the name of a locked object

Synopsis

```
success = NameFromLock(lock, buffer, len)
D0                     D1    D2      D3
```

```
BOOL NameFromLock(BPTR, char *, LONG)
```

Function

Returns a fully qualified path for the lock. This routine is guaranteed not to write more than len characters into the buffer. The name will be null-terminated. Note: if the volume is not mounted, the system will request it (unless, of course, you set pr_WindowPtr to -1). If the volume is not mounted or inserted, it will return an error. If the lock passed in is NULL, "SYS:" is returned. If the buffer is too short, an error will be returned, and IoErr() will return ERROR_LINE_TOO_LONG.

Inputs

lock: lock of object to be examined.

buffer: buffer to store name.

len: length of buffer.

Result

success: success/failure indicator

Bugs

This routine should return the name of the boot volume instead of SYS: for a NULL lock

NewLoadSeg

Name

NewLoadSeg: improved version of LoadSeg for stacksizes

Synopsis

```
seglist = NewLoadSeg(file, tags)
D0                    D1    D2
BPTR NewLoadSeg(UBYTE *, struct TagItem *)
seglist = NewLoadSegTagList(file, tags)
D0                           D1    D2
BPTR NewLoadSegTagList (UBYTE *, struct TagItem *)
```

```
seglist = NewLoadSegTags(file, ...)
BPTR NewLoadSegTags(UBYTE *, ...)
```

Function

Does a LoadSeg() on a file, and takes additional actions based on the tags supplied. Clears unused portions of Code and Data hunks (as well as BSS hunks). (This also applies to InternalLoadSeg and LoadSeg.) NewLoadSeg() does not return seglist in both D0 and D1 as LoadSeg() does. Also, there are no tags defined for NewLoadSeg() at present.

Inputs

file: filename of file to load.

tags: pointer to tagitem array.

Result

seglist: seglist loaded, or NULL

NextDosEntry

Name

NextDosEntry: get the next DOS List entry (V36)

Synopsis

```
newdlist = NextDosEntry(dlist,flags)
D0                       D1     D2
struct DosList *NextDosEntry(struct DosList *,ULONG)
```

Function

Find the next Dos List entry of the right type. You MUST have locked the types you're looking for. Returns NULL if there are no more of that type in the list.

Inputs

dlist: the current device entry.

flags: what type of entries to look for.

Result

newdlist: the next device entry of the right type or NULL

Open

Name

Open: opens a file for input or output

Synopsis

```
file = Open( name, accessMode )
D0             D1    D2
BPTR Open(char *, LONG)
```

Function

The named file is opened and a filehandle returned. If the accessMode is MODE_OLDFILE, an existing file is opened for reading or writing. If the value is MODE_NEWFILE, a new file is created for writing. MODE_READ-WRITE opens a file with a shared lock, but creates it if it didn't exist. Open types are documented in the libraries/dos.h include file and dos/dos.h include files.

The 'name' can be a filename (optionally prefaced by a device name), a simple device such as NIL:, a window specification such as CON: or RAW: followed by window parameters, or *, representing the current window. Note that as of V36, * is obsolete, and CONSOLE: should be used instead. If the file cannot be opened for any reason, the value returned will be zero, and a secondary error code will be available by calling the routine IoErr().

Inputs

name: pointer to a NULL-terminated string.

accessMode: integer.

Result

file: BCPL pointer to a file handle

OpenFromLock

Name

OpenFromLock: opens a file you have a lock on

Synopsis

```
fh = OpenFromLock(lock)
D0                  D1
BPTR OpenFromLock(BPTR)
```

Function

Given a lock, this routine performs an open on that lock. If the open succeeds, the lock is (effectively) relinquished, and should not be UnLock()ed or used. If the open fails, the lock is still usable. The lock associated with the file internally is of the same access mode as the lock you gave up — shared is similar to MODE_OLDFILE, exclusive is similar to MODE_NEWFILE.

Inputs

lock: lock on object to be opened

Result

fh: newly opened filehandle or NULL for failure

Bugs

In the original V36 autodocs, this was shown (incorrectly) as taking a Mode parameter as well. The prototypes and pragmas were also wrong.

Output

Name

Output: identifies the program's initial output file handle

Synopsis

```
file = Output()
D0
BPTR Output(void)
```

Function

Output() is used to identify the initial output stream allocated when the program was initiated. Never close the filehandle returned by Output().

Result

file: BCPL pointer to a filehandle

ParentDir

Name

ParentDir: obtains the parent of a directory or file

Synopsis

```
newlock = ParentDir( lock )
D0                   D1
BPTR ParentDir(BPTR)
```

Function

The argument "lock" is associated with a given file or directory. ParentDir() returns "newlock" which is associated the parent directory of "lock".

Taking the ParentDir() of the root of the current filing system returns a NULL (0) lock. Note this 0 lock represents the root of file system that you booted from (which is, in effect, the parent of all other file system roots.)

Inputs

lock: BCPL pointer to a lock

Result

newlock: BCPL pointer to a lock

ParentOfFH

Name

ParentOfFH: returns a lock on the parent directory of a file

Synopsis

```
lock = ParentOfFH(fh)
D0                D1
BPTR ParentOfFH(BPTR)
```

Function

Returns a shared lock on the parent directory of the filehandle

Inputs

fh: filehandle you want the parent of

Result

lock: lock on parent directory of the filehandle or NULL for failure

ParsePattern

Name

ParsePattern: creates a tokenized string for MatchPattern()

Synopsis

```
IsWild = ParsePattern(Source,Dest,DestLength)
D0                    D1     D2   D3
LONG ParsePattern(UBYTE *, UBYTE *, LONG)
```

Function

Tokenizes a pattern, for use by MatchPattern(). Also indicates if there are any wildcards in the pattern (that is, whether it might match more than one item). Note that Dest must be at LEAST two times as large as Source.

Inputs

source: unparsed wildcard string to search for

dest: output string, gets tokenized version of input

DestLength: length available in destination (should be at least as twice as large as source +2 bytes).

Result

IsWild: 1 means there were wildcards in the pattern, 0 means there were no wildcards in the pattern, -1 means there was a buffer overflow or other error

Bugs

This function should set IoErr() to something useful (not currently set) on an error.

ParsePatternNoCase

Name

ParsePatternNoCase: Create a tokenized string for MatchPatternNoCase() (V36)

Synopsis

```
IsWild = ParsePatternNoCase(Source, Dest, DestLength)
D0                          D1      D2    D3

LONG ParsePatternNoCaae(UBYTE *, UBYTE *, LONG)
```

Function

Tokenizes a pattern, for use by MatchPatternNoCase(). Also indicates if there are any wildcards in the pattern (i.e., whether it might match more than one item). Note that Dest must be at least 2 times as large as Source plus 2 bytes.
  For a description of the wildcards, see ParsePattern().

Inputs

source: unparsed wildcard string to search for.

dest: output string, gets tokenized version of input.
DestLength: length available in destination (should be at least twice as large as source + 2 bytes).

Results

IsWild: 1 means there were wildcards in the pattern,
O means there were no wildcards in the pattern,
-1 means there was a buffer overflow or other error

Bugs

Should set IoErr() to something useful (not currently set) on an error.
See also: ParsePattern(), MatchPatternNoCase(), MatchFirst(), MatchNext()

PathPart

Name

PathPart: returns a pointer to the end of the next-to-last component of a path

Synopsis

```
fileptr = PathPart( path )
D0                  D1
UBYTE *PathPart( UBYTE * )
```

Function

This routine returns a pointer to the character after the next-to-last component of a path specification, which is normally the directory name. If there is only one component, it returns a pointer to the beginning of the string. The only real difference between this and FilePart() is the handling of "/".

Inputs

path: pointer to an path string. May be relative to the current directory or the current disk.

Result

fileptr: pointer to the end of the next-to-last component of the path

Example

PathPart("xxx:yyy/zzz/qqq") would return a pointer to the last "/". PathPart("xxx:yyy") would return a pointer to the first *y*).

See also: FilePart(), AddPart()

PrintFault

Name

PrintFault: returns the text associated with a DOS error code

Synopsis

```
success = PrintFault(code, header)
D0                   D1    D2
BOOL PrintFault(LONG, UBYTE *)
```

Function

This routine obtains the error message text for the given error code. This is similar to the Fault() function, except that the output is written to the default output channel with buffered output. The value returned by IoErr() is set to the code passed in.

Inputs

code: error code.

header: header to output before error text.

Result

success: success/failure code

PutStr

Name

PutStr: writes a string to the default output (buffered)

Synopsis

```
count = PutStr(str)
D0              D1
LONG PutStr(UBYTE *)
```

Function

This routine writes an unformatted string to the default output. No newline is appended to the string and any error is returned. This routine is buffered.

Inputs

str: NULL-terminated string to be written to default output

Result

Error: 0 for success, -1 for any error. This is the opposite of most DOS function returns.

Read

Name

Read: read bytes of data from a file

Synopsis

```
actualLength = Read( file, buffer, length )
D0                   D1    D2      D3
LONG Read(BPTR, void *, LONG)
```

Function

Data can be copied using a combination of Read() and Write(). Read() reads bytes of information from an opened file (represented here by the argument 'file') into the buffer given. The argument "length" is the length of the buffer given.

The value returned is the length of the information actually read.

So, when "actualLength" is greater than zero, the value of "actualLength" is the the number of characters read. Usually Read() will try to fill up your buffer before returning. A value of zero means that end-of-file has been reached. Errors are indicated by a value of -1. This is an unbuffered routine (the request is passed directly to the filesystem). Buffered I/O is more efficient for small reads and writes; see FGetC().

Inputs

file: BCPL pointer to a file handle.

buffer: pointer to buffer.

length: integer.

Result

actualLength: integer

ReadArgs

Name

ReadArgs: parses the command line input

Synopsis

```
result = ReadArgs(template, array, rdargs)
D0                 D1        D2     D3
struct RDArgs * ReadArgs(UBYTE *, LONG *, struct RDArgs *)
```

Function

Parses an argument string according to a template. Normally gets the arguments by reading buffered I/O from Input(), but also can be made to parse a string. MUST be matched by a call to FreeArgs().

ReadArgs parses the commandline according to a template that is passed to it. This specifies the different command-line options and their types. A template consists of a list of options. Options are named in "full" names where possible (for example, "Quick" instead of "Q"). Abbreviations can also be specified by using "abbrev=option" (for example, "Q=Quick").

Options in the template are separated by commas. To get the results of ReadArgs(), you examine the array of longwords you passed to it (one entry per option in the template). This array should be cleared (or initialized to your default values) before passing to ReadArgs(). Exactly what is put in a given entry by ReadArgs() depends on the type of option. The default is a string (a sequence of non-whitespace characters, or delimited by quotes, which will be stripped by ReadArgs), in which case the entry will be a pointer.

Options can be followed by modifiers, which specify things such as the type of the option. Modifiers are specified by following the option with a "/" and a single character modifier. Multiple modifiers can be specified by using multiple "/"s. Valid modifiers are:

/S   Switch. This is considered a boolean variable, and will be set if the option name appears in the command-line. The entry is the boolean (0 for not set, nonzero for set).

/K   Keyword. This means that the option will not be filled unless the keyword appears. For example, if the template is "Name/K", then unless "Name=<string>" or "Name <string>" appears in the command line, Name will not be filled.

/N   Number. This parameter is considered a decimal number, and will be converted by ReadArgs(). If an invalid number is specified, an error is returned. The entry will be a pointer to the longword number (this is how you know if a number was specified).

/T   Toggle. This modifier is similar to a switch, but when specified causes the boolean value to toggle. Similar to /S.

/A   Required. This keyword must be given a value during command-line processing, or an error is returned.

/F   Rest of line. If this modifier is specified, the entire rest of the line is taken as the parameter for the option, even if other option keywords appear in it.

/M   Multiple strings. This means the argument will take any number of strings, returning them as an array of strings. Any arguments not considered to be part of another option will be added to this option. Only one /M should be specified in a template. Example: for a template "Dir/M,All/S" the command-line "foo bar all qwe" will set the boolean "all", and return an array consisting of "foo", "bar", and "qwe". The entry in the array is a pointer to an array of string pointers, the last of which is NULL.

There is an interaction between /M parameters and /A parameters. If there are unfilled /A parameters after parsing, strings will be grabbed from the end of a previous /M parameter list to fill the /A's. This procedure is used for messages like Copy ("From/A/M,To/A"). ReadArgs() returns a struct RDArgs if it succeeds. This action serves as an "anchor" to allow FreeArgs() to free the associated memory. You can also pass in a struct RDArgs to control the operation of ReadArgs() (normally you pass NULL for the parameter, and ReadArgs() allocates one for you).

This mode of action allows you to provide different sources for the arguments, thus providing your own string buffer space for temporary storage, and for extended help text. *See* dos/rdargs.h for more information on this topic.

Note: If you pass in a struct RDArgs, you must still call FreeArgs() to release storage that gets attached to it, but you are responsible for freeing the RDArgs yourself.

Inputs

template: formatting string.

array: array of longwords for results, one per template entry.

rdargs: optional rdargs structure for options. AllocDosObject() should be used for allocating them if you pass one in.

Result

result: a struct RDArgs or NULL for failure

Bugs

Some argument combinations do not work with V36. Use only V37.

ReadItem

Name

ReadItem: reads a single argument/name from command line

Synopsis

```
value = ReadItem(buffer, maxchars, input)
D0                      D1         D2        D3
LONG ReadItem(UBYTE *, LONG, struct CHSource *)
```

Function

Reads a "word" from either Input() (buffered), or via CHSource, if it is non-NULL (*see* dos/rdargs.h for more information). Handles quoting and some "*" substitutions. *See* dos/dos.h for a listing of values returned by ReadItem

(ITEM_XXXX). A "word" is delimited by whitespace, quotes, or EOF. ReadItem() always unreads the last thing read (UnGetC(fh, -1)) so the caller can find out what the terminator was.

Inputs

buffer: buffer to store word in.
maxchars: size of the buffer.
input: CHSource input or NULL (uses FGetC(Input())).

Result

value: *see* dos/dos.h for return values.

ReadLink

Name

ReadLink: Reads the path for a soft filesystem link (V36)

Synopsis

```
success = ReadLink( port, lock, path, buffer, size)
D0                  D1    D2    D3    D4      D5
```

BOOL ReadLink(struct MsgPort *, BPTR, UBYTE *, UBYTE *, ULONG)

Function

ReadLink() takes a lock/name pair (usually from a failed attempt to use them to access an object with packets), and asks the filesystem to find the softlink and fill buffer with the modified path string. You then start the resolution process again by calling GetDeviceProc() with the new string from ReadLink().

Soft-links are resolved at access time by a combination of the filesystem (by returning ERROR_IS_SOFT_LINK to dos), and by Dos (using ReadLink() to resolve any links that are hit).

Inputs

port: msgport of the filesystem
lock: lock this path is relative to on the filesystem

path: path that caused the ERROR_IS_SOFT_LINK
buffer: pointer to buffer for new path from handler
size: size of buffer

Result

Success: boolean

Bugs

In V36, soft-links didn't work in the ROM filesystem. This was fixed for V37.
See also: MakeLink(), Open(), Lock(), GetDeviceProc()

Relabel

Name

Relabel: change the volume name of a volume

Synopsis

```
success = Relabel(volumename,name)
D0                      D1        D2
BOOL Relabel(char *,char *)
```

Function

Changes the name of a volume, if supported by the filesystem

Inputs

volumename: full name of device to rename (with ":").
newname: new name to apply to device (without ":").

Result

success: success/failure indicator

RemAssignList

Name

RemAssignList: Remove an entry from a multi-dir assign (V36)

Synopsis

```
succes = RemAssignList(name, lock)
D0                     D1    D2

BOOL RemAssignList(char *,BPTR)
```

Function

Removes an entry from a multi-directory assign. The entry removed is the first one for which SameLock with 'lock' returns that they are on the same object. The lock for the entry in the list is unlocked (not the entry pased in).

Inputs

name: Name of device to remove lock from (without trailing ':')
lock: Lock associated with the object to remove from the list

Result

success: Success/failure indicator.
See also: Lock(), AssignLock(), AssignPath(), AssignLate(), DupLock(), AssignAdd(), UnLock()

RemDosEntry

Name

RemDosEntry: removes a DOS List entry from its list

Synopsis

```
success = RemDosEntry(dlist)
D0                    D1
BOOL RemDosEntry(struct DosList *)
```

Function

This routine removes an entry from the DOS Device list. The memory associated with the entry is NOT freed. **Note:** You must have locked the DOS List with the appropriate flags before calling this routine.

Inputs

dlist: device list entry to be removed

Result

success: success/failure indicator

RemSegment

Name

RemSegment: removes a resident segment from the resident list

Synopsis

```
success = RemSegment(segment)
D0                   D1
BOOL RemSegment(struct Segment *)
```

Function

Removes a resident segment from the DOS resident segment list, unloads it, and does any other cleanup required. This routine will only succeed if the seg_UC (usecount) is 0.

Inputs

segment: the segment to be removed

Result

success: success or failure

Rename

Name

Rename: renames a directory or file

Synopsis

```
success = Rename( oldName, newName )
D0                 D1        D2
BOOL Rename(char *, char *)
```

Function

Rename() attempts to rename the file or directory specified as "oldName" with the name "newName". If the file or directory "newName" exists, Rename() fails and returns an error. Both "oldName" and the "newName" can contain a directory specification. In this case, the file will be moved from one directory to another.
Note: It is impossible to Rename() a file from one volume to another.

Inputs

oldName: pointer to a null-terminated string.

newName: pointer to a null-terminated string.

Result

success: boolean

ReplyPkt

Name

ReplyPkt: replies a packet to the person who sent it to you

Synopsis

```
ReplyPkt(packet, result1, result2)
         D1      D2       D3
void ReplyPkt(struct DosPacket *, LONG, LONG)
```

Function

This function returns a packet to the process that sent it to you. In addition, it puts your pr_MsgPort address in dp_Port, so using ReplyPkt() again will send the message to you. (This function is used in "ping-ponging" packets between two processes.) ReplyPkt() uses results 1 and 2 to set the dp_Res1 and dp_Res2 fields of the packet.

Inputs

packet: packet to reply, assumed to set up correctly.

result1: first result.

result2: secondary result.

RunCommand

Name

RunCommand: runs a program using the current process (V36)

Synopsis

```
rc = RunCommand(seglist, stacksize, argptr, argsize)
D0                D1         D2          D3       D4
LONG RunCommand(BPTR, ULONG, char *, ULONG)
```

Function

This routine runs a command on your process/CLI. Seglist may be any language, including BCPL programs. Stacksize is in bytes. argptr is a NULLterminated string, argsize is its length. This function returns the returncode the program exited with in d0. It returns -1 if the stack couldn't be allocated. RunCommand also takes care of setting up the current input filehandle in such a way that ReadArgs() can be used in the program, and restores the state of the buffering before returning. It also sets the value returned by GetArgStr(), and restores it before returning. **NOTE:** The setting of the filehandle was added in V37.

Inputs

seglist: seglist of command to run.

stacksize: number of bytes to allocate for stack space.

argptr: pointer to argument command string.

argsize: number of bytes in argument command.

Result

rc: return code from executed command. -1 indicates failure.

SameDevice

Name

SameDevice: Are two locks on a partition of the same device? (V37)

Synopsis

```
same = SameDevice(lockl, lock2)
D0                 D1    D2

BOOL SameDevice( BPTR, BPTR )
```

Function

SameDevice() returns whether two locks refer to partitions that are on the same physical device (if it can figure it out). This may be useful in writing copy routines to take advantage of asynchronous multi-device copies.

Entry existed in V36 and always returned 0.

Inputs

lockl, lock2: locks

Result

same: whether they're on the same device as far as Dos can determine.

SameLock

Name

SameLock: returns whether two locks are on the same object

Synopsis

```
value = SameLock(lock1, lock2)
D0                D1     D2
LONG SameLock(BPTR, BPTR)
```

Function

Compares two locks. Returns LOCK_SAME if they are on the same object, LOCK_SAME_HANDLER if on different objects on the same handler, and LOCK_DIFFERENT if they are on different handlers.

Inputs

lock1: first lock for comparison.

lock2: second lock for comparison.

Result

value: LOCK_SAME, LOCK_SAME_HANDLER, or LOCK_DIFFERENT

Bugs

You should do more extensive checks for NULL against a real lock, checking to see if the real lock is a lock on the root of the boot volume.

Seek

Name

Seek: set the current position for reading and writing.

Synopsis

```
oldPosition = Seek( file, position, mode )
D0                  D1    D2        D3
```

```
LONG Seek(BPTR, LONG, LONG)
```

Function

Seek() sets the read/write cursor for the file "file" to the position "position". This position is used by both Read() and Write() as a place to start reading or writing. The result is the current absolute position in the file, or -1 if an error occurs, in which case IoErr() can be used to find more information. "mode" can be OFFSET_BEGINNING, OFFSET_CURRENT, or OFFSET_END. It is used to specify the relative start position. For example, 20 from current is a position 20 bytes forward from current, -20 is 20 bytes back from current.

To find out where you are, seek zero from current. The end of the file is a Seek() positioned by zero from end. You cannot Seek() beyond the end of a file.

Inputs

file: BCPL pointer to a filehandle.

position: integer.

mode: integer.

Result

oldPosition: integer

SelectInput

Name

SelectInput: select a filehandle as the default input channel

Synopsis

```
old_fh = SelectInput(fh)
D0                    D1
BPTR SelectInput(BPTR)
```

Function

Sets the current input as the default input for the process. This changes the value returned by Input(). old_fh should be closed or saved as needed.

Inputs

fh: newly default input handle

Result

old_fh: previous default input filehandle

SelectOutput

Name

SelectOutput: selects a filehandle as the default input channel

Synopsis

```
old_fh = SelectOutput(fh)
D0                      D1
BPTR SelectOutput(BPTR)
```

Function

SelectOutput() sets the current output as the default output for the process. This routine changes the value returned by Output(). old_fh should be closed or saved as needed.

Inputs

fh : newly desired output handle

Result

old_fh: previous current output

SendPkt

Name

SendPkt: sends a packet to a handler (V36)

Synopsis

```
SendPkt(packet, port, replyport)
         D1       D2      D3
void SendPkt(struct DosPacket *, struct MsgPort *, struct MsgPort *)
```

Function

Sends a packet to a handler and does not wait. All fields in the packet must be initialized before calling this routine. The packet will be returned to replyport. If you wish to use this with WaitPkt(), use the address of your pr_MsgPort for replyport.

Inputs

port: pr_MsgPort of handler process to send to.

packet: packet to send. It must be initialized and have a message.

replyport: MsgPort for the packet to come back to.

SetArgStr

Name

SetArgStr: sets the arguments for the current process

Synopsis

```
oldptr = SetArgStr(ptr)
D0                 D1
UBYTE * void SetArgStr(UBYTE *)
```

Function

This routine sets the arguments for the current program. The ptr MUST be reset to its original value before process exit.

Inputs

ptr: pointer to new argument string.

Result

oldptr: the previous argument string.

SetComment

Name

SetComment: change a file's comment string

Synopsis

```
success = SetComment( name, comment )
D0                    D1     D2
BOOL SetComment(char *, char *)
```

Function

SetComment() sets a comment on a file or directory. The comment is a pointer to a NULL-terminated string of up to 80 characters.

Inputs

name: pointer to a NULL-terminated string.

comment: pointer to a NULL-terminated string.

Result

success: boolean

SetConsoleTask

Name

SetConsoleTask: sets the default console for the process

Synopsis

```
oldport = SetConsoleTask(port)
D0                       D1
struct MsgPort SetConsoleTask(struct MsgPort *)
```

Function

SetConsoleTask() sets the default console task's port (pr_ConsoleTask) for the current process.

Inputs

port: the pr_MsgPort of the default console handler for the process.

Result

oldport: The previous ConsoleTask value.

SetCurrentDirName

Name

SetCurrentDirName: sets the directory name for the process

Synopsis

```
success = SetCurrentDirName(name)
D0                          D1
BOOL SetCurrentDirName(char *)
```

Function

Sets the name for the current dir in the CLI structure. If the name is too long to fit, a failure is returned, and the old value is left intact. It is advised that you inform the user of this condition. This routine is safe to call even if there is no CLI structure.

Inputs

name: name of directory to be set

Result

success: success/failure indicator

Bugs

This function clips to a fixed (1.3-compatible) size

SetFileDate

Name

SetFileDate: sets the modification date for a file or dir (V36)

Synopsis

```
success = SetFileDate(name, date)
D0                    D1    D2
BOOL SetFileDate(char *, struct DateStamp *)
```

Function

Sets the file date for a file or directory. Note that for the Old File System and the Fast File System, the date of the root directory cannot be set. Other filesystems may not support setting the date for all files/directories.

Inputs

name: name of object.

date: new modification date.

Result

success: success/failure indication

SetFileSize

Name

SetFileSize: sets the size of a file

Synopsis

```
newsize = SetFileSize(fh, offset, mode)
D0                    D1  D2      D3
LONG SetFileSize(BPTR, LONG, LONG)
```

Function

Changes the file size, truncating or extending as needed. Not all handlers support this; be careful and check the return code. If the file is extended, no values should be assumed for the new bytes. If the new position is before the filehandle's current position in the file, the file handle will end with a position at the end-of-file.

If there are other filehandles open onto the file, the new size will not leave any filehandle pointing past the end-of-file. You can check for this by looking at the new size.

Do NOT count on any specific values to be in the extended area.

Inputs

fh: file to be truncated/extended.

offset: offset from position determined by mode.

mode: one of OFFSET_BEGINNING, OFFSET_CURRENT, or OFFSET_END.

Result

newsize: position of new end-of-file or -1 for error

SetFileSysTask

Name

SetFileSysTask: sets the default filesystem for the process

Synopsis

```
oldport = SetFileSysTask(port)
D0                       D1
* struct MsgPort void SetFileSysTask(struct MsgPort *)
```

Function

Sets the default filesystem task's port (pr_FileSystemTask) for the current process

Inputs

port: the pr_MsgPort of the default filesystem for the process.

Result

oldport: The previous FileSysTask value.

SetIoErr

Name

SetIoErr: sets the value returned by IoErr() (V36)

Synopsis

```
oldcode = SetIoErr(code)
D0                D1
LONG SetIoErr(LONG);
```

Function

This routine sets up the secondary result (pr_Result2) return code (returned by the IoErr() function).

Inputs

code: code to be returned by a call to IoErr

Result

oldcode: The previous error code.

SetMode

Name

SetMode: Set the current behavior of a handler (V36)

Synopsis

```
success = SetMode(fh, mode)
D0                D1  D2

BOOL SetMode(BPTR, LONG)
```

Function

SetMode() sends an ACTION_SCREEN_MODE packet to the handler in question, normally for changing a CON: handler to raw mode or vice-versa. For CON:, use 1 to go to RAW: mode, 0 for CON: mode.

Inputs

fh: filehandle
mode: The new mode you want

Result

success: Boolean

SetProgramDir

Name

SetProgramDir: sets the directory returned by GetProgramDir (V36)

Synopsis

```
oldlock = SetProgramDir(lock)
D0                      D1
BPTR SetProgramDir(BPTR)
```

Function

Sets a shared lock on the directory the program was loaded from. This lock can be used for a program to find data files, etc. that are stored with the program, or to find the program file itself. NULL is a valid input. This can be accessed via GetProgramDir() or by using paths relative to PROGDIR:.

Inputs

lock: a lock on the directory the current program was loaded from

Result

oldlock: The previous ProgramDir.

SetProgramName

Name

SetProgramName: sets the name of the program being run

Synopsis

```
success = SetProgramName(name)
D0                       D1
BOOL SetProgramName(char *)
```

Function

Sets the name for the program in the CLI structure. If the name is too long to fit, a failure is returned, and the old value is left intact. It is advised that you inform the user if possible of this condition, and/or set the program name to an empty string. This routine is safe to call even if there is no CLI structure.

Inputs

name: name of program to use

Result

success: success/failure indicator

Bugs

This function clips to a fixed (1.3-compatible) size.

SetPrompt

Name

SetPrompt: sets the CLI/Shell prompt for the current process

Synopsis

```
success = SetPrompt(name)
D0                  D1
BOOL SetPrompt(char *)
```

Function

SetPrompt sets the text for the prompt in the CLI structure. If the prompt is too long to fit, a failure is returned, and the old value is left intact. It is advised that you inform the user of this condition. This routine is safe to call even if there is no CLI structure.

Inputs

name: name of prompt to be set

Result

success: success/failure indicator

Bugs

This function clips to a fixed (1.3-compatible) size.

SetProtection

Name

SetProtection: set protection for a file or directory

Synopsis

```
success = SetProtection( name, mask )
D0                      D1    D2:4
BOOL SetProtection (char *, LONG)
```

Function

SetProtection() sets the protection attributes on a file or directory. The lower bits of the mask before V36 are as follows:

bit 4: 1 = file has not changed, 0 = file has been changed.
bit 3: 1 = reads not allowed,   0 = reads allowed.
bit 2: 1 = writes not allowed,   0 = writes allowed.
bit 1: 1 = execution not allowed, 0 = execution allowed.
bit 0: 1 = deletion not allowed, 0 = deletion allowed.

In V36 or later and in the FFS, the read and write bits are respected.

The archive bit is cleared by the file system whenever the file is changed. Backup utilities generally set the bit after backing up each file.

The Fast Filing System looks at the read and write bits, and the Shell looks at the execute bit, and refuses to start a file as a binary executable if it is set.

Other bits may be defined in the dos/dos.h and libraries/dos.h include files. Rather than referring to bits by number you should use the definitions in dos.h.

Inputs

name: pointer to a NULL-terminated string.

mask: the protection mask required.

Result

success: Boolean

SetVar

Name

SetVar: sets a local or environment variable (V36)

Synopsis

```
success = SetVar( name, buffer, size, flags )
D0                D1    D2      D3    D4
BOOL SetVar(UBYTE *, UBYTE *, LONG, ULONG )
```

Function

Sets a local or environment variable. It is advised to only use ASCII strings inside variables, but this is not required.

Inputs

name: pointer to a variable name. Note variable names follow filesystem syntax and semantics.

buffer: a user-allocated area which contains a string that is the value to be associated with this variable.

size: length of the buffer region in bytes. -1 means buffer contains a null-terminated string.

flags: combination of type of var to set (low 8 bits), and flags to control the behavior of this routine. Currently defined flags include:

GVF_LOCAL_ONLY - set a local (to your process) variable.
GVF_GLOBAL_ONLY - set a global environment variable.

The default is to set a local environment variable.

Result

success: if nonzero, the variable was successfully set. FALSE indicates failure.

Bugs

LV_VAR is the only type that can be global.

See also: DeleteVar(), FindVar(), GetVar(), dos/var.h

SetVBuf

Name

SetVBuf: set buffering modes and size (V36)

Synopsis

```
error = SetVBuf(fh, buff, type, size)
D0               D1    D2    D3    D4

LONG SetVBuf(BPTR, UBYTE *, LONG, LONG)
```

Function

Changes the buffering modes and buffer size for a filehandle. With buff == NULL, the current buffer will be deallocated and a new one of (approximately) size will be allocated. If buffer is non-NULL, it will be used for buffering and must be at least max (size,208) bytes long. If buff is NULL and size is -1, then only the buffering mode will be changed.

Inputs

fh: Filehandle
buff: buffer pointer for buffered I/O
type: buffering mode (see <dos/stdio.h>
size: size of buffer for buffered I/O (sizes less than 208 bytes will be ignored).

Result

error: 0 if successful. **NOTE:** opposite of most dos functions!

Bugs

Not implemented yet, always returns 0.
See also: FputC(), FGetC(), UnGetC(), Flush(), Fread(), FWrite(), FGets(), FPuts().

SplitName

Name

SplitName: splits out a component of a pathname into a buffer

Synopsis

```
newpos = SplitName(name, separator, buf, oldpos, size)
D0                 D1       D2       D3    D4     D5
WORD SplitName(UBYTE *, UBYTE, UBYTE *, WORD, LONG)
```

Function

This routine splits out the next piece of a name from a given file name. Each piece is copied into the buffer, truncating at size-1 characters. The new position is then returned so that it may be passed in to the next call to SplitName(). If the separator is not found within 'size' characters, then size-1 characters plus a null are put into the buffer, and the position of the next separator will be returned. If a a separator cannot be found, -1 is returned (but the characters from the old position to the end of the string are copied into the buffer, up to a maximum of size-1 characters). Both strings are null-terminated. This function is mainly intended to support handlers.

Inputs

name: filename being parsed.

separator: separator character to split by.

buf: buffer to hold separated name.

oldpos: current position in the file.

size: size of buf in bytes (including NULL termination).

Result

newpos: new position for next call to SplitName(). -1 is for the last call.

StartNotify

Name

StartNotify: starts notification on a file or directory

Synopsis

```
success = StartNotify(notifystructure)
D0                    D1
BOOL StartNotify(struct NotifyRequest *)
```

Function

Posts a notification request. Do not modify the notify structure while it is active. You will be notified when the file or directory changes. For files, you will be notified after the file is closed. Not all filesystems support this: applications should NOT require it. In particular, most network filesystems won't support it.

Inputs

notifystructure: a filled-in NotifyRequest structure

Result

success: success/failure of request

Bugs

The V36 floppy/HD filesystem doesn't actually send notifications. The V36 ram handler (ram:) does send notifications. This has been fixed in V37.

StrToDate

Name

StrToDate: converts a string to a DateStamp

Synopsis

```
success = StrToDate( datetime )
D0                   D1
BOOL StrToDate( struct DateTime * )
```

Function

StrToDate() converts a human readable ASCII string into an AmigaDOS DateStamp.

Inputs

DateTime: a pointer to an initialized DateTime structure. The DateTime structure should be initialized as follows:

    dat_Stamp: ignored on input.

    dat_Format: a format byte that specifies the format of the dat_StrDat. This can be any of the following. (note: If value used is something other than those below, the default of FORMAT_DOS is used.)

        FORMAT_DOS: AmigaDOS format (dd-mmm-yy).
        FORMAT_INT: International format (yy-mmm-dd).
        FORMAT_USA: American format (mm-dd-yy).
        FORMAT_CDN: Canadian format (dd mm-yy).
        FORMAT_DEF: Default format for locale.

    dat_Flags: a flags byte. The only flags that affect this function are:

DTF_SUBST: ignored by this function.

DTF_FUTURE: if set, indicates that strings such as (stored in dat_StrDate) "Monday" refer to "next" monday. Otherwise, if clear, strings like "Monday" refer to "last" Monday.

dat_StrDay: Ignored by this function.

dat_StrDate: Pointer to valid string representing the date.

This can be a "DTF_SUBST" style string such as "Today" "Tomorrow", "Monday", or it may be a string as specified by the dat_Format byte.This will be converted to the ds_Days portion of the DateStamp. If this pointer is NULL, DateStamp->ds_Days will not be affected.

dat_StrTime: pointer to a buffer that contains the time in the ASCII format hh:mm:ss. This will be converted to the ds_Minutes andds_Ticks portions of the DateStamp. If this pointer is NULL, ds_Minutes and ds_Ticks will be unchanged.

Result

success: a zero return indicates that a conversion could not be performed. A nonzero return indicates that the DateTime. The dat_ Stamp variable contains the converted values.

See also: DateStamp(), DateToStr(), dos/datetime.h

StrToLong

Name

StrToLong: string to long value (decimal)

Synopsis

```
characters = StrToLong(string,value)
D0                    D1      D2
LONG StrToLong(UBYTE *, LONG *)
```

Function

This routine converts decimal string into LONG value. Returns number of characters converted. Skips over leading spaces and tabs (included in count).

If no decimal digits are found (after skipping leading spaces and tabs), StrToLong() returns -1 for characters converted, and puts 0 into value.

Inputs

string: input string.

value: pointer to long value. Set to 0 if no digits are converted.

Result

result: number of characters converted or -1

SystemTagList

Name

SystemTagList: Have a shell execute a command line (V36)

Synopsis

```
error = SystemTagList(command, tags)
D0                    D1       D2

LONG SystemTagList(UBYTE *, struct TagItem *)

error = System(command, tags)
D0             D1       D2

LONG System(UBYTE *, struct TagItem *)

error = SystemTags(command, Tag1, ...)

LONG SystemTags(UBYTE *, ULONG, ...)
```

Function

Similar to Execute(), but does not read commands from the input filehandle. Spawns a Shell process to execute the command, and returns the returncode the command produced, or -1 if the command could not be run for any reason. The input and output filehandles will not be closed by System, you must close them (if needed) after System returns, if you specified them via SYS_INPUT or SYS_OUTPUT.

By default the new process will use your current Input() and Output() filehandles. Normal Shell command-line parsing will be done including redirection on 'command'. The current directory and path will be inherited from your process. Your path will be used to find the command (if no path is specified).

If used with the SYS_Asynch flag, it WILL close both its input and output filehandles after running the command (even if these were your Input() and Output()!).

Normally uses the boot (ROM) Shell, but other shells can be specified via SYS_Usershell and SYS_Customshell. Normally, you should send things written by the user to the Usershell. The UserShell defaults to the same shell as the boot shell.

The tags are passed through to CreateNewProc() (tags that conflict with SystemTagList() will be filtered out). This allows setting things like priority, etc for the new process.

Inputs

command: Program and arguments

tags: See <dos/dostags.h>. Note that both SystemTagList()—specific tags and tags from CreateNewProc() may be passed.

Result

error: 0 for success, result from command, or -1. Note that on error, the caller is responsible for any filehandles or other things passed in via tags.

See also: Execute(), CreateNewProc(), <dos/dostags.h>, Input(), Output()

UnGetC

Name

UnGetC: makes a char available for reading again (buffered)

Synopsis

```
value = UnGetC(fh, character)
D0              D1    D2
LONG UnGetC(BPTR, LONG)
```

Function

Pushes the character specified back into the input buffer. Every time you use a buffered read routine, you can always push back one character. You may be able to push back more, though it is not recommended, since there is no guarantee on how many can be pushed back at a given moment. Passing -1 for the character will cause the last character read to be pushed back.

Note: UnGetC() can be used to make sure that a filehandle is set up as a read filehandle. This is only of importance if you are writing a Shell, and must manipulate the filehandle's buffer.

Inputs

fh: file handle to use for buffered I/O.

character: character to push back or -1.

Result

value: character pushed back, or FALSE if the character cannot be pushed back.

Bugs

In V36, UnGetC(fh, -1) after an EOF would not cause the next character read to be an EOF. This is fixed in V37.

UnLoadSeg

Name

UnLoadSeg: unloads a seglist previously loaded by LoadSeg()

Synopsis

```
success = UnLoadSeg( seglist )
D0                   D1
BOOL UnLoadSeg(BPTR)
```

Function

Unloads a seglist loaded by LoadSeg(). The seglist may be zero. Overlaid segments will have all needed cleanup done, including closing files.

Inputs

seglist: BCPL pointer to a segment identifier

Result

success: returns 0 if a NULL seglist was passed or if it failed to close an overlay file.

Note: This function returned a random value before V36!

UnLock

Name

UnLock: unlocks a directory or file

Synopsis

```
UnLock( lock )
         D1
void UnLock(BPTR)
```

Function

The filing system lock [obtained from Lock(), DupLock(), or CreateDir()] is removed and deallocated.

Inputs

lock: BCPL pointer to a lock.

Note: Passing zero to UnLock() is harmless.

UnLockDosList

Name

UnLockDosList: unlocks the DOS List

Synopsis

```
UnLockDosList(flags)
              D1
void UnLockDosList(ULONG)
```

Function

Unlocks the access on the DOS Device list. You MUST pass the same flags you used to lock the list.

Inputs

flags: MUST be the same flags passed to (Attempt)LockDosList().

UnLockRecord

Name

UnLockRecord: unlocks a record

Synopsis

```
success = UnLockRecord(fh,offset,length)
D0                     D1 D2     D3
BOOL UnLockRecord(BPTR,ULONG,ULONG)
```

Function

This routine releases the specified lock on a file. Note that you must use the same file handle you used to lock the record, and offset and length must be the same values used to lock it. Every LockRecord() call must be balanced with an UnLockRecord() call.

Inputs

> fh: filehandle of locked file.
>
> offset: record start position.
>
> length: length of record in bytes.

Result

> success: success or failure

Bugs

> *See* LockRecord()

UnLockRecords

Name

> UnLockRecords: unlocks a list of records

Synopsis

```
success = UnLockRecords(record_array)
D0                      D1
BOOL UnLockRecords(struct RecordLock *)
```

Function

> This routine releases an array of record locks obtained using LockRecords(). You should NOT modify the record_array while you have the records locked. Every LockRecords() call must be balanced with an UnLockRecords() call.

Inputs

> record_array: list of records to be unlocked

Result

> success: success or failure

Bugs

See LockRecord().

VFPrintf

Name

VFPrintf: formats and prints a string to a file (buffered)

Synopsis

```
count = VFPrintf(fh, fmt, argv)
D0                 D1   D2    D3
LONG VFPrintf(BPTR, char *, LONG *)
count = FPrintf(fh, fmt, ...)
LONG FPrintf(BPTR, char *, ...)
```

Function

VFPrint() writes the formatted string and values to the given file. This routine is assumed to handle all internal buffering so that the formatting string and resultant formatted values can be arbitrarily long. Any secondary error code is returned in IoErr(). This routine is buffered.

Inputs

fh: filehandle to write to.

fmt: RawDoFmt style formatting string.

argv: pointer to array of formatting values.

Result

count: number of bytes written or -1 (EOF) for an error.

VFWritef

Name

VFWritef: writes a BCPL formatted string to a file (buffered)

Synopsis

```
count = VFWritef(fh, fmt, argv)
D0                D1   D2   D3
LONG VFWritef(BPTR, char *, LONG *)
count = FWritef(fh, fmt, ...)
LONG FWritef(BPTR, char *, ...)
```

Function

Writes the formatted string and values to the default output. This routine is assumed to handle all internal buffering so that the formatting string and resultant formatted values can be arbitrarily long. The formats are in BCPL form. This routine is buffered.

Supported formats are: (**Note:** x is in base 36!)

%S—string (CSTR)
%Tx—writes a left-justified string in a field at least x bytes long.
%C—writes a single character
%Ox—writes a number in octal, maximum x characters wide
%Xx—writes a number in hex, maximum x characters wide
%Ix—writes a number in decimal, maximum x characters wide
%N—writes a number in decimal, any length
%Ux—writes an unsigned number, maximum x characters wide
%$—ignore parameter

Inputs

fmt: BCPL style formatting string.

argv: pointer to array of formatting values.

Result

count: number of bytes written or -1 for error.

VPrintf

Name

VPrintf: formats and prints string (buffered)

Synopsis

```
count = VPrintf(fmt, argv)
  D0            D1   D2
LONG VPrintf(char *, LONG *)
count = Printf(fmt, ...)
LONG Printf(char *)
```

Function

Writes the formatted string and values to Output(). This routine is assumed to handle all internal buffering so that the formatting string and resultant formatted values can be arbitrarily long. Any secondary error code is returned in IoErr(). This routine is buffered.

Note: RawDoFmt assumes 16-bit ints, so you will usually need 'l's in your formats (example: %ld versus %d).

Inputs

fmt: exec.library RawDoFmt() style formatting string.

argv: pointer to array of formatting values.

Result

count: number of bytes written or -1 (EOF) for an error.

WaitForChar

Name

WaitForChar: determines if chars arrive within a time limit

Synopsis

```
status = WaitForChar( file, timeout )
D0                    D1    D2
BOOL WaitForChar(BPTR, LONG)
```

Function

If a character is available to be read from "file" within the time (in microseconds) indicated by "timeout", WaitForChar() returns -1 (TRUE). If a character is available, you can use Read() to read it. Note that WaitForChar() is only valid when the I/O stream is connected to a virtual terminal device. If a character is not available within "timeout", a 0 (FALSE) is returned.

Bugs

Due to a bug in the timer.device in V1.2/V1.3, specifying a timeout of zero for WaitForChar() can cause unreliable timer and floppy disk operation.

Inputs

file: BCPL pointer to a file handle.

timeout: integer.

Result

status: Boolean

WaitPkt

Name

WaitPkt: waits for a packet to arrive at your pr_MsgPort

Synopsis

```
packet = WaitPkt()
D0
struct DosPacket *WaitPkt(void);
```

Function

Waits for a packet to arrive at your pr_MsgPort. If anyone has installed a packet wait function in pr_PktWait, it will be called. The message is automatically GetMsg()ed so that it is no longer on the port. It is assumed that the message is a DOS packet. It is NOT guaranteed that the signal will be cleared for the port.

Result

packet: the packet that arrived at the port (from ln_Name of message)

Write

Name

Write: writes bytes of data to a file

Synopsis

```
returnedLength = Write( file, buffer, length )
D0                      D1    D2      D3
LONG Write (BPTR, void *, LONG)
```

Function

Write() writes bytes of data to the opened file "file". "length" indicates the length of data to be transferred; "buffer" is a pointer to the buffer. The value returned is the length of information actually written. So, when "length" is greater than zero, the value of "length" is the number of characters written. Errors are indicated by a value of -1.

Inputs

file: BCPL pointer to a file handle.

buffer: pointer to the buffer.

length: integer.

Result

returnedLength: integer

WriteChars

Name

WriteChars: Writes bytes to the default output (buffered) (V36)

Synopsis

```
count = WriteChars(buf, buflen)
D0                  D1

LONG PutStr(UBYTE *, LONG)
```

Function

This routine writes a number of bytes to the default output. The length is returned. This rountine is buffered.

Inputs

buf: buffer of characters to write
buflen: number of characters to write

Result

count: Number of bytes written. -1 (EOF) indicates an error
See also: FPuts(), FPutC(), FWrite(), PutStr()

AmigaDOS Function Quick Reference

AbortPkt	Aborts an asynchronous packet, if possible.
AddBuffers	Changes the number of buffers for a filesystem.
AddDosEntry	Adds a DOS List entry to the lists.
AddPart	Appends a file/dir to the end of a path.
AddSegment	Adds a resident segment to the resident list.
AllocDosObject	Creates a DOS object.
AssignAdd	Adds a lock to an assign for multidirectory assigns.
AssignLate	Creates an assignment to a specified path later.
AssignLock	Creates an assignment to a locked object.
AssignPath	Creates an assignment to a specified path.
AttemptLockDosList	Attempts to lock the DOS Lists for use.
ChangeMode	Changes the current mode of a lock or filehandle.
CheckSignal	Checks for break signals.
Cli	Returns a pointer to the CLI structure of the process.
Close	Closes an open file.
CompareDates	Compares two datestamps.
CreateDir	Creates a new directory.
CreateNewProc	Creates a new process.
CreateProc	Creates a new process.
CurrentDir	Makes a directory associated with a lock the working directory.
DateStamp	Obtains the date and time in internal format.
DateToStr	Converts a DateStamp to a string.
Delay	Delays a process for a specified time.
DeleteFile	Deletes a file or directory.
DeleteVar	Deletes a local or environment variable.
DeviceProc	Returns the process ID of specific IO handler.
DoPkt	Sends a DOS packet and wait for reply.
DupLock	Duplicates a lock.
DupLockFromFH	Gets a lock on an open file.
EndNotify	Ends a notification request.
ErrorReport	Displays a Retry/Cancel requester for an error.
ExAll	Examines an entire directory.
Examine	Examines a directory or file associated with a lock.
ExamineFH	Gets information on an open file.
Execute	Executes a CLI command.
Exit	Exits from a program.
ExNext	Examines the next entry in a directory.
Fault	Returns the text associated with a DOS error code.
FGetC	Reads a character from the specified input (buffered).

FGets	Reads a line from the specified input (buffered).
FilePart	Returns the last component of a path.
FindArg	Finds a keyword in a template.
FindCliProc	Returns a pointer to the requested CLI process.
FindDosEntry	Finds a specific DOS List entry.
FindSegment	Finds a segment on the resident list.
FindVar	Finds a local variable.
Flush	Flushes buffers for a buffered filehandle.
Format	Causes a filesystem to initialize itself.
FPutC	Writes a character to the specified output (buffered).
FPuts	Writes a string to the specified output (buffered).
FRead	Reads a number of blocks from an input (buffered).
FreeArgs	Free allocated memory after ReadArgs().
FreeDeviceProc	Releases port returned by GetDeviceProc.
FreeDosEntry	Frees an entry created by MakeDosEntry.
FreeDosObject	Frees an object allocated by AllocDosObject.
FWrite	Writes a number of blocks to an output (buffered.)
GetArgStr	Returns the arguments for the process.
GetConsoleTask	Returns the default console for the process.
GetCurrentDirName	Returns the current directory name.
GetDeviceProc	Finds a handler to send a message to.
GetFileSysTask	Returns the default filesystem for the process.
GetProgramDir	Returns a lock on the directory the program was loaded from.
GetProgramName	Returns the current program name.
GetPrompt	Returns the prompt for the current process.
GetVar	Returns the value of a local or global variable.
Info	Returns information about the disk.
Inhibit	Inhibits access to a filesystem.
Input	Identifies the program's initial input file handle.
InternalLoadSeg	Low-level load routine.
InternalUnLoadSeg	Unloads a seglist loaded with InternalLoadSeg.
IoErr	Returns extra information from the system.
IsFileSystem	Returns whether a DOS handler is a filesystem.
IsInteractive	Discovers whether a file is a virtual terminal.
LoadSeg	Loads a load module into memory.
Lock	Locks a directory or file.
LockDosList	Locks the specified DOS Lists for use.
LockRecord	Locks a portion of a file.
MakeDosEntry	Creates a DOSList structure.
MakeLink	Creates a filesystem link.
MatchEnd	Frees storage allocated for MatchFirst/MatchNext.

MatchFirst	Finds file that matches pattern.
MatchNext	Finds the next file or directory that matches pattern.
MatchPattern	Checks for a pattern match with a string.
MatchPatternNoCase	Checks for a pattern match with a string.
MaxCli	Returns the highest CLI process number possibly in use.
NameFromFH	Gets the name of an open filehandle.
NameFromLock	Returns the name of a locked object.
NewLoadSeg	Improved version of LoadSeg for stacksizes.
NextDosEntry	Gets the next DOSList entry.
Open	Opens a file for input or output.
OpenFromLock	Opens a file you have a lock on.
Output	Identifies the program's initial output file handle.
ParentDir	Obtains the parent of a directory or file.
ParentOfFH	Returns a lock on the parent directory of a file.
ParsePattern	Creates a tokenized string for MatchPattern.
ParsePatternNoCase	Create a tokenized string for MatchPatternNoCase().
PathPart	Returns a pointer to the end of the next-to-last component of a path.
PrintFault	Returns the text associated with a DOS error code.
PutStr	Writes a string to the default output (buffered).
Read	Reads bytes of data from a file.
ReadArgs	Parses the command line input.
ReadItem	Reads a single argument/name from command line.
ReadLink	Reads the path for a soft filesystem link.
Relabel	Changes the volume name of a volume.
RemAssignList	Remove an entry from a multi-directory assign.
RemDosEntry	Removes a DOSList entry from its list.
RemSegment	Removes a resident segment from the resident list.
Rename	Renames a directory or file.
ReplyPkt	Replies a packet to the person who sent it to you.
RunCommand	Runs a program using the current process.
SameDevice	Are two locks on a partition of the same device?
SameLock	Returns whether two locks are on the same object.
Seek	Finds and points at the logical position in a file.
SelectInput	Selects a file handle as the default input channel.
SelectOutput	Selects a file handle as the default output channel.
SendPkt	Sends a packet to a handler.
SetArgStr	Sets the arguments for the current process.
SetComment	Changes a file's comment string.
SetConsoleTask	Sets the default console for the process.
SetCurrentDirName	Sets the directory name for the process.

SetFileDate	Sets the modification date for a file or dir.
SetFileSize	Sets the size of a file.
SetFileSysTask	Sets the default filesystem for the process.
SetIoErr	Sets the value returned by IoErr().
SetMode	Set the current behavior of a handler.
SetProgramDir	Sets the directory returned by GetProgramDir.
SetProgramName	Sets the name of the program being run.
SetPrompt	Sets the CLI/Shell prompt for the current process.
SetProtection	Sets protection for a file or directory.
SetVar	Sets a local or environment variable.
SetVBuf	Set buffering modes and size.
SplitName	Splits out a component of a pathname into a buffer.
StartNotify	Starts notification on a file or directory.
StrToDate	Converts a string to a DateStamp.
StrToLong	String to long value (decimal).
SystemTagList	Have a shell execute a command line.
UnGetC	Makes a char available for reading again (buffered).
UnLoadSeg	Unloads a seglist previously loaded by LoadSeg().
UnLock	Unlocks a directory or file.
UnLockDosList	Unlocks the DOSList.
UnLockRecord	Unlocks a record.
UnLockRecords	Unlocks a list of records.
VFPrintf	Formats and prints a string to a file (buffered).
VFWritef	Writes a BCPL formatted string to a file (buffered).
VPrintf	Formats and print string (buffered).
WaitForChar	Determines if chars arrive within a time limit.
WaitPkt	Waits for a packet to arrive at your pr_MsgPort.
Write	Writes bytes of data to a file.
WriteChars	Writes bytes to the default output (buffered).

Chapter 7

The Linker

A **linker** is a tool used to create a single, binary load file from one or more object files generated with C, Assembler, or other Amiga programming languages. This chapter describes the AmigaDOS linker ALINK.

The ALINK linker is supplied by Commodore, however, many programming languages come with their own linker created by the compiler manufacturer. You should refer to your compiler manual for detailed information on the linker used with your programming language.

Introduction

ALINK produces a single binary output file from one or more input files. These input files, known as **object files**, may contain external symbol information. To produce object files, you use your assembler or language translator. Before producing the output, or **load file**, the linker resolves all references to symbols.

The linker can also produce a link map and symbol cross-reference table.

Associated with the linker is an **overlay supervisor**. You can use the overlay supervisor to overlay programs written in a variety of languages. The linker produces load files suitable for overlaying in this way.

You can drive the linker in two ways:

1. As a **Command line**. You can specify most of the information necessary for running the linker in the command parameters.
2. As a **Parameter file**. As an alternative, if a program is being linked repetitively, you can use a parameter file to specify all the data for the linker.

See the description of the WITH option of ALINK below.

These two methods can take three types of input files:

1. **Primary binary input**. This term refers to one or more object files that form the initial binary input to the linker. These files are always output to the load file, and the primary input must not be empty.

2. **Overlay files**. If overlaying, the primary input forms the root of the overlay tree, and the overlay files form the rest of the structure.

3. **Libraries**. This refers to specified code that the linker incorporates automatically. Libraries may be resident or scanned. A **resident library** is a load file that may be resident in memory, or loaded as part of the "library open" call in the operating system. A **scanned library** is an object file within an archive format file. The linker only loads the file if there are any outstanding external references to the library.

The linker works in two passes.

In the first pass, the linker reads all the primary, library, and overlay files, and records the code segments and external symbol information. At the end of the first pass, the linker outputs the map and cross-reference table, if required.

If you specify an output file, then the linker makes a second pass through the input. First it copies the primary input files to the output, resolving symbol references in the process, and then it copies out the required library code segments in the same way. Note that the library code segments form part of the root of the overlay tree. Next, the linker produces data for the overlay supervisor, and finally outputs the overlay files.

In the first pass, after reading the primary and overlay input files, the linker inspects its table of symbols, and if there are any remaining unresolved references, it reads the files, if any, that you specified as the library input. The linker then marks any code segments containing external definitions for these unresolved references for subsequent inclusion in the load file. The linker only includes those library code segments that you have referenced.

Using the Linker

To use the linker, you must know the command syntax, the type of input and output that the linker uses, and the possible errors that may occur. This section attempts to explain these things.

Command Line Syntax

The ALINK command has the following parameters:

```
ALINK [FROM | ROOT] files [TO file] [WITH file]
[VER file] [LIBRARY | LIB files] [MAP file]
[XREF file] [WIDTH n]
```

The keyword template is

```
"FROM = ROOT,TO/K,WITH/K,VER/K,LIBRARY = LIB/K,
MAP/K,XREF/K,WIDTH/K"
```

In the above, "file" means a single file name, "files" means zero or more file names, separated by a comma or plus sign, and "n" is an integer.

The following are examples of valid uses of the ALINK command:

```
ALINK a
ALINK ROOT a +b + c + d MAP map-file WIDTH 120
ALINK a,b,c TO output LIBRARY :flib/lib,obj/newlib
```

When you give a list of files, the linker reads them in the order you specify. The parameters have the following meanings:

FROM: Specifies the object files that you want as the primary binary input. The linker always copies the contents of these files to the load file to form part of the overlay root. At least one primary binary input file must be specified. ROOT is a synonym for FROM.

TO: Specifies the destination for the load file. If this parameter is not given, the linker omits the second pass.

WITH: Specifies files containing the linker parameters, for example, normal command lines. Usually you only use one file here, but, for completeness, you can give a list of files. Note that parameters on the command line override those in WITH files. You can find a full description of the syntax of these files in " WITH Files," below.

VER: Specifies the destination of messages from the linker. If you do not specify VER, the linker sends all messages to the standard output (usually the console).

LIBRARY: Specifies the files that you want to be scanned as the library. The linker includes only reference code segments. LIB is a valid alternative for LIBRARY.

MAP: Specifies the destination of the link map.

XREF: Specifies the destination of the cross-reference output.

WIDTH: Specifies the output width that the linker can use when producing the link map and cross-reference table. For example, if you send output to a printer, you may need this parameter.

WITH Files

WITH files contain parameters for the linker. You use them to save typing a long and complex ALINK command line many times.

A WITH file consists of a series of parameters, one per line, each consisting of a keyword followed by data. You can terminate lines with a semicolon (;), where the linker ignores the rest of the line. You can then use the rest of the line after the semicolon to include a comment. The linker ignores blank lines.

The keywords available are as follows:

```
FROM (or ROOT) files
TO   file
LIBRARY    files
MAP [file]
XREF [file]
OVERLAY
tree specification
#
WIDTH      n
```

where "file" is a single filename, "files" is one or more filenames, "[file]" is an optional filename, and "n" is an integer. You may use an asterisk symbol (*) to split long lines; placing one at the end of a line tells the printer to read the next line as a continuation line. If the filename after MAP or XREF is omitted, the output goes to the VER file (the terminal by default).

Parameters on the command line override those in a WITH file, so that you can make small variations on standard links by combining command line parameters and WITH files. Similarly, if you specify a parameter more than once in WITH files, the linker uses the first occurrence.

Note: In the second example below, this is true even if the first value given to a parameter is null.

Examples of WITH files and the corresponding ALINK calls:

```
ALINK WITH link-file
```

where "link-file" contains

```
FROM obj/main,obj/s
TO   bin/test
LIBRARY   obj/lib
MAP
XREF xo
```

is the same as specifying

```
ALINK FROM obj/main,obj/s TO bin/test LIBRARY obj/lib
XREF xo
```

The command

```
ALINK WITH link LIBRARY ""
```

where "link" contains

```
FROM bin/prog,bin/subs
LIBRARY    nag/fortlib
TO    linklib/prog
```

is the same as the command line

```
ALINK FROM bin/prog,bin/subs TO linklib.prog
```

Note: In the example above, the null parameter for LIBRARY on the command line overrides the value "nag/fortlib" in the WITH file, and so the linker does not read any libraries.

Errors and Other Exceptions

Various errors can occur while the linker is running. Most of the messages are self-explanatory and refer to the failure to open files, or to errors in command or binary file format. After an error, the linker terminates at once.

There are a few messages that are warnings only. The most important ones refer to undefined or multiply defined symbols. The linker should not terminate after receiving a warning.

If any undefined symbols remain at the end of the first pass, the linker produces a warning, and outputs a table of such symbols. During the second pass, references to these symbols become references to **location zero.**

If the linker finds more than one definition of a symbol during the first pass, it puts out a warning, and ignores the later definition. The linker does not produce this message if the second definition occurs in a library file, so that you can replace library routines without it producing spurious messages. A serious error follows if the linker finds inconsistent symbol references, and linking then terminates at once.

Since the linker only uses the first definition of any symbol, it is important that you understand the following order in which files are read.

1. Primary (FROM or ROOT) input.
2. Overlay files.
3. LIBRARY files.

Within each group, the linker reads the files in the order that you specify in the file list. Thus definitions in the primary input override those in the overlay files, and those in the libraries have lowest priority.

MAP and XREF Output

The link map, which the linker produces after the first pass, lists all the code segments that the linker outputs to the load file in the second pass, in the order that they must be written.

For each code segment, the linker outputs a header, starting with the name of the file (truncated to eight letters), the code segment reference number, the type (that is, DATA, CODE, BSS, or COMMON), and size. If the code segment was in an overlay file, the linker also gives the overlay level and overlay ordinate.

After the header, the linker prints each symbol defined in the code segment, together with its value. It prints the symbols in ascending order of their values, appending an asterisk (*) to absolute values.

The value of the WIDTH parameter determines the number of symbols printed per line. If this is too small, then the linker prints one symbol on each line.

The cross-reference output also lists each code segment, with the same header as in the map.

The header is followed by a list of the symbols with their references. Each reference consists of a pair of integers, giving the offset of the reference and the number of the code segment in which it occurs. The code segment number refers to the number given in each header.

Overlays

The automatic overlay system provided by the linker and the overlay supervisor allows programs to occupy less memory when running, without any alterations to the program structure.

When using overlaying, you should consider the program as a **tree** structure. That is, with the **root** of the tree as the primary binary input, together with library code segments and COMMON blocks. This root is always resident in memory. The overlay files then form the other nodes of the tree, according to specifications in the OVERLAY directive.

The output from the linker when overlaying, as in the usual case, is a single binary file, which consists of all the code segments, together with information giving the location within the file of each node of the overlay tree. When you load the program only the root is brought into memory. An overlay supervisor takes care of loading and unloading the overlay segments automatically. The linker includes this overlay supervisor in the output file produced from a link using overlays. The overlay supervisor is invisible to the program running.

OVERLAY Directive

To specify the tree structure of a program to the linker, you use the OVERLAY directive. This directive is exceptional in that you can only use it in WITH files. As with other parameters, the linker uses the first OVERLAY directive you give it.

The format of the directive is:

OVERLAY

Xfiles

.

.

.

#

Note: The overlay directive can span many lines. The linker recognizes a hash sign (#) or the end-of-file as a terminator for the directive.

Each line after OVERLAY specifies one node of the tree, and consists of a count "X" and a file list.

The level of a node specifies its "depth" in the tree, starting at zero, which is the level of the root. The count "X", given in the directive, consists of zero or more asterisks, and the overlay level of the node is given by $X + 1$.

As well as the level, each node other than the root has an **ordinate** value. This refers to the order in which the linker should read the descendents of each node, and starts at 1, for the first "offspring" of a parent node.

Note: There may be nodes with the same level and ordinate, but with different parents.

While reading the OVERLAY directive, the linker remembers the current level, and, for each new node, compares the level specified with this value. If less, then the new node is a descendent of a previous one. If equal, the new node has the same parent as the current one. If greater, the new node is a direct descendent of the current one, and so the new level must be one greater than the current value.

A number of examples may help to clarify this:

THE LINKER

Directive	Level	Ordinate	Tree
OVERLAY			ROOT
a	1	1	/|\
b	1	2	a b c
c	1	3	
#			
OVERLAY			ROOT
a	1	1	/\
b	1	2	a b
*c	2	1	/\
*d	2	2	c d
#			
OVERLAY			ROOT
a	1	1	
b	1	2	//|\\
*c	2	1	a b e f 1
*d	2	2	/\ /|\
e	1	3	c d g h k
f	1	4	/\
*g	2	1	i j
*h	2	2	
**i	3	1	
**j	3	2	
*k	2	3	
1	1	5	
#			

Figure 7-A.

The level and ordinate values given above refer to the node specified on the same line. Note that all the files given in the examples above could have been file lists. Single letters are for clarity. For example, Figure 7-B:

```
ROOT bin/mainaaa
OVERLAY
bin/mainbbb,bin/mainccc,bin/mainddd
*bin/makereal
*bin/trbblock,bin/transint,bin/transr
*bin/transcri
bin/outcode
    #
```

Figure 7-B.

specifies the tree in the following figure:

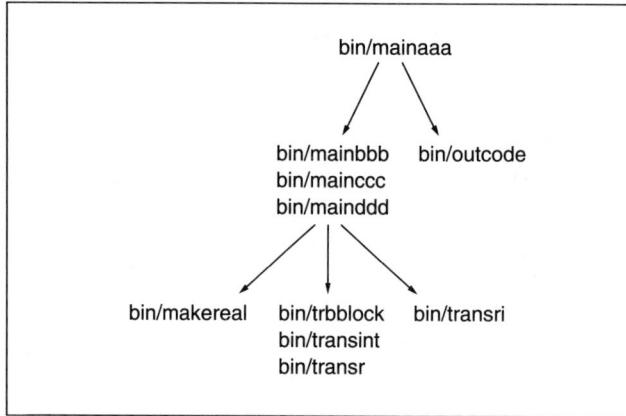

Figure 7-C.

During linking, the linker reads the overlay files in the order you specified in the directive, line by line. The linker preserves this order in the map and cross reference output, and so you can deduce the exact tree structure from the overlay level and ordinate the linker prints with each code segment.

References to Symbols

While linking an overlaid program, the linker checks each symbol reference for validity.

Suppose that the reference is in a tree node "R", and the symbol in a node "S". Then the reference is legal if one of the following statements is true:

1. R and S are the same node.
2. R is a descendent of S.
3. R is the parent of S.

References of the third type above are known as **overlay references**. In this case, the linker enters the overlay supervisor when the program is run. The overlay supervisor then checks to see if the code segment containing the symbol is already in memory. If not, first the code segment, if any, at this level, and all its descendents are unloaded, and then the node containing the symbol is brought into memory. An overlaid code segment returns directly to its caller, and so is not unloaded from memory until another node is loaded on top of it.

For example, suppose that the tree is:

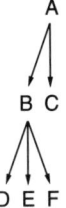

Figure 7-D.

When the linker first loads the program, only A is in memory. When the linker finds a reference in A to a symbol in B, it loads and enters B. If B in turn calls D then again a new node is loaded. When B returns to A, both B and D are left in memory, and the linker does not reload them if the program requires them later. Now suppose that A calls C. First the linker unloads the code segments that it does not require, and which it may overwrite. In this case, these are B and D. Once it has reclaimed the memory for these, the linker can load C.

Thus, when the linker executes a given node, all the node's "ancestors" up to the root are in memory, and possibly some of its descendents.

Cautionary Points

The linker assumes that all overlay references are jumps or subroutine calls, and routes them through the overlay supervisor. Thus, you should not use overlay symbols as data labels.

Try to avoid impure code when overlaying because the linker does not always load a node that is fresh from the load file.

The linker gives each symbol that has an overlay reference an **overlay number**. It uses this value, which is zero or more, to construct the overlay supervisor entry label associated with that symbol. This label is of the form "OVLYnnnn", where nnnn is the overlay number. You should not use symbols with this format elsewhere.

The linker gathers together all program sections with the same section name. It does this so that it can then load them continuously in memory.

Error Codes and Messages

These errors should be rare. If they do occur, the error is probably in the compiler and not in your program. However, you should first check to see that you sent the linker a proper program (for example, an input program must have an introductory program unit that tells the linker to expect a program).

Invalid Object Modules

2	Invalid use of overlay symbol
3	Invalid use of symbol
4	Invalid use of common
5	Invalid use of overlay reference
6	Nonzero overlay reference
7	Invalid external block relocation
8	Invalid bss relocation
9	Invalid program unit relocation
10	Bad offset during 32-bit relocation
11	Bad offset during 6/8-bit relocation
12	Bad offset with 32-bit reference
13	Bad offset with 6/8-bit reference
14	Unexpected end of file
15	Hunk.end missing
16	Invalid termination of file
17	Premature termination of file
18	Premature termination of file

Internal Errors

19	Invalid type in hunk list
20	Internal error during library scan
21	Invalid argument freevector
22	Symbol not defined in second pass

Chapter 8

AmigaDOS Device Input and Output

AmigaDOS uses handlers and filesystems to provide a standard method of interaction with physical I/O devices. Handlers and filesystems are similar; handlers are a subset of a filesystem, supporting only a few I/O operations while filesystems include additional support for file operations as well as directory-type operations. Handlers and filesystems reside either in ROM or in the L: directory.

Handlers and filesystems are often referred to as "AmigaDOS devices" but keep in mind that an AmigaDOS device is different from an Exec device. AmigaDOS devices appear as names within the DOS name space, for example, SER:, RAM: or DF0: (rather than Exec's serial.device or trackdisk.device). AmigaDOS devices are often built on top of Exec devices using the Exec device to perform the low-level functions.

Examples of this type include:

- The Port handler (SER:, PAR:, and PRT:) which is built on top of the serial.device, parallel.device, and printer.device.
- The filesystem, DF0:, DF1: which is built on top of the trackdisk.device.
- CON: (console handler) which is built on top of the console.device.

It is not required for a handler or filesystem to be built on top of an Exec device. In some cases the handler manages its own resources. For example, for the RAM-handler the resource being maintained is RAM. While the memory used by the RAM-handler is still allocated by Exec, there is really no underlying Exec device.

Note that, unlike an Exec device, each handler and filesystem executing must have its own process.

AmigaDOS Devices

Here is a list of AmigaDOS devices implemented as handlers. Note that some handlers have more than one name (RAW: and CON: are the same handler with different names. The port handlers SER:, PAR:, and PRT: are also implemented as a single handler with more than one name).

- AUX: The AUX: handler provides unbuffered serial I/O. It is basically a console handler that uses the serial port rather than the Amiga screen or keyboard. For instance, the command NEWSHELL AUX: allows you to run a SHELL over the serial port.
- CON: Provides buffered keyboard and screen I/O and allows definition of a new window for the output. With CON:, keystrokes are buffered and held back from the application until the user presses the return key. The keyboard input is filtered: function keys and cursor keys are not transmitted. Other keys are automatically echoed in the CON: window.

The window is specified using x/y/width/height/title where x and y are the distance from the top and left edge of the screen the window should open. For instance, the command TYPE >CON:5/5/100/100/Output DEVS:mountlist shows the mountlist file in a new window named Output which is 100 × 100 pixels and is positioned 5 pixels down and to the right of the upper left corner of the screen.

Instead of using a new window for the output, you can send it to the currently selected window by using * instead of CON:x/y/width/height/title.

Under V2.0 and later versions of AmigaDOS, there are new keywords which allow further customizing of the CON: window. These new keywords may appear in any order after the title string in the CON: specifier (use a slash to separate them). The new keywords are:

- AUTO   Don't open window until or unless I/O occurs

CLOSE	Put a close gadget on the window. If the user closes the window, a read from CON: will return -1L; a read from RAW: (or a CON: in raw mode) will return the Raw Event escape string for a Close gadget.
WAIT	Hold off close until user clicks the Close gadget or types control-\.
WINDOW Oxaddr	Use window pointed to by addr (may be a custom screen).
SCREEN name	Open on the public screen specified by name.

The additional CON: keywords BACKDROP, NODRAG, NOBORDER, NOSIZE, SIMPLE, and SMART control the same window attributes as their similarly named Intuition window flags.

Other new features have been added to the CON: handler with V2.0 and later versions of AmigaDOS. The command line can be edited with cursor keys, backspace, and delete. The V2.0 CON: handler supports a 2K line history buffer which allows a line previously typed to be recalled by pressing cursor up. Shift cursor up (or control R) searches back through the line history buffer for the last line entered that matches a partially typed string. Shift cursor down (or control B) brings you to the bottom of the history buffer. Additional edit operations are:

Control K	Deletes everything from the cursor to the end of the line.
Control U	Deletes everything from the cursor to the start of the line.
Control X	Deletes the entire line.
Control W	Moves the cursor to the next tab stop.
Control A	Moves the cursor to the start of the line (Shift cursor left also does this).
Control Z	Moves the cursor to the end of the line (Shift cursor right also does this).

In addition to the line editing features, some text copy and paste features have also been added to the console handler in V2.0. The user can drag-select a text block in a console window with the mouse and then copy the selected text to an internal buffer with Right-Amiga-C. (Extended drag-select is also supported with the Shift keys.) The text may then be pasted into another console window with Right-Amiga-V. Pasted text is inserted into the read stream as if the text had been typed manually.

A special utility called Conclip (part of the standard Startup-sequence in V2.0) provides clipboard support for copy and paste operations. When Conclip is running, console text copied with Right-Amiga-C is placed in the clipboard.device; console paste operations with Right-Amiga-V cause a special code (<CSI>0 v) to be inserted into the read stream instead of the text. The CON: handler reads from the clipboard when this code is received so applications that use CON: get clipboard support automatically. Applications that use the RAW: handler (see below) must provide their own support for clipboard reads.

Note that with the CON: and RAW: handlers, if the SMART flag is used in the window specification then only text paste operations are supported. Text cut operations do not work with the SMART flag.

RAW: Provides unbuffered screen and keyboard I/O and allows definition of a new window for the output just like CON:. (In fact, RAW: and CON: are implemented as a single handler with two names and corresponding modes of operation.) With RAW:, key presses are unbuffered and can be read by an application immediately. The keyboard I/O is unfiltered allowing processing of all key combinations. Keystrokes are not automatically echoed in the RAW: window.

NEWCON: (Obsolete) This handler was included only in V1.3 of the Amiga operating system as an alternative to the original CON: handler. The original CON: handler had no line editing functions but these have been incorporated into CON: in V2.0 and later versions of AmigaDOS.

SER: The SER: handler provides a stream-oriented interface to the serial port (a stream-oriented interface allows you to treat the physical device as a file).

PAR: The PAR: handler provides a stream-oriented interface to the parallel port (a stream-oriented interface allows you to treat the physical device as a file).

PRT: The PRT: handler provides a stream-oriented interface to the printer and also accepts standard printer codes, translating them into the command sequence used for the currently selected printer driver.

NIL: The NIL: handler provides a convenient place to send command output that you are not interested in. For instance, MOUNT>NIL: AUX: mount the AUX: device without printing any diagnostic messages on the screen. Note that the NIL: handler is really a fake handler maintained within AmigaDOS. It is not a separate process.

PIPE: The PIPE: handler is a mechanism meant to provide convenient buffered I/O communication between programs. When the PIPE: is written to, up to 4K bytes of data are buffered before the writing process is blocked. After one process writes to PIPE: any

	other can read from it. This is useful, for instance, when you're using two application programs and want to transfer a large amount of data from one (write) to the other (read) without creating a temporary file in RAM: or on disk.
SPEAK:	The SPEAK: handler provides speech output for the Amiga. With SPEAK you can have the Amiga literally read the contents of a file out loud. For instance, COPY DEVS:mountlist SPEAK:OPT/f/s160 will say the contents of the mountlist in a female voice at a moderate speed. SPEAK accepts all the options of the SAY command and also o0 and o1 (enables or disables processing of options in the input stream), a0 and a1 (toggles direct phoneme mode), and d0 and d1 (enables sentence pause on LF or CR).

Communicating with AmigaDOS Devices

The usual method of communicating with handlers and filesystems is through the AmigaDOS file I/O functions such as Open(), Read(), and Write(). A lower level method is through the DOS packet interface, the basic communication method between different processes. Built on top of the Exec message passing system, the packet interface provides a standard means of interprocess communication.

This communication may take place either synchronously or asynchronously (usually through a routine called DoPkt(), which does the work of finding the task address, sending the message via PutMsg(), and Waiting on the reserved DOS packet signal). The DOS library calls that talk to handlers—Read(), Write(), Open()—use the packet interface.

The dos.library translates these calls into packets, sends them to the appropriate handler process, and returns the results to the calling routine. There is very little extra overhead associated with using the library calls over the using packet interface directly. What is lost, though, is the ability to easily perform asynchronous I/O, so you may want to use the packet interface directly for this instead of using the function interface. For more information on packets, *see* the section entitled "AmigaDOS Packets" in Chapter 11.

Part III

THE TECHNICAL REFERENCE MANUAL

Chapter 9

The Filing System

This chapter describes the AmigaDOS filing system. It includes information on how to patch a disk corrupted by hardware errors.

AmigaDOS File Structure

The AmigaDOS file handler uses a disk that is formatted with blocks of equal size. It provides an indefinitely deep hierarchy of directories, where each directory may contain other directories and files, or just files. The structure is a pure tree—that is, loops are not allowed.

There is sufficient redundancy in the mechanism to allow you to patch together most, if not all, of the contents of a disk after a serious hardware error. Before you can patch together the contents of a disk, you must understand the layout. The subsections below describe the layout of disk blocks.

There are two basic kinds of disk blocks on the Amiga because AmigaDOS has two different filing systems, OFS and FFS. OFS stands for old filing system and is the filing system used in V1.2 and earlier versions of AmigaDOS. FFS stands for fast filing system and is the newer, faster filing system used in V1.3 and all later versions of AmigaDOS. FFS is backward-compatible, which means that it can read and write disks created under the old filing system. For each kind of AmigaDOS disk block both the OFS and FFS structure of the block is listed.

Root Block

The root of the tree is the root block, which is at a fixed place on the disk. The root is like any other directory, except that it has no parent, and its secondary type is different. AmigaDOS stores the name of the disk volume in the name field of the root block.

Each filing system block contains a checksum, where the sum (ignoring overflow) of all the words in the block is zero.

The figures below describe the layout of the root block for the Old Filing System (OFS) and Fast Filing System (FFS).

THE FILING SYSTEM

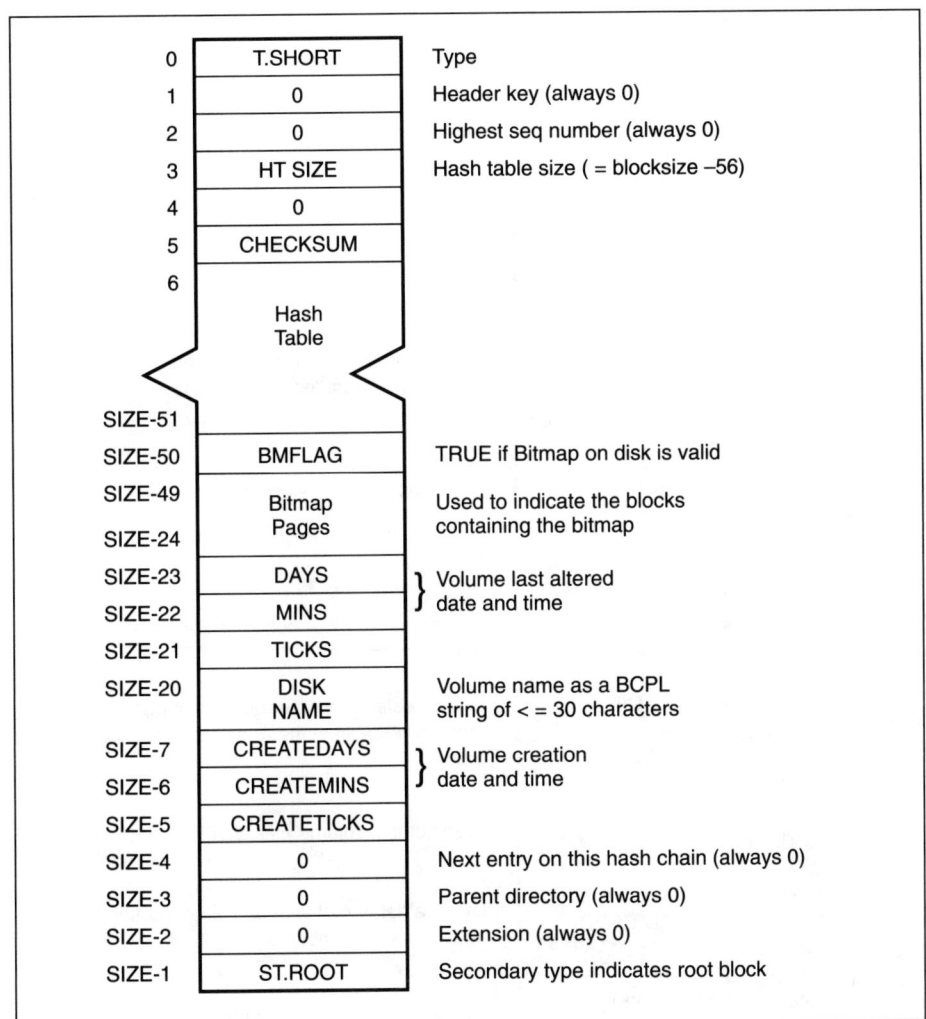

Figure 9-A.
OFS root block.

FFS Root Block

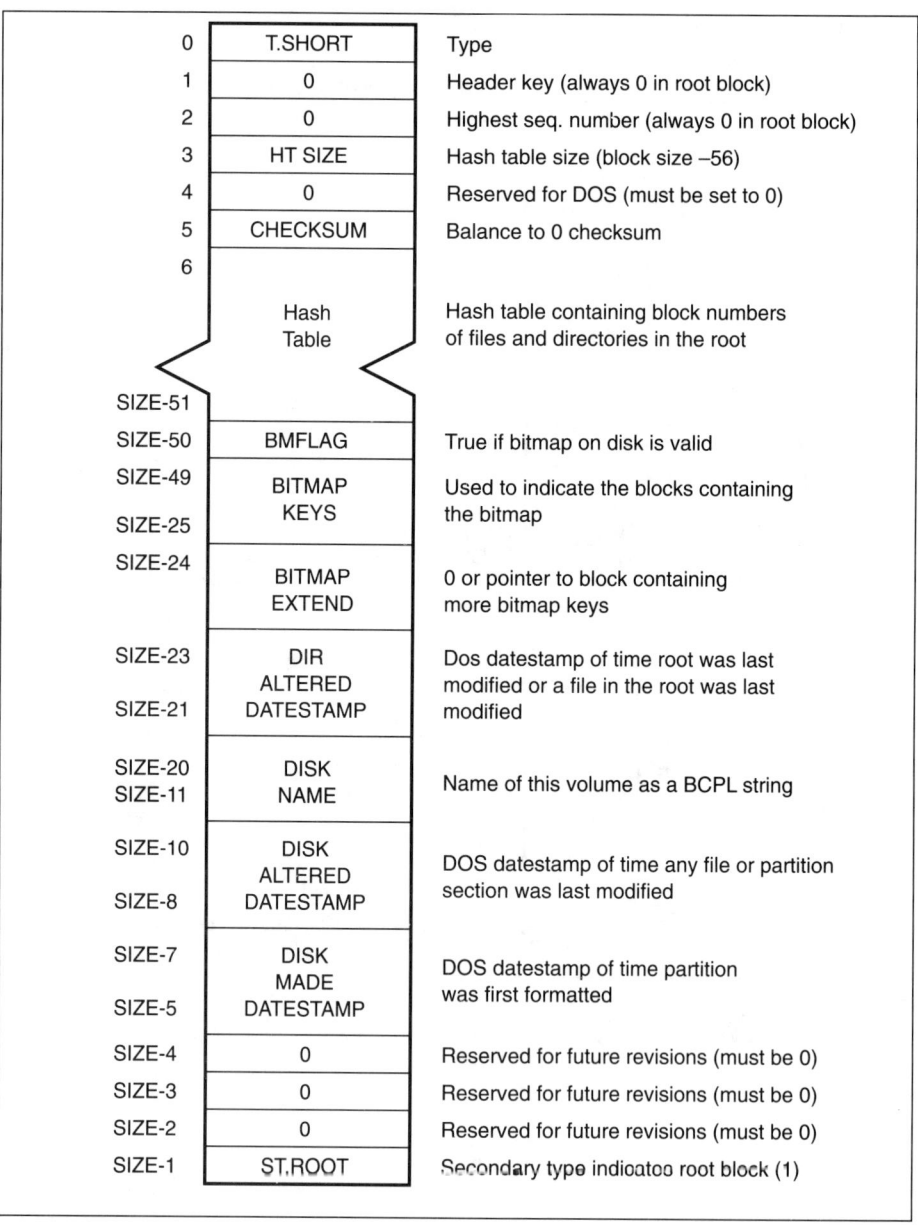

Figure 9-B.
FFS root block.

THE FILING SYSTEM

Shown below is a C language example of how to calculate the location of the root block for an Amiga disk. This program also shows how to extract other useful information from the internal lists maintained by AmigaDOS.

```
;/* rootblock.c - Execute me to compile me with SAS C 5.10
LC -b1 -cfistq -v -y -j73 rootblock.c
Blink  FROM LIB:c.o,rootblock.o  TO  rootblock  LIBRARY
LIB:LC.lib,LIB:Amiga.lib
quit
*/

/* Code to find the root block, Exec device name, unit number, and
 * other information for a DOS drive or partition name
 *
 * REQUIRES V36 or a later version of the dos.library
 */

#include <exec/types.h>
#include <exec/memory.h>
#include <dos/dos.h>
#include <dos/dosextens.h>
#include <dos/filehandler.h>

#include <clib/exec_protos.h>
#include <clib/dos_protos.h>
#include <stdlib.h>
#include <stdio.h>
#include <string.h>

#ifdef LATTICE
int CXBRK(void) { return(0); }    /* Disable Lattice CTRL/C handling */
int chkabort(void) { return(0); }  /* really */
#endif


#define MINARGS 2

UBYTE *vers = "\0$VER: rootblock 37.1";
UBYTE *Copyright -
    "rootblock v37.1\nCopyright (c) 1990 Commodore-Amiga, Inc.  All Rights
Reserved";
UBYTE *usage = "Usage: rootblock drive:";

void bye(UBYTE *s, int e);
void cleanup(void);

#define BTOCSTR(bstr)    ((UBYTE *)((UBYTE *)(BADDR(bstr)) + 1))
```

```
void main(int argc, char **argv)
    {
    extern struct Library *DOSBase;
    struct DosList *doslist;
    struct DeviceNode *dosdev;
    struct FileSysStartupMsg *fss;
    struct DosEnvec *de;
    ULONG   root, blocksPerCyl, blocksPerDisk, bytesPerBlock, bytesPerCyl;
    UBYTE   dosdevname[32];
    int l;

    if(((argc)&&(argc<MINARGS))||(argv[argc-1][0]=='?'))
       {
       printf("%s\n%s\n",Copyright,usage);
       bye("",RETURN_OK);
       }

    if(DOSBase->lib_Version < 36)
       bye("This example requires at least V36 dos.library\n",RETURN_FAIL);

    /* get rid of colon, if any */
    strcpy(dosdevname,argv[1]);
    l = strlen(dosdevname);
    if(dosdevname[l-1]==':') dosdevname[l-1]='\0';

    if(!(doslist = AttemptLockDosList(LDF_DEVICES|LDF_READ)))
       bye("Can't lock dos list\n",RETURN_FAIL);

    if(!(dosdev=(struct DeviceNode *)
       FindDosEntry(doslist,dosdevname,LDF_DEVICES)))
          {
          UnLockDosList(LDF_DEVICES|LDF_READ);
          bye("Can't find device\n",RETURN_FAIL);
          }

    /* dosdev is initialized to point to a DOS DeviceNode */
    fss = (struct FileSysStartupMsg *)BADDR(dosdev->dn_Startup);
    de  = (struct DosEnvec *)BADDR(fss->fssm_Environ);

    blocksPerCyl = de->de_BlocksPerTrack * de->de_Surfaces;
    blocksPerDisk = blocksPerCyl * (de->de_HighCyl - de->de_LowCyl + 1);
    root = (blocksPerDisk - 1 + de->de_Reserved) >> 1;

    /* de_SizeBlock is in longwords */
    bytesPerBlock = de->de_SizeBlock << 2;
    bytesPerCyl = bytesPerBlock * blocksPerCyl;

    printf("Dos Device: %s\n",dosdevname);
    printf("root block: %ld\n",root);
    printf("LowCyl=%ld    HighCyl=%ld    Reserved=%ld\n",
```

```
                de->de_LowCyl, de->de_HighCyl, de->de_Reserved);
        printf("Surfaces=%ld    BlockSize=%ld(longs)    BlocksPerTrack=%ld\n",
                de->de_Surfaces, de->de_SizeBlock, de->de_BlocksPerTrack);

        printf("Exec device name:  %s\n",BTOCSTR(fss->fssm_Device));
        printf("Exec device unit:  %ld\n",fss->fssm_Unit);
        printf("Exec device flags: %ld\n",fss->fssm_Flags);

        /* Unlock doslist it as soon as we are done with it */
        UnLockDosList(LDF_DEVICES|LDF_READ);

        bye("",RETURN_OK);
        }

void bye(UBYTE *s, int e)
        {
        if(*s) printf(s);
        cleanup();
        exit(e);
        }

void cleanup()
        {
        /* nothing */
        }
```

User Directory Blocks

User directory blocks have type T.SHORT and secondary type ST.USERDIR. The six information words at the start of the block also indicate the block's own key (that is, the block number) as a consistency check and the size of the hash table. The 50 information words at the end of the block contain the date and time of creation, the name of the directory, a pointer to the next file or directory on the hash chain, and a pointer to the directory above.

To find a file or subdirectory, you must first apply a hash function to its name. This hash function yields an offset in the hash table, which is the key of the first block on a chain linking those with the same hash value (or zero, if there are none). AmigaDOS reads the block with this key and compares the name of the block with the required name. If the names do not match, it reads the next block on the chain, and so on.

Hashing Algorithm

The hashing algorithm, which is used to determine where a file header goes in the hash table of a directory, is the same for both FFS and the old filing system. The easiest way to describe it is with a small C function. Given a CPTR to a BCPL string, this routine will return the array index into the hash table. This value is used to insert the file header with that name into the appropriate hash table entry in the owning directory.

```
Hash( name )
unsigned char *name;
{
int val,len,i;

    val = len = (int)*name++;
    for(i=0; i<len; i++) val = ((val*13) + (int)toupper( *name++ ))&0x7ff;
    return(val % 72);
}
```

One major difference between FFS and the old filing system is that hash chains must be sorted for FFS. When a hashing collision occurs, files are linked together using the HashChain entry in the FileHeaderBlock or UserDirectoryBlock. The old filing system sticks the new header at the head of the list, while FFS merges the new header into the list in ascending block order.

The figures below show the layout of a user directory block for both the Old Filing System (OFS) and the Fast Filing System (FFS).

THE FILING SYSTEM 343

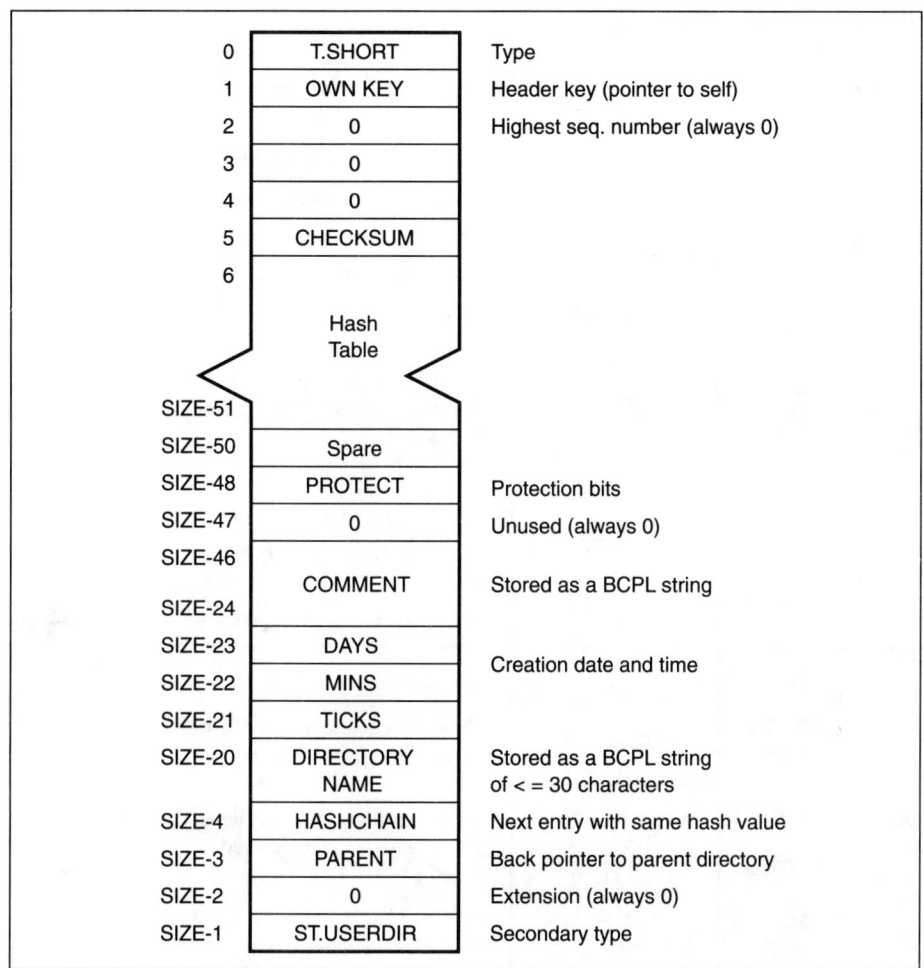

Figure 9-C.
OFS user directory block.

FFS User Directory Blocks

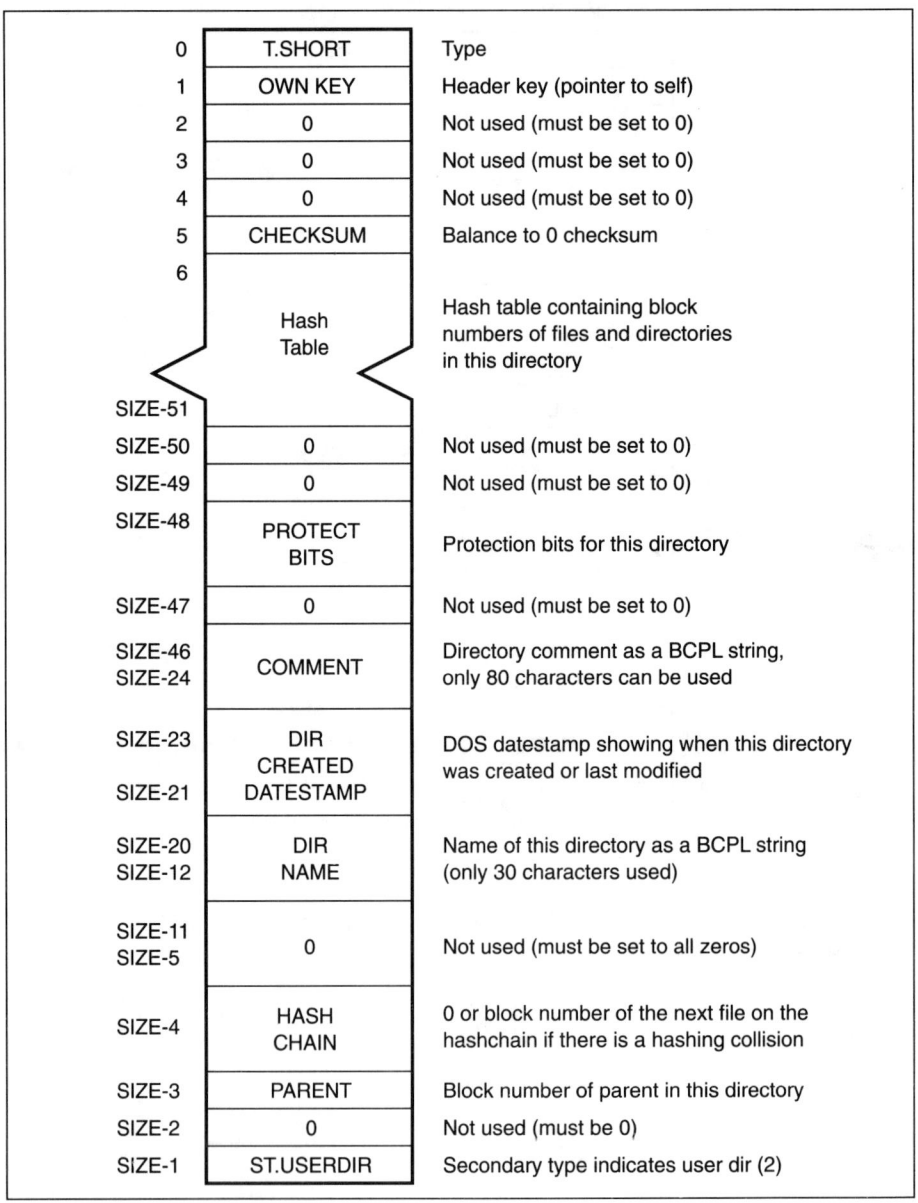

Figure 9-D.
FFS user directory block.

File Header Block

Each terminal file starts with a file header block, which has type T.SHORT and secondary type ST.FILE. The start and end of the block contain name, time, and redundancy information similar to that in a directory block. The body of the file consists of data blocks with sequence numbers from 1 upward. AmigaDOS stores the addresses of these blocks in consecutive words downward from offset size-51 in the block. In general, AmigaDOS does not use all the space for this list and the last data block is not full.

OFS and FFS File Header Block

The following figure describes the layout of the file header block.

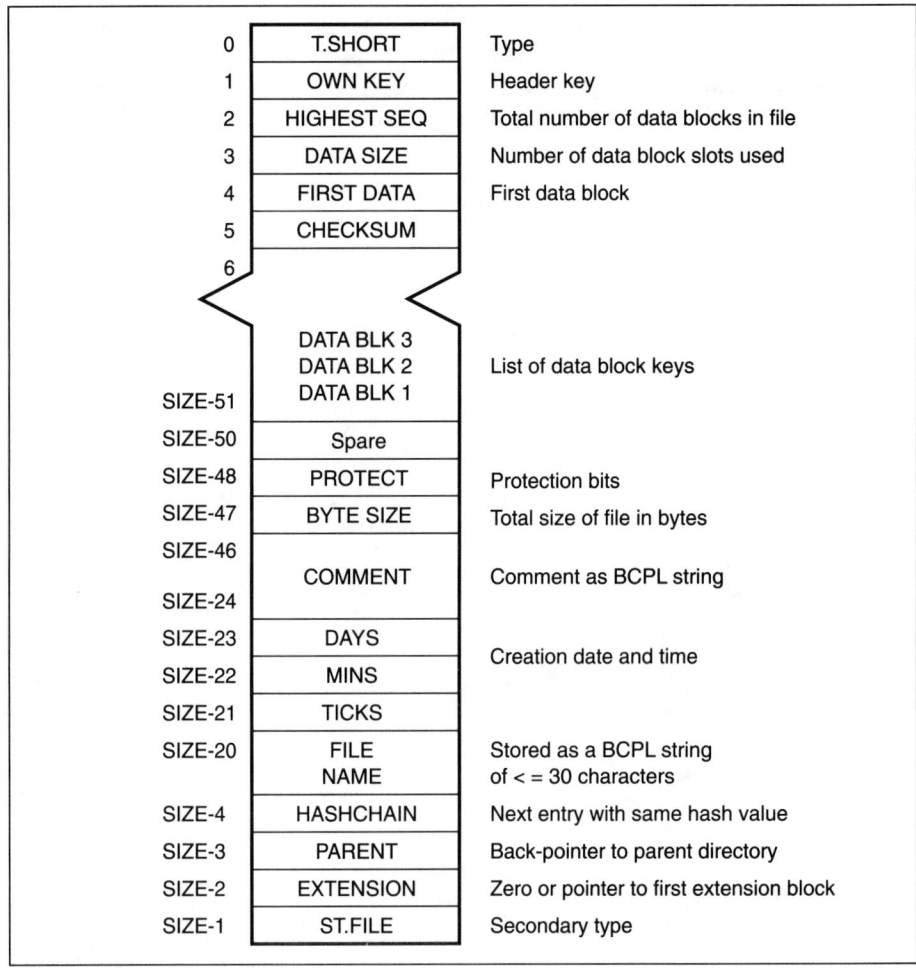

Figure 9-E.
OFS and FFS file header block.

Hard and Soft Links

Hard and soft links are a new feature added to AmigaDOS in V2.0. Hard and soft links allow an AmigaDOS user to refer to a single file or directory by more than one name. A **hard link** associates a new name with a file or directory by linking to its physical location on disk. A **soft link** associates a new name with a file or directory by linking to its path name. Hard and soft links are implemented in the filesystem as modified file header blocks. A new file header block is added for each link created.

The header block for a hard link has a type of T.SHORT (2) and a secondary type of ST_LINKFILE (-4) or ST_LINKDIR (4) depending on whether it is linked to a file or a directory. Hard links point to their object via a block number pointer stored at size-11.

Any AmigaDOS object which has a hard link pointing at it will get a new field at size-10 that is a pointer back to the hard link. In addition, the hard link header block has this new field at size-10 which is used to chain together multiple hard links pointing at the same object.

If a hard link is deleted, it is first removed from the chain of hard links and then its file header block is freed. If the object a hard link points to is deleted, then the first hard link in the chain is altered so that it becomes the new file header block. The original file header block is then freed.

Soft links have type T.SHORT and secondary type of ST_SOFTLINK (3). In this kind of link, the hash table area is used to store a BCPL string representing the path and name of the object being linked to, for example, work:foo/bar/cap. The filesystem does not attempt to access work:foo/bar/cap but tells the caller that the file they are trying to access is a soft link. The caller must then execute the correct DOS call, ReadLink(), to find out what file should really be opened.

If a soft link is deleted then its file header block is freed. If the object a soft link points to is deleted then the soft link is left pointing at a nonexistent file. Subsequent references to the soft link will return the "object not found" error from AmigaDOS. Note that, although soft links are implemented in the filesystem, they are not supported by the MAKELINK command at the time of this writing.

File List Block

If there are more blocks in the file than can be specified in the block list, then the EXTENSION field is nonzero and points to another disk block which contains a further data block list.

OFS and FFS File List Block

The following figure explains the structure of the file list block.

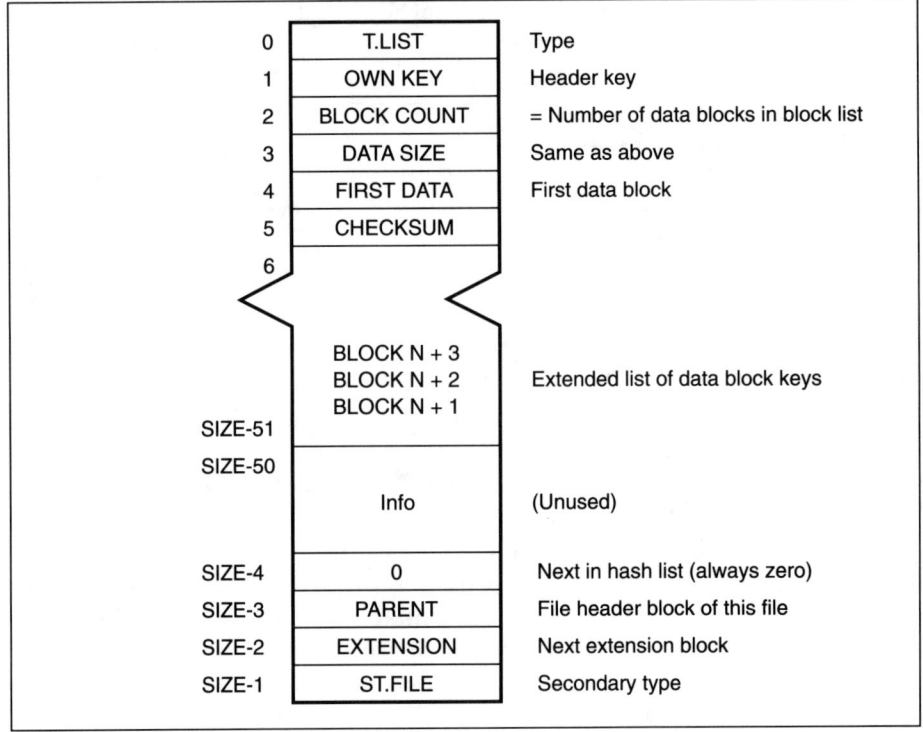

Figure 9-F.
OFS and FFS file list block.

There are as many file extension blocks as required to list the data blocks that make up the file. The layout of the block is very similar to that of a file header block, except that the type is different and the date and filename fields are not used.

Data Block

Data blocks contain only six words of filing system information. These six words refer to the following:

- Type (T.DATA)
- Pointer to the file header block
- Sequence number of the data block
- Number of words of data

- Pointer to the next data block
- Checksum

Normally, all data blocks except the last are full (that is, they have a size =blocksize-6). The last data block has a forward pointer of zero.

FFS data blocks contain only data.

OFS Data Block

The following figure explains the layout of a data block for the Old Filing System (OFS).

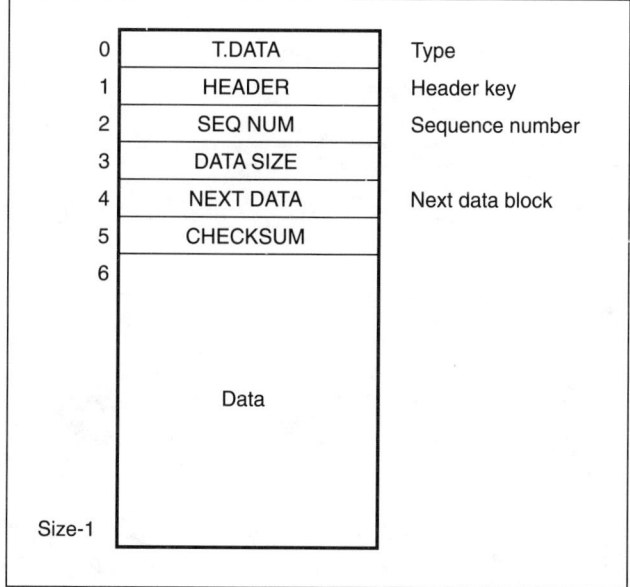

Figure 9-G.
OFS data block.

FFS Data Block

The data block used by the Fast Filing System (FFS) contains only data.

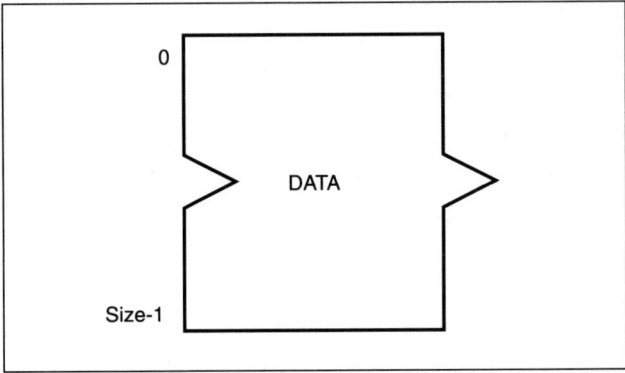

Figure 9-H.
FFS data block.

Chapter 10

Amiga Binary File Structure

Introduction

This chapter details the structure of binary object files for the Amiga, as produced by assemblers and compilers. It also describes the format of binary load files, which are produced by the linker and read into memory by the loader. The format of load files supports overlaying. Apart from describing the format of load files, this chapter explains the use of common symbols, absolute external references, and program units.

Terminology

Some of the technical terms used in this chapter are explained below.

External References

You can use a name to specify a reference between separate program units. The data structure lets you have a name longer than 16M bytes, although the linker restricts names to 255 characters. When you link the object files into a single load file, you must ensure that all external references match corresponding external definitions. The external reference may be of byte size, word, or longword; external definitions refer to relocatable values, absolute values, or resident libraries. Relocatable byte and word references refer to PC-relative address modes and these are entirely handled by the linker. However, if you have a program containing longword relocatable references, relocation may take place when you load the program.

Note that these sizes only refer to the length of the relocation field; it is possible to load a word from a long external address, for example, and the linker makes no attempt to check that you are consistent in your use of externals.

Object File

An assembler or compiler produces a binary image, called an object file. An object file contains one or more program units. It may also contain external references to other object files.

Load File

The linker produces a binary image from a number of object files. This binary image is called a load file. A load file does not contain any unresolved external references.

Program Unit

A program unit is the smallest element the linker can handle. A program unit can contain one or more hunks; object files can contain one or more program units. If the linker finds a suitable external reference within a program unit when it inspects the scanned libraries, it includes the entire program unit in the load file. An assembler usually produces a single program unit from one assembly (containing one or more hunks); a compiler such as FORTRAN produces a program unit for each subroutine, main program, or data block. Hunk numbering starts from zero within each program unit; the only way you can reference other program units is through external references.

Hunks

A **hunk** consists of a block of code or data, relocation information, and a list of defined or referenced external symbols. Data hunks may specify initialized data or uninitialized data (bss). A bss hunk may contain external definitions but no external references nor any values requiring relocation. If you place initialized data blocks in overlays, the linker should not normally alter these data blocks, since it reloads them from disk during the overlay process. Hunks may be named or unnamed, and they may contain a symbol table to provide symbolic debugging information. They may also contain further debugging information for the use of high-level language debugging tools. Each hunk within a program unit has a number, starting from zero.

Resident Library

Load files are also known as resident libraries. Load files may be resident in memory; alternatively, the operating system may load them as part of the "library open" call. You can reference resident libraries through external references; the definitions are in a hunk containing no code, just a list of resident library definitions. Usually, to produce these hunks, you assemble a file containing nothing but absolute external definitions and then pass it through a special software tool to convert the absolute definitions to resident library definitions. The linker uses the hunk name as the name of the resident library, and it passes this through into the load file so that the loader can open the resident library before use.

Scanned Library

A scanned library consists of object files that contain program units which are only loaded if there are any outstanding external references to them. You may use object files as libraries and provide them as primary input to the linker, in which case the input includes all the program units the object files contain. Note that you may concatenate object files.

Node

A node consists of at least one hunk. An overlaid load file contains a root node, which is resident in memory all the time that the program is running, and a number of overlay nodes that are brought into memory as required.

Object File Structure

An object file is the output of the assembler or a language translator. To use an object file, you must first resolve all the external references. To do this, you pass the object file through the linker. An object file consists of one or more program units. Each program unit starts with a header and is followed by a series of hunks joined end to end, each of which contains a number of "blocks" of various types. Each block starts with a longword which defines its type, and this is followed by zero or more additional longwords. Note that each block is always rounded up to the nearest longword boundary. The program unit header is also a block with this format.

The format of a program unit is as follows:

· Program unit header block.
· Hunks.

The basic format of a hunk is as follows:

· Hunk name block.
· Relocatable block.
· Relocation information block.
· External symbol information block.
· Symbol table block.
· Debug block.
· End block.

You may omit all these block types, except the end block.

The following subsections describe the format of each of these blocks. The value of the type word appears in decimal and hex after the type name, for example, hunk_unit has the value 999 in decimal and 3E7 in hex.

hunk_unit (999/3E7)

This block specifies the start of a program unit. It consists of a type word, followed by the length of the unit name in longwords, followed by the name itself padded to a longword boundary with zeros, if required. In diagrammatic form, the format is as follows:

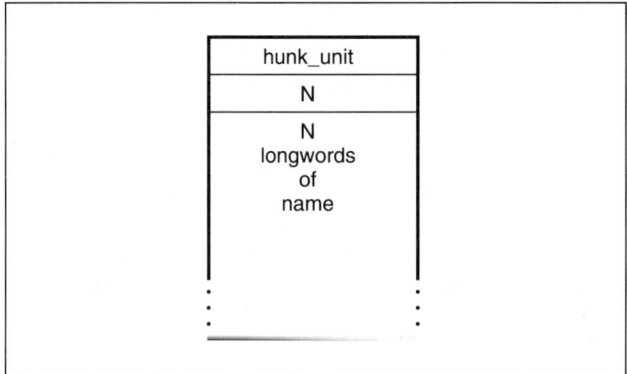

Figure 10-A.
hunk_unit (999/3E7).

hunk_name (1000/3E8)

This block defines the name of a hunk. Names are optional; if the linker finds two or more named hunks with the same name, it combines the hunks into a single hunk. Note that 8- or 16-bit program counter relative external references can only be resolved between hunks with the same name. Any external references in a load format file are between different hunks and require 32-bit relocatable references; although, as the loader scatterloads the hunks into memory, you cannot assume that they are within 32K of each other. Note that the length is in longwords and the name block, like all blocks, is rounded up to a longword boundary by padding with zeros. The format is as follows:

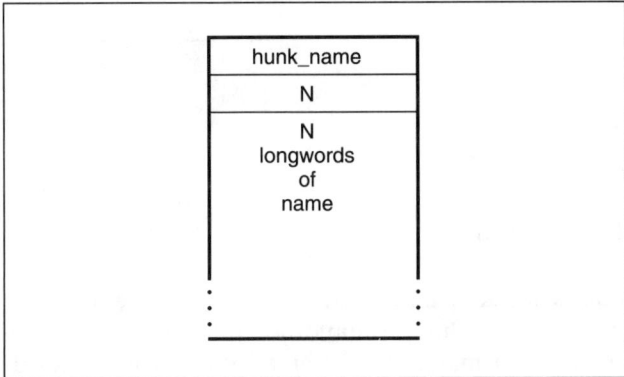

Figure 10-B.
hunk_name (1000/3E8).

hunk_code (1001/3E9)

This block defines a block of code that is to be loaded into memory and possibly relocated. Its format is as follows:

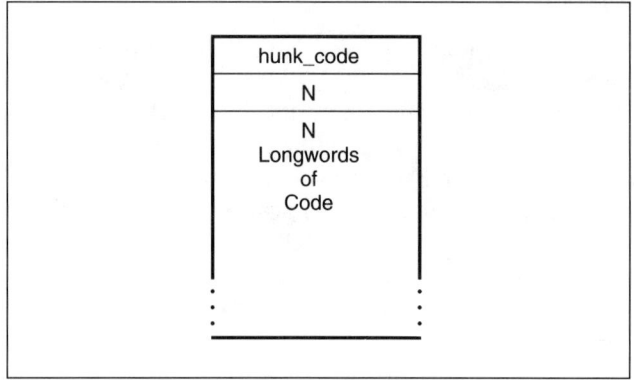

Figure 10-C.

hunk_code (1001/3E9).

hunk_data (1002/3EA)

This block defines a block of initialized data that is to be loaded into memory and possibly relocated. The linker should not alter these blocks if they are part of an overlay node, as it may need to reread them from disk during overlay handling. The format is as follows:

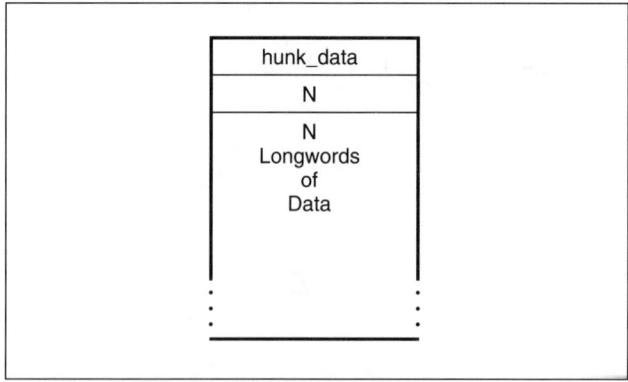

Figure 10-D.

hunk_data (1002/3EA).

hunk_bss (1003/3EB)

This block specifies a block of uninitialized workspace that is allocated by the loader. The hunk_bss blocks are used for such things as stacks and for FOR-TRAN COMMON blocks. It is not possible to relocate inside a bss block, but symbols can be defined within one. Its format is as follows:

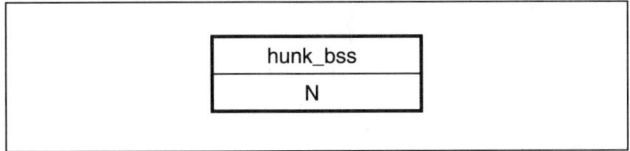

**Figure 10-E.
hunk_bss (1003/3EB).**

where N is the size of block you require in longwords. The memory used for bss blocks is zeroed by the loader when it is allocated.

The relocatable block within a hunk must be one of hunk_code, hunk_data, or hunk_bss. A hunk_code contains executable machine language. A hunk_data contains initialized data (constants, etc.) and a hunk_bss contains uninitialized data (arrays, variables, etc.).

For these three hunk types, the size longword of the hunk is interpreted in a special way based on the two most significant bits:

```
+------------Bit 31 MEMF_FAST
1 +----------Bit 30 MEMF_CHIP
```

0 0 If neither bit is set, then the loader gets whatever memory is available (this is backward compatible). Preference is given to Fast memory.
1 0 Loader must use Fast memory or fail.
0 1 Loader must use Chip memory or fail.
1 1 If bit 31 and bit 30 are both set then there is extra information available in the next longword. The lower 24 bits of the next longword are passed as a type to AllocMem (), the upper 8 bits are reserved for future expansion (not used currently).

hunk_reloc32 (1004/3EC)

A hunk_reloc32 block specifies 32-bit relocation that the linker is to perform within the current relocatable block. The relocation information is a reference to a location within the current hunk or any other within the program unit. Each hunk within the unit is numbered, starting from zero. The linker adds the address of the base of the specified hunk to each of the longwords in the preceding relocatable block that the list of offsets indicates. The offset list only includes referenced hunks and a count of zero indicates the end of the list. Its format is as follows:

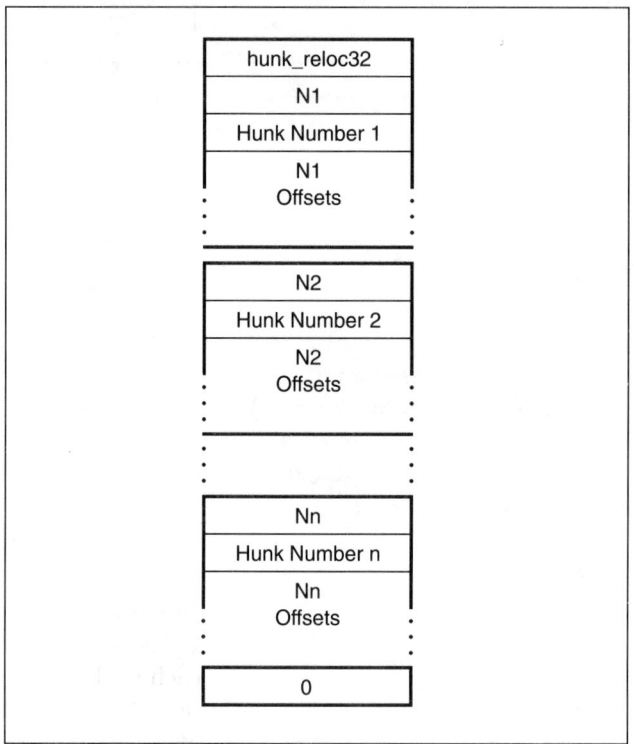

**Figure 10-F.
hunk_reloc32 (1004/3EC).**

hunk_reloc32short (1020/3FC)

A hunk_reloc32short specifies 32-bit relocation that the linker is to perform within the current relocatable block using 16-bit quantities. It has the same format as a hunk_reloc32 (that is, the fields to be modified are 32 bits long), but the actual offsets and hunk numbers are 16 bits wide to save space, and make loading faster.

This is a more efficient way of encoding the relocation information in a file (hunk_reloc32's mostly consist of 0's, since almost all hunks are less than 64K long) and serves as an alternative to hunk_reloc32 for the final output of a linker. This is a new hunk available in V2.0 and later versions of AmigaDOS only.

hunk_reloc16 (1005/3ED)

A hunk_reloc16 block specifies 16-bit relocation that the linker should perform within the current relocatable block. The relocation information refers to 16-bit program counter relative references to other hunks in the program unit. The format is the same as hunk_reloc32 blocks. These references must be to hunks with the same name, so that the linker can perform the relocation while it coagulates (that is, gathers together) similarly named hunks.

hunk_reloc8 (1006/3EE)

A hunk_reloc8 block specifies 8-bit relocation that the linker should perform within the current relocatable block. The relocation information refers to 8-bit program counter relative references to other hunks in the program unit. The format is the same as hunk_reloc32 blocks. These references must be to hunks with the same name, so that the linker can perform the relocation while it coagulates similarly named hunks.

hunk_dreloc32 (1015/3F7)

A hunk_dreloc32 block specifies 32-bit data section relative relocation that the linker is to perform within the current block. This hunk type is used to implement base-relative addressing on the Amiga. The linker adds the offset of the base of the specified hunk (that is, the number of bytes from the base of hunk "_MERGED" to the base of the specified hunk) to each of the longwords in the preceding relocatable block that the list of offsets indicates. The specified hunk must be merged with the data hunk named "_MERGED". The hunk format is identical to "hunk_reloc32".

hunk_dreloc16 (1016/3F8)

A hunk_dreloc16 block specifies 16-bit data section relative relocation that the linker is to perform within the current block. Exept for relocation size, this block is identical to "hunk_dreloc32".

hunk_dreloc8 (1017/3F9)

A hunk_dreloc8 block specifies 8-bit data section relative relocation that the linker is to perform within the current block. Except for relocation size, this block is identical to "hunk_dreloc32".

hunk_ext (1007/3EF)

This block contains external symbol information. It contains entries both defining symbols and listing references to them. Its format is as follows:

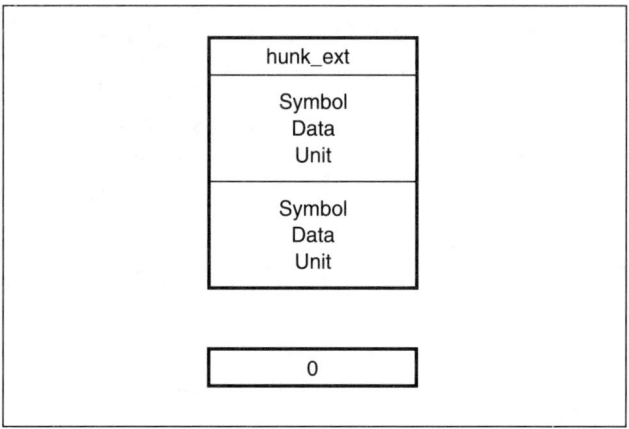

Figure 10-G.
hunk_ext (1007/3EF).

where there is one "symbol data unit" for each symbol used, and the block ends with a zero word.

Each symbol data unit consists of a type byte, the symbol name length (3 bytes), the symbol name itself, and further data. You specify the symbol name length in longwords, and pad the name field to the next longword boundary with zeros.

The type byte specifies whether the symbol is a definition or a reference, and so forth. AmigaDOS uses values 0–127 for symbol definitions, and 128–255 for references.

At the time of writing, the values are as follows:

Name	Value	Meaning
ext_symb	0	Symbol table—see symbol block below
ext_def	1	Relocatable definition
ext_abs	2	Absolute definition
ext_res	3	Resident library definition
ext_ref32	129	32-bit reference to symbol
ext_common	130	32-bit reference to COMMON
ext_ref16	131	16-bit reference to symbol
ext_ref8	132	8-bit reference to symbol
ext_dref32	133	32-bit base relative reference to symbol
ext_dref16	134	16-bit base relative reference to symbol
ext_dref8	135	8-bit base relative reference to symbol

Table 10-A.
External Symbols

The linker faults all other values. For ext_def there is one data word, the value of the symbol. This is merely the offset of the symbol from the start of the hunk. For ext_abs there is also one data value, which is the absolute value to be added into the code. The linker treats the value for ext_res in the same way as ext_def, except that it assumes the hunk name is the library name and it copies this name through to the load file. The type bytes ext_ref32, ext_ref16, and ext_ref8 are followed by a count and a list of references, again specified as offsets from the start of the hunk.

The type ext_common has the same structure except that it has a COMMON block size before the count. The linker treats symbols specified as common in the following way: if it encounters a definition for a symbol referenced as common, then it uses this value (the only time a definition should arise is in the FORTRAN Block Data case). Otherwise, it allocates suitable bss space using the maximum size you specified for each common symbol reference.

The linker handles external references differently according to the type of the corresponding definition. It adds absolute values to the longword, or byte field and gives an error if the signed value does not fit. Relocatable 32-bit references have the symbol value added to the field and a relocation record is produced for the loader. 16- and 8-bit references are handled as PC-relative references and may only be made to hunks with the same name so that the hunks are coagulated by the linker before they are loaded. It is also possible for PC-relative references to fail if the reference and the definition are too far apart. The linker may only access resident library definitions with 32-bit references, which it then handles as relocatable 32-bit references. The symbol data unit formats are as follows:

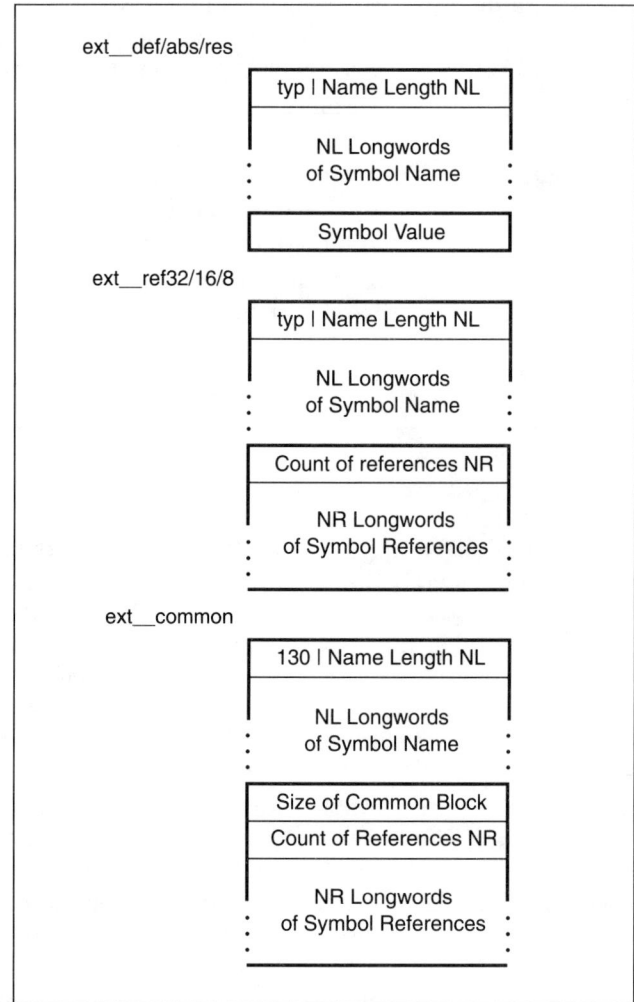

Figure 10-H.
Symbol data unit.

hunk_symbol (1008/3F0)

You use this block to attach a symbol table to a hunk so that you can use a symbolic debugger on the code. The linker passes symbol table blocks through attached to the hunk and, if the hunks are coagulated, coagulates the symbol tables. The loader does not load symbol table blocks into memory; when this is required, the debugger is expected to read the load file. The format of the symbol table block is the same as the external symbol information block with symbol table units for each name you use. The type code of zero is used within the symbol data units. The value of the symbol is the offset of the symbol from the start of the hunk. Thus the format is as follows:

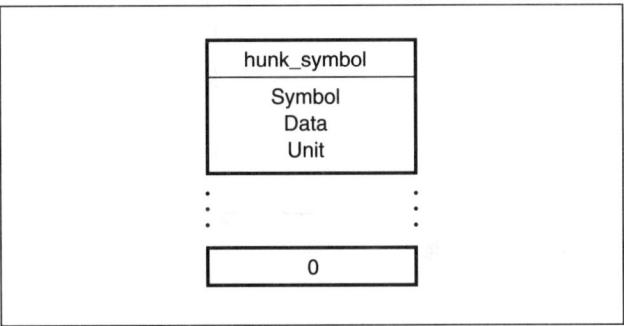

Figure 10-I.
hunk_symbol (1008/3F0).

where each symbol data unit has the following format:

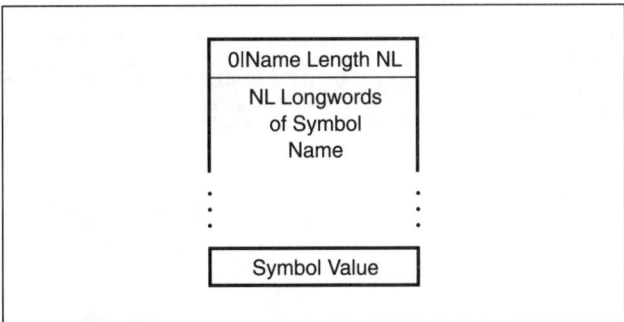

Figure 10-J.
Symbol data unit.

hunk_debug (1009/3Fl)

AmigaDOS provides the debug block so that an object file can carry further debugging information. For example, high-level language compilers may need to maintain descriptions of data structures for use by high-level debuggers. The debug block may hold this information. AmigaDOS does not impose a format on the debug block except that it must start with the hunk_debug longword and be followed by a longword that indicates the size of the block in longwords. Thus the format is as follows:

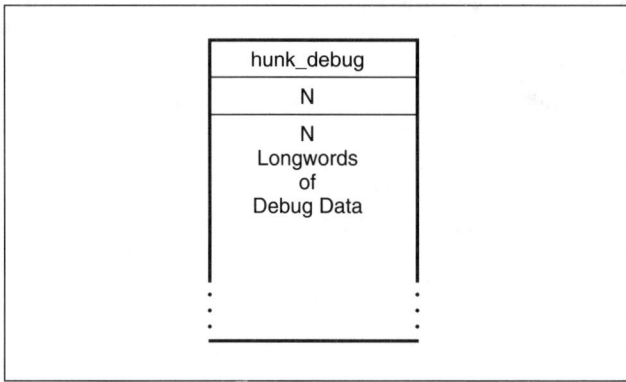

Figure 10-K.

hunk_debug (1009/3Fl).

hunk_end (1010/3F2)

This block specifies the end of a hunk. It consists of a single longword, hunk_end.

Load Files

The format of a load file (that is, the output from the linker) is similar to that of an object file. In particular, it consists of a number of hunks with a similar format to those in an object file. The main difference is that the hunks never contain an external symbol information block, as all external symbols have been resolved, and the program unit information is not included. In a simple load file that is not overlaid, the file contains a header block which indicates the total number of hunks in the load file and any resident libraries the program referenced. This block is followed by the hunks, which may be the result of coagulating a number of input hunks if they had the same name. This complete structure is referred to as a node. Load files may also contain overlay information. In this case, an overlay table follows the primary node, and a special break block separates the overlay nodes. Thus the load file structure can be summarized as follows, where the items marked with an asterisk (*) are optional.

- Primary node.
- Overlay table block (*).
- Overlay nodes separated by break blocks (*).

The relocation blocks within the hunks are always of type hunk_reloc32, and indicate the relocation to be performed at load time. This includes both the 32-bit relocation specified with hunk_reloc32 blocks in the object file and extra relocation required for the resolution of external symbols.

Each external reference in the object files is handled as follows. The linker searches the primary input for a matching external definition. If it does not find one, it searches the scanned library and includes in the load file the entire program unit where the definition was defined. This may make further external references become outstanding. At the end of the first pass, the linker knows all the external definitions and the total number of hunks that it is going to use. These include the hunks within the load file and the hunks associated with the resident libraries. On the second pass, the linker patches the longword external references so that they refer to the required offset within the hunk which defines the symbol. It produces an extra entry in the relocation block so that, when the hunks are loaded, it adds to each external reference the base address of the hunk defining the symbol. This mechanism also works for resident libraries.

Before the loader can make these cross-hunk references, it needs to know the number and size of the hunks in the nodes. The header block provides this information, as described below. The load file may also contain overlay information in an overlay table block. Break blocks separate the overlay nodes.

hunk_header (1011/3F3)

This block gives information about the number of hunks that are to be loaded, and the size of each one. It also contains the names of any resident libraries which must be opened when the node is loaded.

The format of the hunk_header is described in Figure 10-L. The first part of the header block contains the names of resident libraries that the loader must open when this node is loaded. Each name consists of a longword indicating the length of the name in longwords and the text name padded to a longword boundary with zeros. The name list ends with a longword of zero. The names are in the order in which the loader is to open them.

When it loads a primary node, the loader allocates a table in memory which it uses to keep track of all the hunks it has loaded. This table must be large enough for all the hunks in the load file, including the hunks in overlays. The loader also uses this table to keep a copy of the hunk tables associated with any resident libraries. The next longword in the header block is therefore this table size, which is equal to the maximum hunk number referenced plus one.

The next longword F refers to the first slot in the hunk table the loader should use when loading. For a primary node that does not reference a resident library, this value is zero; otherwise, it is the number of hunks in the resident libraries. The loader copies these entries from the hunk table associated with the library following a library open call. For an overlay node, this value is the number of hunks in any resident libraries plus the number of hunks already loaded in ancestor nodes.

The next longword L refers to the last hunk slot the loader is to load as part of this loader call. The total number of hunks loaded is therefore L - F + 1.

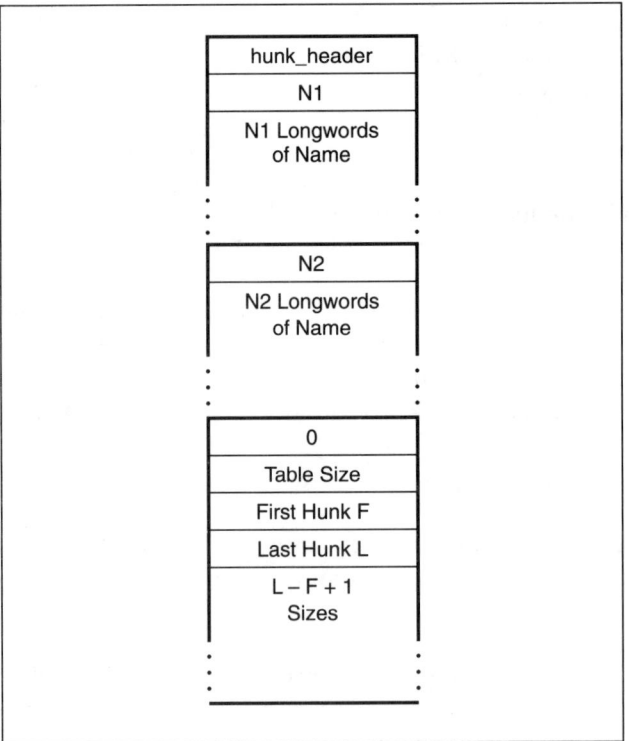

Figure 10-L.
hunk_header (1011/3F3).

The header block continues with L - F + 1 longwords that indicate the size of each hunk that is to be loaded as part of this call. This enables the loader to pre-allocate the space for the hunks and hence perform the relocation between hunks that is required as they are loaded.

hunk_overlay (1013/3F5)

The overlay table block indicates to the loader that it is loading an overlaid program, and contains all the data for the overlay table. On encountering it, the loader sets up the table, and returns, leaving the input channel to the load file still open. Its format is as follows:

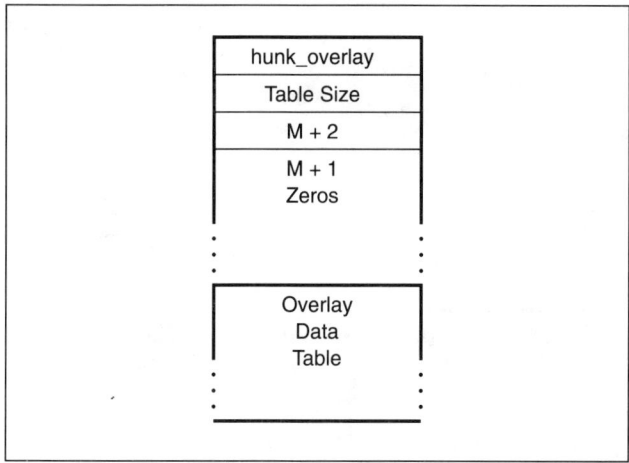

Figure 10-M.
hunk_overlay (1013/3F5).

The first longword is the upper bound of the complete overlay table (in longwords).

M is the maximum level of the overlay tree uses with the root level being zero. The next M + 1 words form the ordinate table section of the overlay table.

The rest of the block is the overlay data table, a series of eight-word entries, one for each overlay symbol. If 0 is the maximum overlay number used, then the size of the overlay data table is (0 + 1)*8, since the first overlay number is zero. So, the overlay table size is equal to (0 + 1) * 8 + M + 1.

hunk_break (1014/3F6)

A break block indicates the end of an overlay node. It consists of a single longword, hunk_break.

Examples

The following simple sections of code show how the linker and loader handle external symbols. For example,

```
                            IDNT        A
                            XREF        BILLY, JOHN
                            XDEF        MARY
* The next longword requires relocation
0000'0000 0008              DC.L        FRED
0004'123C 00FF              MOVE.B      #$FF,D1
0008'7001       FRED        MOVEQ       #1,D0
*External entry point
000A'4E71       MARY        NOP
000C'4EB90000 0000          JSR         BILLY       Call external
0012' 2239 0000 0000        MOVE.L      JOHN,D1     Reference external
                            END
```

produces the following object file:

```
hunk_unit
00000001    Size in longwords
41000000    Name, padded to longword
hunk_code
00000006    Size in longwords
00000008    123C00FF  70014E71  4EB90000  00002239  00000000
hunk_reloc32
00000001    Number in hunk 0
00000000    hunk 0
00000000    Offset to be relocated
00000000    Zero to mark end
hunk_ext
01000001    XDEF, Size 1 longword
4D415259    MARY
0000000A    Offset of definition
81000001    XREF, Size 1 longword
4A4F484E    JOHN
00000001    Number of references
00000014    Offset of reference
81000002    XREF, Size 2 longwords
```

AMIGA BINARY FILE STRUCTURE

```
42494C4C   BILLY
59000000   (zeros to pad)
00000001   Number of references
0000000E   Offset of reference
00000000   End of external block
hunk_end
```

The matching program to this is as follows:

```
                          IDNT     B
                          XDEF     BILLY,JOHN
                          XREF     MARY
0000' 2A3C AAAA AAAA      MOVE.L   #$AAAAAA,D5
* External entry point
0006' 4E71          BILLY NOP
* External entry point
0008' 7201          JOHN  MOVEQ    #1,D1
*Call external reference
OOOA' 4EF9 0000 0000      JMP      MARY
                          END
```

and the corresponding output code would be:

```
hunk_unit
00000001   Size in longwords
42000000   Unit name
hunk_code
00000004   Size in longwords
2A3CAAAA AAAA4E71 72014EF9 00000000
hunk_ext
01000001   XDEF, Size 1 longword
4A4F484E   JOHN
00000008   Offset of definition
01000002   XDEF, Size 2 longwords
42494C4C   BILLY
59000000   (zeros to pad)
00000006   Offset of definition
81000001   XREF, Size 1 longword
4D415259   MARY
00000001   Number of references
0000000C   Offset of reference
```

```
00000000   End of external block
hunk_end
```

Once you passed this through the linker, the load file would have the following format:

```
hunk_header
00000000   No hunk name
00000002   Size of hunk table
00000000   First hunk
00000001   Last hunk
00000006   Size of hunk 0
00000004   Size of hunk 1
hunk_code
00000006 Size of code in longwords
00000008 123C00FF 70014E71 4EB90000 00062239 00000008
hunk_reloc32
00000001   Number in hunk 0
00000000   hunk 0
00000000   Offset to be relocated
00000002   Number in hunk 1
00000001   hunk 1
00000014   Offset to be relocated
0000000E   Offset to be relocated
00000000   Zero to mark end
hunk_end
hunk_code
00000004   Size of code in longwords
2A3CAAAA AAAA4E71 72014EF9 0000000A
hunk_reloc32
00000001   Number in hunk 0
00000000   hunk 0
0000000C   Offset to be relocated
00000000   Zero to mark end
hunk_end
```

When the loader loads this code into memory, it reads the header block and allocates a hunk table of two longwords. It then allocates space by calling an operating system routine and requesting two areas of sizes 6 and 4 longwords, respectively. Assuming the two areas it returned were at locations 3000 and 7000, the hunk table would contain 3000 and 7000.

The loader reads the first hunk and places the code at 3000; it then handles relocation. The first item specifies relocation with respect to hunk 0, so it adds 3000 to the longword at offset 0 converting the value stored there from 00000008 to 00003008. The second item specifies relocation with respect to hunk 1. Although this is not loaded, we know that it will be loaded at location 7000, so this is added to the values stored at 300E and 3014. Note that the linker has already inserted the offsets 00000006 and 00000008 into the references in hunk 0 so that they refer to the correct offset in hunk 1 for the definition. Thus the longwords specifying the external references end up containing the values 00007006 and 00007008, which is the correct place once the second hunk is loaded.

In the same way, the loader loads the second hunk into memory at location 7000 and the relocation information specified alters the longword at 700C from 0000000A (the offset of MARY in the first hunk) to 0000300A (the address of MARY in memory).

The loader handles references to resident libraries in the same way, except that, after it has opened the library, it copies the locations of the hunks comprising the library into the start of the hunk table. It then patches references to the resident library to refer to the correct place by adding the base of the library hunks.

Amiga Library File Structure

There are two kinds of Amiga library file structures: the original format used with both ALINK and BLink, and the new indexed format used with BLink versions 7.2 and later.

The original Amiga library file structure is essentially one or more object modules concatenated together into one file. This structure has the appeal of simplicity. More object modules can be added to a library by appending them to the end of the library file.

In this format, the initial pass performed by a linker must process the library file sequentially to find the program units that it needs to link in.

Example Library File

Thus, a typical library might look as follows:

```
HUNK_UNIT              2,    "First PU"
HUNK_NAME,             3,    "First Hunk"
HUNK_CODE,            20,    20 longwords of code...
HUNK_RELOC32,          3,    3, 12, 22, 48
                       2,    2, 4, 34
                       0
HUNK_EXT,    EXT_DEF|2,      "FirstDef", 0
             EXT_DEF|3,      "SecondDef", 38
           EXT_REF32|2,      "ThirdDef", 2, 12, 48
           EXT_REF32|3,      "FourthDef", 1, 4
                       0
HUNK_DEBUG,            7,    7 longwords of debugging information...
HUNK_END
HUNK_NAME,             3,    "Second Hunk"
HUNK_DATA,            30,    30 longwords of data...
HUNK_EXT,    EXT_DEF|3,      "FirstConst", 0
             EXT_DEF|3,      "FourthDef", 4
             EXT_DEF|3,      "LongString", 8
                       0
HUNK_END

HUNK_BSS,             40
HUNK_EXT,    EXT_DEF|2,      "workStr", 0
                       0
HUNK_END

HUNK_UNIT,             3,    "Second PU"
HUNK_NAME,             3,    "Third Hunk"
HUNK_CODE,            64,    64 longwords of code...
HUNK_RELOC32,          2,    0, 14, 54
                       4,    1, 4, 22, 28, 44
                       3,    2, 10, 38, 100
                       0
HUNK_EXT,  EXT_REF32|2,      "FirstDef", 2, 14, 54
           EXT_REF32|3,      "LongString", 3, 22, 28, 44
             EXT_DEF|2,      "ThirdDef", 0
                       0
HUNK_END
```

The New Library File Structure

The new library file format is very much like the old, except that there is an extra level of encapsulation, through the use of two new hunk types. Users may still merge libraries by simply concatenating files and old or new format libraries can be appended together.

The new format is more compact and faster for the linker to process. It achieves its performance and flexibility by adding two additional hunk types: hunk_lib and hunk_index. Like all basic Amiga hunk types, these consist of a longword type value, followed by a 32-bit value for the number of subsequent longwords in the hunk. Further, they always occur in pairs, hunk_lib first, hunk_index following. Nothing comes between.

hunk_lib (1019/3FB)

The format of hunk_lib is shown in Figure 10-N.

hunk_lib
N
N Longwords of Contained Hunks

Figure 10-N.
hunk_lib (1019/3FB).

The size field (N) of the hunk_lib structure must be a count of ALL of the longwords belonging to the structure, excluding the type and size field. Thus, the longword count given in the size field can be greater than 65,535, however, note that the offset, in longwords, to the last code, data, or bss hunk be no greater than 65,535 (see hunk_index, below). If the contained hunk (or its constituent hunks) extend beyond that point, the hunk_lib size field MUST still include them in the count.

hunk_index (1020/3FC)

The hunk_index provides an index to all the hunks concatenated in hunk_lib. hunk_index format is shown in Figure 10-O.

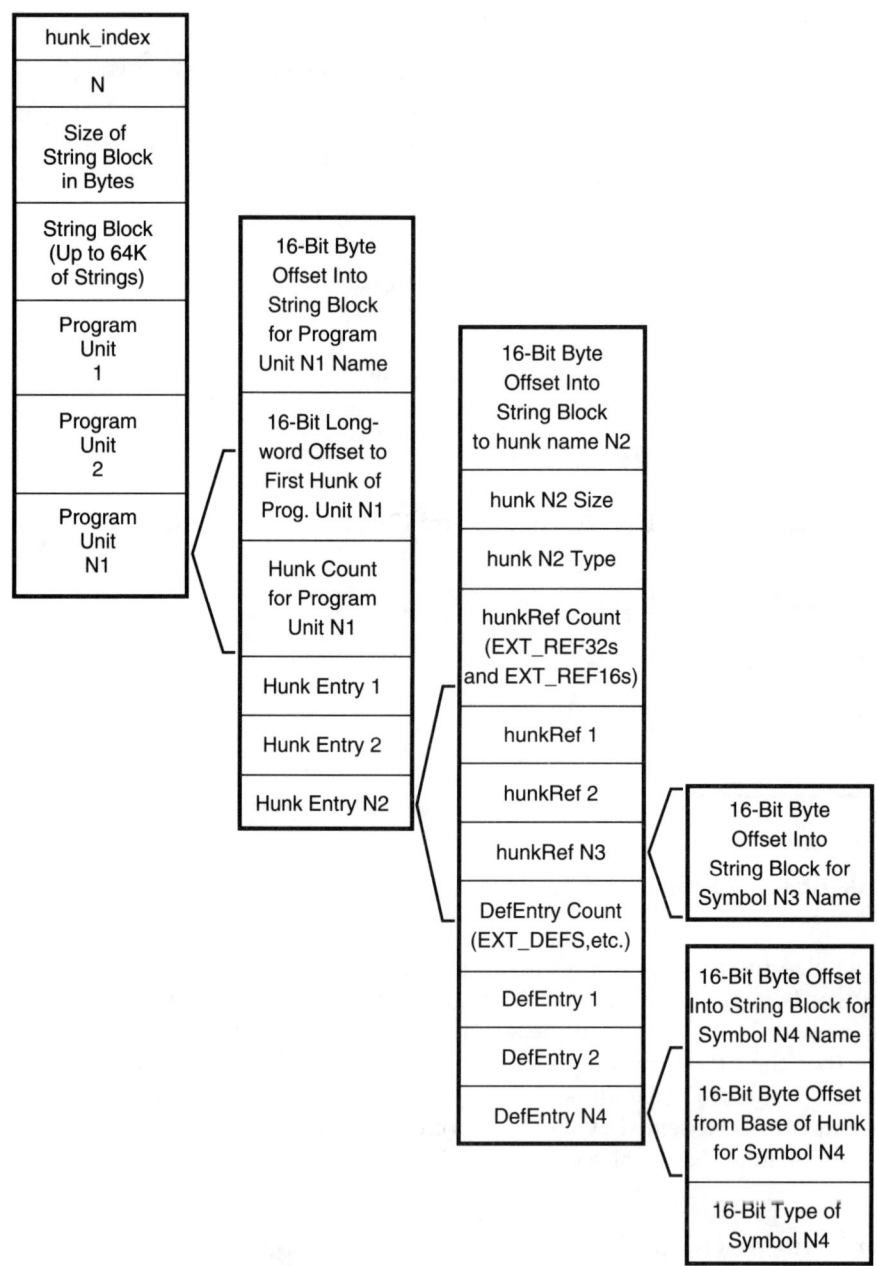

Figure 10-O.
hunk_index format.

Example of hunk_lib

Here's an example of a new format library, based on the previous example given in "Example Library File," above. The library is formed by pairing of hunk_lib and a hunk_index. Here's the hunk_lib:

```
HUNK_LIB,               191
HUNK_CODE,              20,   20 longwords of code...
HUNK_RELOC32,           3,    3, 12, 22, 48
                        2,    2, 4, 34
                        0
HUNK_EXT,   EXT_REF32|2,      "ThirdDef", 2, 12, 48
            EXT_REF32|2,      "FourthDef", 1, 4
                        0
HUNK_DEBUG,             7,    7 longwords of
                              debugging information...
HUNK_END
HUNK_DATA,              30,   30 longwords of data...
HUNK_END
HUNK_BSS,               40
HUNK_END
HUNK_CODE,              64,   64 longwords of code...
HUNK_RELOC32,           2,    0, 14, 54
                        4,    1, 4, 22, 28, 44
                        3,    2, 10, 38, 100
                        0
HUNK_EXT,   EXT_REF32|2,      "FirstDef", 2, 14, 54
            EXT_REF32|3,      "LongString", 3, 22, 28, 44
                        0
HUNK_END
```

Example of hunk_index

The hunk_index for the library is more complicated. It follows the general format:

- hunk_index.
- Size.
- 16-bit word aligned string block.
- one or more punit structures.

where the string block consists of a 16-bit word value, representing the size of the rest of the block, in bytes, and the rest of the block consists of null-terminated (C-style) strings, where the first string must be the null string. Strings are NOT word-boundary aligned. If necessary, the block is padded on the end with a single 0 byte, to align to a word boundary. Thus the string block for the above example would resemble the following:

```
122
""               at offset      0
"First PU"       at offset      1
"First Hunk"     at offset     10
"FirstDef"       at offset     21
"SecondDef"      at offset     30
"ThirdDef"       at offset     40
"FourthDef"      at offset     49
"Second Hunk"    at offset     59
"FirstConst"     at offset     71
"LongString"     at offset     82
"workStr"        at offset     93
"Second PU"      at offset    101
"Third Hunk"     at offset    111
```

This block needed no trailing 0 byte for alignment to a 16-bit word boundary. Note that this block, excluding its length field, can be no larger than 65,534 bytes (64K −2 bytes). The trailing pad byte, if present, is included in the size field for the block.

What follows the string block is one or more punit structures with the following format:

- Punit header.
- One or more hunk entries.
- If necessary, a padding 16-bit 0 value, to realign the hunk_index hunk to a longword boundary.

where a punit header consists of:
1. A 16-bit offset of a program unit name string in preceding string block (0 is the offset to the first string; -2 is the offset to the length of the block). This offset is in bytes, and is signed. Thus, the total string space available for any one hunk_lib's symbol names is 65,534 bytes.
2. A 16-bit offset of first hunk (code, data, or bss) to a program unit within the preceding hunk_lib structure. This offset is in longwords, meaning that

no hunk in the corresponding hunk_lib can begin beyond a byte offset of 262,140).

3. A 6-bit count of the number of hunks in the preceding hunk_lib structure (code, data, and bss).

and a hunk entry consists of:

1. A 16-bit offset to hunk name string in string block (or 0—the null string).
2. The 16-bit size of the hunk, in longwords.
3. A 16-bit type of the hunk (hunk_code, hunk_data, hunk_bss), with any Fast or Chip flag settings moved into the upper 2 bits of the type word.
4. A 16-bit count of the number of references. This information is duplicated from the EXT_REFs of any hunk_ext associated with the hunk. This particular field is followed by the 16-bit string offsets of the symbols being referenced in the string block (the string itself if a 32-bit reference).
5. The 16-bit count of the number of definitions. This information is moved completely out of the hunk_exts of the hunk (which is why they are so much shorter in the example of the hunk_lib above). This field is followed by 0 or more entries of three words:

    a.) A 16-bit offset to defined symbol name string in string block (most significant bit always clear).

    b.) A 16-bit offset (in bytes) of symbol from base of hunk.

    c.) A 16-bit type of the symbol definition. Note that type has been extended. In some instances of EXT_ABS values, most notably the _CIA references in amiga.lib, the ABS value has significant bits which take up to 25 bits to store.

Since the type field value will fit comfortably into 1 byte, the upper byte is reserved for bits 16–23 of EXT_ABS values, and bit 6 in the type byte is used to note the state of the uppermost 8 bits of the original 32-bit value of the EXT_ABS (that is, all 1's, or all 0's). This permits 25 bits' worth of EXT_ABS information to be stored in the existing structures. Thus, for EXT_ABS data, the following is the format:

```
original EXT_ABS values:   abs1 = $c709d3
                           abs2 = -14872941    ($ff1d0e93)
resultant EXT_ABS values:  abs1 = $09d3              (word)
                                  $c7                (byte)
                                  EXT_ABS            (byte)
```

```
            abs2 = $0e93              (word)
                   $1d                (byte)
                   EXT_ABS | 64       (byte)
```

Note that in all hunk_index structures, a 16-bit value of 0 for the count of array elements of a given type means that NO array elements of that type are present in the structure.

Thus, the hunk_index for the above given hunk_lib is:

```
hunk_index, 57
   122
   " "                      at offset  0
   "First PU"                          1
   "First Hunk"                       10
   "FirstDef"                         21
   "SecondDef"                        30
   "ThirdDef"                         40
   "FourthDef"                        49
   "Second Hunk"                      59
   "FirstConst"                       71
   "LongString"                       82
   "workStr"                          93
   "Second PU"                       101
   "Third Hunk"                      111
   1, 0, 3                 program unit w/3 hunks...
      10, 20, HUNK_CODE     hunk info
         2, 40, 49           2 refs...
         2, 21, 0, EXT_DEF   2 defs...
         30, 38, EXT_DEF
      59, 30, HUNK_DATA     hunk info
         0                   no refs
         3, 71, 0, EXT_DEF   3 defs...
         49, 4, EXT_DEF
         82, 4, EXT_DEF
      0, 40, HUNK_BSS       hunk info
         0                   no refs
         1, 93, 0, EXT_DEF   1 def...
   101, 92, 1              program unit w/1 hunk...
      111, 64, HUNK_CODE    hunk info
         2, 21, 82           2 refs...
         1, 40, 0, EXT_DEF   1 def...
```

```
0                         16-bit pad for longword alignment
                          of hunk
```

Note from the examples that the hunk_lib structure still contained the hunk_ends, the hunk_reloc32's, the hunk_debug, and part of some of the hunk_exts; if a hunk_symbol had been present, it would also have to be in the hunk_lib with its corresponding code, data, or bss hunk.

These hunks—hunk_code, hunk_data, hunk_bss, hunk_reloc32, hunk_reloc16, hunk_reloc8, hunk_symbol, hunk_debug, and hunk_end—must be present exactly as if they weren't in a hunk_lib. A hunk_unit, hunk_name must be removed entirely, replaced by program unit entries in the hunk_index associated with the hunk_lib. The hunk_ext must lose any EXT_DEFs, the information for which is instead found in the hunk entries in the hunk_index. EXT_REF32s and/or EXT_REF16s must be present in a hunk_ext in order for the hunk_ext to remain at all in the hunk_lib, and EXT_REF32s and EXT_REF16s must be noted as well in the reference list in the hunk entry found in the hunk_index for the hunk. EXT_REF8s are not supported.

Chapter 11

AmigaDOS Data Structures

This chapter describes AmigaDOS data structures in memory and in files. The layout of a disk is described in Chapter 9.

Introduction

AmigaDOS provides device independent input and output. It achieves this by creating a handler process for each device you use. The handler process accepts a standard set of I/O requests and converts these to device specific requests where required. All AmigaDOS clients refer to the handler process rather than the device directly, although it is possible to use a device without a handler if this is required. This chapter describes the data structure within AmigaDOS, including the format of a process, central shared data structures, and structure of handler requests.

In addition to normal Amiga value such as LONG and APTR, AmigaDOS uses BPTRs. A BPTR is a BCPL pointer, which is a pointer to longword-aligned memory block divided by 4. So, to read a BPTR in C, you simply shift the left by 2. To create a BPTR, you should use memory obtained via a call to ALLOC-Mem. You could also use stack memory, but you must ensure that the starting address is on a longword boundary.

AmigaDOS also has a BSTR, which is a BCPL string. BSTR consists of a BPTR to memory that contains the length of the string in the first byte, and the bytes within the string following.

A number of references to the Global Vector appear within this chapter. The Global Vector is a jump table used by BCPL and is a pointer to a standard shared Global Vector. Some processes, such as the file handler, use a private global vector. In either case, you should never access the Global Vector from your code since it is for the private use of AmigaDOS only. Under 2.0 and later versions of AmigaDOS, the Global Vector is used only for backwards-compatibility with old BCPL programs. The new AmigaDOS is written in C and Assembler and does ont use the Global Vector.

Process Data Structures

These values are created as part of an AmigaDOS process; there is a complete set for each process.

A process is an Exec task with a number of extra data structures appended. The process structure consists of:

- Exec task structure
- Exec message port
- AmigaDOS process value

The process identifier AmigaDOS uses internally is a pointer to the Exec message port (pr_MessagePort) from which the Exec task may be obtained.

AmigaDOS process values are as follows:

Value	Name	Description
BPTR	pr_SegList	Array of seg lists used by this process
LONG	pr_StackSize	Size of process stack in bytes
APTR	pr_GlobVec	Global vector for this process (BCPL)
LONG	pr_TaskNum	CLI task number of zero if not a CLI
BPTR	pr_StackBase	Ptr to high memory end of process stack
LONG	pr_Result2	Value of secondary result from last call
BPTR	pr_CurrentDir	Lock associated with current directory
BPTR	pr_CIS	Current CLI Input Stream
BPTR	pr_COS	Current CLI Output Stream

APTR	pr_ConsoleTask	Console handler process for current window
APTR	pr_FileSystemTask	File handler process for current drive
BPTR	pr_CLI	Pointer to CLI
APTR	pr_ReturnAdd	Pointer to previous stack frame
APTR	pr_PktWait	Function to be called when awaiting msg
APTR	pr_WindowPtr	Window for error printing

These new definitions have been appended to the process data structure with release V2.0 and later versions of AmigaDOS.

Value	Name	Description
BPTR	pr_HomeDir	Home directory of executing program
LONG	pr_Flags	Flags telling DOS about process
LONG	(*pr_ExitCode) (LONG returncode, LONG pr_ExitData)	Code to call on exit of program or NULL
LONG	pr_ExitData	Passed as an argument to pr_ExitCode
UBYTE *	pr_Arguments	Arguments passed to the process at start
struct MinList	pr_LocalVars	Local environment variables
ULONG	pr_ShellPrivate	For the use of the current Shell
BPTR	pr_CES	Error stream—if NULL, use pr_COS

To identify the segments that a particular process uses, you must use pr_SegList. pr_SegList is an array of longwords with its size in Seg_List[0]. Other elements are either zero or a BPTR to a SegList. CreateProc() and CreateNewProc() create this array with the first two elements of the array pointing to resident code and the third element, being the SegList, passed an argument. When a process terminates, FreeMem() is used to return the space for the pr_SegList.

The pr_StackSize field indicates the size of the process stack, as supplied by the user when calling CreateProc() or CreateNewProc(). Note that the process stack is not the same as the command stack a CLI uses when it calls a program.

The CLI obtains its command stack just before it runs a program and you may alter the size of this stack with the STACK command. When you create a process, AmigaDOS obtains the process stack and stores the size in pr_StackSize. The pointer to the space for the process control block and the stack is also stored in the MemEntry field of the task structure. When the process terminates this space is returned via a call to FreeVec. You can also chain any memory you obtain into this list structure so that it, too, gets put back when the task terminates. But be careful, this method won't work for a program run from the CLI since memory is not freed until the process goes away.

If a call to CreateProc() or CreateNewProc() creates the process, GlobVec is a pointer to the Shared Global Vector. However, some internal handler processes use a private global vector.

The value of pr_TaskNum is normally zero; a CLI process stores the small integer that identifies the invocation of the CLI here.

The pointer pr_StackBase points to the high-memory end of the process stack. This is the end of the stack when using languages such as C or assembler; it is the base of the stack for languages such as BCPL. Note that pr_StackBase may not be the same as the one your application uses (e.g., if your program is started from the CLI).

The pr_Result2 and pr_CurrentDir fields are handled by the AmigaDOS functions IoErr() and CurrentDir(), respectively. pr_CIS and pr_COS are the values Input and Output return and refer to the filehandles you should use when running a program under the CLI. Never access pr_CIS and pr_COS directly. Instead use the AmigaDOS functions provided for this purpose.

The pr_ConsoleTask field refers to the console handler for the current window. The pr_FileSysytemTask field refers to the file handler for the boot device. You use these values when attempting to open the * device or a file by a relative path name when pr_CurrentDir is null.

The pr_CLI pointer is nonzero only for CLI processes. In this case it refers to a further structure the CLI uses with the following format:

Value	Name	Description
LONG	cli_Result2	Value of IoErr from last command
BSTR	cli_SetName	Name of current directory
BPTR	cli_CommandDir	BPTR to CLI path
LONG	cli_ReturnCode	Return code from last command
BSTR	cli_CommandName	Name of current command
LONG	cli_FailLevel	Fail level (set by FAILAT)
BSTR	cli_Prompt	Current prompt (set by PROMPT)
BPTR	cli_StandardInput	Default (terminal) CLI input

BPTR	cli_CurrentInput	Current CLI input
BSTR	cli_CommandFile	Name of EXECUTE command file
LONG	cli_Interactive	Boolean; True if prompts required
LONG	cli_Background	Boolean; True if CLI created by RUN
BPTR	cli_CurrentOutput	Current CLI output
LONG	cli_DefaultStack	Stack size to be obtained in longwords
BPTR	cli_StandardOutput	Default (terminal) CLI output
BPTR	cli_Module	SegList of currently loaded command

The exit function uses the value of pr_ReturnAddr which points to just above the return address on the currently active stack. If a program exists by performing an RTS on an empty stack, the control passes to the code address pushed onto the stack by CreateProc() or by the CLI. If a program terminates with a call to Exit, then AmigaDOS uses this pointer to extract the same return address. Note that the AmigaDOS function Exit() is inappropriate for most programs which should use the exit function provided by the compiler manufacturer instead.

The value of pr_PktWait is normally zero. If it is nonzero, then AmigaDOS calls pr_PktWait whenever a process is about to go to sleep to await a signal indicating that a message has arrived. In the same way as GetMsg(), the function should return a message when one is available. Usually you use this function to filter out any private messages arriving at the standard process message port that are not intended for AmigaDOS.

The value of pr_WindowPtr is used when AmigaDOS detects an error that normally requires the user to take some action. Examples of these errors are attempting to write to a write-protected disk, or when the disk is full. If the value of pr_WindowPtr is -1, then the error is returned to the calling program as an error code from the AmigaDOS call of Open(), Write(), or whatever. If the value is zero, then AmigaDOS places a request box on the Workbench screen informing the user of the error and providing the opportunity to retry the operation or to cancel it. If the user selects to cancel, then AmigaDOS returns the error code to the calling program. If the user selects retry, or insert a disk, then AmigaDOS attempts the operation once more. Under V2.0 and later versions of AmigaDOS, if a pr_WindowPtr is zero then AmigaDOS will put requesters on the default public screen.

If you put a positive value into the pr_WindowPtr field, then AmigaDOS takes this to be a ponter to a window structure. Normally you would place the Window structure of the window you are currently using here. In this case,

AmigaDOS displays the error message within the window you have specified, rather than using the Workbench screen. You can always leave the pr_WindowPtr field as zero, but if you are using another screen, then the messages AmigaDOS displays appear on the Workbench screen, possibly obscured by your own screen.

The initial value of pr_WindowPtr is inherited from the process that created the current one. If you decide to alter pr_WindowPtr from within a program that runs under the CLI, then you must save the original value and restore it when you finish; otherwise, the CLI process contains a pr_WindowPtr that refers to a window that is no longer present.

The rest of the fields in the process structure are brand new and appear only in V2.0 and later versions of AmigaDOS. The pr_HomeDir field is the directory from which the program associated with this process was loaded. This field is referenced when the progdir: feature of V2.0 is used. The pr_Flags field is a private field containing flags for AmigaDOS.

The field named (*pr_ExitCode)() is a LONG pointing to the cleanup code to be called after the program exits. It takes as a parameter the return code of the program and may return a modified return code when the process terminates. The pr_ExitData is provided as a convenience and allows you to pass additional information to your pr_ExitCode automatically.

Another new field is pr_Arguments. This is a null terminated string of the register level arguments passed to the process when the program was started. You can modify this field using the SetArguments() function but if you do, you must restore it to its original value before exiting.

pr_LocalVars is used to implement process local variables. Do not access these directly. Use the new calls GetVar(), SetVar(), and DeleteVar() instead.

The pr_ShellPrivate field is for the private use of the Shell associated with this process. Never access it.

The value in pr_CES points to an error stream to use for this process separate from pr_CIS and pr_COS. This field is not fully implemented in AmigaDOS at the time of this writing.

Redirecting System Requesters

On the Amiga, when a user or a program requests a file on a volume that is not currently mounted, AmigaDOS brings up a System Request on the Workbench screen asking the user to insert the disk.

The pr_WindowPtr field of the Process structure determines where most process-related system requesters appear. The normal value is 0L which causes the requesters to come up on the Workbench screen (the default public screen).

If your application has its own custom screen, and you perform any actions that might cause a System Request (such as loading of files or printing) you should redirect such requesters for your Process so that the requesters related to your Process are brought up on your application screen.

To do this, first find your Process:

```
proc = (struct Process *)FindTask(NULL);
```

Save the old value of proc->pr_WindowPtr, and replace it with a pointer to one of the Intuition Windows on your custom screen. The requesters will come up on the same screen (and with the same title as) that Window. Be sure to replace the original pr_WindowPtr value before closing your window or exiting your program.

Other applications may wish to temporarily disable such requesters so that attempts to Open() or Lock() unmounted volumes simply return an error without bringing up a requester. To do this, save the old value of pr_WindowPtr and store -1L there instead. Before exiting your program, replace the original value of pr_WindowPtr.

DOS Library Structure

This data structure only exists once; however, all AmigaDOS processes use it. If you make a call to OpenLibrary(), you can obtain the library base pointer. The base of the data structure is a positive offset from the library base pointer. The library base pointer points to the following structure:

Library Node structure

APTR to DOS RootNode

APTR to DOS Shared Global Vector

DOS private register dump

Many internal AmigaDOS calls use the Shared Global Vector, which is a jump table. You should not normally use it, except through the supplied interface calls, as it is liable to change without warning.

The RootNode structure is as follows:

Value	Name	Description
BPTR	rn_TaskArray	Array of CLI processes
BPTR	rn_ConsoleSegment	SegList for the CLI
struct DateStamp	rn_Time	Current time

LONG	rn_RestartSeg	SegList for the disk validator process
BPTR	rn_Info	Pointer to the Info structure

These fields have been appended to the RootNode structure in V2.0 and later versions of AmigaDOS.

BPTR	rn_FileHandlerSegment	Segment for a file handler
struct MinList	rn_CliList	New list of all CLI processes the first cpl_Array is also rn_TaskArray
struct MsgPort *	rn_BootProc	Private pointer to msgport of boot filesystem
BPTR	rn_ShellSegment	SegList for Shell (for NewShell)
LONG	rn_Flags;	DOS Flags

The rn_TaskArray is an array with its size stored in rn_TaskArray [0]. The process ID (in other words the MsgPort associated with the process) for each CLI is stored in the array. The process ID for CLI n is stored in rn_TaskArray [n]. An empty slot is filled with zero. Under AmigaDOS 2.0, TaskArray is duplicated and extended with the rn_CliList structure. The commands RUN and NEWCLI scan the rn_TaskArray table for the next free slot and use this for the CLI created. You should not access the TaskArray table directly from your code. Instead use the AmigaDOS functions provided for this purpose.

The rn_ConsoleSegment is the SegList for the code of the CLI. RUN and NEWCLI use this value to create a new instance of a CLI.

The RootNode stores the current date and time; normally you should use the AmigaDOS function DateStamp() to return a consistent set of values. The values Days, Mins, and Ticks specify the date and time. The value of Days is the number of days since January 1st, 1978. The value of Mins is the number of minutes since midnight. A tick is one-fiftieth of a second, but the time is only updated anytime DateStamp is called.

The RestartSeg is the SegList for the code of the disk validator, which is a process that AmigaDOS creates whenever you insert a new disk into a drive. In V2.0 and later versions of AmigaDOS this field is null since the disk validator process is no longer separate.

The rest of the fields in the RootNode structure are brand new and appear only in V2.0 and later versions of AmigaDOS.

The field named rn_FileHandlerSegment is a seglist of the ROM filesystem.

The rn_CliList field is a list of tables of CLI pointers. This supplants rn_TaskArray method used in previous versions of AmigaDOS and eliminates the limit on the number of CLIs that can run at the same time. Note that the first table in the rn_CliList is also stored in TaskArray for the sake of backward compatibility. This list should be accessed using FindCli() and MaxCli() only. Do not directly access it from your code.

The rn_ BootProc field is a private pointer to the filesystem process that the system was booted off of. This is not necessarily the same as the ROM filesystem.

The rn_ShellSegment field is the SegList for the boot Shell and rn_Flags contains new flags used by AmigaDOS for future expansion. Currently it contains only one flag which determines whether * or #? is used as the AmigaDOS wildcard.

Info Substructure

To access the Info substructure with the following format, you use the rn_Info pointer.

Value	Name	Description
BPTR	di_McName	Pointer to the resident list
BPTR	di_DevInfo	Device list
BPTR	di_Devices	Currently zero
BPTR	di_Handlers	Currently zero
APTR	di_NetHand	Currently zero

Most of the fields in the Info substructure are empty at this time, and Commodore-Amiga will use them for expanding the system.

The DevInfo structure is a linked list. You use it to identify all the device names that AmigaDOS knows about; this includes ASSIGN names and disk volume names. To access the information in the DevInfo structure under V1.3 and earlier versions of AmigaDOS, you must first call Forbid(). This means no Wait() calls or message passing are allowed while you access the structure (and you must also call Permit() when you are finished).

In V2.0 and later versions of AmigaDOS you must call LockDosList() before accessing the DevInfo structure. This allows you to call Wait() and do message passing in the code that accesses DevInfo. You must call UnLockDosList() when you are finished. For compatibility with V1.3 programs, LockDosList() calls

Forbid() and UnLockDosList() calls Permit(). However, this will be removed in a future release of AmigaDOS.

There are three possible formats for the linked list entries in DevInfo depending on whether the entry refers to a disk volume, an assign, or a device or directory. For an entry describing a device or directory (via ASSIGN) the entry is as follows:

Value	Name	Description
BPTR	dvi_Next	Pointer to next list entry or zero
LONG	dvi_Type	List entry type (device or dir)
APTR	dvi_Task	Handler process or zero
BPTR	dvi_Lock	Filesystem lock or zero
BSTR	dvi_Handler	Filename of handler or zero
LONG	dvi_StackSize	Stack size for handler process
LONG	dvi_Priority	Priority for handler process
LONG	dvi_Startup	Startup value to be passed to handler process
BPTR	dvi_SegList	SegList for handler process or zero
BPTR	dvi_GlobVec	Global Vector for handler process or zero
BSTR	dvi_Name	Name of device or ASSIGNed name

The dvi_Next field links all the list entries together and the name of the logical device is held in the dvi_Name field. Although the dvi_Name field is a BSTR, note that it must end with a zero byte and this extra byte should not be included in the length count.

The dvi_Type field is 0 (dt_device) or 1 (dt_dir). You can make a directory entry with the ASSIGN command. This command allocates a name to a directory that you can then use as a device name. If the list entry refers to a directory, then the Task field refers to the filesystem process handling that disk, and the dvi_Lock field contains a pointer to a lock on that directory.

If the list entry refers to a device, then the device may or may not be resident. If it is resident, the dvi_Task identifies the handler process, and the dvi_Lock is normally zero. If the device is not resident, then dvi_Task is zero and AmigaDOS uses the rest of the list structure.

If the dvi_SegList is zero, then the code for the device is not in memory. The Handler field is a string specifying the file containing the code (for example, SYS:L/ram-handler). A call to LoadSeg() loads the code from the file and inserts the result into the SegList field.

AmigaDOS now creates a new handler process with the dvi_SegList, dvi_StackSize, and dvi_Priority values. The new process is a BCPL process and requires a Global Vector; this is either the value you specified in dvi_GlobVec or a new private global vector if dvi_GlobVec is zero. If dvi_GlobVec is -1 then the process is not a BCPL process but is one created by CreateProc().

The new process is passed a message containing the name originally specified, the value stored in Startup and the base of the list entry. The new handler process may then decide to patch into the Task slot the process ID or not as required. If the dvi_Task slot is patched, then subsequent references to the device name use the same handler task; this is what the RAM: device does. If the dvi_Task slot is not patched, then further references to the device result in new process invocations; this is what the CON: device does.

If the dvi_Type field within the list entry is equal to 2 (dt_volume), then the format of the list structure is slightly different.

Value	Name	Description
BPTR	dvi_Next	Pointer to next list entry or zero
LONG	dvi_Type	List entry type (volume)
APTR	dvi_Task	Handler process or zero
BPTR	dvi_Lock	File system lock
struct DateStamp	dol_VolumeDate	Volume creation date
BPTR	dol_LockList	List of active locks for this volume
LONG	dol_DiskType	Type of disk
LONG	Spare	Not used
BSTR	dvi_Name	Volume name

In this case, the dvi_Name field is the name of the volume, and the Task field refers to the handler process if the volume is currently inserted; or to zero if the volume is not inserted. To distinguish disks with the same name, AmigaDOS timestamps the volume on creation and then saves the timestamp in the list structure. AmigaDOS can therefore compare the timestamps of different volumes whenever necessary.

If a volume is not currently inserted, then AmigaDOS saves the list of currently active locks in the dol_LockList field. Note that dol_LockList is private and should never be accessed directly. Not all filesystems support the dol_LockList field. AmigaDOS uses the dol_DiskType field to identify the type of disk. The disk type is up to four characters packed into a longword and padded on the right with nulls.

If the dvi_Type field within the list entry is equal to 3 or 4 (dt_nonbinding or dt_late) then the format of the list structure is as follows:

Value	Name	Description
BPTR	dvi_Next	Pointer to the next list entry or zero
LONG	dvi_Type	List entry type (late- or nonbinding assign)
APTR	dvi_Task	Handler process or zero
BPTR	dvi_Lock	Filesystem lock
UBYTE*	dol_AssignName	Name for late- or nonbinding assigns
struct AssignList *	dol_List	For multidirectory assigns (regular)
LONG	Spare	Not used
LONG	Spare	Not used
LONG	Spare	Not used
LONG	Spare	Not used
BSTR	dvi_Name	Volume name

For multidirectory assigns, the additional locks are strung off of dol_Llist. For late and nonbinding assigns, dol_AssignName has the string for the assign (path). Late-binding assigns turn into regular assigns once they bind. Also note that any normal assign can have more locks strung off of the dol_List.

Memory Allocation

AmigaDOS obtains all the memory it allocates by calling the AllocMem() function provided by Exec. In this way, AmigaDOS obtains structures such as locks and file handles; it usually places them back in the free pool by calling FreeMem. Under V2.0 and later versions of AmigaDOS AllocVec() and FreeVec() are available to do this. In either case, each memory segment allocated by AmigaDOS is identified by a BPTR to the second longword in the structure. The first longword always contains the length of the entire segment in bytes. Thus the structure of allocated memory is as follows:

Value	Name	Description
LONG	BlockSize	Size of memory block
LONG	FirstData	First data segment, BPTR to block points here

Segment Lists

To obtain a segment list, you call LoadSeg. The result is a BPTR to allocated memory, so that the length of the memory block containing each list entry is stored at -4 from the BPTR. This length is 8 more than the size of the segment list entry, allowing for the link field and the size field itself.

The SegList is a list linked together by BPTRs and terminated by zero. The remainder of each segment list entry contains the code loaded. Thus the format is:

Value	Name	Description
LONG	NextSeg	BPTR to next segment or zero
LONG	FirstCode	First value from binary file

File Handles

File handles are created by the AmigaDOS function Open(), and you use them as arguments to other functions such as Read() and Write(). AmigaDOS returns them as a BPTR to the following structure:

Value	Name	Description
struct Message *	fh_Link	Reserved for AmigaDOS
struct Message *	fh_Key	Reply port for the packet
struct Message *	fh_Port	Process ID of handler
LONG	fh_Buf	Buffer for internal use
LONG	fh_Pos	Character position for internal use
LONG	fh_End	End position for internal use
LONG	fh_Func1	Function called when buffer exhausted
LONG	fh_Func2	Function called when buffer is full

LONG	fh_Func3	Function called when handle is closed
LONG	fh_Arg1	Argument depends on file handle type
LONG	fh_Arg2	Argument depends on file handle type

Most of the fields are only used by AmigaDOS internally; normally Read() or Write() uses the file handle to indicate the handler process and any arguments to be passed. Values should not be altered within the file handle by user programs. In general, you should not read the values either (except fh_Arg1 which is used for direct packet I/O).

Locks

The filing system extensively uses a data structure called a lock. This structure serves two purposes. First, it serves as the mechanism to open files for multiple reads or a single write. Note that obtaining a shared read lock on a directory does not stop that directory being updated.

Second, the lock provides a unique identification for a file. Although a particular file may be specified in many ways, the lock is a simple handle on that file. The lock contains the actual disk block location of the directory or file header and is thus a shorthand way of specifying a particular filesystem object. The structure of a lock is as follows:

Value	Name	Description
BPTR	fl_Link	BPTR to next lock in chain, else zero
LONG	fl_Key	Block number of directory or file header
LONG	fl_Access	Shared or exclusive access
struct MsgPort *	fl_Task	Process ID of handler
BPTR	fl_Volume	BPTR to dlt_volume DOS list entry

Because AmigaDOS uses the fl_Link field to chain locks together, you should not alter it. The filing system fills in fl_Key field to represent the location on disk of the directory block or the file header block. The fl_Access serves to indicate whether this is a shared read lock, when it has the value -2, or an exclusive write lock when it has the value -1. The fl_Task field contains a pointer to the handler process for the device containing the file to which this lock refers. Finally the fl_Volume field points to the node in the DevInfo structure that identifies the volume to which this lock refers. Volume entries in the DevInfo structure remain there if a disk is inserted or if there are any locks open on that volume.

Note that a lock can also be a zero. The special case of lock zero indicates that the lock refers to the root of the initial filing system, and the pr_FileSystemTask field within the process data structure gives the handler process. None of the fields in the Lock structure should be changed by your code. The Lock structures is strictly handler-private and read-only.

AmigaDOS Packets

Packet passing handles all communication performed by AmigaDOS between processes. The functional diagram below shows how packets fit in with the other components of the Amiga operating system.

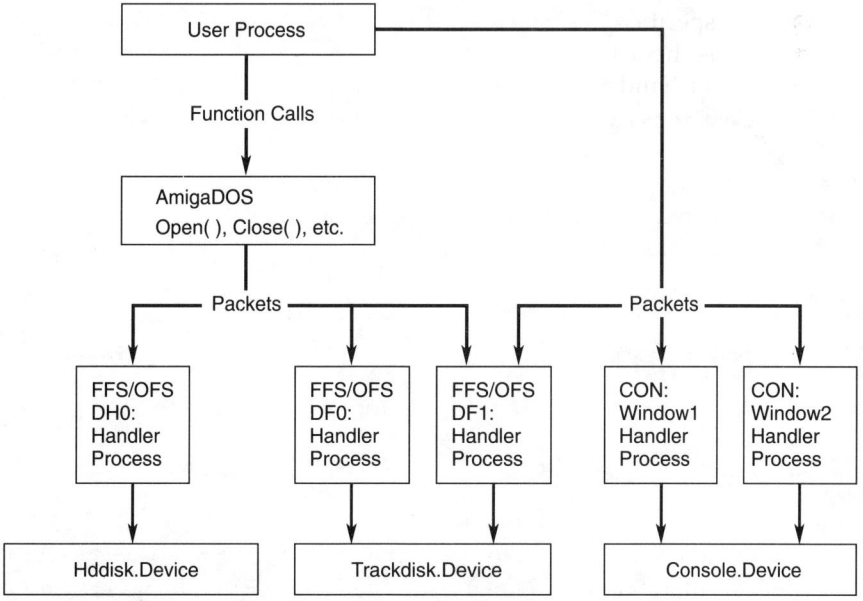

Figure 11-1.

A StandardPacket (defined in dos/dosextens.h) is used to send packet commands to a process's MsgPort. The StandardPacket structure contains an Exec Message structure and an AmigaDOS DOSPacket structure:

```
struct StandardPacket {
struct Message    sp_Msg;
struct DOSPacket  sp_Pkt;
};
```

This structure must be longword-aligned, and initialized to link the Message and DOSPacket sections to each other:

```
packet->sp_Msg.mn_Node.ln_Name = (char *)&(packet->sp_Pkt);
packet->sp_Pkt.dp_Link         = &(packet->sp_Msg);
```

Packets must also be initialized with a ReplyPort which can be created with the amiga.lib function CreatePort():

```
if(replyport = (struct MsgPort *) CreatePort(NULL,0))
{
    packet->sp_Pkt.dp_Port        = replyport;
}
```

The DOSPacket portion of the StandardPacket structure is used to pass the packet type and arguments, and to receive the results of the packet. The arguments types, number of arguments, and results vary for different packet types and are documented with each packet description. A DOSPacket must be longword-aligned and has the following general structure.

Value	Name	Description
struct Message *	dp_Link	Pointer back to Exec message structure
struct MsgPort *	dp_Port	Reply port for the packet. Must be filled in each send
LONG	dp_Type	Packet type
LONG	dp_Res1	For filesystem calls this is the result that would have been returned by the function, e.g., Write ("W") returns actual length written.

LONG		dp_Res2	For filesystem calls this is what would have been returned by IoErr()
LONG		dp_Arg1	Argument (depends on packet type)
LONG		dp_Arg2	Argument 2 (depends on packet type)...
LONG		dp_Arg7	Argument 7 (depends on packet type)

The format of a specific packet depends on its type; but in all cases it contains a back-pointer to the Message structure, the MsgPort for the reply, and two result fields. When AmigaDOS sends a packet, the reply port is overwritten with the process ID of the sender so that the packet can be returned. Thus, when sending a packet to an AmigaDOS handler process, you must fill in the reply MsgPort each time; otherwise when the packet returns, AmigaDOS has overwritten the original port. AmigaDOS maintains all other fields except the result fields.

All AmigaDOS packets are sent to the message port created as part of a process; this message port is initialized so that arriving messages cause signal bit 8 to be set. An AmigaDOS process that is waiting for a message waits for signal 8 to be set. When the process wakes up because this event has occurred, GetMsg() takes the message from the message port and extracts the packet address. If the process is an AmigaDOS handler process, then the packet contains a value in the PktType field that indicates an action to be performed, such as reading some data. The argument fields contain specific information such as the size of the buffer where the characters go.

When the handler process has completed the work required to satisfy this request, the packet returns to the sender, using the same message structure. Both the message structure and the packet structure must be allocated by the client and not deallocated before the reply has been received. Normally AmigaDOS is called by the client to send the packet, such as when a call to Read() is made. However, there are cases where asynchronous I/O is required, and in this case the client may send packets to the handler process as required. The packet and message structures must be allocated, and the process ID field filled in with the message port where this packet must return. A call to PutMsg() then sends the message to the destination. Note that many packets may be sent out, returning to either the same or different message ports.

Packet Types

Packets sent to a filesystem or handler can be divided into several basic categories:

- Basic Input/Output. These actions deal with transferring data to and from objects controlled by the handler.
- File/Directory Manipulation/Information. These actions are used to gain access to and manipulate the high-level structures of the filesystem.
- Volume Manipulation/Information. These actions allow access to the specific volume controlled by the filesystem.
- Handler Maintenance and Control. These actions allow control over the handler/filesystem itself, independent of the actual volume or structure underneath.
- Handler Internal. These actions are never sent to the handler directly. Instead they are generally responses to I/O requests made by the handler. The handler makes these responses look like packets to simplify processing.
- Obsolete Packets. These packets are no longer valid for use by handlers and filesystems.
- Console Only Packets. These packets are specific to console handlers. Filesystems can ignore these packets.

Each packet type documented in this section is listed with its action name, its corresponding number, any AmigaDOS routines that use this packet, and the list of parameters that the packets uses. The C variable types for the packet parameters are one of the following types:

BPTR   This is BCPL pointer (the address of the given object shifted right by 2). **Note:** This means that the object must be aligned on a longword boundary.

LOCK   This is a BPTR to a FileLock structure returned by a previous ACTION_LOCATE_OBJECT. A lock of 0 is legal, indicating the root of the volume for the handler.

BSTR   This is a BPTR to a string where the first byte indicates the number of characters in the string. A byte of this length is unsigned but because the information is stored in a byte, the strings are limited to 255 characters in length.

BOOL   A 32-bit Boolean value either containing DOSTRUE (-1) or DOSFALSE (0). **Note:** Equality comparisons with DOSTRUE should be avoided.

CODE   A 32-bit error code as defined in the dos/dos.h include file. Handlers should not return error codes besides those defined in dos/dos.h.

ARG1   The FileHandle->fh_Arg1 field.

LONG   A 32-bit integer value.

Basic Input/Output

The Basic Input/Output actions are supported by both handlers and filesystems. In this way, the application can get a stream level access to both devices and files. One difference that arises between the two is that a handler does not necessarily support an ACTION_SEEK while it is generally expected for a filesystem to do so.

These actions work based on a FileHandle which is filled in by one of the three forms of opens:

```
ACTION_FINDINPUT     1005    Open(..., MODE_OLDFILE)
ACTION_FINDOUTPUT    1006    Open(..., MODE_NEWFILE)
ACTION_FINDUPDATE    1004    Open(..., MODE_READWRITE)
ARG1:   BPTR    FileHandle to fill in
ARG2:   LOCK    Lock on directory that ARG3 is relative
                to
ARG3:   BSTR    Name of file to be opened (relative to
                ARG1)

RES1:   BOOL    Success/Failure (DOSTRUE/DOSFALSE)
RES2:   CODE    Failure code if RES1 is DOSFALSE
```

All three actions use the lock (ARG2) as a base directory location from which to open the file. If this lock is NULL, then the filename (ARG3) is relative to the root of the current volume. Because of this, filenames are not limited to a single filename but instead can include a volume name (followed by a colon) and multiple slashes allowing the filesystem to fully resolve the name. This eliminates the need for AmigaDOS or the application to parse names before sending them to the filesystem. Note that the lock in ARG2 must be associated with the filesystem in question. It is illegal to use a lock from another filesystem.

The calling program owns the file handle (ARG1). The program must initialize the filehandle before trying to open anything (in the case of a call to Open(), AmigaDOS allocates the file handle automatically and then frees it in Close()). All fields must be zero except the fh_Pos and fh_End fields which should be set to -1. On a successful open, the handler is responsible for filling in the fh_Type field with a pointer to the MsgPort of the handler process. Lastly, the handler must initialize fh_Arg1 with something that allows the handler to uniquely locate the object being opened (normally a file). This value is implementation specific. This field is passed to the READ/WRITE/ SEEK/END/TRUNCATE operations and not the file handle itself.

FINDINPUT and FINDUPDATE are similar in that they only succeed if the file already exists. FINDINPUT opens with a shared lock while FINDUPDATE opens it with a shared lock but if the file doesn't exist, FINDUPDATE will create the file. FINDOUTPUT always opens the file (deleting any existing one) with an exclusive lock.

```
ACTION_READ       'R'      Read(...)
ARG1:    ARG1    fh_Arg1 field of the opened FileHandle
ARG2:    APTR    Buffer to put data into
ARG3:    LONG    Number of bytes to read

RES1:    LONG    Number of bytes read. 0 indicates EOF. -1
                 indicates ERROR
RES2:    CODE    Failure code if RES1 is -1
```

This action extracts data from the file (or input channel) at the current position. If fewer bytes remain in the file than requested, only those bytes remaining will be returned with the number of bytes stored in RES1. The handler indicates an error by placing a -1 in RES1 and the error code in RES2. If the read fails, the current file position remains unchanged. Note that a handler may return a smaller number of bytes than requested, even if not at the end of a file. This happens with interactive-type file handles which may return one line at a time as the user hits return, for example, the console handler, CON:.

```
ACTION_WRITE      'W'       Write(...)
ARG1:    ARG1    fh_Arg1 field of the opened file handle
ARG2:    APTR    Buffer to write to the file handle
ARG3:    LONG    Number of bytes to write

RES1:    LONG    Number of bytes written.
RES2:    CODE    Failure code if RES1 not the same as ARG3
```

This action copies data into the file (or output channel) at the current position. The file is automatically extended if the write passes the end of the file. The handler indicates failure by returning a byte count in RES1 that differs from the number of bytes requested in ARG3. In the case of a failure, the handler does not update the current file position (although the file may have been extended and some data overwritten) so that an application can safely retry the operation.

```
ACTION_SEEK       1008      Seek(...)
ARG1:    ARG1    fh_Arg1 field of the opened FileHandle
ARG2:    LONG    New Position
```

```
ARG3:     LONG   Mode: OFFSET_BEGINNING,OFFSET_END, or
                 OFFSET_CURRENT

RES1:     LONG   Old Position. -1 indicates an error
RES2:     CODE   Failure code if RES1 = -1
```

This packet sets the current file position. The new position (ARG2) is relative to either the beginning of the file (OFFSET_BEGINNING), the end of the file (OFFSET_END), or the current file position (OFFSET_CURRENT), depending on the mode set in ARG3. Note that ARG2 can be negative. The handler returns the previous file position in RES1. Any attempt to seek past the end of the file causes an error and leaves the current file position in an unknown location.

```
ACTION_END        1007       Close(...)
ARG1:     ARG1   fh_Arg1 field of the opened FileHandle

RES1:     LONG   DOSTRUE
```

This packet closes an open file handle. This function generally returns a DOSTRUE as there is little the application can do to recover from a file closing failure. If an error is returned under 2.0, DOS does not deallocate the file handle. Under 1.3, it does not check the result.

```
ACTION_SET_FILE_SIZE   1022   SetFileSize(file,off,mode)
ARG1:     BPTR   FileHandle of opened file to modify
ARG2:     LONG   New end of file location based on mode
ARG3:     LONG   Mode. One of OFFSET_CURRENT, OFFSET_BEGIN,
                 or OFFSET_END

RES1:     BOOL   Success/Failure (DOSTRUE/DOSFALSE)
RES2:     CODE   Failure code if RES1 is DOSFALSE
```

This function is used to change the physical size of an opened file. ARG2, the new end-of-file position, is relative to either the current file position (OFFSET_CURRENT), the beginning of the file (OFFSET_BEGIN), or the end of the file (OFFSET_END), depending on the mode set in ARG3. The current file position will not change unless the current file position is past the new end-of-file position. In this case, the new file position will move to the new end of the file. If there are other open file handles on this file, ACTION_SET_FILE_SIZE sets the end-of-file for these alternate file handles to either their respective current file position or to the new end-of-file position of the file handle in ARG1, whichever makes the file appear longest.

2.0 only

ACTION_LOCK_RECORD   2008   LockRecord(fh,pos,len,mod,tim)
ARG1:   BPTR   FileHandle to lock record in
ARG2:   LONG   Start position (in bytes) of record in the file
ARG3:   LONG   Length (in bytes) of record to be locked
ARG4:   LONG   Mode
        0 = Exclusive
        1 = Immediate Exclusive (timeout is ignored)
        2 = Shared
        3 = Immediate Shared (timeout is ignored)
ARG5:   LONG   Timeout period in AmigaDOS ticks (0 is legal)

RES1:   BOOL   Success/Failure (DOSTRUE/DOSFALSE)
RES2:   CODE   Failure code if RES1 is DOSFALSE

This function locks an area of a file in either a shareable (indicating read-only) or exclusive (indicating read/write) mode. Several shareable record locks from different file handles can exist simultaneously on a particular file area but only one file handle can have exclusive record locks on a particular area at a time. The ``exclusivity'' of an exclusive file lock only applies to record locks from other file handles, not to record locks within the file handle. One file handle can have any number of overlapping exclusive record locks. In the event of overlapping lock ranges, the entire range must be lockable before the request can succeed. The timeout period (ARG5) is the number of AmigaDOS ticks (1/50 second) to wait for success before failing the operation.

2.0 only

ACTION_FREE_RECORD   2009   FreeRecord(file,pos,len)
ARG1:   BPTR   FileHandle to unlock record in
ARG2:   LONG   Start position (in bytes) of record in the file
ARG3:   LONG   Length of record (in bytes) to be unlocked

RES1:   BOOL   Success/Failure (DOSTRUE/DOSFALSE)
RES2:   CODE   Failure code if RES1 is DOSFALSE

This function unlocks any previous record lock. If the given range does not represent one that is currently locked in the file, ACTION_FREE_RECORD returns an error. In the event of multiple locks on a given area, only one lock is freed.

Directory/File Manipulation/Information

The directory/file actions permits an application to make queries about and modifications to handler objects. These packets perform functions such as creating subdirectories, resolving links, and filling in FileInfoBlock structures for specific files.

```
ACTION_LOCATE_OBJECT       8          Lock(...)
ARG1:    LOCK   Lock on directory to which ARG2 is relative
ARG2:    BSTR   Name (possibly with a path) of object to
                lock
ARG3:    LONG   Mode: ACCESS_READ/SHARED_LOCK,
                ACCESS_WRITE/EXCLUSIVE_LOCK

RES1:    LOCK   Lock on requested object or 0 to indicate
                failure
RES2:    CODE   Failure code if RES1 = 0
```

The AmigaDOS function Lock() uses this action to create its locks. Given a name for the object, which may include a path, (ARG2) and a lock on a directory from which to look for the name (and path), ACTION_LOCATE_OBJECT will locate the object within the filesystem and create a FileLock structure associated with the object. If the directory lock in ARG1 is NULL, the name is relative to the root of the file handler's volume (a.k.a. ``:''). The memory for the FileLock structure returned in RES1 is maintained by the handler and freed by an ACTION_FREE_LOCK. Although it's not a requirement, if a handler expects to support the pre-1.3 FORMAT command, it must accept any illegal mode as ACCESS_READ.

A handler can create an exclusive lock only if there are no other outstanding locks on the given object. Once created, an exclusive lock prevents any other locks from being created for that object. In general, a handler uses the FileLock->fl_Key field to uniquely identify an object. Note that some applications rely on this (although it is not required to be implemented by the handler).

The fl_Volume field of the returned FileLock structure should point to the DOS device list's volume entry for the volume on which the lock exists. In addition, there are several diagnostic programs that expect all locks for a volume to be chained together off the dl_LockList field in the volume entry. Note that relying on this chaining is not safe, and can cause serious problems including a system crash. No application should use it.

ACTION_COPY_DIR   19   DupLock(...)
ARG1:   LOCK   Lock to duplicate

RES1:   LOCK   Duplicated Lock or 0 to indicate failure
RES2:   CODE   Failure code if RES1 = 0

This action's name is misleading as it does not manipulate directories. Instead, it creates a copy of a shared lock. The copy is subsequently freed with an ACTION_FREE_LOCK. Note that it is valid to pass a NULL lock. Currently, the DupLock() call always returns 0 if passed a 0, although a handler is not required to return a 0.

ACTION_FREE_LOCK   15   UnLock(...)
ARG1:   LOCK   Lock to free

RES1:   BOOL   TRUE

This action frees the lock passed to it. The AmigaDOS function Unlock() uses this packet. If passed a NULL lock, the handler should ignore the packet and return success.

ACTION_EXAMINE_OBJECT   23   Examine(...)
ARG1:   LOCK   Lock of object to examine
ARG2:   BPTR   FileInfoBlock to fill in

RES1:   BOOL   Success/failure (DOSTRUE/DOSFALSE)
RES2:   CODE   Failure code if RES1 = DOSFALSE

This action fills in the FileInfoBlock with information about the locked object. The Examine() function uses this packet. This packet is actually used for two different types of operations. It is called to obtain information about a given object while in other cases, it is called to prepare for a sequence of EXAMINE_NEXT operations to traverse a directory.

This seemingly simple operation is not without its quirks. One in particular is the FileInfoBlock->fib_Comment field. This field used to be 116 bytes long, but was changed to 80 bytes in release 1.2. The extra 36 bytes lie in the fib_Reserved field. Another quirk of this packet is that both the fib_EntryType and the fib_DirEntryType fields must be set to the same value, as some programs look at one field while other programs look at the other.

Filesystems should use the same values for fib_DirEntryType as the ROM filesystem and RAM-handler do. These are as follows:

ST_ROOT	1
ST_USERDIR	2
ST_SOFTLINK	3
ST_LINKDIR	4
ST_FILE	–3
ST_LINKFILE	–4

Note: This shows up as a directory unless checked for explicitly

Also note that for directories, handlers must use numbers greater than 0, since some programs test to see if fib_DirEntryType is greater than 0, ignoring the case where fib_DirEntryType equals 0. Handlers should avoid using 0 because it is not interpreted consistently.

```
ACTION_EXAMINE_NEXT    24      ExNext(...)
ARG1:      LOCK    Lock on directory being examined
ARG2:      BPTR    BPTR FileInfoBlock

RES1:      BOOL    Success/failure (DOSTRUE/DOSFALSE)
RES2:      CODE    Failure code if RES1 = DOSFALSE
```

The ExNext() function uses this packet to obtain information on all the objects in a directory. ACTION_EXAMINE fills in a FileInfoBlock structure describing the first file or directory stored in the directory referred to in the lock in ARG1. ACTION_EXAMINE_NEXT is used to find out about the rest of the files and directories stored in the ARG1 directory. ARG2 contains a pointer to a valid FileInfoBlock field that was filled in by either an ACTION_EXAMINE or a previous ACTION_EXAMINE_NEXT call. It uses this structure to find the next entry in the directory. This packet writes over the old FileInfoBlock with information on the next file or directory in the ARG2 directory. ACTION_EXAMINE_NEXT returns a failure code of ERROR_NO_MORE_ENTRIES when there are no more files or directories left to be examined. Unfortunately, like ACTION_EXAMINE, this packet has its own peculiarities. Among the quirks that ACTION_EXAMINE_NEXT must account for are:

- The situation where an application calls ACTION_ EXAMINE_NEXT one or more times and then stops invoking it before encountering the end of the directory.
- The situation where a FileInfoBlock passed to ACTION_ EXAMINE_NEXT is not the same as the one passed to ACTION_EXAMINE or even the previous EXAMINE_NEXT operation. Instead, it is a copy of the FileInfoBlock with only the fib_DiskKey and the first 30 bytes of the fib_FileName fields

copied over. This is now considered to be illegal and will not work in the future. Any new code should not be written in this manner.
- Because a handler can receive other packet types between ACTION_EXAMINE_NEXT operations, the ACTION_EXAMINE_NEXT function must handle any special cases that may result.
- The LOCK passed to ACTION_EXAMINE_NEXT is not always the same lock used in previous operations. It is, however, a lock on the same object.

Because of these problems, ACTION_EXAMINE_NEXT is probably the trickiest action to write in any handler. Failure to handle any of the above cases can be quite disastrous.

```
ACTION_CREATE_DIR      22      CreateDir(...)
ARG1:       LOCK    Lock to which ARG2 is relative
ARG2:       BSTR    Name of new directory (relative to ARG1)

RES1:       LOCK    Lock on new directory
RES2:       CODE    Failure code if RES1 = DOSFALSE

ACTION_DELETE_OBJECT   16      DeleteFile(...)
ARG1:       LOCK    Lock to which ARG2 is relative
ARG2:       BSTR    Name of object to delete (relative to
                    ARG1)

RES1:       BOOL    Success/failure (DOSTRUE/DOSFALSE)
RES2:       CODE    Failure code if RES1 = DOSFALSE

ACTION_RENAME_OBJECT   17      Rename(...)
ARG1:       LOCK    Lock to which ARG2 is relative
ARG2:       BSTR    Name of object to rename (relative to
                    ARG1)
ARG3:       LOCK    Lock associated with target directory
ARG4:       BSTR    Requested new name for the object

RES1:       BOOL    Success/failure (DOSTRUE/DOSFALSE)
RES2:       CODE    Failure code if RES1 = DOSFALSE
```

These three actions perform most of the work behind the AmigaDOS commands MAKEDIR, DELETE, and RENAME (for single files). These packets take as their parameters a lock describing where the file is and a name relative to that lock. It is the responsibility of the filesystem to ensure that the operation is not going to cause adverse effects. In particular, the RENAME_OBJECT action allows moving files across directory bounds and as such must ensure that it doesn't create hidden directory loops by renaming a directory into a child of itself.

For Directory objects, the DELETE_OBJECT action must ensure that the directory is empty before allowing the operation.

```
ACTION_PARENT          29      Parent(...)
ARG1:     LOCK    Lock on object to get the parent of

RES1:     LOCK    Parent Lock
RES2:     CODE    Failure code if RES1 = 0
```

This action receives a lock on an object and creates a shared lock on the object's parent. If the original object has no parent, then a lock of 0 is returned. Note that this operation is typically used in the process of constructing the absolute path name of a given object.

```
ACTION_SET_PROTECT     21      SetProtection(...)
ARG1:     Unused
ARG2:     LOCK    Lock to which ARG3 is relative
ARG3:     BSTR    Name of object (relative to ARG2)
ARG4:     LONG    Mask of new protection bits

RES1:     BOOL    Success/failure (DOSTRUE/DOSFALSE)
RES2:     CODE    Failure code if RES1 = DOSFALSE
```

This action allows an application to modify the protection bits of an object. The 4 lowest-order bits [read, write, execute, delete (RWED)] are a bit peculiar. If their respective bit is set, that operation is not allowed (that is, if a file's delete bit is set the file is not deleteable). By default, files are created with the RWED bits set and all others cleared. Additionally, any action that modifies a file is required to clear the A (archive) bit. *See* the dos/dos.h include file for the definitions of the bit fields.

```
ACTION_SET_COMMENT     28      SetComment(...)
ARG1:     Unused
ARG2:     LOCK    Lock to which ARG3 is relative
ARG3:     BSTR    Name of object (relative to ARG2)
ARG4:     BSTR    New Comment string

RES1:     BOOL    Success/failure (DOSTRUE/DOSFALSE)
RES2:     CODE    Failure code if RES1 = DOSFALSE
```

This action allows an application to set the comment string of an object. If the object does not exist then DOSFALSE is returned in RES1 with the failure code in RES2. The comment string is limited to 79 characters.

```
ACTION_SET_DATE        34      SetFileDate(...) in 2.0
ARG1:      LOCK    Object
ARG2:      BPTR    DateStamp

RES1:      BOOL    Success/failure (DOSTRUE/DOSFALSE)
RES2:      CODE    Failure code if RES1 = DOSFALSE
```

This action allows an application to set an object's creation date.

```
2.0 only
ACTION_FH_FROM_LOCK    1026   OpenFromLock(lock)
ARG1:      BPTR    BPTR to filehandle
ARG2:      BPTR    Lock on file to open.

RES1:      BOOL    Success/failure (DOSTRUE/DOSFALSE).
RES2:      CODE    Failure code if RES1 = NULL
```

This action opens a file from a given lock. If this action is successful, the filesystem essentially steals the lock so a program should not use it anymore. If ACTION_FH_FROM_LOCK fails, the lock is still usable by an application.

```
2.0 only
ACTION_SAME_LOCK       40     SameLock(lock1,lock2)
ARG1:      BPTR    Lock 1 to compare
ARG2:      BPTR    Lock 2 to compare

RES1:      LONG    Result of comparison, one of LOCK_SAME
                   (0) if locks are for the same object
                   LOCK_SAME_HANDLER (1) if locks are on
                   different objects of the same handler
                   LOCK_DIFFERENT (-1) otherwise
RES2:      CODE    Failure code if RES1 is LOCK_DIFFERENT
```

This action compares the targets of two locks. If they point to the same object, ACTION_SAME_LOCK should return LOCK_SAME.

```
2.0 only
ACTION_MAKE_LINK       1021   MakeLink(name,targ,mode)
```

```
ARG1:     BPTR    Lock on directory ARG2 is relative to
ARG2:     BSTR    Name of the link to be created (relative
                  to ARG1)
ARG3:     BPTR    Lock on target object or name (for soft
                  links)
ARG4:     LONG    Mode of link, either LINK_SOFT or
                  LINK_HARD

RES1:     BOOL    Success/Failure (DOSTRUE/DOSFALSE)
RES2:     CODE    Failure code if RES1 is DOSFALSE
```

This packet causes the filesystem to create a link to an already existing file or directory. There are two kinds of links, hard links and soft links. The basic difference between them is that a filesystem resolves a hard link itself, while the filesystem passes a string back to DOS telling it where to find a soft-linked file or directory. To the packet level programmer, there is essentially no difference between referencing a file by its original name or by its hard link name. In the case of a hard link, ARG3 is a lock on the file or directory that the link is ``linked'' to, while in a soft link, ARG3 is a pointer to a C-style string.

In an oversimplified model of the ROM filesystem, when it is asked to locate a file, the system scans a disk looking for a file header with a specific (file) name. That file header points to the actual file data somewhere on the disk. With hard links, more than one file header can point to the same file data, so data can be referenced by more than one name. When the user tries to delete a hard link to a file, the system first checks to see if there are any other hard links to the file. If there are, only the hard link is deleted, the actual file data the hard link used to reference remains, so the existing hard links can still use it. In the case where the original link (not a hard or soft link) to a file is deleted, the filesystem will make one of its hard links the new "real" link to the file. Hard links can exist on directories as well. Because hard links "link" directly to the underlying media, hard links in one filesystem cannot reference objects in another filesystem.

Soft links are resolved through DOS calls. When the filesystem scans a disk for a file or directory name and finds that the name is a soft link, it returns an error code (ERROR_IS_SOFT_LINK). If this happens, the application must ask the filesystem to tell it what the link refers to by calling ACTION_READ_LINK. Soft links are stored on the media, but instead of pointing directly to data on the disk, a soft link contains a path to its object. This path can be relative to the lock in ARG1, relative to the volume (where the string will be prepended by a colon ":"), or an absolute path. An absolute path contains the name of another volume, so a soft link can reference files and directories on other disks.

2.0 only

ACTION_READ_LINK   1024   ReadLink(port,lck,nam,buf,len)
ARG1:   BPTR   Lock on directory that ARG2 is relative to
ARG2:   CPTR   Path and name of link (relative to ARG1).
               Note: This is a C string not a BSTR
ARG3:   APTR   Buffer for new path string
ARG4:   LONG   Size of buffer in bytes

RES1:   LONG   Actual length of returned string, -2 if there isn't enough space in buffer, or -1 for other errors
RES2:   CODE   Failure code

This action reads a link and returns a path name to the link's object. The link's name (plus any necessary path) is passed as a CPTR (ARG2) which points to a C-style string, rather than a BSTR. This is an exceptional case; only the ACTION_READ_LINK packet uses a CPTR instead of a BSTR. ACTION_READ_LINK returns the path name in ARG3. The length of the target string is returned in RES1 (or a -1 indicating an error).

ACTION_CHANGE_MODE   1028   ChangeMode(type,obj,mode)
ARG1:   LONG   Type of object to change—either CHANGE_FH or CHANGE_LOCK
ARG2:   BPTR   object to be changed
ARG3:   LONG   New mode for object—see ACTION_FINDINPUT, and ACTION_LOCATE_OBJECT

RES1:   BOOL   Success/Failure (DOSTRUE/DOSFALSE)
RES2:   CODE   Failure code if RES1 is DOSFALSE

This action requests that the handler change the mode of the given file handle or lock to the mode in ARG3. This request should fail if the handler can't change the mode as requested (for example, an exclusive request for an object that has multiple users).

2.0 only

ACTION_COPY_DIR_FH   1030   DupLockFromFH(fh)
ARG1:   BPTR   filehandle

RES1:   BPTR   Lock associated with file handle or NULL
RES2:   CODE   Failure code if RES1 = NULL

This action requests that the handler return a lock associated with the currently opened file handle. The request may fail for any restriction imposed by the filesystem (for example, when the file handle is not opened in a shared mode). The file handle is still usable after this call, unlike the lock in ACTION_FH_FROM_LOCK.

2.0 only
ACTION_PARENT_FH   1031   ParentOfFH(fh)
ARG1:   BPTR   File handle is fh_Arg1.

RES1:   BPTR   Lock on parent of a file handle
RES2:   CODE   Failure code if RES1 = NULL

This action obtains a lock on the parent directory (or root of the volume if at the top level) for a currently opened file handle. The lock is returned as a shared lock and must be freed. Note that unlike ACTION_COPY_DIR_FH, the mode of the file handle is unimportant. For an open file, ACTION_PARENT_FH should return a lock under all circumstances.

2.0 only
ACTION_EXAMINE_ALL   1033   ExAll(lock,buff,size,type,ctl)
ARG1:   BPTR   Lock on directory to examine
ARG2:   APTR   Buffer to store results
ARG3:   LONG   Length (in bytes) of buffer (ARG2)
ARG4:   LONG   Type of request—one of the following:
                  ED_NAME Return only file names
                  ED_TYPE Return above plus file type
                  ED_SIZE Return above plus file size
                  ED_PROTECTION Return above plus file protection
                  ED_DATE Return above plus 3 longwords of date
                  ED_COMMENT Return above plus comment or NULL
ARG5:   BPTR   Control structure to store state information. The control structure must be allocated with AllocDOSObject()!

RES1:   LONG   Continuation flag—DOSFALSE indicates termination
RES2:   CODE   Failure code if RES1 is DOSFALSE

This action allows an application to obtain information on multiple directory entries. It is particularly useful for applications that need to obtain information on a large number of files and directories.

This action fills the buffer (ARG2) with partial or whole ExAllData structures. The size of the ExAllData structure depends on the type of request. If the request type field (ARG4) is set to ED_NAME, only the ed_Name field is filled in. Instead of copying the unused fields of the ExAllData structure into the buffer, ACTION_EXAMINE_ALL truncates the unused fields. This effect is cumulative, so requests to fill in other fields in the ExAllData structure cause all fields that appear in the structure before the requested field will be filled in as well. Like the ED_NAME case mentioned above, any field that appears after the requested field will be truncated (see the ExAllData structure below).

For example, if the request field is set to ED_COMMENT, ACTION_EXAMINE_ALL fills in all the fields of the ExAllData structure, because the ed_Comment field is last. This is the only case where the packet returns entire ExAllData structures.

```
struct ExAllData {
    struct ExAllData *ed_Next;
    UBYTE   *ed_Name;
    LONG    ed_Type;
    ULONG   ed_Size;
    ULONG   ed_Prot;
    ULONG   ed_Days;
    ULONG   ed_Mins;
    ULONG   ed_Ticks;
    UBYTE   *ed_Comment;
        /* strings will be after last used field */
};
```

Each ExAllData structure entry has an ead_Next field which points to the next ExAllData structure. Using these links, a program can easily chain through the ExAllData structures without having to worry about how large the structure is. Do not examine the fields beyond those requested as they certainly will not be initialized (and will probably overlay the next entry).

The most important part of this action is the ExAllControl structure. It must be allocated and freed through AllocDOSObject()/FreeDOSObject(). This allows the structure to grow if necessary with future revisions of the operating and filesystems. Currently, ExAllControl contains four fields:

Entries: This field is maintained by the filesystem and indicates the actual number of entries present in the buffer after the action is complete. Note that a value of zero is possible here as no entries may match the match string.

LastKey: This field must be initialized to 0 by the calling application before using this packet for the first time. This field is maintained by the filesystem as a state indicator of the current place in the list of entries to be examined. The filesystem may test this field to determine if this is the first or a subsequent call to this action.

MatchString: This field points to a pattern matching string to control which directory entries are returned. If this field is NULL, then all entries are returned. Otherwise, this string is used to pattern match the names of all directory entries before putting them into the buffer. The default AmigaDOS pattern match routine is used unless MatchFunc is not NULL (see below). Note that it is not acceptable for the application to change this field between subsequent calls to this action for the same directory.

MatchFunc: This field contains a pointer to an alternate pattern matching routine to validate entries. If it is NULL then the standard AmigaDOS wildcard routines will be used. Otherwise, MatchFunc points to a hook function that is called in the following manner:

```
BOOL = MatchFunc(hookptr, data,typeptr)
                 A0       A1   A2
hookptr    Pointer to the hook being called
data       Pointer to the (partially) filled in ExAll
           data for the item being checked
typeptr    Pointer to the longword indicating the type
           of the ExAll request (ARG4)
```

This function is expected to return DOSTRUE if the entry is accepted and DOSFALSE if it is to be discarded.

```
2.0 only
ACTION_EXAMINE_FH      1034   ExamineFH(fh,fib)
ARG1:    BPTR    File handle on open file
ARG2:    BPTR    FileInfoBlock to fill in

RES1:    BOOL    Success/Failure (DOSTRUE/DOSFALSE)
RES2:    CODE    Failure code if RES1 is DOSFALSE
```

This function examines a filehandle and fills in the FileInfoBlock (found in ARG2) with information about the current state of the file. This routine is analogous to the ACTION_EXAMINE_OBJECT action for locks. Because it is not always possible to provide an accurate file size (for example, when buffers have not been flushed or two processes are writing to a file), the fib_Size field (see dos/dos.h) may be inaccurate.

```
2.0 only
ACTION_ADD_NOTIFY         4097   StartNotify(NotifyRequest)
ARG1:     BPTR    NotifyRequest structure

RES1:     BOOL    Success/Failure (DOSTRUE/DOSFALSE)
RES2:     CODE    Failure code if RES1 is DOSFALSE
```

This action asks a filesystem to notify the calling program if a particular file is altered. A filesystem notifies a program either by sending a message or by signaling a task.

```
struct NotifyRequest {
        UBYTE *nr_Name;
        UBYTE *nr_FullName; /* set by DOS - don't touch */
        ULONG nr_UserData; /* for applications use */
        ULONG nr_Flags;

        union {
          struct {
            struct MsgPort *nr_Port;/* for SEND_MESSAGE */
          } nr_Msg;

          struct {
            struct Task *nr_Task;   /* for SEND_SIGNAL */
            UBYTE nr_SignalNum;     /* for SEND_SIGNAL */
            UBYTE nr_pad[3];
          } nr_Signal;
        } nr_stuff;

        ULONG nr_Reserved[4];       /* leave 0 for now */

                                    /* internal use by handlers */
```

```
    ULONG nr_MsgCount;                  /* # of outstanding msgs */
    struct MsgPort *nr_Handler;         /* handler sent to (for
                                           EndNotify) */
};
```

To use this packet, an application needs to allocate and initialize a NotifyRequest structure (see above). As of this writing, NotifyRequest structures are not allocated by AllocDOSObject(), but this may change in the future. The handler gets the watched file's name from the nr_FullName field. The current filesystem does not currently support wildcards in this field, although there is nothing to prevent other handlers from doing so.

The string in nr_FullName must be an absolute path, including the name of the root volume (no assigns). The absolute path is necessary because the file or its parent directories do not have to exist when the notification is set up. This allows notification on files in directories that do not yet exist. Notification will not occur until the directories and file are created.

An application that uses the StartNotify() DOS call does not fill in the NotifyRequest's nr_FullName field, but instead fills in the nr_Name field. StartNotify() takes the name from the nr_Name field and uses GetDeviceProc() and NameFromLock() to expand any assigns (such as ENV:), storing the result in nr_FullName. Any application utilizing the packet level interface instead of StartNotify() must expand their own assigns. Handlers must not count on nr_Name being correct.

The notification type depends on which bit is set in the NotifyRequest.nr_Flags field. If the NRF_SEND_MESSAGE bit is set, an application receives notification of changes to the file through a message (see NotifyMessage from dos/notify.h). In this case, the nr_Port field must point to the message port that will receive the notifying message. If the nr_Flags NRF_SEND_SIGNAL bit is set, the filesystem signals a task instead of sending a message. In this case, nr_Task points to the task and nr_SignalNum is the signal number. Only one of these 2 bits should be set!

If a program sets the NRF_WAIT_REPLY bit, the handler must wait to send pending notifications until previous ones are returned. When a handler receives a notification request with the NRF_NOTIFY_INITIAL bit set, the handler sends an initial message or gives an initial signal if the watched file already exists.

Handlers should only perform a notification when the actual contents of the file have been changed. This includes ACTION_WRITE, ACTION_TRUNCATE, ACTION_SET_DATE, ACTION_DELETE, ACTION_RENAME, ACTION_FINDUPDATE, ACTION_FINDINPUT, and ACTION_FINDOUTPUT. It may also include other actions such as ACTION_SET_COMMENT or

ACTION_SET_PROTECT, but this is not required (and may not be expected by the application as there is no need to reread the data).

```
2.0 only
ACTION_REMOVE_NOTIFY   4098   EndNotify(NotifyRequest)
ARG1:      BPTR    Pointer to previously added notify request

RES1:      BOOL    Success/Failure (DOSTRUE/DOSFALSE)
RES2:      CODE    Failure code if RES1 is DOSFALSE
```

This action cancels a notification (see ACTION_ADD_NOTIFY). ARG1 is the NotifyRequest structure used to initiate the notification. The handler should abandon any pending notification messages. Note that it is possible for a file system to receive a reply from a previously sent notification message even after the notification has been terminated. It should accept these messages silently and throw them away.

Volume Manipulation/Information

The Volume Manipulation and Information actions are used to allow access to the underlying volume currently being manipulated by the file system.

```
ACTION_CURRENT_VOLUME  7       <sendpkt only>
RES1:      BPTR    Pointer to volume node of current volume
```

This action returns a pointer to the volume node (from the DOS device list) associated with the file system. As the volume node may be removed from the device list when the file system mounts a different volume (such as when directed to by an ACTION_INHIBIT) there is no guarantee that this pointer will remain valid for any amount of time. This action is generally used by AmigaDOS to provide the volume line of a requester.

```
ACTION_DISK_INFO        25      Info(...)
ARG1:      BPTR    Pointer to an InfoData structure to fill in

RES1:      BOOL    Success/Failure (DOSTRUE/DOSFALSE)

ACTION_INFO             26      <sendpkt only>
ARG1:      LOCK    Lock
ARG2:      BPTR    Pointer to a InfoData Structure to fill in

RES1:      BOOL    Success/Failure (DOSTRUE/DOSFALSE)
```

AMIGADOS DATA STRUCTURES

These actions are used to get information about the device and status of the file handler. ACTION_DISK_INFO is used by the info command to report the status of the volume currently in the drive. It fills in an InfoData structure about the volume the file system currently controls. ACTION_INFO fills in an InfoData structure for the volume the lock (ARG1) is on instead of the volume currently in the drive. These actions are generally expected to return DOSTRUE.

The ACTION_DISK_INFO packet has a special meaning for console style handlers. When presented with this packet, a console style handler should return a pointer to the window associated with the open handle.

```
ACTION_RENAME_DISK     9      Relabel(...) in 2.0
ARG1:      BSTR    New disk name

RES1:      BOOL    Success/Failure (DOSTRUE/DOSFALSE)
```

This action allows an application to change the name of the current volume. A filesystem implementing this function must also change the name stored in the volume node of the DOS device list.

```
2.0 only
ACTION_FORMAT          1020   Format(fs,vol,type)
ARG1:      BSTR    Name of device (with trailing ':')
ARG2:      BSTR    Name for volume (if supported)
ARG3:      LONG    Type of format (file system specific)

RES1:      BOOL    Success/Failure (DOSTRUE/DOSFALSE)
RES2:      CODE    Failure code if RES1 is DOSFALSE
```

This packet tells a file system to perform any device or file system specific formatting on any newly initialized media. On receiving this action, a file system can assume that the media has already been low-level formatted and should proceed to write out any high-level disk structure necessary to create an empty volume.

Handler Maintenance and Control

A number of packets are defined to give an application some control over a filesystem:

ACTION_DIE   5   <sendpkt only>
RES1:   BOOL   DOSTRUE

As its name implies, the ACTION_DIE packet tells a handler to quit. All new handlers are expected to implement this packet. Because of outstanding locks and the fact that the handler address is returned by the DeviceProc() routine, it is unlikely that the handler can disappear completely, but instead will have to release as many resources as possible and simply return an error on all packets sent to it.

In the future, the system may be able to determine if there are any outstanding DeviceProc() references to a handler, and therefore make it safe to shut down completely.

ACTION_FLUSH   27   <sendpkt only>
RES1:   BOOL   DOSTRUE

This action causes the file system to flush out all buffers to disk before returning this packet. If any writes are pending, they must be processed before responding to this packet. This packet allows an application to make sure that the data that is supposed to be on the disk is actually written to the disk instead of waiting in a buffer.

ACTION_MORE_CACHE   18   AddBuffers(...) in 2.0
ARG1:   LONG   Number of buffers

RES1:   BOOL   DOSTRUE
RES2:   LONG   New number of buffers

This action allows an application to change the number of internal buffers used by the filesystem for caching. Note that a positive number increases the number of buffers while a negative number decreases the number of buffers. In all cases, the number of current buffers are returned in RES2. This allows an application to inquire the number of buffers by sending in a value of 0 (resulting in no change). Note that the OFS and FFS in 1.3 do not accept a negative number of buffers.

ACTION_INHIBIT   31   Inhibit(...) in 2.0
ARG1:   BOOL   DOSTRUE = inhibit,   DOSFALSE = uninhibit

RES1:   BOOL   Success/failure (DOSTRUE/DOSFALSE)

This action is probably one of the most dangerous that a file system has to handle. When inhibited (ARG1 = DOSTRUE), the filesystem must not access any underlying media and return an error code on all attempts to access the device. Once uninhibited (ARG1 = DOSFALSE), the file system must assume that the media has been changed. The file system must flush the buffers before the ACTION_INHIBIT, popping up a requester demanding that the user put back the current disk, if necessary. The handler may choose to reject an inhibit request if any objects are open for writing.

Although it's not required, a handler should nest inhibits. Prior to 2.0, the system handlers did not keep a nesting count and were subject to some obscure race conditions. The 2.0 ROM filing system introduced a nesting count.

```
ACTION_WRITE_PROTECT    1023    <sendpkt only>
ARG1:       BOOL    DOSTRUE/DOSFALSE (write protect/un-write protect)
ARG2:       LONG    32 Bit pass key

RES1:       BOOL    DOSTRUE/DOSFALSE
```

This is a new packet defined for the Fast File System. This packet allows an application to change the write protect flag of a disk (if possible — applications cannot write to floppies that have their write-protect tabs set). This packet is primarily intended to allow write-protecting nonremovable media such as hard disks. The value in ARG1 toggles the write status. The 32-bit passkey allows a program to prevent other programs from unwrite-protecting a disk. To unlock a disk, ARG2 must match the passkey of the packet that locked the disk, unless the disk was locked with a passkey of 0. In this case, no passkey is necessary to unlock the disk.

```
2.0 only
ACTION_IS_FILESYSTEM    1027    IsFileSystem(devname)

RES1:       BOOL    Success/Failure (DOSTRUE/DOSFALSE)
RES2:       CODE    Failure code if RES1 is DOSFALSE
```

Through this function, a handler can indicate whether or not it is a filesystem (whether or not it can support separate files for storing information). Programs will assume a handler can create multiple, distinct files through calls to Open() if the handler returns this packet with a DOSTRUE value. A handler does not need to support directories and subdirectories in order to qualify as a filesystem. It does have to support the Examine()/ExNext() calls.

Note that the AmigaDOS routine IsFileSystem() will attempt to use Lock(":",SHARED_ACCESS) if this packet returns ERROR_ACTION_NOT_KNOWN.

Handler Internal

There are several actions that are generally used by handlers to allow messages returning from requested services (typically an Exec device) to look like incoming request packets. This allows the handler to request that an asynchronous operation be notified of the completion. For example, a handler sends the serial.device a request for a read, but instead of sending a plain I/O request, it sends a DOS packet disguised as an I/O request. The serial.device treats the packet like a normal I/O request, returning it to the handler when it is finished. When the handler gets back its disguised DOS packet, it knows that the read has completed.

ACTION_NIL   0   <internal>

Although not specifically an action, many returns look like this value because the action field has not been filled in.

ACTION_READ_RETURN   1001   <internal>

This return is generally used to indicate the completion of an asynchronous read request.

ACTION_WRITE_RETURN   1002   <internal>

This return is generally used to indicate the completion of an asynchronous write request.

ACTION_TIMER   30   <internal>

This return is used to indicate the passage of a time interval. Many handlers have a steady stream of ACTION_TIMER packets so that they can schedule house keeping and flush buffers when no activity has occurred for a given time interval.

Obsolete Packets

There are several packet types that are documented within the system that include files that are obsolete. A file system is not expected to handle these packets, and any program that sends these packets cannot expect them to work:

```
ACTION_DISK_CHANGE       33            <Obsolete>
ACTION_DISK_TYPE         32            <Obsolete>
ACTION_EVENT              6            <Obsolete>
ACTION_GET_BLOCK          2            <Obsolete>
ACTION_SET_MAP            4            <Obsolete>
```

Of particular note here is ACTION_DISK_CHANGE. The DiskChange command uses the ACTION_INHIBIT packet to accomplish its task.

Console Only Packets

The remaining packets are only used for console handlers and do not need to be implemented by a file system.

```
ACTION_SCREEN_MODE      994     <sendpkt only>
ARG1:      LONG    Mode (zero or one)

RES1:      BOOL    Success/Failure (DOSTRUE/DOSFALSE)
RES2:      CODE    Failure code if RES1 is DOSFALSE
```

Switch the console to and from RAW mode. An ARG1 of 1 indicates the unprocessed, raw mode while an ARG1 of zero indicates the processed, ``cooked'' mode.

```
ACTION_WAIT_CHAR         20     WaitForChar()
ARG1:      ULONG   Timeout in microseconds

RES1:      BOOL    Success/Failure (DOSTRUE/DOSFALSE)
RES2:      CODE    Failure code if RES1 is DOSFALSE
```

Performs a timed read of a character. The WaitForChar() function uses this packet.

Summary of Defined Packet Numbers

This is a listing of all the DOS packets defined by Commodore. Packets 0-2049 are reserved for use by Commodore. Unless otherwise noted, packets 2050-2999 are reserved for use by third-party developers (see table N below). The remaining packets are reserved for future expansion. (Note: packets 2008, 2009, 4097, and 4098 are in use by Commodore.)

Decimal	Hex	Action #define
0	0x0000	ACTION_NIL
1		<Reserved by Commodore>
2	0x0002	ACTION_GET_BLOCK
3		<Reserved by Commodore>
4	0x0004	ACTION_SET_MAP
5	0x0005	ACTION_DIE
6	0x0006	ACTION_EVENT
7	0x0007	ACTION_CURRENT_VOLUME
8	0x0008	ACTION_LOCATE_OBJECT
9	0x0009	ACTION_RENAME_DISK
10–14		<Reserved by Commodore>
15	0x000F	ACTION_FREE_LOCK
16	0x0010	ACTION_DELETE_OBJECT
17	0x0011	ACTION_RENAME_OBJECT
18	0x0012	ACTION_MORE_CACHE
19	0x0013	ACTION_COPY_DIR
20	0x0014	ACTION_WAIT_CHAR
21	0x0015	ACTION_SET_PROTECT
22	0x0016	ACTION_CREATE_DIR
23	0x0017	ACTION_EXAMINE_OBJECT
24	0x0018	ACTION_EXAMINE_NEXT
25	0x0019	ACTION_DISK_INFO
26	0x001A	ACTION_INFO
27	0x001B	ACTION_FLUSH
28	0x001C	ACTION_SET_COMMENT
29	0x001D	ACTION_PARENT
30	0x001E	ACTION_TIMER
31	0x001F	ACTION_INHIBIT
32	0x0020	ACTION_DISK_TYPE
33	0x0021	ACTION_DISK_CHANGE
34	0x0022	ACTION_SET_DATE
35–39		<Reserved by Commodore>
40	0x0028	ACTION_SAME_LOCK
41–81		<Reserved by Commodore>
82	0x0052	ACTION_READ
83–86		<Reserved by Commodore>

87	0x0057	ACTION_WRITE
88–993		<Reserved by Commodore>
994	0x03E2	ACTION_SCREEN_MODE
995–1000		<Reserved by Commodore>
1001	0x03E9	ACTION_READ_RETURN
1002	0x03EA	ACTION_WRITE_RETURN
1003		<Reserved by Commodore>
1004	0x03EC	ACTION_FINDUPDATE
1005	0x03ED	ACTION_FINDINPUT
1006	0x03EE	ACTION_FINDOUTPUT
1007	0x03EF	ACTION_END
1008	0x03F0	ACTION_SEEK
1009–1019		<Reserved by Commodore>
1020	0x03FC	ACTION_FORMAT
1021	0x03FD	ACTION_MAKE_LINK
1022	0x03FE	ACTION_SET_FILE_SIZE
1023	0x03FF	ACTION_WRITE_PROTECT
1024	0x0400	ACTION_READ_LINK
1025		<Reserved by Commodore>
1026	0x0402	ACTION_FH_FROM_LOCK
1027	0x0403	ACTION_IS_FILESYSTEM
1028	0x0404	ACTION_CHANGE_MODE
1029		<Reserved by Commodore>
1030	0x0406	ACTION_COPY_DIR_FH
1031	0x0407	ACTION_PARENT_FH
1032		<Reserved by Commodore>
1033	0x0409	ACTION_EXAMINE_ALL
1034	0x040A	ACTION_EXAMINE_FH
1035–2007		<Reserved by Commodore>
2008	0x07D8	ACTION_LOCK_RECORD
2009	0x07D9	ACTION_FREE_RECORD
2010–2049		<Reserved by Commodore>
2050-2999		<Reserved for 3rd Party Handlers>
4097	0x1001	ACTION_ADD_NOTIFY
4098	0x1002	ACTION_REMOVE_NOTIFY
4099-		<Reserved by Commodore for Future Expansion>

Using Packets Directly

AmigaDOS contains many features that can only be accessed by sending a packet directly to a process. For example, the ACTION_DISK_INFO packet may be used to find the Intuition window pointer of a CON: or RAW: window. This is useful for redirecting system requesters so that they appear where the user can see them (see Redirecting System Requesters, above). The Window pointer will be returned in the ID_VolumeNode field, and a pointer to the console's I/O request will be returned in the ID_InUse field. Note that auxiliary consoles (AUX:) can return a NULL Window pointer, and also may have no ConUnit (io_Unit) associated with their I/O request block. Be careful to check for these possibilities when you use this packet. If your application runs in a CLI window, a user may be running you in an auxiliary (AUX:) CLI.

Another example is the ACTION_SCREENMODE_MODE packet which can be sent to the handler process of a CON: window to put the console into raw or cooked mode.

By default, CON: provides mapped keyboard input which is filtered, buffered, and automatically echoed. Many of the special key escape sequences (such as those generated by the function, cursor, and help keys) are filtered out; all strokes are buffered and held back from the reader until the user hits the Return key; and the nonfiltered keypresses (such as alphanumeric keys and backspace) are automatically echoed to the CON: window. This "cooked" mode is perfect for general line input from a user because it provides automatic line editing features (same as in the Shell command line).

Sometimes, however, an application needs to get individual keys immediately from a CON: window, or control its own echoing, or receive the escape strings that the keymap generates for special keys such as the Help key or cursor keys.

In this case, an ACTION_SCREEN_MODE packet with the argument DOSTRUE (-1L) may be sent to the MsgPort of a CON: window to put the CON: into "raw" mode. In raw mode, a CON: behaves much like a RAW: window. Keyboard console input is not automatically filtered, buffered, or echoed. When reading a CON: which has been set to "raw" mode, each keypress can be read immediately as the ASCII value or string to which the key is mapped by the keymap.

For some applications, it may be convenient to toggle a CON: window between cooked and raw modes, to use cooked mode for user line input, and raw mode when keypresses should cause immediate actions.

ACTION_SCREEN_MODE with the argument DOSFALSE (0L) will place a CON: window in cooked mode. Note that the ACTION_SCREEN_MODE packet may also be used on auxiliary (AUX:) consoles.

The handler MsgPort of most named AmigaDOS devices (like DF0:) can be found with the DeviceProc() function. Note that DeviceProc() cannot be used to find a CON: or RAW: handler because there may be many handlers for each of these. The handler MsgPort(ProcessID) of a CON: or RAW: window is in its FileHandle structure (fh_Type). The MsgPort of a CLI process's "*" window is process->pr_ConsoleTask.

Here's how to find the MsgPort of a handler process (in all cases make sure that port is non-NULL before using it):

1. Finding the MsgPort of a unique named handler process such as "DF0:"
   port = (struct MsgPort *)DeviceProc("DF1:").

2. Finding the MsgPort of the handler process for an open file:

```
fh = Open("CON:0/40/640/140/Test",MODE_NEWFILE);
if((fh)&&(fh->Type))
        /* if Open succeeded and fh_Type is non-NULL */
{
              port = (struct MsgPort *)(((struct
              FileHandle *)
              (fh<<2))->fh_Type);
}
```

3. Finding the MsgPort of your process's console handler:

```
struct Task *task = FindTask(NULL);
if(task->tc_Node.ln_Type == NT_PROCESS)
{
      /* port may be NULL - check before using ! */
      port = ((struct Process *)task)->pr_ConsoleTask;
}
```

Packets are sent by initializing a longword-aligned StandardPacket structure and sending the packet to the MsgPort of a handler process.

The 2.0 DOS.library provides new simple functions for sending and replying to packets:

```
SendPkt() - asynchronously send your initialized packet
WaitPkt() - wait for asynchronous packet to complete
```

ReplyPkt() - reply a packet which has been sent to you
DoPkt() - creates and sends a packet, and waits for completion

Refer to section 2.2 (AmigaDOS Functions) for a full description of these functions and their arguments.

If you need to send packets in a 1.3-compatible manner, the following function may be used rather than the new 2.0 dos.library functions.

```
#include <exec/types.h>
#include <exec/memory.h>
#include <libraries/DOS.h>
#include <libraries/DOSextens.h>
 *  dopkt() by A. Finkel, P. Lindsay, C. Scheppner
 *  Send a packet in a 1.3-compatible manner
 *  and wait for completion; returns Res1 of the
 *  reply packet
 */

LONG dopkt(pid,action,args,nargs)
struct MsgPort *pid;    /* process indentifier    */
                        /* (handler message port) */
LONG action,            /* packet type (desired action) */
     args[],            /* a pointer to an argument list*/
     nargs;             /* number of arguments in list */
{
   struct MsgPort        *replyport;
   struct StandardPacket *packet;

   LONG  count, *pargs, res1;

   replyport = (struct MsgPort *) CreatePort(NULL,0);
   if(!replyport) return(NULL);

   packet = (struct StandardPacket *)
            AllocMem((long)sizeof(struct StandardPacket),MEMF_PUBLIC|MEMF_CLEAR);
   if(!packet)
       {
       DeletePort(replyport);
       return(NULL);
       }
```

```
packet->sp_Msg.mn_Node.ln_Name = (char *)&(packet->sp_Pkt);
packet->sp_Pkt.dp_Link         = &(packet->sp_Msg);
packet->sp_Pkt.dp_Port         = replyport;
packet->sp_Pkt.dp_Type         = action;

/* copy the args into the packet */
pargs = &(packet->sp_Pkt.dp_Arg1); /* address of first arg */
for(count=0;count < nargs;count++)
    pargs[count]=args[count];

PutMsg(pid,packet); /* send packet */


WaitPort(replyport);
GetMsg(replyport);

res1 = packet->sp_Pkt.dp_Res1;

FreeMem(packet,(long)sizeof(struct StandardPacket));
DeletePort(replyport);

return(res1);
}
```

Chapter 12

Additional Information for the Advanced Developer

This chapter describes certain topics that are likely to be of interest to the advanced developer who may wish to create new devices to be added to the Amiga or who wish their code to run with Amiga computers which have been expanded beyond a 512K memory size.

The following topics are covered here:

Overlay Hunk Description
  for developers putting together large programs

Linking in a new disk-device to AmigaDOS
  lets a developer add a hard disk or disk-like device as a name-addressable part of the filing system.

Linking in a new non-disk-device to AmigaDOS
  lets a developer add such things as additional serial ports, parallel ports, graphics tablets, RAM-disks, or what-have-you to AmigaDOS (non–filing–system related).

Using AmigaDOS without using Intuition
  for developers who may prefer to install and use their own screen handling in place of that provided by Intuition.

Hunk Overlay Table—Overview

When overlays are used, the linker basically produces one very large file containing all of the object modules as hunks of relocatable code. The hunk overlay table contains a data structure that describes the hunks and their relationship to each other.

When you are designing a program to use overlays, you must keep in mind how the overlay manager (also called the overlay supervisor) handles the interaction between the various segments of the file. What you must do, basically, is build a tree that reflects the relationships between the various code modules that are a part of the overall program and tell the linker how this tree should be constructed.

The hunk overlay table is generated as a set of 8 long words, each describing a particular overlay node that is part of the overall file. Each 8 long word entry is comprised of the following data:

Hunk Overlay Symbol–Table Entry Data Structure:

```
long seekOffset;     /* where in the file to find this node */
long dummy1;         /* a value of 0 ... compatibility item */
long dummy2;         /* a value of 0 ... compatibility item */
long level;          /* level in the tree */
long ordinate;       /*f item number at that level */
long firstHunk;      /* hunk number of the first hunk containing
                      * this node. */
long symbolHunk;     /* the hunk number in which this symbol is
                      * located */
long symbolOffsetX;  /* (offset + 4), where offset is the offset
                      * within the symbol hunk at which this
                      * symbol's entry is located. */
```

Each of these items is explained further in the sections that follow.

Designing an Overlay Tree

Let's say that you have, for example, the files main, a, b, c, d, e, f, g, h, i, and j, and that main can call a, b, c, and d and that each of these files can call main. Additionally let's say that routine e can be called from a, b, c, d, or main, but has no relationship to routine f. Thus, if a routine in e is to be run, then a, b, c, and d need to be memory-resident as well. Routine f is like e; that is, it needs nothing in e to be present, but can be called from a, b, c, or d. This means that the overlay manager can share the memory space between routines e and f, since neither need ever be memory-coresident with the other to run.

If you consider routine g to share the same space as the combination of a, b, c, and d and routines h, i, and j sharing the same space, you have the basis for constructing the overlay tree for this program structure:

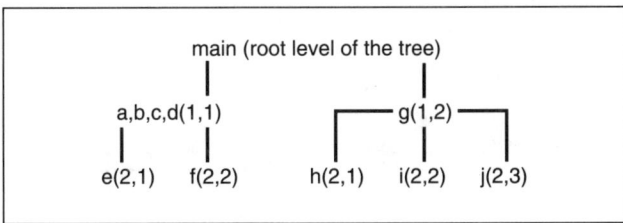

Figure 12-1.

Not only have we drawn the tree, but we have also labeled its branches to match the hunk overlay (level, ordinate) numbers that are found in the hunk overlay table that matches the nodes to which they are assigned.

From the description above, you can see that if main is to call any routine in program segment a–d, then all of those segments should be resident in memory at the same time. Thus they have all been assigned to a single node by the linker. While a–d are resident, if you call routines in e, the linker will automatically load routine e from disk, and reinitialize the module (each time it is again brought in), so that its subroutines will be available to be run. If any segment a–d calls a routine in f, the linker replaces e with the contents of f and initializes it. Thus a–d are at level 1 in the overlay tree, and routines e and f are at level 2, requiring that a–d be loaded before e or f can be accessed and loaded for execution.

Note: A routine can only perform calls to routines in other nodes that either are currently memory-resident (the ancestors of the node in which the routine now in use is located), or a routine in a direct child node. That is , main cannot call e directly, but e can call routines in main since main is an ancestor.

Note also that within each branch of each subnode, the ordinate numbers begin again with number 1 for a given level.

Describing the tree

You create the tree by telling the overlay linker about its structure. The numerical values, similar to those noted in the figure above, are assigned sequentially by the linker itself and appear in the hunk node table. Here is the sequence of overlay link statements that cause the figure above to be built:

```
OVERLAY
a,b,c,d
*e
*f
g
*h
*i
*j
```

Figure 12-2.

This description tells the linker that a, b, c, d are part of a single node at a given level (in this case level 1), and the asterisk in front of e and f each say that these are one each on the next level down from a–d, and accesible only through a–d or anything closer toward the root of the tree. The name g has no asterisk, so it is considered on the same level as a–d, telling the linker that either a-d or g will be memory-resident, but not both simultaneously. Names h, i, and j are shown to be related to g, one level down.

The above paragraphs have explained the origin of the hunk node level and the hunk ordinate in the hunk overlay symbol table.

seekOffset Amount

The first value for each node in the overlay table is the seek offset. As specified earlier, the overlay linker builds a large single file containing all of the overlay nodes. The seek offset number is that value that can be given to the seek(file, byte_offset) routine to point to the first byte of the hunk header of a node.

firstHunk

The firstHunk value in the overlay symbol table is used by the overlay manager when unloading a node. It specifies the initial hunk that must have been loaded in order to have loaded the node that contains this symbol. When a routine is called at a different level and ordinate (unless it is a direct, next level, child of the current node), it is necessary to free the memory utilized by invalid hunks, so as to make room to overlay with the hunk(s) containing the desired symbol.

symbolHunk and symbolOffsetX

These table entries for the symbols are used by the overlay manager to actually locate the entry point once it has either determined it is already loaded or has loaded it. The symbolHunk shows in which hunk to locate the symbol. symbolOffsetX-4 shows the offset from the start of that hunk at which the entry point is actually located.

Overlay Nodes and the Linker

While linking an overlaid program, the linker checks each symbol reference for validity. Suppose that the reference is in a tree node R, and the symbol is in a node S. Then the reference is legal if one of the following is true:

1. R and S are the same node.
2. R is a descendant of S.
3. R is the parent of S.

References of the third type above are known as overlay references. In this case, the linker enters the overlay supervisor when the program is run. The overlay supervisor then checks to see if the code segment containing the symbol is already in memory. If not, first the code segment, if any, at this level, and all its descendants are unloaded, and then the node containing the symbol is brought into memory. An overlaid code segment returns directly to its caller, and so is not unloaded from memory until another node is loaded on top of it.

For example, suppose that Figure 12-3 is the tree:

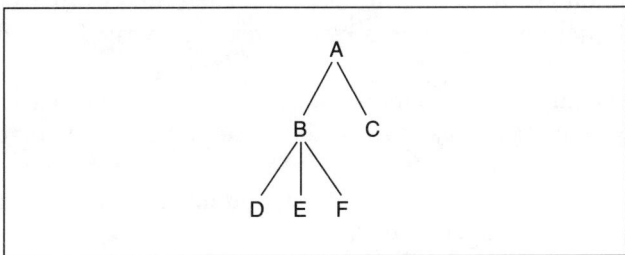

Figure 12-3.
The tree.

When the linker first loads the program, only A is in memory. When the linker finds a reference in A to a symbol in B, it loads and enters B. If B, in turn, calls D then again a new node is loaded. When B returns to A, both B and D are left in memory, and the linker does not reload them if the program requires them later. Now suppose that A calls C. First the linker unloads the code segments that it does not require, and which it may overwrite. In this case, these are B and D. Once it has reclaimed the memory for these, the linker can load C.

Thus, when the linker executes a given node, all the node's "ancestors," up to the root are in memory, and possibly some of its descendants.

The linker assumes that all overlay references are jumps or subroutine calls, and routes them through the overlay supervisor. Thus, you should not use overlay symbols as data labels.

Try to avoid impure code when overlaying because the linker does not always load a node that is fresh from the load file.

The linker gives each symbol that has an overlay reference an overlay number. It uses this value, which is zero or more, to construct the overlay supervisor entry label associated with that symbol. This label is of the form "OVLYnnnn", where nnnn is the overlay number. You should not use symbols with this format elsewhere.

The linker gathers together all program sections with the same section name. It does this so that it can load them continuously in memory.

Delete all the material on "ATOM: (Alink Temporary Object Modifier)". It describes a product no longer sold or supported by Commodore.

Creating a New Device to Run Under AmigaDOS

This section provides information about adding devices that are NOT part of the DOS filing system like the console and port handlers. The next section provides information about adding file-system-related devices (hard disks, floppy disks)—that is, devices that DOS can use to read and write files with their associated directories.

You would want to use this information to add a new device such as a new serial port or a new parallel port. In this case you may be creating a device named "SER2:" which is to act just like "SER:" as far as DOS is concerned.

There are two steps involved here. First, you must create a suitable device, a process that is not addressed here.

Second, you must make this new device available as an AmigaDOS device. This process involves writing a suitable device handler and installing it into the AmigaDOS structures. You install a new device and its handler under AmigaDOS with the MOUNT command. You need to put the device in the DEVS: directory, the handler in the L: directory, and add an entry for the device in DEVS: mountlist.

The device handler is the interface between your device and an application program. The AmigaDOS kernel will attempt to load the code of the handler and create a new process for it when it is first referenced. This is handled automatically when the kernel notices that the Task field in the DevInfo structure is zero. If the code is already loaded, the code segment pointer is placed in the SegList field. If this field is zero, the kernel loads the code from the filename given in the filename field and updates the SegList field.

Making New Disk Devices

To create a new disk device, you must construct a new device node as described in "Info Substructure," Chapter 11 of this book. You must also write a device driver for the new disk device.

A device driver for a new disk device must mimic the calls that are performed by the trackdisk device. It must include the ability to respond to commands such as Read(), Write(), Seek(), and return status information in the same way as described for the trackdisk driver.

Using AmigaDOS Without Workbench/Intuition

This information is provided to give developers some information about how AmigaDOS and Intuition interact with each other. As of this writing, it is not possible to fully close down Intuition or the input device. It is possible to install one's own input handler within the input stream and thereby handle input events yourself, after your program has been loaded and started by AmigaDOS. If, after that point, you take over the machine in some manner, you can prevent AmigaDOS from trying to put up system requesters or otherwise interacting with the screen by modifying DOS as shown below. Basically, your own program must provide alternate ways to handle errors that would normally cause DOS to put up a requester.

Another alternative for taking over the machine is to ignore the AmigaDOS filing system altogether, and use the trackdisk.device to boot your code and data on your own.

Here are the details about AmigaDOS and Intuition:

AmigaDOS initializes itself and opens Intuition. It then attempts to open the configuration file (created by Preferences) and passes this to Intuition. It then opens the initial CLI window via Intuition and attempts to run the first CLI command. This is commonly a loadwb (load Workbench), followed by an endcli on the initial CLI.

An application program can be made to behave like Workbench, in that it spawns a new process. The next CLI command is then endcli, which closes everything down, leaving only the new process running (along with the filesystem processes). This process would set the pr_WindowPtr field to -1, which indicates that the DOS should report errors quietly. Note that the application MUST handle all errors. There are further details on this in Chapter 11. DOS will also have initialized the TrapHandler field of the user task to point to code that will display a requester after an error; this should be replaced by a user-provided routine. This will stop all uses of Intuition from the user task, provided there are no serious memory corruption problems found, in which case DOS will call Exec Alert directly.

There is still the problem that the filesystem processes may ask for a requester, in the event of a disk error or if the filesystem task crashes due to memory corruption. To stop this, the pr_WindowPtr and tc_TrapHandler fields of the filesystem tasks must be set to -1 and a private Trap handler must be provided in the same way as was done for the user task. This is easily done as shown below.

Find the message port for each filesystem task by calling DeviceProc(), passing it each of the devices AmigaDOS is running (DF0:, DF1:, etc.). You get the device names by walking the device list pointed to by the Info structure. An error indicates that the device is not present. From the message port you can find the task base for each filesystem task, and hence patch these two slots. This procedure should be repeated for each disk unit.

The application program can now close Intuition. Workbench has, of course, never been invoked. Note that as of this writing, it is not possible to stop DOS from opening Intuition.

Note that if the applications want to use any other device such as SER:, the handler process must be patched in exactly the same way as the filesystem processes. The application should obviously not attempt to open the CON: or RAW: once Intuition has become inactive.

Index

A

AbortPkt, description of, 188–189
ADDBUFFERS, 43
  description of, 189–190
AddDosEntry, description of, 190
ADDMONITOR, 44
AddPart, description of, 191
AddSegment, description of, 192
ALIAS, 45–46
Aliases
  removing, UNALIAS, 147–148
  setting, ALIAS, 45–46
ALINK
  command line syntax, 317
  parameters, 317–318
  WITH files, 318–322
AllocDosObject, description of, 193
AmigaDOS
  commands, 19–21
  console handling, 6–8
  filing system, 8–18
  processes of, 5–6
  updating, 21–22
AmigaDOS devices, 327–331
  communication with, 331
  listing of, 328–331
Amiga linker, 170
Angle brackets, in format listings of commands, 41
ARG1, 398
Arguments, 8
Arrow symbols, redirection of input/output, 21, 30
ASCII files, displaying contents, MORE, 118–119
ASK, 46
Assembler, 170, 352
ASSIGN, 35–37, 46–50
AssignAdd, description of, 193–194
AssignLate, description of, 194–195
AssignLock, description of, 195–196

AssignPath, description of, 196
Asterisk (*), 16
  as device name, 16
  and filenames, 8–9
AttemptLockDosList, description of, 196–197
Automatic overlay system, linker, 321
AUTOPOINT, 51
AUX, 328
AVAIL, 51–52

B

Background
  running commands in, 20
  RUN, 134–135
Background patterns, creating, WBPATTERN, 151–152
Basic Input/Output, packet, 398, 399–402
BCPL, 381–382
BINDDRIVERS, 52
BINDMONITOR, 52–53
BLANKER, 53–54
BOOL, 398
Boolean returns, functions, 188
Bootable disks
  creating, INSTALL, 105–106
  creating CLI disk, 26
  INSTALL, 25–26
Booting, automation of boot sequence, 35
BPTR, 381, 392, 393, 398
Braces, in format listings of commands, 41
Brackets, in format listings of commands, 41
BREAK, 54–55
BSTR, 381, 398
Buffered I/O, 179–180
Buffers, adding cache buffers, ADDBUFFERS, 43–44
Burst mode, 62–63

C

C, logical device, 17

437

Caches
    clearing CPU caches, CPU, 62–64
    instruction cache, 62
Calculations, on-screen, CALCULATOR, 55
CALCULATOR, 55
CAMG chunk, 72
Caps lock key, disabling, NOCAPSLOCK, 121
CD, 56
C directory, 18
ChangeMode, description of, 197–198
CHANGETASKPRI, 57
Characters, alternative character set, 7
CheckSignal, description of, 198
Cli, description of, 199
CLOCK, 57–58
Close, description of, 199–200
CMD, 58–59
CODE, 398
COLORS, 59–60
    changing
        COLORS, 59–60
        PALETTE, 123
Command history, use of, 6
Command line, and linker, 315
Command line buffer, 6
Command Line Interface
    activation of, 3
    creating CLI disk, 26
    See also Shell
Command path, search of, WHICH, 152
Commands, 19–21
    ADDBUFFERS, 43
    ADDMONITOR, 44
    ALIAS, 45–46
    ASK, 46
    ASSIGN, 46–50
    AUTOPOINT, 51
    AVAIL, 51–52
    BINDDRIVERS, 52
    BINDMONITOR, 52–53
    BLANKER, 53–54
    BREAK, 54–55
    CALCULATOR, 55
    CD, 56
    CHANGETASKPRI, 57
    CLOCK, 57–58
    CMD, 58–59
    COLORS, 59–60
    conventions related to, 40
    COPY, 60–62
    CPU, 62–64
    DATE, 64–65
    DELETE, 65–66
    DIR, 66–68

directing input/output, 21
DISKCHANGE, 68–69
DISKCOPY, 69–70
DISKDOCTOR, 70–71
DISPLAY, 71–73
ECHO, 73
ED, 74–77
EDIT, 78–81
ELSE, 82
ENDCLI, 82–83
ENDIF, 83
ENDSHELL, 83
ENDSKIP, 84
EVAL, 84–86
EXCHANGE, 86–87
EXECUTE, 87–91
execution of, 19, 20, 39–40
FAILAT, 91–92
FAULT, 93
FILENOTE, 93–94
FIXFONTS, 94
FKEY, 94–95
FONT, 95–96
FORMAT, 96–97
format listings, 41
format of, 41
GET, 97
GETNV, 97–98
GRAPHICDUMP, 98–99
ICONEDIT, 99
ICONTROL, 99–100
ICONX, 100
IF, 100–102
IHELP, 102–103
INFO, 103
INITPRINTER, 104
INPUT, 104
INSTALL, 105
instructing command sequence to fail, FAILAT, 91–92
interactive running of, 19
interrupting current command, 21
IPREFS, 106
JOIN, 106
KEYSHOW, 107
LAB, 107
LIST, 107–110
listing of commands, 153–157
loading commands faster, 19
LOADWB, 110–111
LOCK, 111
MAKEDIR, 112
MAKELINK, 112
MEMACS, 113–118
MORE, 118–119
MOUNT, 119

NEWCLI, 119–120
NEWSHELL, 120–121
NOCAPSLOCK, 121
NOFASTMEM, 122
OVERSCAN, 122
PALETTE, 123
PATH, 123–124
POINTER, 125
PRINTER, 125
PRINTERGFX, 126
PRINTFILES, 126–127
PROMPT, 127–128
PROTECT, 128–129
QUIT, 129–130
RELABEL, 130
REMRAD, 131
RENAME, 131–132
RESIDENT, 132–134
RUN, 134–135
running in background, 20
   RUN, 134–135
SAY, 135
SCREENMODE, 136
SEARCH, 136–138
SERIAL, 138
SET, 138–139
SETCLOCK, 139–140
SETDATE, 140
SETENV, 141
SETFONT, 141–142
SETMAP, 142–143
SETPATCH, 143
SKIP, 143–144
SORT, 144–145
STACK, 145
STATUS, 146
template, 42
template of command, accessing, 24
TIME, 146–147
TYPE, 147
UNALIAS, 147–148
UNSET, 148
UNSETENV, 148
VERSION, 148
WAIT, 149–150
WBCONFIG, 150
WBPATTERN, 151–152
WHICH, 152
WHY, 153
Commodity Exchange programs, control of, EXCHANGE, 86–87
Communication specifications, setting, SERIAL, 138
CompareDates, description of, 200
CON, 15, 328–330
Conclip, 329–330

Console
   console handler, 6
   packets for, 398, 421
Control key combinations, 6–8
   editing commands, 7–8
COPY, 19, 32–33, 60–62
Copying directories, COPY, 60–62
Copying disks, DISKCOPY, 24–25
Copying files, COPY, 32–33, 60–62
C programming, initial environment in, 172
CPU, 62–64
CreateDir, description of, 201
CreateNewProc, description of, 201–202
CreateProc, description of, 202–203
CurrentDir, description of, 203–204
Current directory, changing, CD, 10–11, 29–30
Current drive, setting, 12–13
Cursor, moving with ED, 75

D

Data blocks, 348–350
Data structure
   file handles, 393–394
   library structure, 387–392
   locks, 394–395
   packets, 395–427
   process data structure, 382–387
   segment lists, 393
DATE, 22, 30, 64–65
   changing datestamp, SETDATE, 140
   setting, DATE, 30, 64–65
DateStamp, description of, 204–205
DateToStr, description of, 205–206
Delay, description of, 206–207
DELETE, 31–32, 65–66
Delete character, 6
Delete directories, DELETE, 65–66
DeleteFile, description of, 207
Delete files, DELETE, 31–32, 65–66
Delete line, 6, 7
DeleteVar, description of, 207–208
Device drivers, binding to hardware, BINDDRIVERS, 52
Device names, 13, 13–16
   asterisk (*), 16
   CON, 15
   NIL, 14
   PAR, 14
   PRT, 14–15
   RAM, 14
   RAW, 15
   SER, 14
   use of, 13–14
DeviceProc, description of, 208–209

Devices
  device names, 13–16
  disk devices, creating new device, 435
  logical devices, 16–19
   making available to system, MOUNT, 119
  new device to run under AmigaDos, creating, 434–435
  See also AmigaDOS devices
DEVS, 17
DIR, 4, 27, 66–68
Directories
  C directory, 18
  changing, CD, 56
  changing name of, RENAME, 131–132
  copying directories, COPY, 60–62
  creation of, MAKEDIR, 33–34, 112
  and current drive, 12
  deleting directories, DELETE, 65–66
  directory list for search to find commands, PATH, 123–124
  displaying files in, DIR, 27, 34, 66–68
  listing information about, 107–110
  root directory, 9
  search of, 11
  setting current directory, 10–11
  structure of, 9–10
  and subdirectories, 10
  T directory, 18
Directory/file manipulation/information, packet, 398, 403–416
DISKCHANGE, 68–69
DISKCOPY, 24–25, 69–70
Diskcopy program, 4
Disk devices, creating new device, 435
DISKDOCTOR, 70–71
Disks
  assigning disks, ASSIGN, 35–37
  changing in disk drive, DISKCHANGE, 68–69
  changing volume name, RELABEL, 130
  copying contents, DISKCOPY, 69–70
  formatting, FORMAT, 96–97
  repair of corrupted disk, DISKDOCTOR, 70–71
  viewing contents of disk, 34
  write-protection, setting, LOCK, 111
DISPLAY, 71–73
  changing size of, OVERSCAN, 122
  selecting mode, SCREENMODE, 136
DoPkt, description of, 209–210
Dos.library, and programming, 170, 174–176
DOS packet interface, 331
DupLockFromFH, description of, 211
DupLock, description of, 210–211

E

ECHO, 73
ED, 34–35, 74–77
  extended mode commands, 76–77
  immediate mode commands, 75–76
  moving cursor, 75
EDIT, 78–81
  character positioning commands, 80
  current line commands, 80
  file commands, 81
  global commands, 81
  positioning commands, 79
  search commands, 79–80
  text verification commands, 81
Editing
  icons, ICONEDIT, 99
  summary of editing commands, 7–8
  text files, ED, 74–77
  text files by processing source files, EDIT, 78–81
ELSE, 82
ENDCLI, 35, 82–83
ENDIF, 83
EndNotify, description of, 212
End-of-file indicator, 7
ENDSHELL, 3, 22, 83
ENDSKIP, 84
Error codes, printing messages for, FAULT, 93
Error messages
  listing of, 157–161
  printing, WHY, 153
ErrorReport, description of, 212–213
EVAL, 84–86
ExAll, description of, 213–216
Examine, description of, 216–217
ExamineFH, description of, 217–218
EXCHANGE, 86–87
Exclusive locks, 174
EXECUTE, 17, 20, 33, 35, 87–91
  dot commands, 90
  description of, 218–219
Exit, description of, 219–220
Exiting, programs, 172–173
ExNext, description of, 220–221
Expression, evaluation of, EVAL, 84–86
External references, 351–352
External symbols, 361
  handling by linker/loader, example, 368–371

F

FAILAT, 20, 91–92
Failure, of programming routine, 172

FAULT, 93
  description of, 221–222
FGetC, description of, 222–223
FGets, description of, 223–224
File description, 12
File handles
  data structure, 393–394
  input/output programming, 174, 177–179
  structure of, 393–394
File header block, 345–347
File list block, 347–348
Filenames
  changing, RENAME, 31, 131–132
  creation of, 8–9
  warning about creating new files, 9
Filenotes, attaching to files, FILENOTE, 13, 93–94
FilePart, description of, 224
Files
  accessing from disk, 13
  attaching note to, FILENOTE, 93–94
  changing protection bits, PROTECT, 128–129
  combining two files, JOIN, 106
  copying files, COPY, 60–62
  deleting files, DELETE, 65–66
  displaying files in directory, DIR, 66–68
  linking, MAKELINK, 112–113
  listing information about, LIST, 107–110
  viewing contents of, ED, 34–35
Filesystem. *See* AmigaDOS devices
File system information
  INFO, 29, 103–104
  LIST, 27–28
Filing system
  attaching filenotes, 13
  device names, 13–16
  directories, 9–10
  disk blocks
    data blocks, 348–350
    file header block, 345–347
    file list block, 347–348
    root block, 336–341
    user directory blocks, 341–344
  function of, 327
  logical drives, listing of, 16–19
  naming files, 8–9
  setting current device, 12–13
  setting current directory, 10–11
FindArg, description of, 225
FindCliProc, description of, 225–226
FindDosEntry, description of, 226
FindSegment, description of, 227
FindVar, description of, 228
FIXFONTS, 94

FKEY, 94–95
Flags, setting, BREAK, 54–55
Flush, description of, 228–229
FONT, 95–96
Fonts
  changing Shell font, SETFONT, 141–142
  specifying, FONT, 95–96
  updating files, FIXFONTS, 94
FORMAT, 25, 96–97
  description of, 229–230
Format listings, 41
Formatting disks, FORMAT, 25, 96–97
FPutC, description of, 230
FPuts, description of, 231
FRead, description of, 231–232
FreeArgs, description of, 232–233
FreeDeviceProc, description of, 233
FreeDosEntry, description of, 233–234
FreeDosObject, description of, 234
Function keys, assigning text strings to, FKEY, 94–95
Functions
  description of
    AbortPkt, 188–189
    AddBuffers, 189–190
    AddDosEntry, 190
    AddPart, 191
    AddSegment, 192
    AllocDosObject, 193
    AssignAdd, 193–194
    AssignLate, 194–195
    AssignLock, 195–196
    AssignPath, 196
    AttemptLockDosList, 196–197
    ChangeMode, 197–198
    CheckSignal, 198
    Cli, 199
    Close, 199–200
    CompareDates, 200
    CreateDir, 201
    CreateNewProc, 201–202
    CreateProc, 202–203
    CurrentDir, 203–204
    DateStamp, 204–205
    DateToStr, 205–206
    Delay, 206–207
    DeleteFile, 207
    DeleteVar, 207–208
    DeviceProc, 208–209
    DoPkt, 209–210
    DupLockFromFH, 211
    DupLock, 210–211
    EndNotify, 212
    ErrorReport, 212–213
    ExAll, 213–216
    Examine, 216–217

ExamineFH, 217–218
Execute, 218–219
Exit, 219–220
ExNext, 220–221
Fault, 221–222
FGetC, 222–223
FGets, 223–224
FilePart, 224
FindArg, 225
FindCliProc, 225–226
FindDosEntry, 226
FindSegment, 227
FindVar, 228
Flush, 228–229
Format, 229–230
FPutC, 230
FPuts, 231
FRead, 231–232
FreeArgs, 232–233
FreeDeviceProc, 233
FreeDosEntry, 233–234
FreeDosObject, 234
FWrite, 235
GetFileSysTask, 238–239
GetArgStr, 235–236
GetConsoleTask, 236
GetCurrentDirName, 236–237
GetDeviceProc, 237–238
GetProgramDir, 239
GetProgramName, 239–240
GetPrompt, 240–241
GetVar, 241–242
Info, 242–243
Inhibit, 243
Input, 243–244
InternalLoadSeg, 244–245
InternalUnLoadSeg, 245–246
IoErr, 246
IsFileSystem, 247
IsInteractive, 247–248
LoadSeg, 248–249
Lock, 249
LockDosList, 249–250
LockRecord, 250–251
LockRecords, 251–252
MakeDosEntry, 252–253
MakeLink, 253–254
MatchEnd, 254
MatchFirst, 254–256
MatchNext, 256
MatchPattern, 257
MatchPatternNoCase, 257–258
MaxCli, 258–259
NameFromFH, 259
NameFromLock, 259–260
NewLoadSeg, 260–261

NextDosEntry, 261–262
Open, 262
OpenFromLock, 263
Output, 263–264
ParentDir, 264
ParentOfFH, 265
ParsePattern, 265–266
ParsePatternNoCase, 266–267
PathPart, 267–268
PrintFault, 269
PutStr, 268–269
Read, 269–270
ReadArgs, 270–272
ReadItem, 272–273
ReadLink, 273–274
Relabel, 274
RemAssignList, 275
RemDosEntry, 275–276
RemSegment, 276
Rename, 277
ReplyPkt, 277–278
RunCommand, 278–279
SameDevice, 279
SameLock, 280
Seek, 280–281
SelectInput, 281–282
SelectOutput, 282
SendPkt, 282–283
SetArgStr, 283–284
SetComment, 284
SetConsoleTask, 284–285
SetCurrentDirName, 285
SetFileDate, 286
SetFileSize, 286–287
SetFileSysTask, 287–288
SetIoErr, 288
SetMode, 288–289
SetProgramDir, 289
SetProgramName, 290
SetPrompt, 290–291
SetProtection, 291–292
SetVar, 292–293
SetVBuf, 293–294
SplitName, 294–295
StartNotify, 295–296
StrToDate, 296–297
StrToLong, 297–298
SystemTagList, 298–299
UnGetC, 299–300
UnLoadSeg, 300–301
UnLock, 301
UnLockDosList, 302
UnLockRecord, 302–303
UnLockRecords, 303
VFPrintf, 304
VFWritef, 304–305

VPrintf, 305–306
WaitForChar, 306–307
WaitPkt, 307–308
Write, 308
WriteChars, 308–309
listing of, 310–313
syntax of
Boolean returns, 188
register values, 187
values, 188
FWrite, description of, 235

G

GetFileSysTask, description of, 238–239
GET, 97
GetArgStr, description of, 235–236
GetConsoleTask, description of, 236
GetCurrentDirName, description of, 236–237
GetDeviceProc, description of, 237–238
GETNV, 97–98
GetProgramDir, description of, 239
GetProgramName, description of, 239–240
GetPrompt, description of, 240–241
GetVar, description of, 241–242
Global variables
getting value of, 97–98
removing, UNSETENV, 148
setting, SETENV, 141
GRAPHICDUMP, 98–99
Graphics
display and IFF ILBM format, DISPLAY, 71–73
printing, specifying, PRINTERGFX, 126

H

Handler internal, packets, 398, 420–421
Handlers
file handlers, 178–179
function of, 178, 327
handler maintenance, packets, 398, 417–420
See also AmigaDOS devices
Hard link, 346–347
Hash function, 341
Hashing algorithm, 342
Header, 320
Header files, 170
Hunks, 353
format of, 354
hunk overlay table, 430–433
of library files, 373–379
of load files, 365–367
of object files, 354–364

I

ICONEDIT, 99

Icons
editing, ICONEDIT, 99
execution of script file from, ICONX, 100
ICONTROL, 99–100
ICONX, 100
IF, 100–102
alternative to IF, ELSE, 82
termination of, ENDIF, 83
IHELP, 102–103
INFO, 103
description of, 242–243
Inhibit, description of, 243
INITPRINTER, 104
INPUT, 104
description of, 243–244
Input/output
redirection of, 21, 30
redirection of output, CMD, 58–59
Input/output programming, 173–186
buffered I/O, 179–180
dos.library functions, use of, 174–176
example of basic I/O file, 176–177
file handles, 174, 177–179
locks, 174
standard command line parsing, 181–186
INSTALL, 25–26, 105
Instruction cache, 62
InternalLoadSeg, description of, 244–245
InternalUnLoadSeg, description of, 245–246
IoErr, description of, 246
IPREFS, 106
IsFileSystem, description of, 247
IsInteractive, description of, 247–248

J

JOIN, 106

K

Keyboard
setting speed, INPUT, 104–105
taking over mouse operations, IHELP, 102–103
Keymap
changing, SETMAP, 142–143
displaying, KEYSHOW, 107
KEYSHOW, 107
Kickstart process, 25

L

L, logical device, 17
LAB, 107
Libraries
and linker, 315
resident library, 315

scanned library, 315
Library data structure, 387–392
   Info substructure, 389–392
Library files
   example of, 372
   hunks of, 373–379
   new structure of, 373–379
   original format, 371
LIBS, 17
Linker
   automatic overlay system, 321
   caution related to, 325
   driving linker, methods of, 315–316
   errors, types of, 325–326
   errors and, 320
   function of, 315
   input files and, 316
   order for reading files, 320
   output of, 320–321
   OVERLAY directive, 321–324
   overlay supervisor, 315
   processes in, 316
   references to symbols, 324–325
   See also ALINK
Linking
   hard link, 346–347
   linking files, MAKELINK, 112–113
   soft link, 347
Link map, 315, 320
LIST, 27–28, 107–110
Load files, 315, 353
   format of, 364–365
   hunks, listing of, 365–367
   structure of, 364–365
LoadSeg, description of, 248–249
LOADWB, 35, 110–111
Local variables
   getting value of, GET, 97
   removing, UNSET, 148
   setting, SET, 138–139
LOCK, 111, 398
   description of, 249
LockDosList, description of, 249–250
LockRecord, description of, 250–251
LockRecords, description of, 251–252
Locks
   data structure, 394–395
   exclusive locks, 174
   functions of, 394
   input/output programming, 174
   shared locks, 174
   zero lock, 395
Logical devices, 16–19
   assigning to directories, ASSIGN, 47–50
   C, 17
   DEVS, 17

FONTS, 17
L, 17
LIBS, 17
S, 17
SYS, 16–17
LONG, 398
Loops, counter for, 85–86

M

MAKEDIR, 33–34, 112
MakeDosEntry, description of, 252–253
MAKELINK, 112
   description of, 253–254
MatchEnd, description of, 254
MatchFirst, description of, 254–256
MatchNext, description of, 256
MatchPattern, description of, 257
MatchPatternNoCase, description of, 257–258
MaxCli, description of, 258–259
MEMACS, 35, 113–118
   editing commands, 114–115
   extra commands, 117–118
   filing commands, 114
   line commands, 116
   move commands, 116
   search commands, 117
   window commands, 115–116
   word commands, 116–117
Memory
   allocation of, 392–393
   buffers, 43
   creating devices in, 14
   report of information, AVAIL, 51–52
   use of only resident Chip RAM, NOFASTMEM, 122
Monitor
   assigning names to display modes, BINDMONITOR, 52–53
   blanking screen, BLANKER, 53–54
   changing colors, COLORS, 59–60
   non–RGB, ADDMONITOR, 44–45
MORE, 118–119
MOUNT, 119
Mouse, setting speed, 104–105
Mouse operation, keyboard assignment of, IHELP, 102–103
Multitasking
   nature of, 5
   and priority numbers, 57

N

NameFromFH, description of, 259
NameFromLock, description of, 259–260
NEWCLI, 119–120
NEWCON, 330

NewLoadSeg, description of, 260–261
NEWSHELL, 120–121
NextDosEntry, description of, 261–262
NIL, 14, 330
NOCAPSLOCK, 121
Node, 354
NOFASTMEM, 122

O

Object files, 315, 352
    hunks, listing of, 354–364
    structure of, 353–354
Open, description of, 262
OpenFromLock, description of, 263
Output, description of, 263–264
OVERLAY directive, linker, 321–324
Overlay files, 320
    and linker, 315
Overlay number, 325
Overlay reference, 324
Overlay supervisor, linker, 315
Overlay table, hunk overlay table, generation of, 430–433
OVERSCAN, 122

P

Packets, 395–427
    Basic Input/Output, 398, 399–402
    categories of, 397–398
    console only packets, 398, 421
        directory/file manipulation/information, 398, 403–416
    direct use of, 424–427
    handler internal, 398, 420–421
    handler maintenance, 398, 417–420
    listing of, 398
    obsolete packets, 398, 421
    operation of, 395–396
    relationship to operating system, 395
    StandardPacket, 395
    summary of defined packet numbers, 421–423
    volume Manipulation/Information, 398, 416–417
PALETTE, 123
PAR, 14, 330
Parameter file, and linker, 315
ParentDir, description of, 264
ParentOfFH, description of, 265
ParsePattern, description of, 265–266
ParsePatternNoCase, description of, 266–267
Parsing, standard command line parsing, 181–186
PATH, 123–124
PathPart, description of, 267–268

Patterns, background patterns, WBPATTERN, 151–152
PIPE, 330–331
POINTER, 125
Preferences, communicating information to Workbench, IPREFS, 106
Primary binary input, and linker, 315
PRINTER, 125
    initializing, INITPRINTER, 104
    sending files to, PRINTFILES, 126–127
    specifying/setting options, PRINT, 125–126
PRINTERGFX, 126
PrintFault, description of, 269
PRINTFILES, 126–127
Printing
    error messages, WHY, 153
    graphics printing, PRINTERGFX, 126
Processes
    beginning new process, NEWCLI, 119–120
    changing priorities, CHANGETASKPRI, 57
    data structure, 382–387
    listing of information, STATUS, 146
    nature of, 5–6
    process values, 382–383
    redirecting system requests, 386–387
Programming
    creating executable program, steps in, 171
    getting started, 169–170
    input/output programming, 173–186
    resident libraries, calling, 170
    running program
        under Shell, 171–173
        under Workbench, 173
Program unit, 353
PROMPT, 19, 127–128
    changing, PROMPT, 127–128
PROTECT, 28, 128–129
Protecting files, PROTECT, 28–29
Protection bits of file, changing, PROTECT, 128–129
Protection flags, 28
PRT, 14–15, 330
PutStr, description of, 268–269

Q

QUIT, 129–130

R

RAM, 14, 32
Ramdisk, 32
Ramdrive, removing recoverable device, REMRAD, 131

RAW, 15, 330
Read, description of, 269–270
ReadArgs, description of, 270–272
ReadItem, description of, 272–273
ReadLink, description of, 273–274
Redirection, of input/output, 21, 30
References to symbols, linker, 324–325
Register values, functions, 187
RELABEL, 28, 130
   description of, 274
Relabeling disks, RELABEL, 26–27
RemAssignList, description of, 275
RemDosEntry, description of, 275–276
REMRAD, 131
RemSegment, description of, 276
RENAME, 31, 131–132
   description of, 277
Repair of corrupted disk, DISKDOCTOR, 70–71
ReplyPkt, description of, 277–278
RESIDENT, 19, 132–134
Resident commands, display/modification of, RESIDENT, 132–134
Resident library, 315, 354
   See also Functions
Return Code Limit, 92
ROM patches, creating, SETPATCH, 143
Root block, 336–341
Root directory, 9
RUN, 20, 134–135
RunCommand, description of, 278–279

S

S, logical device, 17
SameDevice, description of, 279
SameLock, description of, 280
SAY, 135
Scanned library, 315, 354
Screen dump, GRAPHICDUMP, 98–99
SCREENMODE, 136
Screen pointer, changing, POINTER, 125
Script files, 35–36
   alternative to IF, ELSE, 82
   evaluating conditional operations, IF, 100–102
   execution from icon, ICONX, 100
   exiting with return code, EXIT, 129–130
   getting user input, ASK, 46
   skipping label, SKIP, 143–144
   specifying labels, LAB, 107
   termination of IF, ENDIF, 83
   termination of SKIP block, ENDSKIP, 84
Scripts, execution of, EXECUTE, 87–91
SEARCH, 136–138
   of command path, WHICH, 152

   of directories, 11
   last occurrence of command, 6
   text strings, SEARCH, 136–138
Seek, description of, 280–281
Segment lists, 393
   data structure, 393
SelectInput, description of, 281–282
SelectOutput, description of, 282
SendPkt, description of, 282–283
SER, 14, 330
SERIAL, 138
Serial port, setting communication specs, SERIAL, 138
SET, 138–139
SetArgStr, description of, 283–284
SETCLOCK, 22, 30, 139–140
SetComment, description of, 284
SetConsoleTask, description of, 284–285
SetCurrentDirName, description of, 285
SETDATE, 140
SETENV, 141
SetFileDate, description of, 286
SetFileSize, description of, 286–287
SetFileSysTask, description of, 287–288
SETFONT, 141–142
SetIoErr, description of, 288
SETMAP, 142–143
SetMode, description of, 288–289
SETPATCH, 143
SetProgramDir, description of, 289
SetProgramName, description of, 290
SetPrompt, description of, 290–291
SetProtection, description of, 291–292
SetVar, description of, 292–293
SetVBuf, description of, 293–294
Shared Global Vector, 387
Shared locks, 174
Shell
   ending process
      ENDCLI, 82–83
      ENDShell, 3, 22, 83
   opening new window, NEWShell, 3, 22, 120–121
   processes, 5–6
   prompt, 19
   running program under, 171–173
      failure of routines, 172
      initial environment in assembler, 171–172
      initial environment in C, 172
      terminating program, 172–173
680X0 processors, 62–63
SKIP, 143–144
Soft link, 347
SORT, 144–145
   alphabetical, SORT, 144–145

SPEAK, 331
Speech capabilities, use of, SAY, 135–136
Speed, loading commands faster, 19
SplitName, description of, 294–295
Square brackets, in format listings of commands, 41
STACK, 145
Stack pointer, 172
Stacks, 171
   setting size, STACK, 145
StartNotify, description of, 295–296
Startup-sequence, 35, 52
Static Column Dynamic RAM (SCRAM), 62–63
STATUS, 55, 146
Strings, display of, ECHO, 73
StrToDate, description of, 296–297
StrToLong, description of, 297–298
Symbol cross-reference table, 315
SYS, 16–17
SystemTagList, description of, 298–299

T

T directory, 18
Template, 42
   accessing, 24
   codes of, 42
   example of, 42
Temporary files, directory for, 18
Text files
   creating/editing, MEMACS, 113–118
   display of, TYPE, 147
   editing, ED, 74–77
   editing by processing source files, EDIT, 78–81
   typing to screen, TYPE, 31
TIME, 22, 146–147
   on-screen clock, CLOCK, 57–58
      setting/reading hardware clock, SETCLOCK, 30, 139–140
   setting system clock, TIME, 146–147
   waiting period for specified time, WAIT, 149–150
Tree structure, 321
TYPE, 31, 147

U

UNALIAS, 147–148
UnGetC, description of, 299–300
UnLoadSeg, description of, 300–301
UnLock, description of, 301
UnLockDosList, description of, 302
UnLockRecord, description of, 302–303
UnLockRecords, description of, 303
UNSET, 148
UNSETENV, 148

Updating AmigaDOS, 21–22
User directory blocks, 341–344

V

Validation process, restarting, 21–22
Values, functions, 188
VERSION, 148–149
Version of software, finding, VERSION, 148–149
Vertical bars, in format listings of commands, 41
VFPrintf, description of, 304
VFWritef, description of, 304–305
Volume Manipulation/Information, packet, 398, 416–417
Volume name, 13
   changing, RELABEL, 130
VPrintf, description of, 305–306

W

WAIT, 149–150
WaitForChar, description of, 306–307
Waiting period, for specified time, WAIT, 149–150
WaitPkt, description of, 307–308
WBCONFIG, 150
WBPATTERN, 151–152
WHICH, 152
WHY, 153
Wildcards, 9
Windows
   background patterns, WBPATTERN, 151–152
   control of backdrop window, WBCONFIG, 150
   opening new window, NEWSHELL, 120–121
   selection of, AUTOPOINT, 51
WITH files, ALINK, 318–322
Workbench
   background patterns, WBPATTERN, 151–152
   changing colors, PALETTE, 123
   communicating preferences information to, IPREFS, 106
   relationship to subdirectories, 4
   running program under, 171–173
   setting parameters, ICONTROL, 99–100
   starting, LOADWB, 110–111
   using AmigaDos without, 435–436
Write, description of, 308
WriteChars, description of, 308–309
Write-protection, setting, LOCK, 111